Is there a Judeo-Christian Tradition?

Perspectives on Jewish Texts and Contexts

Edited by
Vivian Liska

Volume 4

Is there a Judeo-Christian Tradition?

A European Perspective

Edited by
Emmanuel Nathan
Anya Topolski

DE GRUYTER

Volume inspired by the international workshop "Is there a Judeo-Christian tradition?" as part of the UCSIA/IJS Chair for Jewish-Christian Relations, organized by the Institute of Jewish Studies of the University of Antwerp and the University Centre Saint Ignatius Antwerp (UCSIA).

ISBN 978-3-11-057870-6
e-ISBN (PDF) 978-3-11-041659-6
e-ISBN (EPUB) 978-3-11-041667-1
ISSN 2199-6962

Library of Congress Cataloging-in-Publication Data
A CIP catalog record for this book has been applied for at the Library of Congress.

Bibliographic information published by the Deutsche Nationalbibliothek
The Deutsche Nationalbibliothek lists this publication in the Deutsche Nationalbibliografie; detailed bibliographic data are available on the Internet at http://dnb.dnb.de.

This volume is text- and page-identical with the hardback published in 2016.
Cover image: bpk / Hamburger Kunsthalle / Elke Walford
Typesetting: fidus Publikations-Service GmbH, Nördlingen
Printing and binding: CPI books GmbH, Leck

♾ Printed on acid-free paper
Printed in Germany

www.degruyter.com

Acknowledgments

On 12 and 13 February 2014, the Institute of Jewish Studies (IJS) and the University Centre Saint Ignatius Antwerp (UCSIA) jointly organized a two-day international workshop at the University of Antwerp, Belgium, entitled "Is there a Judeo-Christian tradition?" This conference was organized as part of the annual UCSIA/IJS joint Chair for Jewish-Christian Relations 2013-2014. Instead of one scholar holding the chair for that academic year (as had been done annually up to that point since 2008-2009), both institutes decided to invite a number of scholars to examine and question the assumption of a shared Judeo-Christian tradition from a variety of interdisciplinary perspectives. We are grateful to the directors of both institutes, Prof. Dr. Vivian Liska (IJS) and Prof. Dr. Jacques Haers, sj (then director of UCSIA), for taking the lead on this venture. In addition to their input, the conference would not have been possible without the expert organizational help from Mr. Jan Morrens (IJS) and Ms. Barbara Segaert (UCSIA), and of course the invaluable input from the scholars who participated in this workshop in a most dynamic way.

Resulting from this workshop, Vivian approached both of us to produce an edited volume for her series, "Perspectives on Jewish Texts and Contexts," published by De Guyter. Since some readers may wonder how this volume is relevant to Judaism today, we offer four possible reasons. First, a careful study of the Judeo-Christian signifier indicates that it should resist a Christian supersession of Judaism, the signifier should not be used as a synonym for Christianity. Second, this study recognizes that Judaism has been an inextricable part of the 'Judeo-Christian' signifier when in Christian western lands. It may not always have been part of the conversation on that signifier, yet as this volume has made amply clear, when Jews have not been part of that conversation, others have stepped in to decide the conversation for them. In many ways, the latter half of the 20th century has seen a conscious attempt by Jewish scholars to rectify and correct this bias. Third, it should not go unsaid that the 'floating signifier' of 'Judeo-Christian' has also resignified Judaism and this has not only been negative. To be sure, Christianity has quite often undervalued and, at some points sought to eradicate, its Jewish roots. Yet rabbinic Judaism has from its inception been in a reciprocal dialogue with Christianity (and, when living in Islamic lands, with Islam). As such it should not be forgotten that Christianity and Islam have been Judaism's other and both these religious traditions can impact Judaism (and have done so) also for the better. Fourth, and finally, examining the 'Judeo-Christian' signifier up close has revealed that neither side of that hyphen harbours a stable category. That is to say, neither Judaism nor Christianity is one stable, homogenous, category. There are Judaisms and Christianities. Vive les differences!

We were also very grateful that Vivian allowed us free rein, as the volume's editors, to conceptualize the volume into the shape it now has. From the outset, we were quite clear not simply to produce a conference proceedings volume, but rather a book dedicated to exploring the signifier 'Judeo-Christian' in greater detail, especially from its rich and turbulent origins on the European continent before it gained currency across the Atlantic in the United States. We produced a book concept, presented it to Vivian and the editorial board, and – once accepted – proceeded to invite contributors to the volume. We are deeply appreciative to all the contributors who accepted our invitation and, with great generosity of spirit, allowed us to hold them to a rather quick turnaround. As deadlines gathered pace, we were also grateful for the proofreading skills offered by Mr. Jeremy Schreiber on some of the finalized manuscripts. Needless to say, Dr. Ulrike Krauss and Ms. Katja Lehming from De Gruyter were invaluable for their advice and customary professionalism in getting this book to print.

Looking back, much has transpired in the short time that has elapsed from the book's conceptualization to finalization. Separated by continents and time zones, we have relied on technology to overcome geographical and temporal distances. We have both marked milestones in our personal and professional lives. Through it all, this book has been the bridge – indeed the hyphen – that has kept us connected. To have facilitated and fostered a deep conversation on this topic has been our greatest joy and reward.

Emmanuel Nathan and Anya Topolski

Contents

Emmanuel Nathan and Anya Topolski

1 The Myth of a Judeo-Christian Tradition: Introducing a European Perspective

Since the fall of the Iron Curtain there has been a steady rise in the use of the term 'Judeo-Christian' by European theologians, politicians, historians and philosophers. Is it possible that such divergent public figures as Geert Wilders, a right-wing populist politician in The Netherlands, Jacques Derrida, a left-leaning French philosopher, and Pope Emeritus Benedict XVI, use the term 'Judeo-Christian tradition' in the same manner? Is there any means to pin down the meaning of this term as it is now being used in Europe? Or is this term, which 'has achieved considerable currency' throughout Europe – both popular and scholarly, a shibboleth as was claimed by Mark Silk in his 1984 'Notes on the Judeo-Christian Tradition in America' (Silk 1984, 65). Silk was responding to Arthur Cohen's American-based analysis of this term in 'The Myth of the Judeo-Christian tradition' (Cohen 1971, original essay 1957). Cohen decried the use and abuse of the term 'Judeo-Christian Tradition' in North America in the post-Shoah decades. He was quite explicit with regard to his thesis.

> And it is here that we can identify the myth. Jews and Christians have conspired together to promote a tradition of common experience and common belief, whereas in fact they have joined together to reinforce themselves in the face of a common disaster ... before a world that regards them as hopelessly irrelevant, and meaningless. The myth is a projection of the will to endure of both Jews and Christians, an identification of common enemies, an abandonment of millennial antagonisms in the face of threats which do not discriminate between Judaism and Christianity. (Cohen 1971, xix)

According to Cohen there is no Judeo-Christian tradition; this tradition is an ideologically motivated myth. For those unfamiliar with this essay and its historical context, the common enemy Cohen refers to is the rise of atheism and its ties to 'the Red Threat' of Communism. Given that Cohen was writing not only from an American perspective, but also in the 1950s, it is worth considering if his thesis is still accurate. He writes: "It is in our time that the 'Judeo-Christian tradition' has come to full expression. ... [and] has particular currency and significance in the Unites States. It is not a commonplace in Europe as it is here" (*ibid.* xviii–xix). While this may have been true in the 1950s, it is no longer the case sixty years later. The term 'Judeo-Christian tradition' was central to the debates about the EU Constitution between 2003 and 2005[1] and is currently used by politicians from all parties as well as religious leaders of all denominations. As such it has become part of common parlance in all European languages in the 21st century. It is this European 'coming to full expression' in the 21st century that is central to this current volume.

***

Before trying to disentangle the many diverse uses of the term 'Judeo-Christian' in contemporary European discourse, let us briefly consider the possible origins of the concept or signification of Judeo-Christianity.[2] To help navigate this complex concept, we begin by sifting through the theological, philosophical, and political literature on the notion of Judeo-Christianity. Three possible historical origins emerge: the early Church period prior to the 'parting of the ways' between Judaism and Christianity (200–400 CE) (Dunn 1999; Boyarin 2006; Becker and Reed 2007), 17th century Enlightenment thought, and 19th century theology (greatly inspired by German Idealism). As there is a clear theological connection between the first and third hypothesis, we can consider them together by way of the writings of Bernard Heller and Simon Claude Mimouni, both theologians, the former in Jewish studies in the US and the latter in early Christianity in France (Heller 1951; Mimouni 2012). As a second step, we consider the authors that locate the origins of this tradition in the Enlightenment period (very broadly construed) such as: Joel Sebban, Isaac Rottenberg, Marshall Grossman, and Arthur A. Cohen (Sebban 2012; Gover 1989; Rottenberg 2000; Grossman 1989; Cohen, Stern, and Mendes-Flohr 1998). Within this group, Sebban is the only author writing about this signifier on the (European) Continent. All the other authors are explicitly interested in the role of this term in American public discourse. What we hope to make clear is that these distinctions, European or American, theological or political, Jewish or

1 Please see part 2 of chapter 14 for more on this.

2 This attempt, not surprisingly, has many potential pitfalls and problems. How arbitrary is one's stating point? While arbitrariness is potentially unavoidable, transparency may partially serve to offset it by allowing each choice to be acknowledged, justified and scrutinised. From among the many attempts to trace the notion of Judeo-Christianity (or the Judeo-Christian tradition or heritage etc.), there are two dominant albeit intertwined lines. *First* there are those authors that have sought to understand how this term arose in the contemporary American political context (Cohen; Rottenberg; Gover in his response to Grossman); *second* are those authors interested in the transformations of the theological significance of this concept (Teixiodor, Heller, Mimouni). Another possible frame, explored in this volume, lies at the intersection of these two lines, in the realm of the theological-political.

Christian, affect the frame of each author and as such influences what they take to be the origins and meaning of this signifier.

Heller's 1951 piece, 'The Judeo-Christian tradition concept: air or deterrent to goodwill?', published in the journal *Judaism*, ambitiously claims that this tradition has "a long and cherished history" (Heller 1951, 133). This history has four phases: its origin in the period directly following the birth of Jesus, 19th century German theological supersessionism, 20th century racial anti-Semitism (which he connects to Nietzsche), and most recently political Orientalism. Explicitly demarcated by the horrors of the Shoah, Heller's frame leads him to narrate the transformations of the notion of Judeo-Christianity in terms of shifting anti-Semitism e.g. from theological to political via racial anti-Semitism. Framed in a similar vein to Marshall Grossman's 1989 deconstructive analysis of the 'violence of the hyphen in Judeo-Christian', Heller's ideological motivation to prove that anti-Semitism is as old as Christianity prevents him from appreciating the Foucauldian inspired concern in Grossman's analysis – the role of power, and its relation to discourse. Concretely, Heller wants to paint a picture of 2000 years of uninterrupted anti-Semitism from the birth of Christianity to the Shoah. He thus fails to acknowledge the radical difference between Early Church (pre-Constantine) inter-community tensions and the latter three phases. While there was undoubtedly a great deal of anti-Judaism in the period when Christianity was born, this phase of Judeo-Christianity was one in which there was an unambiguous relationship between these communities and their followers, an ambiguity that caused tension and sometimes led to violence, but was by no means – in terms of power dynamics – an early form of anti-Semitism (Boyarin 2006). Heller's account of the origin and history of the term 'Judeo-Christianity' is entirely focused on anti-Semitism and its roots in Christianity.

This type of bias is clearly avoided by Claude Mimouni in his highly detailed analysis of the concept of Judeo-Christianity. He corrects Heller's anachronistic error by tracing its origins to the 19th century and specifically the writings of F.C. Baur (influenced by both Schleiermacher and Hegel), who he claims was the first person to use this term *in print*. Mimouni thus demonstrates that the term Judeo-Christianity was introduced by the 19th century German Protestant theologians who sought to bring attention to the period of the early Church in which there was much tension between the competing notions of Christianity (many of which were seeking to define themselves *vis-a-vis* Judaism). In this vein, the first use of this term was theological in origin and served to identify different early Christian communities that were close to Judaism in terms of either *praxis* or *dogma*. While Baur's later usage of this term varies, its original purpose was one of classification, part and parcel of the new academic discipline of religious studies (*Religionsgeschichte*). It is perhaps Mimouni's restricted interest in the discipline of theology that accounts for his neglect of the term's pre-theological origins in the wider political space. Yet if one does not take this wider context into consideration, one could just as easily declare its origin to be much earlier given that scholars several centuries before began to study these same early Christian communities and their relationship to Judaism showing a surprisingly strong interest in Hebrew and scripture. It is upon this basis that Javier Teixiodor dates Judeo-Christianity's conceptual origin to the authors of the 15th and early 16th century engaged in translating the Bible, such as Valla and Erasmus, who emphasised the importance of its Hebraic or Judaic roots (Teixidor 2006). While Mimouni is correct to acknowledge that Baur was the first to explicitly use this term Judeo-Christianity, he (and Teixiodor) fails to appreciate the *political* motives that led to a renewed interest in these early Christian communities, and the reading of the Bible in Hebrew, its original language (Nelson 2011; Topolski 2016).

One of the most significant contributions to the discussion about the origins of the term 'Judeo-Christian' that does consider the *political* motives is that by Joël Sebban (Sebban 2012). With an explicitly French focus, Sebban locates the roots of this term in the emancipation of the Jews in the year 1791. The French context is clearly influenced by events on the European continent and the role of the Catholic Church (as the writings of Jacques Maritain demonstrate, see (Maritain 2012; Andras and Hubert 1996)). In this vein, 'la morale judéo-chrétienne' has several ideologically different manifestations. Sebban develops several of these political responses to the idea of a Judeo-Christian tradition such as: a liberal Christian ideology (at the turn of the 20th century), a last attempt to save the life of the spirit by religious philosophers in the 19th century, and most recently in the form of a discourse of civilisations. While it is clear that, as Sebban argues, these competing ideas all came to the surface during the French Revolution, Sebban does not consider the events and intellectual climate prior to the French Revolution. Instead, he moves quickly from 1791 to 1831, Baur's first usage of the term only then slowing down and engaging in a very close analysis of 'la morale judéo-chrétienne' from Baur to Renan via Nietzsche, an analysis that is confirmed in several contributions to this volume. As many scholars examining this term contend, its origins cannot be fully appreciated without its connection to questions first raised in the 17th century about the relationship between Church and State, between Judaism and Christianity, and between monarchists and republicans. For this reason it is surprising that Sebban does not connect the events of 1791 to the earlier debates about the role of religion in philosophy or the dialogue on modern forms of statecraft. To do so, we now turn to contributions by Gover, Rottenberg, and Cohen who all situate the origins of this term in the Enlightenment.

As Sebban demonstrates, the concept of Judeo-Christianity certainly goes beyond the boundaries of theology, a fact which all of the authors who locate its origins in the period between the 17th and 18th century equally appreciate. Yerach Gover, who shares Mimouni's interest in theology, traces the origins of the concept of Judeo-Christianity from the renewed interest in Hebrew, the Bible and its critical study during the Reformation to the thinkers of the Enlightenment. While he recognises the essential connection between theology and philology in the 16th century, he neither connects this to the political project it enabled – the *Respublica Hebraeorum*, an integral part of the genealogy of the notion of Judeo-Christianity, nor does he connect the upsurge in interest in Hebrew, language and texts, to the Protestant Reformation. Instead he focuses on their role as the founders of several new fields of study, such as comparative religions. The latter is undoubtedly related to the political tensions within the Church, yet Gover's frame does not call for a closer political analysis (in this vein his analysis is close to Mimouni's). In the 16th century, primarily in Protestant milieu, the academic interest in other religions, both Christian and non-Christian, is facilitated by the political campaigns for tolerance and separation between Church and State as well as the search for a *prisca theoloigca* (an *ur*-religion). Evidence of this lineage are two students of John Selden (1584–1654), who wrote many renowned writings on the *Hebrew Republic*, James Harrington and Thomas Hobbes, both of whom also sought to draw political lessons from the Hebrew scriptures.[3]

While Cohen's analysis is US-centred, he does state that there is more to the myth of the Judeo-Christian tradition than the American tale he tells. As such he dedicates a few paragraphs to the European history of the Judeo-Christian tradition. Drawing an analogy to its usage in the US in the 1950s, Cohen states that, "The Judeo-Christian connection was formed by the opponents of Judaism and Christianity, by the opponents of a system of unreason which had nearly destroyed Western Europe" (Cohen 1971, xviii). He refers specifically to both the rise of atheist thinkers in Europe from the 17th and 18th centuries, such as Spinoza and Voltaire, as well as those trying to carve an intellectual space for a rational religion in the 18th and 19th century such as Kant and Hegel. Though Cohen is less interested in the genealogy of the Judeo-Christian myth, he does clearly indicate that – for those interested in its historical origins – one ought to begin in the 17th century.

3 For more on the relationship between Hebraic texts and European political thought see Eric Nelson's *The Hebrew Republic* (2010).

> It could not be helped that in the attack on Christianity Judaism should suffer, for Christianity depended upon Judaism for the internal logic of its history ... It could not be otherwise, then, but that a 'Christo-Jewish tradition' should come to be defined and characterized as one of irrationality and fanaticism. (Cohen, Stern, and Mendes-Flohr 1998, 34–5)

Cohen refers to this 'Christo-Jewish tradition' as the origins of the myth in that this link between Judaism and Christianity eventually leads to the ideological myth he seeks to debunk. While this strikes us as a plausible explanation, it would have been inconceivable in the 16th century. While 15th century scholars were keen to read the Bible in Hebrew, it would be a stretch to claim that Christians would have recognised that their inner logic is Judaic (this remains contested by thinkers today such as Marcel Gauchet and Charles Taylor). In this context, Cohen refers to Spinoza as a Jewish precursor to the Enlightenment who played a particular role in bringing together the Hebrew Bible and the Christian religion. While we agree that Spinoza played a pivotal role in the melding of Judaism and Christianity, we do so with more care and attention to detail. Writing with broad brushstrokes, Cohen states that, "the Christo-Jewish legacy was both affirmed and opposed" (Cohen, Stern, and Mendes-Flohr 1998, 35) by the thinkers of the Enlightenment. The question he fails to consider, however, is: why was this 'Christo-Jewish' tradition defined and what exactly did it mean (at the time)? Likewise Cohen fails to consider the aims of Spinoza's sparring partners. Did all those that affirmed this tradition seek to oppose it? To answer this and other related questions, a closer analysis of Spinoza's *Tractatus Theologico-Politicus* and its reception history are necessary. In any case, the importance of this period, during which Christians found new ideas and inspiration from the Jewish texts and tradition, and specifically Spinoza's *Tractatus*, for the origin of the idea of the Judeo-Christian tradition or heritage, should not be underestimated (Topolski 2015; Topolski, 2016).

In his article 'The Idea of a Judeo-Christian Worldview', Isaac Rottenberg claims that it was during the 17th century that "the religiopolitical foundations were laid for the future shape of American society" (Rottenberg 2000, 403). Accordingly, the theological-political roots of the US were to be found in the Protestant interpretations of Hebrew Scriptures as models for political constitutions. This is what he refers to as the Judeo-Christian worldview which was born in Europe in the 17th century. In this vein, Rottenberg contests Cohen's claim that this tradition is a myth or that it was forged out of self-defence. Without focusing on any specific philosopher or text, Rottenberg paints a picture of the thinkers and questions being debated by intellectuals, who were often politically involved or influential, during this period in European history. Along similar lines, he refers to Spinoza and Locke (influenced by Hobbes and Grotius – both Christian Hebraists) as "two advocates of religiopolitical theories" (Rottenberg 2000, 404) who found themselves in a milieu overflowing with religious fervour. While the Enlightenment is often characterised as a period in which reason reigned and the state freed itself from the grips of the Church (as Cohen assumes), one could contend that this is perhaps a prime example of history being written by the victors. It is worth recalling, as both Nelson and Rottenberg highlight, that there was an upsurge in religious zeal, and specifically in mystical and millennialist dreams in the 17th century in both England and The Netherlands (Nelson 2011; Rottenberg 2000). It is in response to this surge, and its connection to sectarian conflict, that Spinoza and Locke both made demands for religious tolerance and a critical approach to scriptures. While Rottenberg does little to distinguish between their particular approaches (which are quite different), he acknowledges the different role of the "'new theology' and it socio-political implications" (Rottenberg 2000, 406) for Catholics and Protestants. Similarly, the mainly Protestant interest in Judaism and Hebrew blossomed into groups of Hebraic Christians or Christian Hebraists who found arguments for democracy, participation, and religious tolerance in the Bible. Accordingly he connects these groups to the foundations of America. In this scheme, Europe is ruled by a Catholic hegemony, America by the Protestants.[4]

***

Fortuitously, Rottenberg's trans-Atlantic 'parting of the ways', between Catholics and Protestants, sets the scene for this volume with its explicitly European (and implicit Germanic) focus. This latter 'parting of the ways' parallels the 2nd – 4th century 'parting of the ways' between Jews and Christians which was the focus, and point of dispute, between Catholic and Protestant theologians in the 19th century. Before immersing ourselves in these debates, let us consider what this overview of the major contributions on the origins of the concept of Judeo-Christianity makes clear. While there is clearly no consensus on the meaning of this term, there is a scholarly consensus on the importance of Enlightenment political-theology and its 19th century coinage by F.C. Baur. In this vein, we can conclude that while there are many accounts of the importance of the 17th century thinkers for

---

4 So what about the minorities on both sides of the ocean? Glossing over the fact that Spinoza was Jewish, albeit only as a fact of birth, Rottenberg does not consider how this struggle between Church and state was viewed or experienced by those who were excluded from both. This fact is one that we must take into consideration when analysing Spinoza's *Tractatus Theologico-Politicus*, the only contribution to the *Respublica Hebraeorum* literature written by a Jew.

the roots of the connection between Jewish and Christian texts, beliefs etc., the term itself only arises in the 19th century.[5]

As this volume aims to tell the European tale of the Judeo-Christian tradition, our starting point is the *attribution* of its coinage in 1831 in a publication by Ferdinand Christian Baur (1792–1860), the founder of the German Protestant Tübingen School. The essay *Die Christuspartei in der korinthischen Gemeinde, der Gegensatz des paulinischen und petrinischen Christentums in der ältesten Kirche, der Apostel Petrus in Rom* (The Christ Party in the Corinthian Community, the Opposition of Pauline and Petrine Christianity in the earliest Church, the apostle Peter in Rome or abbreviated 'The Christ Party') was published in the *Tübinger Zeitschrift*. It is necessary to stress that the term 'Judeo-Christian' is attributed to Baur and that it most likely was used before (Jones 2012). There is also much to be said about how the German terms '*jüdisch-christliche*', '*judenchristen*' and '*judenchristlich*' are translated. Baur, like Nietzsche in the *Anti-Christ* (paragraph 24) and 'The Genealogy of Morals' uses the former terms, which can be translated as either Jewish Christian or Judeo-Christian. David Lincicum (Lincicum 2012), a Baur expert, translates the term as 'Jewish Christianity' rather than Judeo-Christian. However, in the 19th century, translations into English of works using these terms used the term 'Judeo-Christian' which is why Baur, and the Tübingen School he founded, are credited with its coinage.

> It was only in the late nineteenth century in Germany that the Judeo-Christian tradition, as such, was first defined. It was introduced by German Protestant scholarship to account for the findings developed by the Higher Criticism of the Old Testament and achieved considerable currency as a polemical term in that period. There, quite clearly, the negative significance of the expression became primary. The emphasis fell not on the communality of the word 'tradition' but to the accented stress of the hyphen. The Jewish was latinized and abbreviated into 'Judeo' to indicate a dimension, albeit a pivotal dimension, of the explicit Christian experience. ... It was no less for all its efforts to be scholarly, an exhibition of what Solomon Schechter called 'Higher Anti-Semitism,' for the Jewish in the Jewish experience was all but obliterated. (Cohen 1971, xviii)

The essays collected in this volume speak to the three claims made by Cohen in this paragraph. These three claims are:

1) The term 'Judeo-Christian' was coined in Germany in the 19th century by Protestant theological scholars – more specifically by F.C. Baur, founder of the Tübingen School.

5 For this reason, we begin this volume with a contribution that explicitly connects an important early 18th century thinker, John Toland, to F.C. Baur.

2) The term, unlike its (re)appearance in the United States (concurrent with the rise of the Nazis), had a decidedly negative usage – popularised by Nietzsche by means of the notion of *ressentiment* or slave morality.
3) This term is anti-Semitic. While Cohen uses the term to refer specifically to the exclusion of Jews, several of the essays in this volume consider its connection to another related form of exclusion in Europe today – Islamophobia. Given that the term 'Semite' was used in Germany in the 19th century by orientalists, theologians and philologists to include Arabs and Muslims, Cohen's claim rings as true today as sixty years ago.

Broadly speaking, these three claims can be categorised into (1) issues of historical context, (2) lines of theological and philosophical inquiry, or (3) political implications. For this reason, the contributions in this volume have been grouped under these three major headings. Understandably, while several of the articles in this book are able to dialogue with more than just one of these three considerations, what follows is a brief summary of each contribution that clarifies why we have chosen to order them in this way.

1 History

Four contributions make up this first part. **Stanley Jones** traces the term 'Jewish Christianity,' from its first use by John Toland to its use a century later by Ferdinand Christian Baur. By looking at the historical contexts of both their writings, Jones concludes that while both authors were interested in ancient Jewish Christianity, they were both not interested in the Judeo-Christian tradition as such. **Peter Hodgson**, in his turn, examines Baur's interpretation of Christianity's relationship to Judaism and argues that, taken on its own merits (without the subsequent reception of Baur by later scholars), Baur strived hard to strike an appropriate balance when describing Christianity's relationship to Judaism. **Ivan Kalmar** takes a closer look at 19th century Orientalism and, in so doing, shows that Jews of that 'long century' were associated in the Christian mind with Muslims, but such was the attraction to the Orient that 'self-orientalizing Jews' would themselves have seen greater affinity with a shared Judeo-Muslim tradition than the Judeo-Christian tradition of today's European discourse. **Noah Strote** then analyzes the logic of Judeo-Christianity as it developed in the latter half of the 20th century in post-war Germany and how that was shaped by a post-Shoah and Cold War context.

Taken as a whole, these four contributions offer a broad historical view of events from the turn of the 18th century, through the so-called 'long 19th century', to the latter half of the 20th century. They also help situate and contextualise the influence that Baur would have on later uses of the term 'Judeo-Christian'. Another observation is the distinctly European (even German) context to such discussions, well before the term 'Judeo-Christian' would become a 'floating signifier' and cross into other continents and contexts.

2 Theology and Philosophy

Another way of looking at the signifier 'Judeo-Christian' is to parse its significance in theological and philosophical terms. The second part of the volume comprises five contributions. **Emmanuel Nathan** examines the Apostle Paul, often seen as the first embodiment of the 'Judeo-Christian' before Judaism and Christianity formally parted ways. In particular, Nathan looks at the reclamation of the 'Jewish Paul' in biblical studies and argues that a Christian tendency persists in situating the Apostle between law and love. From another angle, **Gesine Palmer** analyses the new Paulinism – a philosophical interest in the Apostle Paul coming from such philosophers as Giorgio Agamben, Slavoj Žižek, and Alain Badiou. She warns, however, against a new kind of antinomianism to be found in their works, which these thinkers associate with Jewish law. **Marianne Moyaert** reflects on the theological significance of the 'Judeo-Christian' tradition as a Catholic theologian conscious of writing in the post-Shoah period and following the Second Vatican Council. She cautions, however, against an over-enthusiasm within some Catholic circles to celebrate Christian Seder Meals and uses this concrete instance to reflect more deeply on the challenges of stressing too much continuity between Judaism and Christianity. **Christoph Schmidt** takes as his starting point a debate between Jürgen Habermas and Joseph Ratzinger on a post-secular relation between secular society and religion. In light of this he examines the demand for an alternative reconstruction of the classical enlightened canon of modernity created at the end of the 18th century by Gotthold Ephraim Lessing, in which Judaism is succeeded by Christianity and the latter in turn by modern enlightened culture. **Michael Fagenblat** commences his contribution by outlining Emmanuel Levinas's 'research project' on Judeo-Christianity based on Levinas' notes during his time as a prisoner of war (between 1940 and 1945). From there, Fagenblat traces Levinas' phenomonology of Judeo-Christianity, particularly in light of Israel's 'Passion' in the Shoah, but concludes that discussion on this fraught 'fraternal existence' between Judaism and Christianity should also nowadays include Islam, so that it may offer a corrective to the otherwise one-sided binary opposition of today's geo-political alliances. In this way, Fagenblat sets the stage to move on to the third political part of the volume.

Read together, these five contributions occupy a fitting 'middle section' to the volume, reflecting as they do on theological and philosophical currents in the latter half of the 20th century, but at the same time looking back to their 19th (sometimes even 18th) century antecedents, and then forward to realities and challenges in the 21st century. Starting the section with biblical studies also offered a linking function to the preceding chapters on the origins of the signifier 'Judeo-Christian' and their rootedness in philological and history-of-religions approaches. At the same time, kicking off the section with the apostle Paul also revealed how he embodies an apt intersection of historical, theological, and philosophical discourses (with even a faint nod to potential political implications), and these theological and philosophical discourses then continued to unwind and rewind through the remaining section. Taken together, the contributions in this section also reflect how discussions on the 'Judeo-Christian' signifier have changed in the aftermath of the Shoah. In addition, what equally becomes apparent are the subtle differences between Protestant and Catholic approaches on the 'Christian' side of this hyphen, inasmuch as the 'Jewish' side equally attests to a rich diversity of opinions and positions.

3 Contemporary Political Implications

The third and final part is comprised of four contributions. **Warren Zev Harvey** takes us through the understanding of the Judeo-Christian tradition in the USA since the 1940s and how its usage has been contrasted against five 'others': (1) the Christian tradition; (2) Hellenism; (3) modern secularism; (4) other religious traditions; and (5) the Judeo-Christo-Islamic tradition, i.e., the Abrahamic or monotheistic tradition. Not all of its uses are praiseworthy, just as some are not entirely blameworthy either. Other uses are simply indifferent. The context in which it is used is therefore of paramount importance. **Itzhak Benyamini** takes as his starting point Lyotard's notion of the hyphen in the signifier 'Judeo-Christian' and asks whether, in light of the long theological and historical encounters between the two religious traditions, the relations between them need to be reconsidered in a more complex way than simply their connection, or disconnection, through a hyphen. The political ramifications of Benyamini's reflections become immediately clear in the contribution by **Amanda Kluveld.** She analyzes the different uses of the signifier 'Judeo-Christian' in debates on European current affairs. She also compares how the European usage of the term differs from its usage in the USA. In the United States the idea of a Judeo-Christian tradition is part of a civil religion. In Europe, however, the term is not connected to either the Christian or the Jewish tradition. It is an instrument in a toolbox of political rhetoric that appeals to a secular search for an identity or even Europe's soul. Finally, **Anya Topolski** traces the genealogy of the signifier Judeo-Christianity in order expose the problematic political stakes of European identity constructions. Topolski argues that the signifier creates only an illusory unity since it does so by exclusionary means. A signifier that was previously used to exclude Jews is now being used to exclude Muslims, another of Europe's historical others. Both Kluveld and Topolski's contributions close the circle begun by Warren Zev Harvey's contribution in this section, but also link back to earlier discussions on Baur, supersessionism, Orientalism, anti-Semitism, and Islamophobia that have arisen in previous sections of this volume.

While the contributions in this section can certainly be read on their own terms, they cohere well together in reflecting on the broader societal and political implications of the signifier 'Judeo-Christian' once their historical origins, and theological-philosophical connotations have been adequately considered. This is also reflected in the chronology of this section. The political implications of the Judeo-Christian signifier have their roots and antecedents in the 19th and 20th centuries, but the contributions in this section are resolute in discussing its impact on current affairs in today's 21st century context. In addition, whereas due recognition is given to the usage of the signifier in the United States, the majority of the contributions return the discussion to its European origins and choose to reflect upon the impact it has on contemporary European political discourse. In doing so, the 'contemporary floating signifier' has come full circle, returning to its Europeans origins.

***

In lieu of an epilogue or conclusion, which might imply that this inquiry into the European genealogy of the signifier 'Judeo-Christian' tradition is complete (or can be completed), we would like to reiterate a few insights gathered from this volume that we hope will contribute to a continuing conversation. As the third section in this volume makes clear, the signifier in Europe today has found itself confronted with new realities and challenges. What is often overlooked is how complex and significant its European story was and is, a story that weaves itself through centuries of theology, philosophy, philology, and politics. What is clear is that it has had and continues to have many different meanings and usages and, if there is one lesson we must carry forward, it is that if one should choose to use this term (in spite of all the reasons not to do so), then it is imperative that we qualify what we mean when doing so. Moreover, when we hear others using this term, especially in academic circles, it would be good to ask for clarification for as, Condorcet wisely remarked in 1793, "the corruption of the meaning of words hints at the corruption of things in themselves" (71).

Bibliography

Andras, Charles, and Bernard Hubert. *Jacques Maritain en Europe: la réception de sa pensée*. Paris: Editions Beauchesne, 1996.

Becker, Adam H., and Annette Yoshiko Reed, eds. *The Ways That Never Parted: Jews and Christians in Late Antiquity and the Early Middle Ages*. Fifth or Later Edition. Minneapolis: Fortress Press, 2007.

Boyarin, Daniel. *Border Lines: The Partition of Judaeo-Christianity*. Philadelphi, NJ: University of Pennsylvania Press, 2006.

Cohen, Arthur Allen. *The Myth of the Judeo-Christian Tradition, and Other Dissenting Essays*. New York: Schocken Books, 1971.

Cohen, Arthur Allen, David Stern, and Paul R. Mendes-Flohr. *An Arthur A. Cohen Reader: Selected Fiction and Writings on Judaism, Theology, Literature, and Culture*. Detroit , MI: Wayne State University Press, 1998.

Condorcet, Antoine-Nicolas De. *Sketch for the Progress of the Human Mind*. New York: Noonday, 1955.

Dunn, James D. G. *Jews and Christians: The Parting of the Ways, A. D. 70 to 135*. Grand Rapids, Mich: Wm. B. Eerdmans Publishing Co., 1999.

Gover, Yerach. "Why Be a Nebbish? A Response to Marshall Grossman." *Social Text* 22 (1989): 123–9.

Grossman, Marshall. "The Violence of the Hyphen in Judeo-Christian." *Social Text* 22 (1989): 115–22.

Heller, Bernard. "About the Judeo-Christian Tradition." *Judaism* 1 (1951): 260–1.

Jones, F. Stanley. *The Rediscovery of Jewish Christianity from Toland to Baur*. Atlanta: Society of Biblical Literature, 2012. *Open WorldCat*. Web. 12 Nov. 2013. http://www.sbl-site.org/assets/pdfs/pubs/063705P.front.pdf October 20th 2015.

Lincicum, David. "F. C. Baur's Place in the Study of Jewish Christianity." *The Rediscovery of Jewish Christianity from Toland to Baur*. Ed. F. Stanley Jones. Atlanta: Society of Biblical Literature, 2012. 137–66. *Open WorldCat*. Web. 12 Nov. 2013. http://www.sbl-site.org/assets/pdfs/pubs/063705P.front.pdf October 20th 2015.

Maritain, Jacques. *Christianity and Democracy, and The Rights of Man and Natural Law*. San Francisco, CA: Ignatius Press, 2012.

Mimouni, S. C. *Early Judaeo-Christianity: Historical Essays*. Leuven: Peeters Publishers, 2012.

Nelson, Eric. *The Hebrew Republic: Jewish Sources and the Transformation of European Political Thought*. Reprint. Boston: Harvard University Press, 2011.

Rottenberg, Isaac. "The Idea of a Judeo-Christian Worldview: Religiopolitical Reflections." *Journal of Ecumenical Studies* 37.3/4 (2000): 401–420.

Sebban, Joel. "Genèse de La 'Morale Judéo-Chrétienne': étude Sur L'origine D'une Expression Dans Le Monde Intellectuel Français." *Revue de L'histoire Des Religions* (2012): Volume I, 85–133.
Silk, Mark. 'Notes on the Judeo-Christian Tradition in America.' American Quarterly 36, no. 1 (1 April 1984): 65–85. doi:10.2307/2712839.
Teixidor, Javier. *Judeo-Christianisme*. Paris: Gallimard Education, 2006.
Topolski, Anya. "Spinoza's True Religion: The Modern Origins of a Contemporary Floating Signifier." *Society and Politics* 8.1: 41–59, 2014.
Topolski, Anya. "Tzedakah: The True Religion of Spinoza's Tractatus?" *History of Political Thought* (2016): Vol. XXXVII. No. 1. Spring 2016, pp 78–106.

Part 1: **History**

F. Stanley Jones

2 Jewish Christianity and the Judeo-Christian Tradition in Toland and Baur

Modern scholarship on the New Testament and early Christianity is accustomed to employ the concept of "Jewish Christianity" in its historical discussions. The term has also been adopted in treatments of rabbinic writings.[1] This concept of Jewish Christianity would seem to be relevant also for examination of the notion of a Judeo-Christian tradition and thus merits closer evaluation.

Since about the middle of the twentieth century, however, the category "Jewish Christianity" has itself been subject to increasing scrutiny. Scholars of religions in antiquity have felt under mounting pressure to define the term before using it, and quite different definitions have been formulated and deployed.[2] The formulation of definitions has led to brief overviews of the other competing definitions and thus to the rudiments of a history of scholarship. More recently, the history of research has been pursued in and of itself and has led to considerable revision of accepted wisdom about the subject (Carleton Paget 2010). In particular, the conventional view that a German theologian–New Testament and church historian Ferdinand Christian Baur–initiated the study of Jewish Christianity in an article from 1831 (Baur 1831b)[3] has now been thoroughly debunked (Jones 2012 and cf., e.g., Lieu 2013). Through the use of an increasing number of books available on the Internet, it seems to have been possible to locate the first usage of the term "Jewish Christianity" and to isolate the introduction of the category in historical investigations of early Christianity in the work of the Irish-born freethinker John Toland, well over a hundred years before Baur. Neither Toland nor Baur, however, wrote of a Judeo-Christian tradition.[4] It nevertheless seems well worth exploring why they did not and whether they approximated the notion

1 E.g., Visotzky 1989.

2 Carleton Paget 2010, 297–316, provides a recent review with copious references to the literature.

3 See the documentation for this view in Carleton Paget 2010, 290.

4 For details on terminological issues, see the historical review in Lemke 2001, especially for usage in German theological writings, where the term "Judenchristentum" gradually becomes dominant especially via Baur and his student Albert Schwegler; see further specifics in Jones 2012, 128 n. 28, 133 with n. 65. In Romance languages, the terminological situation is somewhat different insofar as phrases corresponding to "Judeo-Christianity" predominate (e.g., "judéo-christianisme" in French).

of such a tradition, especially when they treated the historical phenomenon of Jewish Christianity.

John Toland (1670–1722) has, in fairly recent times, become the subject of growing international interest for students of the Enlightenment. The neglect of Toland, whatever its exact origins, has been found to be historically indefensible, and productive studies of this historical figure have flourished.[5] The present essay will examine only a few aspects of Toland's thought and writings, though it rests upon the results of the broader rediscovery of Toland in recent times.

Of particular concern here is that Toland seems to have been the first writer to have used the term "Jewish Christianity," featured not least in the title of his *Nazarenus: Or, Jewish, Gentile, and Mahometan Christianity* (1718). Furthermore, Toland is renowned for having written a treatise entitled *Reasons for Naturalizing the Jews in Great Britain and Ireland, On the Same Foot with All Other Nations. Containing also, A Defence of the Jews against All Vulgar Prejudices in All Countries* (1714). These two facts alone would seem to provide sufficient reason to ask if Toland was familiar with a notion of a Judeo-Christian tradition and if he promoted such.

A beginning of the inquiry may be made with Toland's introduction of the term "Jewish Christianity" (Myllykoski 2012, 35). It is true that in exegetical commentary on the Bible before the time of Toland, terms such as Christian Jew, Hebrew Christian, Jew Christian, and Jewish Christian had been used to describe those early Christians who were of Jewish descent and upbringing. Such terms had also been used to describe Jews who had converted to Christianity in the sixteenth and seventeenth centuries (Myllykoski 2012, 5–7) and furthermore to describe Christians of the radical reformation who adopted Jewish customs in conformity with the Hebrew Bible (Myllykoski 2012, 7–9). Some accounts indicate that a portion of the latter actually called themselves "Christian Jews" (Myllykoski 2012, 8), while elsewhere the terms were used in a pejorative manner to describe Christians with whom one disagreed, usually because they observed something considered too "ceremonial." At this time, the correlation of the ancient Jewish Christians with the contemporary "Jewish Christians" was evident to all sides.

Indeed, the young Toland likely gained an interest in the ancient Jewish Christians through his encounters with contemporary "Jewish Christians." After his Masters degree in Edinburgh, Toland moved to London and came into close relations with Daniel Williams (Sullivan 1982, 3); Toland states that he also became intimately acquainted with Williams's brother-in-law, Joseph Stennett, the famous pastor and hymnwriter of the Baptist Sabbatarian congregation in

5 A substantial foundation for this work was laid by Carabelli 1975, 1978.

London (Toland 1718, 53–54). Williams assisted in gaining financial support for Toland to pursue theological studies in the Netherlands (Sullivan 1982, 3–4). And Toland himself expressly connects his initial studies of the Jewish Christians with this time of his with Frederick Spanheim in Leiden:

> I was long before directed to my materials [sc. on the ancient Jewish Christians] by the celebrated FREDERIC SPANHEMIUS, when I study'd Ecclesiastical History under him at Leyden, tho I differ widely from my master in this point. (Toland 1718, iii–iv)[6]

Coming from the background just described, Toland had, from the start, personal reasons to question Spanheim's view that the Ebionites and Nazoraeans were a *later* perversion (a heretical misunderstanding) of the gospel (Spanheim 1829, 216–217, listed here with other "aberrations from Christian simplicity" and the qualification that "the heresy of the Ebionites [...] sprang up after the destruction of Jerusalem").[7]

Toland's positive attitude towards the Jews–to look now at another part of the equation–has been seen as an element that sharply distinguishes him from other Enlightenment thinkers (Wiener 1941, 215, 219–220; Flusser 1988, 208). It seems quite likely that the background and original fount for Toland's attitude is also connected with the religious environment Toland experienced in London in the early 1690s. Millennialism (the belief that Christ was about to return to set up an earthly kingdom) flourished around the time of the execution of Charles I (January 1649), and though a series of (inevitable) disappointments ensued, certain themes surfaced that endured variously. One topic was an increased inter-

---

6 Toland goes to the Netherlands and flourishes in the aftermath of the writings of Baruch Spinoza. By this time, distance from Spinoza had been variously established or proclaimed in Protestant theological circles in the Netherlands (e.g., by Jean LeClerc). Spinoza's influence on Toland's historical work has been variously estimated, from central and decisive (following the lead of Colie 1959) to rather mitigated. One issue is that Toland apparently never directly acknowledges Spinoza in this context and mentions instead figures such as Spanheim, whereas he directly takes issue with Spinoza in his version of pantheism. See also n. 9, below, for another aspect of the problem.

7 Here Spanheim essentially presents the standard view of his time regarding the ancient Jewish Christians. This perspective on the Jewish Christians established itself among the ancient Christian heresiologists and dominated throughout the Middle Ages into the early modern period. According to this view, some Jewish followers of Jesus were unable to abandon their attachment to the Jewish law and thus reintroduced elements of the Jewish law back into the message of Jesus. Some of these Jewish Christians were said to have held a low opinion of Christ (as a normal human, born of natural human intercourse), in line with their inability to comprehend his spiritual message.

est in the status of the Jews and the notion that their conversion would remove a final major obstacle to the coming of the millennium.[8]

Toland's difference from other Enlightenment thinkers with respect to the Jews is based, in his mature thought, on his understanding of religious universalism and particularism, which he connected with Cicero (G. Palmer 1996, 107–110).[9] Toland thought that the universal law found necessary and particular expression in the traditions of the various nations and therefore that it was contrary to reason to ask the various nations to abandon their particular traditions that incorporated the universal law. Applied to the Jews, this perspective meant for Toland that the Jews should always subsist as a distinct nation, as heirs to their particular traditions[10] that incorporate the universal law. Jesus, in Toland's view (1718, 39), was "a reformer of the abuses which had gradually crept in upon it [the Jewish Law]." The ancient Jewish Christians thus properly continued to "observe their own country rites" (1718, 39), and this was indeed the original plan of Christianity (1718, 64) in which Jewish Christians would stand in "Union without Uniformity" with Gentile Christians (1718, v [in italics in the original]). Jewish Christians were "the first Christians and consequently the only Christians for some time" (1718, 25). "Jewish Christianity" was thus postulated by Toland to be an entity unto itself–a justifiable distinctive type of Christianity. Jews and Jewish Christians then should not have been forced to give up their particular tradition (1718, 50: "the Levitical Law"), nor is it reasonable or right to ask Jews to give up their particular tradition now (1718, 56). Jewish Christians in this perspective form a type of Judaism. In principle, one could think of this type of Judaism as a representative of a Judeo-Christian tradition, though this concept does not match Toland's usage and, indeed, surprisingly seems foreign to his thought, as will be seen.

Gentile Christianity, in Toland's view, is derivative from Judaism and, in a sense, is based on it. Thus, Toland wrote (1720, i) that his investigations of the Mosaic theocracy was "my duty, as the Religion I profest was founded on the MOSAIC *Institution*." Yet according to the original plan of Christianity, "the dis-

8 See, e.g., Katz 1994, 112–113; newer literature is documented in Shear 2011, 96–97 n. 15.

9 Wiener 1941, 217–218, sees the background for Toland's thought here in Spinoza but has difficulty in explaining the principles by which Toland moved beyond Spinoza ("his [sc. Toland's] evaluations and conclusions differ widely [sc. from Spinoza's]" (217), though he briefly mentions Cicero (231); this is where G. Palmer's insights are particularly helpful. See also the more radical exposition of Toland's relevant thought in terms of political philosophy/theology in M. Palmer 2002, 106–151.

10 "This Law they look'd upon to be [...] expressive of the history of their peculiar nation" (1718, 38).

ciples from among the Gentiles do stand under no obligation to keep that Law, either as it is ceremonial or judicial" (1718, 72). While original Gentile Christianity was indeed obliged to obey the Noachide laws, insofar as they lived among the Jewish Christians (1718, 65, 69), even this original plan of Christianity has been disrupted: there are effectively no Jewish Christians anymore[11] (living in one society with Gentile Christians), so Gentile Christians are not even under the Noachide laws.[12] By its observance of Noachide laws, Islam proves itself to be a "peculiar Christianity" that deserves toleration "as any other Sectaries"(1718, 61).[13] For Toland (1696, 46) the essence of Christianity would seem to be a proclamation of natural reason[14] that takes root in various ethnic contexts.

All in all, Toland does not spell out the Judeo-Christian-Muslim tradition[15] as such, which possibly could have included, for example, the "notion of one God"[16] (Toland would perhaps have ascribed this notion to natural religion). Accord-

---

11 Toland variously raises the possibility that Jews might become Christians. He says this would have been the case with himself, if he had been born a Jew (1720, 217), and he states that all Jews would now also be Christians, if the Gentile Christians had not persisted in forcing them to abandon their law (1718, 56; 1720, 219), but he leaves such cases theoretical.

12 Toland struggled somewhat with this point, as is apparent in the additions to the English version of *Nazarenus* (e.g., at 1718, 47–50; cf. esp. the comparative edition of the earlier French with the second edition of the English in G. Palmer 1996) as well as in the alterations/additions to the second English edition. In an addition, Toland (1718, 49) mentions the possibility that "shou'd all the Jews become Christian, and be resettl'd in Judea" matters would be different for the Gentile Christians living there.

13 See Toland 1718, 5, where it is stated that "you'll discover some of the fundamental doctrines of Mahometanism to have their rise [...] from the earliest monuments of the Christian religion." Throughout *Nazarenus*, Toland points out the precedence for Muslim beliefs in early Christianity; see, e.g., 1718, 17 (Muslim accounts that another person was crucified in the stead of Jesus), 1718, 24 (Muslim accounts of Paul). Thus, "the Mahometans may not improperly be reckon'd and call'd a sort or sect of Christians" (1718, 4).

14 Cf. Toland 1718, v: "Now, this *Gospel* consists not in words but in virtue; tis inward and spiritual, abstracted from all formal and outward performances" (in italics in the original). Cf. Toland 1726, 139: "JESUS CHRIST taught a reasonable Doctrine"; Toland 1718, 67: "one main design of Christianity was to improve and perfect knowledge of the Law of nature."

15 This concept is being introduced here in retrospect; it is not a phrase that Toland himself uses, though it seems to lie at hand for the modern reader. What is being pursued here is an attempt to work out exactly why Toland did not think in these terms.

16 Cf. Toland 1726, 130, where he summarizes one aspect of the teaching of Jesus as "he fixt the true notion of one God." In general, Toland (1726, 130) views Jesus as having undertaken a radical cleansing when he "begun to disperse those thick clouds of ignorance which from the Jews and Gentiles had much obscur'd the perfect truth." Jesus's mission is thus viewed as a qualitatively distinct restoration of natural religion, with the resultant true Christianity as "a perfect Religion" (1726, 132).

ingly, in his presentation of "The Primitive Constitution of the Christian Church" there is essentially no talk of a tradition inherited from Judaism (Toland 1726).[17] In his plea for the naturalization of the Jews, Toland similarly does not appeal to a common Judeo-Christian tradition; rather, he asserts (1714, 12) that the Jews will "never join any Party in civil Affairs, but that which patronizes LIBERTY OF CONSCIENCE and the NATURALIZATION, which will ever be the side of Liberty and the Constitution" and argues extensively (1714, 50–56) that Jews have little intention of proselytizing.[18] Indeed, Toland's promotion of differences and diversity serves his larger vision of "Union without Uniformity."[19]

Thus, for all of Toland's glorification of the Mosaic republic,[20] Toland makes little room for a Judeo-Christian tradition in his thought on this subject. Other ethnic groups (historic nations) should perhaps be inspired by the Judaic tradition (the incredible Mosaic republic), but Christian groups are not viewed as the direct extension of this tradition.[21] Thus, the study of ancient Irish Christianity that follows in *Nazarenus* may be viewed a sample of how an early Christianity flourished in a particular ethnic setting "before the Papal corruptions and Usurpations."[22]

---

17 Toland (1726, 199–200) discusses the "imposition of hands" as "a ceremony peculiarly us'd by the Jews" that has been widely used among the Christians, but he denies it to be "a necessary Rite of divine Institution."

18 Toland (1714, 54) states: "were they now in full possession of their old Government and Country, they wou'd not endeavor to convert all the world to their THEOCRACY."

19 The expression "Union without Uniformity" is found in Toland 1718, v, where it is applied to the original plan of Christianity with respect to Jews and Gentiles.

20 In this regard, see particularly G. Palmer's poignant reconstruction of what Toland's never written work "The Mosaic Republic" intended to express (1996, 94–117), "damit andere Gesellschaften sich an ihrem Beispiel orientieren können (so that other societies could orient themselves through their [sc. the Jews'] example)" (111). (Translations from German and Latin throughout this article are my own and have been provided for possible assistance to the reader.)

21 Cf. Wiener 1941, 241: "Unfettered by Church dogma he [Toland] refuses to see in Judaism the precursor of Christianity, with Judaism yielding its place to the new faith, as had been taught by the Church." But it is skewed and not fully adequate when Wiener (1941, 242) writes: "Christianity is nothing but Judaism without the specific ritual Law." G. Palmer (1996, 111 n. 279) writes: "Wie sehr de facto die jüdischen Traditionen in Tolands England als Bestandteile der christlichen Überlieferung die ursprünglichen Traditionen der verschiedenen Völker überdecken, denen doch, nach dem nazarenischen Plan, ein eigener Platz durchaus zustünde [...] (However much, in Toland's England, Jewish traditions as pieces of the Christian heritage overlay the various nations' original traditions, which according to the program of *Nazarenus* supposedly deserved their own place [...])." One can compare and contrast with Toland his near contemporary William Whiston; see Shear 2011.

22 So the individual title page before "Letter II" (1718).

When approaching F. C. Baur (1792–1860) with the question of whether he approximated the notion of a Judeo-Christian tradition, one is taken back, of course, to an earlier stage in German historical study of early Christianity. Many issues that are taken for granted today as self-evident simply had not been raised in Baur's day; indeed, a number of these issues were first raised and established as givens in response to Baur.

Of importance for an understanding of Baur's work is consideration of his often-neglected starting point in the broader history of religions. Baur's first work entitled *Symbolik und Mythologie oder die Naturreligion des Alterthums* (1824–1825) is a broad comparison of world religions organized under a systematizing scheme of thought guided by the (Schleiermachian) "feeling of dependency" (doctrine of God, doctrine of the world, doctrine of the human, doctrine of immortality), following upon extensive terminological prolegomena (clarification of the concepts of mythology and religion) and a general historical overview of the world's religions and their possible relations with each other.[23] The presupposition of this massive endeavor is that Christianity is the most perfect form of religion in both its interior and exterior aspects (1:161, where Baur proceeds from "dem Christenthum als derjenigen Religionsform aus, in welcher, wie die innere Einheit, so auch die äussere die vollkommenste seyn muß [Christianity as that form of religion in which, just as the internal unity, so also the external (unity) must be the most perfect]"). Christ is readily seen as "the founder of a new religion and church (Stifter einer neuen Religion und Kirche)" (ibid.) and as differing "in a totally distinctive manner (auf eine ganz ausgezeichnete Weise)" even from the religions that similarly call on a founder (ibid., mentioning Moses and

---

23 One can see a (quite conservative, even reactionary) starting point for this approach and presentation in his earlier extensive review of C. Kaiser, *Die biblische Theologie, oder Judaismus und Christianismus nach der grammatisch-historischen Interpretations-Methode, und nach einer freimüthigen Stellung in die kritisch-vergleichende Universalgeschichte der Religionen und in die universale Religion*, vol. 1: *Erster oder theoretischer Theil* (Baur 1818). As is perhaps partially apparent from the title, Kaiser's first volume is itself a quite exceptional and remarkable attempt to present Christianity in the context of the general history of religions. On Kaiser and this volume, see Kantzenbach 1960, 87–98.

It seems that young Baur was assigned (or assumed for himself) the task of critiquing Kaiser's rationalistic foray and, through his extensive remarks, got himself into the bind of needing to offer a better definition of religion, etc., which found expression in *Symbolik und Mythologie*. For a general presentation of what Baur is up to in *Symbolik und Mythologie*, see Hester 1994, who in n. 25 on p. 73 also points to the review of Kaiser as well as another, unpublished work by Baur for the background of this study. A sympathetic presentation of Baur's development is found in Zeller 1865, which is essential reading on Baur (Zeller, an acclaimed scholar in his own right, was Baur's son-in-law).

Muhammed).[24] This work, with its idealistic vocabulary and forms of thought, stems from Baur's decade in Blaubeuren at a small Protestant preparatory school where he taught Classics and focused on comparative mythology. Only upon his appointment in Tübingen, to the established theological faculty in the midst of a major university, was Baur's area of teaching specified as the historical theological disciplines (church history, New Testament history, history of dogma, etc.; Hodgson 1966, 16–17).

For the current investigation, what is particularly noteworthy in *Symbolik und Mythologie oder die Naturreligion des Alterthums* is the modest role played by Judaism. In his survey of world religions,[25] Judaism is never treated as a (significant) entity in itself.[26] Judaism is rather subsumed under the broader category of oriental religion.[27] His idealistic form of thinking "erlaubt Baur, den Eintritt des Christentums in die Welt als den Angelpunkt der ganzen Weltgeschichte darzustellen (allows Baur to present the entrance of Christianity into the world as the pivotal points of the entire history of the world)."[28] The contrast of Christianity to the *entire* pre-Christian history of humanity is actually Baur's motivating impulse.[29]

Once Baur reaches Tübingen (again), he starts to focus in on the historical studies for which he is famous, though he never abandons the notion of identifying the grand ideas at work in history–especially as postulated in Schelling's idealistic philosophy, with the absolute or universal coming to self-consciousness

---

24 See similar remarks such as "der entschiedene Vorzug des Christenthums vor allen andern Religionen (the distinct superiority of Christianity over all other religions)" in 1824–1825, 1:164, and comments in 1824–1825, 1:211 (distinguishing Christianity rather strongly from Judaism and Islam).

25 Hester 1994, 75, properly points out that Baur did not intend to write a comprehensive history of religions; see Baur 1824–1825, 1:221–222, for some indication of what he is including and why (he is focused on what he perceives to be the grand developments in human religious history).

26 As something of a background for this, see Baur 1818, 701, 714–715, where he questions Kaiser's case for developments in Judaism that set the path for Jesus and earliest Christianity.

27 See, e.g., mention of Judaism in Baur 1824–1825, 1:210–211, 222, 2.2: 454.

28 Hester 1994, 79.

29 Hester 1994, 79–80, concludes his overview of *Symbolik und Mythologie oder die Naturreligion des Alterthums* with these words: "Baurs historische Konstruktion der Mythologie wurde demgemäß von zwei Grundpfeilern getragen, von einem orientalisch-griechischen Gegensatz innerhalb der symbolisch-mythischen Periode und von dem wesentlich höheren Gegensatz zwischen der vorchristlichen und der christlichen Periode überhaupt (Baur's historical treatment of mythology was accordingly founded on two basic pillars: on an Oriental-Greek contrariety during the symbolic-mythical period and on the significantly greater overall contrariety between the pre-Christian period and the Christian period)."

via the particular, which is thereby overcome.[30] A clear expression of this philosophical/theological foundation is Baur's early work in Tübingen *Die christliche Gnosis oder die christliche Religions-Philosophie in ihrer geschichtlichen Entwicklung* (1835), which closes with nearly two hundred pages devoted to a discussion of the "neuere Religions-Philosophie" of J. Böhme, Schelling, Schleiermacher, and Hegel. Baur states here (1835, VII–VIII) that only this newest philosophy of religion allows a proper understanding of the internal organism of the (ancient) gnostic systems.

Of interest in this study for the current question is Baur's presentation of Judaism as one of the three forms of religion behind gnosticism. Baur equates gentile religion with nature or material, Judaism with the notion of a creator god, and Christianity with Christ or redemption (1835, 25). For Baur, these three forms of religion form a ladder from lower to higher, and Baur expressly recognizes "mediating Judaism" (27). A couple of factors, however, keep Baur from speaking of a Judeo-Christian tradition. One the one hand, Baur found his "mediating Judaism" not generally in "common Judaism" (47) but rather in "a completely different form" (46), Alexandrian Judaism and the two earlier sects, the Essenes and the Therapeuts. These sects "rejected all animal sacrifices and the related temple cult in such a decisive way that we gain a very clear concept of the contrariety that they established against common Judaism" (46–47). On the other hand, Baur still sees in Christianity something essentially new, worthy of not only being termed a third major form of religion but of being called the absolute (26–27). It is apparent that only Baur's idealistic forms of thought and reasoning are what allows the determinations of such absolute distinctions and contrarieties.

During this period, Baur argued that the Ebionites (the distinctive Jewish Christians)[31] represented an extension of this "completely different form" of Judaism (1831a; 1835, 403). Nevertheless, for the Baur of this period the Ebionites were considered to be a group that arose *after* the first Jewish war with Rome (1831a, 24–25; as indicated above, in the discussion of Spanheim and Toland, this was the standard view of church historians from antiquity through the early modern period). The Ebionites thus do not represent the main Christian development but rather an attempt to re-Judaize Christianity insofar as they "were

---

30 Cf. a statement to this effect in Baur 1835, 22–23. For straightforward praise of Schelling's perspective as expressive of Baur's historical work later in his career, see the long footnote in Baur 1852, 248–249 n. 1.

31 In this study (1831a), Baur is not readily using the term "Jewish Christians" but is still employing the ancient heresiological designations. Baur 1831b, in contrast, more readily uses the term "Judenchristen," apparently prompted by his attempt to deal with the earlier period; cf., e.g., 1831b, 82–83, 108.

mixing in doctrines and practices of the Essenes with Christian doctrine (Essenorum dogmata et præcepta cum christiana doctrina miscebant)."[32] Accordingly, there would seem to be no true continuous Judeo-Christian tradition at work in earliest Christianity. Thus, when Baur deals with the pre-war Jewish Christians ("Judenchristen") reflected in Paul's letters, he similarly distances them from Peter, the disciple of Jesus, and James, the brother of Jesus, whom he nevertheless calls "Jewish apostles" ("Judenapostel"; 1831b, 114), and views these Jewish Christians as "judaizing" (1831b, 107: "Dieselben judaisirenden Gegner [the same judaizing opponents]") or *introducing* their brand of Judaism (1831b, 108–109).

Later, Baur (1863, 17) gave greater recognition to the Jewish heritage of Christianity, particularly the monotheistic notion of God: "In seinem Gottesbewusstsein weiss sich daher das Christenthum vor allem mit dem Judenthum Eins (Thus, in its consciousness of God, Christianity knows itself to be one, above all, with Judaism)." Nevertheless, Baur (1863, 17) qualified this heritage in a major way: "Aber der alttestamentliche Gottesbegriff hat auf der andern Seite auch ein so ächt nationales Gepräge, dass der ganze damit zusammenhängende und daraus hervorgegangene Particularismus in dem entschiedensten Gegensatz zum Christentum steht (But, on the other hand, the Old Testament concept of God also has such a genuinely national profile that the entire particularism, which is connected with it and issues from it, stands in the most decisive contrariety to Christianity)." Admittedly, Alexandrian Judaism, "a completely new form of Judaism," had already broken through the old Jewish particularism (1863, 19). "A deeply religious outlook on life" developed among the Essenes and is very close to Christianity, even if one cannot say that Christianity has its origin in Essenism (1863, 20). Despite these developments, Baur (1863, 22–23) found the essential element of Christianity not in these points of contact but rather in the unique person of Jesus and his proclamation.[33] Though the idea of the Messiah closely connects Judaism and Christianity and enables Christianity to be understood only on the background of Judaism (1863, 36), the death of Jesus meant the complete break with Judaism (1863, 39: "so war jetzt sein Tod der vollendete Bruch zwischen ihm

---

32 Baur 1831a, 31.

33 The answer to the question raised on these pages is partially found in Baur 1863, 28–29, where Baur asserts that the proclamation was "ein neues Prinzip (a new principle)" (28), "ein wesentlich Neues (something essentially new)" (29) that "wird von selbst zum qualitativen Gegensatz (develops of itself to the qualitative opposite)" (29). On p. 36, Baur states in summary: "Betrachtet man den Entwicklungsgang des Christenthums, so ist es doch nur die Person seines Stifters, an welcher seine ganze geschichtliche Bedeutung hängt (When one observes the developmental path of Christianity, its entire historical importance is finally dependent solely on the person of its founder)."

und dem Judenthum [thus his death was now the completed break between him and Judaism]").[34]

For the later Baur (1863, 44), Paul was the first to verbalize "Christian universalism in its fundamental distinction from Jewish particularism" (cf., however, inklings of this view already in 1831b, 109). Also at this late stage in his career, Baur (1863, 50) recognized that the opponents of Paul were none other than "the older apostles themselves" who had not overcome their Jewish particularism (1863, 51).[35] In contrast to Toland, Baur sees a radical opposition between Paul and the Jewish Christians. Indeed, the entire history of early Christianity is to be understood as the resolution and mediation of these two tendencies (1863, 72). What arises is Catholic Christianity (1863, 98–99), which picks up and transcends the particularism of Judaism (this is "im Universalismus des Christentums aufgehoben (transcended in the universalism of Christianity)"; 1863, 172). From this point on, Jewish Christianity can no longer be considered part of the Catholic church (1863, 173). These sorts of metaphysical transformations of the Spirit can leave mere historical realities (particularisms) in the dust, and thus, for Baur, the Jewish heritage of Christianity is entirely "aufgehoben" and no longer really relevant. Jewish Christianity was merely a stage in the development of Christianity that it passed through.[36] The principle of Christian universalism is superior to particularisms and will always overcome any particular expression of Christianity (1863, 107–108). For Baur (1852, 250), another such significant transformation occurred at the time of the Reformation, when Catholicism and the Papacy were transcended in a new form of Christian consciousness.

In conclusion, despite their attention to ancient Jewish Christianity, neither Toland nor Baur had much to say about the Judeo-Christian tradition. The reason for this silence differs in each case. For Toland, the view that historic nations had each developed their own particular tradition to embody the universal law hindered the idea that one of these particular traditions should be shared with extra-

---

34 The next sentence here (1863, 39) reads: "Ein Tod, wie der seinige, machte es für den Juden, so lange er Jude blieb, zur Unmöglichkeit, an ihn als seinen Messias zu glauben (A death such as his made it impossible for the Jew, to the degree that he remained a Jew, to believe in him as his Messiah)."

35 Baur 1865, 143, phrases it this way: "Das christliche Bewusstsein war in den Judenchristen noch nicht so erstarkt, dass man das Gesetz hätte fallen lassen können (Christian awareness among the Jewish Christians was not yet strong enough to allow the dropping of the law)."

36 Baur 1865, 161–162, writes: "Der Ebionitismus und Paulinismus sind der erste grosse Gegensatz, in welchem die Entwicklung des Christenthums und des christlichen Dogma sich bewegte (Ebionism and Paulinism make up the first great contrariety in which the development of Christianity and Christian dogma moved)."

neous nations to create a hybrid tradition. For Baur, idealistic forms of thought held him to the notion that Christianity was something absolutely new and similarly hindered him from giving greater weight to any shared traditions. Examination of these two cases brings to light important aspects of Western religious thought that still reverberate and resonate variously. In any event, they form a significant piece of the historical background for the modern discussion. While Toland was instrumental in the establishment of the historical category "Jewish Christianity," Baur's work, with its sharp emphasis on metaphysical distinctions and transformations, provoked as a counter-reaction the increasing study of Judaism at the time of Jesus and the exploration of the commonalities between the two[37] that are now standard for the field.

Bibliography

Baur, Ferdinand Christian. Review of C. Kaiser, *Die biblische Theologie, oder Judaismus und Christianismus nach der grammatisch-historischen Interpretations-Methode, und nach einer freimüthigen Stellung in die kritisch-vergleichende Universalgeschichte der Religionen und in die universale Religion*, vol. 1: *Erster oder theoretischer Theil. Archiv für die Theologie und ihre neuste Literatur* 2 (1818): 656–717.

Baur, Ferdinand Christian. *Symbolik und Mythologie oder die Naturreligion des Alterthums.* 2 vols. Stuttgart: J. B. Metzler, 1824–1825.

Baur, Ferdinand Christian. *De Ebionitarum origine et doctrina, ab Essenis repetenda.* Tübingen: Typis Hopferi de L'Orme, 1831a.

Baur, Ferdinand Christian. "Die Christuspartei in der korinthischen Gemeinde, der Gegensatz des petrinischen und paulinischen Christentums in der ältesten Kirche, der Apostel Petrus in Rom." *Tübinger Zeitschrift für Theologie* 4 (1831b): 61–206.

Baur, Ferdinand Christian. *Die christliche Gnosis oder die christliche Religions-Philosophie in ihrer geschichtlichen Entwicklung.* Tübingen: C. F. Osiander, 1835.

Baur, Ferdinand Christian. *Die Epochen der kirchlichen Geschichtschreibung.* Tübingen: Ludwig Friedrich Fues, 1852. English translation: "The Epochs of Church Historiography." *Ferdinand Christian Baur on the Writing of Church History.* Ed. and trans. Peter C. Hodgson. A Library of Protestant Thought. New York: Oxford University Press, 1968. 41–257.

Baur, Ferdinand Christian. *Kirchengeschichte der drei ersten Jahrhunderte.* 3rd ed. Tübingen: L. F. Fues, 1863. English translation: *The Church History of the First Three Centuries.* Trans. Allan Menzies. 2 vols. Theological Translation Fund Library. London: Williams and Norgate, 1878.

37 One thinks particularly of the work of Georg Heinrich August Ewald.

Baur, Ferdinand Christian. *Von der apostolischen Zeit bis zur Synode in Nicäa*. Pt. 1 of *Das Dogma der alten Kirche*. Vol. 1 of *Vorlesungen über die christliche Dogmengeschichte*. Ed. Ferd. Fr. Baur. Leipzig: Fues's Verlag (L. W. Reisland), 1865.

Carabelli, Giancarlo. *Tolandiana: Materiali bibliografici per lo studio dell'opera e della fortuna di John Toland (1670–1722)*. Florence: La Nuova Italia Editrice, 1975.

Carabelli, Giancarlo. *Tolandiana: Materiali bibliografici per lo studio dell'opera e della fortuna di John Toland (1670–1722), Errata, addenda e indici*. Pubblicazioni della Facoltà di Magistero dell'Università di Ferrara 4. Ferrara: Università degli studi di Ferrara, 1978.

Carleton Paget, James. "The Definition of the Term 'Jewish Christian'/'Jewish Christianity' in the History of Research." *Jews, Christians and Jewish Christians in Antiquity*. Wissenschaftliche Untersuchungen zum Neuen Testament 251. Tübingen: Mohr Siebeck, 2010. 289–324.

Colie, Rosalie L. "Spinoza and the Early English Diests." *Journal of the History of Ideas* 20 (1959): 23–46.

Flusser, David. "John Toland oder die ursprüngliche Absicht des Christentums." *Das jüdisch-christliche Religionsgespräch*. Ed. Heinz Kremers and Julius H. Schoeps. Stuttgart: Burg, 1988. 198–209.

Hester, Carl E. "Baurs Anfänge in Blaubeuren." *Historisch-kritische Geschichtsbetrachtung: Ferdinand Christian Baur und seine Schüler*. Ed. Ulrich Köpf. Contubernium 40. Sigmaringen: Jan Thorbecke, 1994. 67–82.

Hodgson, Peter C. *The Formation of Historical Theology: A Study of Ferdinand Christian Baur*. Makers of Modern Theology. New York: Harper & Row, 1966.

Jones, F. Stanley, ed. *The Rediscovery of Jewish Christianity: From Toland to Baur*. History of Biblical Studies 5. Atlanta, GA: The Society of Biblical Literature, 2012.

Kantzenbach, Friedrich Wilhelm. *Die Erlanger Theologie: Grundlinien ihrer Entwicklung im Rahmen der Geschichte der theologischen Fakultät 1743–1877*. Munich: Evang. Presseverband für Bayern, 1960.

Katz, David S. *The Jews in the History of England 1485–1850*. Oxford: Clarendon, 1994.

Lemke, Hella. *Judenchristentum zwischen Ausgrenzung und Integration: Zur Geschichte eines exegetischen Begriffes*. Hamburger Theologische Studien 25. Münster: Lit, 2001.

Lieu, Judith M. Review of *The Rediscovery of Jewish Christianity: From Toland to Baur*, ed. F. Stanley Jones. *Journal of Ecclesiastical History* 64 (2013): 647–648.

Myllykoski, Matti. "'Christian Jews' and 'Jewish Christians': The Jewish Origins of Christianity in English Literature from Elizabeth I to Toland's *Nazarenus*." *The Rediscovery of Jewish Christianity: From Toland to Baur*. Ed. F. Stanley Jones. History of Biblical Studies 5. Atlanta, GA: The Society of Biblical Literature, 2012. 3–41.

Palmer, Gesine. *Ein Freispruch für Paulus: John Tolands Theorie des Judenchristentums mit einer Neuausgabe von Tolands 'Nazarenus' von Claus-Michael Palmer*. Arbeiten zur neutstamentlichen Theologie und Zeitgeschichte 7. Berlin: Institut Kirche und Judentum, 1996.

Palmer, Michael. "Adeisidaemon, Vernunft zwichen Atheismus und Aberglauben: Materialismus & Commenwealth bei John Toland." Ph.D. diss., Technische Universität Berlin, 2002.

Shear, Adam. "William Whiston's Judeo-Christianity: Millenarianism and Christian Zionism in Early Enlightenment England." *Philosemitism in History*. Ed. Jonathan Karp and Adam Sutcliffe. Cambridge: Cambridge University Press, 2011.

Spanheim, Frederick. *Ecclesiatical Annals*. Trans. George Wright. Cambridge: T. Tevenson, 1829.

Sullivan, Robert E. *John Toland and the Deist Controversy: A Study in Adaptations*. Harvard Historical Studies 101. Cambridge, MA, and London: Harvard University, 1982.
Toland, John. *Christianity Not Mysterious*. London, 1696.
Toland, John. *Reasons for Naturalizing the Jews in Great Britain and Ireland, On the Same Foot with All Other Nations. Containing also, A Defence of the Jews against All Vulgar Prejudices in All Countries*. London: J. Roberts, 1714.
Toland, John. *Nazarenus: Or, Jewish, Gentile, and Mahometan Christianity*. 2nd ed., rev. London: J. Brotherton, J. Roberts, and A. Dodd, 1718. (Reproduced also in Jones 2012, 167–242)
Toland, John. *Tetradymus*. London: J. Brotherton, J. Roberts, and A. Dodd, 1720.
Toland, John. "The Primitive Constitution of the Christian Church." *A Collection of Several Pieces of Mr. John Toland*. 2 vols. London: J. Peele, 1726. 2:120–200.
Visotzky, Burton L. "Prolegomenon to the Study of Jewish-Christianities in Rabbinic Literature." *Association for Jewish Studies Review* 14 (1989): 47–70. (Reprinted in his *Fathers of the World: Essays in Rabbinic and Patristic Literature*. Wissenschaftliche Untersuchungen zum Neuen Testament 80. Tübingen: J. C. B. Mohr [Paul Siebeck], 1995. 129–149.)
Wiener, Max. "John Toland and Judaism." *Hebrew Union College Annual* 16 (1941): 215–242.
Zeller, Eduard. "Ferdinand Christian Baur." *Vorträge und Abhandlungen geschichtlichen Inhalts*. Leipzig: Fues's Verlag (L. W. Reisland), 1865. 354–434. (Originally published in *Preußische Jahrbücher* 7 [1861]: 495–512; 8 [1861]: 206–223, 283–314.)

Peter C. Hodgson

3 F. C. Baur's Interpretation of Christianity's Relationship to Judaism

In his lectures on New Testament theology, Ferdinand Christian Baur (1792–1860) emphasizes the differences that distinguish the authors of the individual New Testament writings from each other. The greatest difference bears upon "Christianity's relationship to Judaism," along with "all that bears upon the person of Jesus" and on how the "Christian principle" is grasped.[1] Baur's identification of the Jewish question as front and center for New Testament research explains why a renewed interest in the study of Jewish Christianity on the part of contemporary scholars finds itself engaged, positively or negatively, with Baur.[2]

The Racialist, Orientalist Critique of Baur

My concern at the outset is with the negative engagement from a perspective known as "Orientalism," which criticizes Western stereotypes about the East. This perspective is well represented by Shawn Kelley.[3] He says that Hegel's "racialized views" of history are transferred into the arena of biblical scholarship especially under the influence of Baur, who takes over Hegel's "fundamental antithesis between the Western (free) Greeks and the nonWestern (servile) Orientals and interjects it into the very heart of his analysis of emerging Christianity." Much as I would like to defend Hegel against such an assertion,[4] my focus in this essay is solely on Baur. Of Baur, Kelley writes:

---

1 *Vorlesungen über neutestamentliche Theologie*, ed. Ferdinand Friedrich Baur (Leipzig: Fues's Verlag, 1864), 20. Subsequent citations are abbreviated as *VNTTh*. Robert F. Brown and I are presently working on a translation of these lectures.

2 See James Carleton Paget, "The Reception of Baur in Britain," in *Ferdinand Christian Baur und die Geschichte des frühen Christentums*, ed. Martin Bauspiess, Christoph Landmesser, and David Lincicum (Tübingen: Mohr Siebeck, 2014), 380–86. Brown and I also plan to translate this collection.

3 Shawn Kelley, *Racializing Jesus: Race, Ideology and the Formation of Modern Biblical Scholarship* (London and New York: Routledge, 2002), quotations below from 6–7.

4 It could be pointed out, for example, that Hegel favorably compares the "breadth," "infinitude," and "free universality" of the Orient with the "abstract rigidity or finitude" of the West. Thus when Christianity first appears, in the Roman world, its highest ideals and deepest spirit-

> … He combined the antiJudaism of Christian theology (where the Jew, the repudiator of Jesus, comes to symbolize the antithesis to all that is good and honorable) with the racialized Orientalism of his day. He interjected this narrative into early Christianity by arguing that the fundamental divide within early Christianity was between the (despotic, fleshly, backwards, Eastern) Jewish Christianity and the (free, spiritual, dynamic, Western) Hellenistic Christians. Early Christianity, for Baur, is fueled by a conflict between Hebrew and Hellenist, which means between a slave and a free consciousness. The conflict of earliest Christianity eventually gives way to compromise, as the Western spirit of freedom makes its peace with the despotic spirit of the East and transforms itself in early Catholicism. It becomes the task of radical biblical scholars to strip away the Eastern and Catholic debris that impedes access to the authentic Western core of the New Testament.

In this summary form, such a critique is a gross caricature. But still there is a valid issue at stake. For our early-twenty-first century sensibilities, Baur's mid-nineteenth century interpretation of Judaism is problematic on at least two counts. First, the characteristic mark of Judaism is often described as "particularistic," by which Baur means that the God of Israel is understood to be the God of the Jewish people alone (the "chosen people") rather than the God of human beings as such, including Gentiles. Second, Baur understands Christianity to be the "absolute religion," which supersedes not only Jewish religion but other religions too, absorbing them into itself and transforming them. If particularism and supersession are markers of "Orientalism," so be it. But Baur's views are not racialist or crypto-racist.[5] He is not motivated by racial prejudice or religious antagonism, but by the attempt to understand how Christianity emerged as a religion distinct from Judaism, while at the same time Jewish factors remained an essential component of it. This is a legitimate historical question. How does historical novelty occur within the ongoing continuum of history? It does so (and here Baur acknowledges his indebtedness to Hegel) not through a supernatural incursion of the divine but through the process by which history changes – the interplay of powers and interpretations – or in logical terms the process of identity, difference, and mediation. Because history is unending, so also this process repeats itself in endless configurations. The unity of logic and history indicates (for Baur as well as Hegel) that the ideal and the real are inextricably intertwined. Logic is historicized, and reason is introduced into history.

---

uality come from the East, specifically from Judaism. Greece is seen to have a mediating role between East and West and becomes a factor only later in the history of Christianity. Georg Wilhelm Friedrich Hegel, *Lectures on the Philosophy of World History*, vol. 1, ed. and trans. Robert F. Brown and Peter C. Hodgson (Oxford: Clarendon Press, 2011), 451–2.

5 The term "race" is introduced into the translation of Baur's church history at points where it is not found in the German text. See below, n. 10.

Today we are inclined to think in terms of "identity" rather than "particularity," and we affirm the equivalent validity of the major world religions rather than the superiority of one over the others. The language of "identity," while neutral, leaves the question open as to, for example, how the identity of Christianity differs from the identity of Judaism – a question that contemporary scholarship rather prefers to avoid. But arguments about the superiority or inferiority of religions have proven to be fruitless and harmful, and most serious religious scholars today embrace some form of pluralism or recognition of equivalent validity. In this respect, Baur's approach is no longer acceptable. He views the religions in a progressive scheme, and indeed seems to make negative generalized remarks about Judaism, exaggerated perhaps by his dialectical oppositions. But if we look below the surface and at detailed analyses, we get a different picture.

Overview of Baur's Thesis about the Interaction between Jewish and Pauline Christianity in the Formation of the Early Church

Baur's critical New Testament studies began with his lengthy article of 1831 on the "Christ party" in the Corinthian church.[6] Here he engaged several of his predecessors (Gottlob Christian Storr, Johann Gottfried Eichhorn, Johann Ernst Christian Schmidt, and August Neander) on the question as to who the opponents were of Paul in Corinth (1 Corinthians 1:12), and in particular whether the Christ party represented Jewish Christianity. The question was not an original one for Baur, but he advanced the discussion of it in ways that became foundational for subsequent research. Much of this article was incorporated into his book on Paul in 1845,[7] and the results were summarized in his church history. As we shall see,

6 "Die Christuspartei in der korinthischen Gemeinde, der Gegensatz des petrinischen und paulinischen Christenthums in der ältesten Kirche, der Apostel Petrus in Rom," *Tübinger Zeitschrift für Theologie*, 5:4 (1831), 61–206.

7 *Paulus, der Apostel Jesu Christi: Sein Leben und Wirken, seine Briefe und seine Lehre*, 1st edn (Stuttgart: Becher und Müller, 1845); 2nd edn, ed. Eduard Zeller, 2 vols (Leipzig: Fues's Verlag, 1866–67). *Paul the Apostle of Jesus Christ, His Life and Works, His Epistles and Teachings*, trans. from the 2nd edn by Allan Menzies, 2 vols (London and Edinburgh: Williams & Norgate, 1873–75). Baur was working on revisions to this book when he suffered a stroke. He completed the revisions only for the first part (the life and work of the Apostle) and the beginning of the second part (the Pauline epistles), not for the third part (the theological framework of Paul). The *Vorlesungen über neutestamentliche Theologie* incorporate Baur's latest revisions to his treatment of Pauline

Baur came to regard the conflict between opposing tendencies as the driving force of early Christianity, and indeed of the whole of history.

The following summary of his thesis is based on the first volume of the church history.[8] Baur begins by claiming that the two parties – the Jewish Christians and the Pauline Christians – both have their origin in the figure of Jesus, one side focusing more on his moral-religious teaching and the other on his messianic person. In Antioch, fourteen years after Paul's conversion, the issue was whether Gentiles could become Christians without circumcision. We may deduce from the Corinthian epistles that a heated confrontation occurred between Peter and Paul, with Peter insisting that Gentile Christians cannot be on the same level with Jewish Christians, and Paul holding that all Christians are of equal status (*KG* 44–53, *CH* 51–5).

Paul attacked the foundations of the argument that salvation must include observance of the law and circumcision in his earliest epistle, Galatians (*KG* 53–57, *CH* 56–60). Even within the sphere of Jewish history the law is not the primary and original element. Above it stands the promise to Abraham, which points toward the time when righteousness will become the blessing of all nations. This promise can be fulfilled only when the law gives way to faith. The purpose of the law is a transitional one, to expose sin and prepare humanity to be set free from it. Judaism holds promise and fulfillment apart until the fullness of time has arrived. In the new community of Christ, there are no differences between Jew and Greek, circumcision and uncircumcision, rather all are one in faith manifesting itself as love. One should keep in mind that these ideas are expressed by Paul, a Jew by birth who argues for Christianity on the basis of his knowledge of the Hebrew scriptures (from his rabbinic training) and his conversion and missionary experience. The conflict here is between two ways of interpreting Judaism in relationship to Christianity, not between Judaism and Hellenism.[9] Paul too could

---

theology, and they are the only source for this revised presentation. See Zeller's Preface to *Paulus* 1: iii–iv; and F. F. Baur's Preface to *VNTTh* iii–iv.

8 *Das Christenthum und die christliche Kirche der drei ersten Jahrhunderte*, 1st edn (Tübingen: L. F. Fues, 1853), 2nd edn (1860), 3rd edn, identical with 2nd, published under the title *Kirchengeschichte der drei ersten Jahrhunderte* (1863). *The Church History of the First Three Centuries*, trans. from the 3rd edn, ed. by Allan Menzies, 2 vols (London and Edinburgh: Williams & Norgate, 1878–79). Subsequent citations are abbreviated as *KG* and *CH* (all the *CH* citations are from the first volume of the English translation).

9 Compare Anders Gerdmar's critique of Baur as the creator of "the Judaism-Hellenism dichotomy," in *Baur und die Geschichte des frühen Christentums*, 107–28, with Christof Landmesser's view of Baur as a modern interpreter of the Pauline idea of freedom, ibid., 161–94. See also W. D.

be regarded as a Jewish Christian, but with a radically new interpretation, one emphasizing the presence of the fulfillment in Christ.

To advance such a bold claim, Paul also had to claim an apostolic authority equal to or greater than that of the older apostles, who had known Jesus in the flesh. This is the issue that came up in Corinth and surfaces in the Corinthian epistles (*KG* 57–62, *CH* 60–65). Here the topics of law and circumcision have completely disappeared. Rather the question concerns the apostolic authority of Paul. Is Paul a true and genuine apostle at all? Paul has no empirical proof, apart from the results of his missionary labor, but only his subjective experience of seeing the Lord and being called by him. Here conflicting principles of authority oppose each other; the principle of Paulinism, writes Baur, is the emancipation of consciousness from every external authority and the elevation of the human spirit to freedom and light.

The height of the conflict between Jewish and Pauline Christianity occurs after the death of Paul and continues into the second century (*KG* 71–93, *CH* 76–98). The Pauline side is expressed in the Gospel of Luke and the deutero-Pauline epistles; the Jewish side in Revelation and Hebrews, Papias and Hegesippus, the Ebionites and Simon Magus. The virulent attacks on Paul found in the Pseudo-Clementine Homilies have Gnostic associations. The Ebionites consider Paul an apostate and false teacher, reject all his epistles, slander his memory, and claim that he was a Gentile by birth, not a Jew. In the Homilies and Recognitions, Paul appears in the character of Simon Magus, preaching a lawless doctrine. The Magus is nothing other than a caricature of Paul and becomes the great father of heretics, representing the views with which Paul is associated by his opponents.

But a reconciliation or mediation (*Vermittlung*) must also have occurred, otherwise a Catholic Church could never have arisen, a church that "cut off from itself everything extreme and united opposites within itself" (*KG* 94–106, *CH* 99–111). Baur hypothesizes that there must have been steps of reconciliation, from both sides but in different ways. The two parties sense that they belong together, act upon each other in the living process of development, each modifying and being modified by the other. The first step occurs when baptism comes to replace circumcision as the outward sign of initiation into the saving community. With increasing numbers of Gentiles converting without circumcision, the issue is resolved, as it were, on the ground. A second step occurs when Pauline universalism is transferred from Paul to Peter. According to the Clementine writ-

---

Davies, *Paul and Rabbinic Judaism: Some Rabbinic Elements in Pauline Theology*, 4th edn (Philadelphia: Fortress Press, 1980).

ings, Peter (not Paul) is the apostle to the Gentiles, and his mission ends with his alleged martyrdom in Rome.

Baur appreciates the contribution of Jewish Christianity to the formation of the Catholic Church (*KG* 106–109, *CH* 112–14). Without its hierarchical organization, which derives from Jewish theocracy, the church could never have survived against hostile forces and become a viable historical institution. Thus Jewish Christianity remains a permanent and essential feature of Christianity, and the tension between it and Paulinism furnishes the dynamic by which the church exists in the world. They are "the two factors of its historical movement" (*KG* 130, *CH* 137), the ideal factor and the real factor. When one factor threatens to submerge the other, resistance occurs and a new balance is established, for the church is and remains an ideal-real community, even after the Reformation when it assumes a new ecclesial form.

Baur summarizes his ecclesiology at the beginning of the third part of the church history, where he addresses the antithesis between Gnosticism and the Catholic Church.

> The very idea of the Catholic Church is that it should seek to rise above everything particular and merge it in the universality of the Christian principle; but on the other hand it is a no less essential part of its task to maintain and hold fast the positive elements of Christianity. In fact, what constitutes it a Catholic Church is that it stands in the middle to harmonize all tendencies and reject the one extreme as much as the other. Had not the idea that developed itself out of Christianity, the idea of the Catholic Church, overcome the particularism of Judaism, Christianity itself would have been a mere sect of Judaism. But on the other side, where it came into contact with paganism, it was threatened by a danger no less serious, namely the generalization and evaporation (*Verallgemeinerung und Verflüchtigung*) of its content by ideas through which Christian consciousness, spreading out in limitless expansion, would entirely lose its specific historical character. Now this was the tendency of Gnosticism. (*KG* 175–6, *CH* 185)

Gnosticism introduces speculative and philosophical considerations into Christian theology and stimulates its development in many ways, positive and negative. For example, the major Christian doctrines are first formulated in opposition to Gnostic heresies. Baur remains alert to the fact that *gnosis* is a powerful but dangerous tool, and that a balance has to be found between faith and thought, history and reason.

Baur's Interpretation of the Teaching of Jesus

Regarding the entrance of Christianity into the world as simply and absolutely a miracle requires stepping at once outside all historical connection, and the same interruption of the historical process is then equally possible at later stages as well. From Baur's historical-critical perspective, such a view is unacceptable, so the historian must view the so-called absolute beginning as itself "a link of the chain of history," and resolve it insofar as possible into its "natural elements" (*KG* 1, *CH* 1–2). These natural elements include the political universalism of the Roman Empire into which Christianity was born and the pre-Christian religions from which Christianity evolved. Baur discusses Christianity's anticipation in Greek philosophy and culture, but no direct influence from Greece occurs until the end of the second century (*KG* 3–16, *CH* 3–16). Its true antecedent is Judaism:

> Christianity arose on Jewish soil, and is connected with Judaism far more closely and directly. It professes to be nothing other than spiritualized Judaism: it strikes its deepest roots in the soil of the Old Testament religion... The special superiority that distinguishes Judaism from all the religions of the pagan world is its pure and refined monotheistic idea of God... In its consciousness of God, therefore, Christianity knows itself to be at one with Judaism. The God of the Old Testament is the God of the New, and all the teaching of the Old Testament concerning the essential distinctness of God from the world, and the absolute sublimity and holiness of God's nature, is also an essential part of Christian teaching. But on the other hand the Old Testament concept of God has so much a national stamp that the particularism connected with and ensuing from it stands in the most decisive antithesis to Christianity. (*KG* 16–17, *CH* 17–18)[10]

My purpose in quoting this passage is to emphasize not (in this instance) Baur's critique of Jewish particularism – which is certainly present in his writings along with the view that Christianity as the absolute religion supersedes previous religions – but rather his insistence that Christianity, not being miraculous in origin, does indeed arise on Jewish soil and is deeply connected with it. In other words, it is precisely Baur's historical-critical approach that drives him to a serious engagement with Judaism.

The teaching of Jesus, writes Baur, "is the foundation and presupposition for all that belongs to the history of the development of Christian consciousness. That is precisely why his teaching is what stands above and beyond all such development, what is immediate to it, is its origin. As such, Jesus' teaching is not theology but is instead religion. Jesus is the founder of a new religion" (*VNTTh* 45). For this

---

10 The English translation introduces extraneous language, including the category of "race," which is not found in the German text.

reason Baur treats only Jesus in Part One of his *Lectures on New Testament Theology*.[11] Theology starts in Part Two of the *Lectures* with the interpretation of Jesus on the part of the New Testament authors, initially Paul. As the founder, Jesus does not stand above history as such but constitutes one of its decisive turning points, the emergence of a new possibility (a *kairos* in Paul Tillich's sense[12]). This new possibility appears not simply out of the blue but only in relation to the existing form of religion.

The Relation of Jesus' Teaching to the Old Testament and to the Law

In the Sermon on the Mount, Jesus announces that he has come not to abolish the law and the prophets but to fulfill them (*VNTTh* 46–60). The Sermon makes it clear that Jesus stands wholly on the soil of the Old Testament, and that his relationship to it is not destructive but constructive. The law cannot be abolished until it has become actual truth and reality, and it does so when people adhere to it and abide by it. This in turn involves their becoming members of the kingdom of God, which in Matthew Jesus calls the kingdom of heaven. With his radical demands in the Sermon on the Mount, Jesus insists on a pure and sincere conscience (*Gesinnung*), a morality (*Sittlichkeit*) not made up of outward acts but one subsisting in the inner recesses of conscience. Such conduct gives human beings absolute moral worth in the eyes of God, or what Jesus calls "righteousness." This is not merely a quantitative extension of the law but a qualitative antithesis. The essential principle of Christianity involves setting "the inner element over against the outer one, conscience over against the act, the spirit of the law over against the letter of the law." Thus on the one hand Jesus does not acknowledge the Mosaic law as having absolutely binding authority, but on the other hand he never speaks of abolishing the law as a whole, and he does not deny its validity for those who trust it. He stops short of an open break with the law and leaves further development to the spirit of his teaching. "Since new wine belongs in new wineskins, the spirit of the new teaching cannot be put into a vessel for the old teaching. On its own, the new spirit will burst that old vessel and create a new

11 The *Lectures* contain by far Baur's most extended treatment of the teaching of Jesus, which is not intended as a "life" of Jesus. The latter is not attainable from the sources.
12 Paul Tillich, "Kairos," in *The Protestant Era*, trans. James Luther Adams (Chicago: University of Chicago Press, 1948), 32–51.

form for itself." With this simple, familiar image, drawn directly from Jewish practice, Jesus positions himself in relation to Judaism.

The Moral and Religious Teaching of Jesus

Jesus' Fundamental Moral Vision (*VNTTh* 60–65). What gives human beings their moral-religious worth is conscience alone, conscience directed to God as its *own* absolute content. The summary of the law is that one should love God and one's neighbor as oneself. "The universal element is the action's formal aspect in virtue of which one treats others the same way that one wants to be treated by them ... This is the formal principle of action that essentially coincides with the Kantian imperative so to act that the maxim of your own action can be the universal law of action." The Christian principle elevates itself to what is universal, unconditional, intrinsically subsistent. The purest expression of the principle is found in the beatitudes of the Sermon on the Mount.

> As an affirmation of the Old Testament law, and as the antithesis to Pharisaic legalism, Christianity appeared foremost as a strengthening of moral consciousness, as a moral power that sought to arouse in human beings the awareness of their moral self-determination, the energy of their own moral freedom and autonomy. This moral element ... is the substantial core of Christianity, and all else, howsoever great its significance may be, stands in a more or less secondary and incidental relationship to this moral element. It is the foundation on which everything else first can be built. Even though it hardly has the form and the complexion of what Christianity became historically, it nevertheless already is implicitly the whole of Christianity. All too soon it was able to be suppressed by the dogmatism developing from Christian consciousness, to be set in its shadow, to be overlaid and stifled. Yet this moral element ever remained the firmly unshakable point to which people always had to return again – to turn back from all the aberrations in dogma and life and return to that in which authentic Christian consciousness expresses itself in its most direct, original form and its simplest truth, infinitely exalted above all the self-deceptions of dogmatism. (*VNTTh* 64–65)

Baur's critique of the aberrations of dogmatism is noteworthy for one who also devoted a large portion of his scholarly attention to the development of the Christian principle in the history of dogma. Such a development was essential, and dogma gradually acquired a critical consciousness. The greatest thinkers always recognized their dependence on the original gospel, a gospel that stood in the closest proximity to Judaism.

Righteousness (*VNTTh* 65–69). In righteousness (*dikaiosunē*), the moral element receives a *religious* content. Righteousness involves not merely one's relationship to oneself (moral self-consciousness) but also one's relationship to God, without which there is no religious consciousness. Indeed, such righteousness is the very completion and fulfillment of the law that Jesus claims is at hand. It is the state of adequacy in which one is subjectively what the kingdom of God is objectively. As a post-Enlightenment Protestant thinker, Baur argues that Christianity sublates (annuls and preserves[13]) the Old Testament's separation of the divine and the human. The two sides coincide inasmuch as the subjective possibility of the consummate fulfilling of the law is also given together with this completion. "The subjective possibility of *dikaiosunē*, the power of reconciliation with God, which consciousness, when further developed, calls 'grace,' is simply included in the other aspect, the objective carrying-out of the consummated law." Jesus speaks only of fulfilling the law perfectly, although he is in fact revealing a new and universal power of reconciliation. His consciousness still stands within the Old Testament perspective insofar as it sticks with the countervailing objectivity of God's law. Pauline theology is the first to make righteousness, as a new principle, into the object of Christian consciousness and to understand it as grace.

Righteousness or grace is the objective divine power working within and as human subjectivity, and it is the category that links the teaching of Jesus and the thought of Paul. Paul simply expresses for consciousness what was posited implicitly and factually in the teaching of Jesus.

The Kingdom of God (*VNTTh* 69–75). The concept of the kingdom of God is taken over wholly from the Old Testament's religious and political system. For Jesus it is simply the *moral-religious community* of those who make up the people of God. He has so spiritualized the concept of the messianic kingdom that in his sense it is just a community resting on moral-religious qualifications, with its ultimate goal not in the sensible but in the supersensible world. "What takes place in heaven is the paradigm for what ought to take place on earth. So ... when the will of God is also fulfilled on earth, the kingdom of God is made actual on earth; it comes unto us, unfolding and spreading itself more and more in humankind... This purely moral-religious concept of the kingdom of God contrasts with the Jews' customary representations of it." Be like children, says Jesus; do not claim the kingdom for it grows on its own, it has "its own inner motive power and endlessly produces its widespread effect" (as seen in the parables of the kingdom). The kingdom of God is simply "the divine principle instilled into humankind and working, as the substantial element in it, with an overarching power." The only

13 The German term *Aufhebung* has this double meaning. The distinction between the divine and the human is not collapsed into an identity; rather the two are understood to be inwardly related.

real question is whether, for Jesus, it extends to the Gentiles or merely includes Jews.

When Baur says that Jesus' concept of the kingdom of God contrasts with the Jews' customary representations of it, he probably is thinking more of its theocratic aspect than its apocalyptic-eschatological aspect (its supernatural, cataclysmic arrival). In any event, eschatology is not a prominent feature of Baur's Jesus. He allows that apocalyptic motifs come later, for example in the Book of Revelation, and that they provide a backdrop to other New Testament writings as well. But Jesus himself is not an apocalyptic figure. Baur's moral-religious interpretation aligns more with the existential interpretation of Rudolf Bultmann than with the eschatological interpretation still favored by many New Testament scholars today.

Jesus' Person and Messianic Self-Consciousness

Baur provides an extensive discussion of Jesus' conception of his person and his messianic self-consciousness (*VNTTh* 75–121). He acknowledges that much is found in the Synoptic Gospels on this subject that was first formed subsequent to the death of Jesus and in light of the messianic beliefs of the apostles, so a critical winnowing is required with only approximate results. But Baur allows for a messianic consciousness far more liberally than many New Testament scholars do today.

Son of Man and Son of God (*VNTTh* 75–84). Jesus chooses for himself the expression "son of man" taken from Daniel 7:13–14, not with the intention of saying directly that he is the Messiah, but only to refer to himself as a human being sharing in everything human. Being son of man does not involve coming in glory on the clouds of heaven, but rather only involves the fullness of human suffering and lowliness. The so-called earthly son of man sayings are the ones that Baur regards as being an authentic self-reference of Jesus. Likewise, Jesus is a "son of God" in the sense of belonging among the "children of God" as those who, by their moral conduct, make themselves worthy of the divine favor.

Statements about Jesus' Person and His Messianic Consciousness (*VNTTh* 85–96). Baur infers from the Matthean tradition that Jesus becomes aware of his messianic identity only gradually. He acknowledges and discloses it for the first time in Matthew 16:13–20, when he asks his disciples who they say that he is and affirms Peter's avowal that he is the Messiah, the Son of God. Baur's explanation is as follows. Jesus can only have discerned his messianic calling in the process of actualizing the idea of the kingdom of heaven in the sense of all the moral and religious demands he lays upon his followers. He is at odds with his nation or people in that he wants to be its Messiah solely in the spiritual sense in which he grasps the Messiah-idea. The nation's belief in the Messiah is the necessary medium by which alone he can hope for the realization of his spiritual idea of the kingdom of heaven. Since he does not wish to be a Messiah in the people's sense, he can decisively express the messianic consciousness that at first develops in him gradually only after he has provided the requisite foundation for it. He spiritualizes the Messiah-idea in accord with the moral-religious concept he links to the kingdom of heaven.

Jesus' Death and Resurrection; the Second Coming and Last Judgment (*VNTTh* 96–113). Jesus may have had intimations that he would be the sacrificial victim of his messianic vocation, but he does not possess a higher, supernatural knowledge that enables him to foresee the future. He has a presentiment of his death, but not of its significance. He just assumes that all who acknowledge their sins and repent of them with true humility may be assured of their forgiveness. His vocation is that of a teacher; the substance is his teaching, not his fate.

With respect to his alleged pronouncements about his resurrection, his second coming and last judgment, as found in the Synoptic tradition, all we can say is that Jesus' person belongs essentially together with his teaching. He is himself "the concrete demonstration of the absolute truth of his teaching." He internalizes his awareness of his role by applying to himself the popular views of the Messiah current at his time. But he does not predict any of the events following upon his death, and he does not use the vivid and sensible eschatological imagery found in the Gospels. These are products of the writers who were articulating the interests and convictions of their own time.

The Father, the Son, and the Children of God (*VNTTh* 113–21). One of Jesus' most original ideas is that of God as "Father" (anticipations are found in the Psalms, Isaiah, and Jeremiah). This term expresses the direct relationship in which a human being stands to God. From God's side it entails love and goodness; from the human side, trust and dependence, freely resting on the awareness of one's need. This relationship is not only immediate but also universal. No one is excluded from the relationship to God the Father; it transcends every national limitation. God, as the universal Father of everyone, "makes his sun rise on the evil and the good, and sends rain on the righteous and the unrighteous" (Matthew 5:45).

> Here Jesus draws out the moral consequences of the idea of God as Father, the consequences of the universality of God's relationship to human beings: that we ought also to love our enemy and do good to those who hate us, certainly inasmuch as God too treats everyone, good and evil, righteous and unrighteous, in the same way. So this moral bond linking human beings with God is, as such, a further element of the idea of God as Father

in Jesus' sense. If God is the Father of human beings, then they are God's children, as God's sons [and daughters].

If God the Father is the moral idea in itself, then the Son is the idea realizing itself in God's children. This moral concept of the Son of God must be distinguished from both the metaphysical concept of the Gospel of John and the Jewish national concept.

Thus Jesus does not limit his messianic plan to a particular nation. He does not refuse or exclude Gentiles. Even so, he may have considered it his distinctive task to make the lost sheep of the house of Israel the focus of his personal activity, for they need his care first and foremost. As to the Canaanite woman, he affirms that even Gentiles ought not to be excluded from the messianic kingdom, if only their faith is great enough. He praises faith wherever it is found. "The prophets of old" – Isaiah, Jeremiah, Amos, Malachi – "had already raised the hope that in the messianic age the Gentiles will turn to the true religion." Universalism is implicit in their message, just as it is explicit in that of Jesus. "But it cannot be determined precisely in what way he sought to expand Jewish particularism to Christian universalism" because we are left in doubt as to whether Jesus anticipated replacing Jewish circumcision with the Christian rite of baptism.

Baur's Interpretation of the Pauline Theological Framework

The first period of Part Two of the *Lectures on New Testament Theology* addresses the "theological frameworks" (*Lehrbegriffe*) of the Apostle Paul and the Book of Revelation.[14] The second and third periods address the theological frameworks of the remaining books of the New Testament canon, with the individual writings treated in the order of composition as Baur reconstructed it. My concern in this essay is limited to Paul.

14 Baur's discussion of Revelation and Hebrews (*VNTTh* 207–56) further reveals his familiarity with the Old Testament, prophetic and priestly Judaism, rabbinic teaching, Talmudic tradition, etc.

The Transition from the Teaching of Jesus to the Teaching of the Apostles

The original form in which Christianity appears as a new religion is quite different from a dogmatically-expounded theological framework (*VNTTh* 122–6). Jesus' death and resurrection are the intervening factors. Because of his death, Christianity receives a shape essentially different from its original form: the focus shifts from Jesus' teaching to his person, its absolute significance and saving work. However, the validity of Jesus' teaching itself is in no way dependent on his death, so this shift represents a very sharp difference of perspective. With respect to the resurrection, the question is whether it is a factual event that happens to his body or a spiritual process in the minds of the disciples. In either case, the disciples turn to passages from the Old Testament to make sense of his death and to support their experience that he lives on. Thus, "if Christ did not rise again bodily, he had to rise again spiritually in the faith of the disciples." This faith is the absolute presupposition for the whole of New Testament theology. "The doctrine of the person of Jesus is the fundamental dogma on which everything rests. In this doctrine Christianity's difference in principle from the Old Testament comes to light in its full compass, a difference nevertheless played down in the teaching of Jesus."

In the New Testament theology lectures, Baur organizes the presentation not by treating the authentic Pauline epistles[15] separately, as he does in his *Paulus* and *Kirchengeschichte*, but by combining the teaching of Paul from these epistles under several interpretative categories or logical steps.

Christianity's Relation to Judaism and the Meaning of Jesus' Death

Baur claims that, while "Jesus' original teaching presents Christianity's inner connection and essential identity with Old Testament religion," Paulinism by contrast "is the most decisive break of Christian consciousness from the law and the whole of Judaism resting on the Old Testament" (*VNTTh* 127–32). Observe,

15 The four assuredly Pauline letters are Galatians, 1 and 2 Corinthians, and Romans. All the other letters attributed to him fall under the category of "Deutero-Pauline" (or non-Pauline in the case of the Pastoral Epistles) because of evidence that they are written at a later time or exhibit a different theological framework. See Christof Landmesser in *Baur und die Geschichte des frühen Christentums*, 169–72.

however, that the categories and problematics with which Paul works are wholly Jewish because the Old Testament is his principal source; and, in addition, he adopts one of the central categories of Jesus' teaching, "righteousness" (*dikaiosunē*). Thus Baur goes on to say that Paul "has only expressed, simply for consciousness, what was inherently, in principle and in fact, in other words *implicitly*, already contained in the teaching of Jesus." Such statements are characteristic of Baur's dialectical way of thinking.

For the Jewish view of the Messiah, the death of Jesus is the greatest of scandals, the most obvious proof that Jesus cannot be the Messiah. But suddenly the thought occurs to Paul (his conversion experience, interpreted as intellectual insight) that the Messiah's destiny is precisely to die, and that his death could have an entirely different religious meaning, a sacrificial death in exchange for people's sins. As such it would accomplish for the first time what the entire religious institution of the Old Testament had not and could not accomplish, the realization of righteousness. After his conversion, Paul believes he is called to be the Apostle to the Gentiles, and he becomes aware of the universal significance of Christianity.

Righteousness as the Essence of Religion

Judaism and Christianity are placed by Paul under the higher concept of the idea of religion, and religion is about righteousness (or reconciliation), that is, the relationship in a which a human being ought to stand vis-à-vis God (*VNTTh* 132–3). There must be righteousness both in human interrelationships (each person lets the other partake of what is inherently the other's due) and in the divine-human relationship (only when humans are as God wills can there be a relationship of oneness between them and God). Religion's purpose is to realize righteousness. Up to this point Judaism and Christianity "wholly share the same ground." But the paths to righteousness diverge: being declared righteous by works of the law as opposed to being declared righteous by faith.

The Impossibility of Becoming Righteous by Works of the Law

If there is a righteousness that does place human beings in an adequate relationship to God, it is a righteousness based on faith, or the "righteousness of God" (*VNTTh* 133–48). Baur explains that the "of" is a genitive of the subject, meaning that God's essential being is righteousness, so that in righteousness by faith the active subject is not the human being but is instead God. God is both the subject and the object of righteousness: this is the insight of faith.

Paul proves his thesis that a human being is not made righteous by works of the law in three steps: the empirical proof (the unrighteousness of humanity is a historical fact acknowledged by both Jews and Gentiles), the proof from religious history (the development from Adam onwards ends only in sin and death), and the anthropological proof (the concept of the human being as *sarx*, "flesh," as well as *nous*, "mind"). These proofs, set forth in the first chapters of Romans, draw almost exclusively from Judaism, its history and literature.

Works of the law become works of the flesh, and in place of the righteousness that is supposed to be the outcome of works of the law, there appears only its opposite, sin. The power of the law founders on the resistance of the flesh. But the law still has a real effect: it brings about sin, first making sin to be what it is. Consciousness of sin comes from the law, and without consciousness of sin there is no sin. The law is the norm of moral conduct, but it condemns us. In the condition of a divided, unhappy consciousness (awareness of the difference between what we ought to be and what we actually are), we can only cry out in anguish. "This is the point at which Judaism and Christianity come into the closest and most direct contact. But it is also the furthermost point beyond which the religious consciousness of Judaism cannot go." Jews, of course, would insist that Judaism can and does go further, but along a different path – the path of the Torah rather than the path of Christ. The issue for Jews is with Pauline theology itself, not just with Baur.

Righteousness by Faith

Launching into a lengthy discussion of the meaning of "righteousness by faith," (*VNTTh* 153–82), Baur distinguishes among different usages of the word "faith," for which the distinctive Pauline meaning is trust or confidence in the grace of God; and such faith brings freedom. What matters is what human beings believe, what they receive as purely a gift of grace, not what is ascribed to them as their own works. Faith is an inward receiving and holding firm to what one has been offered. This would appear to represent the height of Paul's critique of Judaism.

> But however decisively, with his principle of faith, the Apostle has parted ways with Judaism as the religion of the law, and has adopted a standpoint wholly opposed to it, this is nevertheless not so radical a break that it would make the fundamental outlook on which his new theory of justification rests something other than an essentially Jewish view. Not only is Jesus – as the Messiah promised in the Old Testament and appearing in the Jewish nation – the object of faith, the *genomenos ek spermatos David kata sarka*, the one descended from

> David according to the flesh (Romans 1:3), the *sperma* or offspring of Abraham (Galatians 3:16), the second Adam. Also, the significance the Apostle's theory assigns to Jesus' death is grounded in a concept taken from Judaism as the religion of the law. (*VNTTh* 155)

This is a classically Baurian statement, reflecting his recognition of the complexity of the issue and his striving to get the balance right. He elaborates on this balance by distinguishing three aspects, juridical, anthropological, and historical.

The Factual or Juridical Aspect: Christ's Death as Substitution (*VNTTh* 156–60). The curse of the law is executed not on those who deserve it but on Jesus in their place. His death is the purchase price for setting human beings free, an equivalent payment, a sacrificial offering, a substitution. Human enmity toward God is overcome through the death of God's Son. But it is not God who needs to be reconciled; rather what allows humans to be reconciled with God is God's constant disposition toward them, made known through Christ and allowing their sins to be overlooked. Just as Christ's death provides satisfaction with respect to God, it is vicarious with respect to human beings: he has died *huper hēmōn*, for us or in place of us. Thus Christ has to be a human being, but not equal to humans in sin. His is a "likeness of sinful flesh." Baur himself is critical of the juridical view of atonement as substitution or satisfaction, but he regards Paul's espousal of it as an indication of his Jewish heritage.

The Anthropological Aspect: Christ's Death and the Flesh (*VNTTh* 160–3). If Jesus' death nullifies the flesh, so too sin is cut off from the root of its existence in the flesh. Believers are so strictly one with the dead Christ that the bond linking them with sin is to be seen as severed, and they themselves are to be *viewed* as righteous. The death of Christ involves only the negative aspect, the removal of the guilt for sin. The resurrection involves the declaration that believers are *in fact* righteous and share in the living Spirit of the one risen from the dead.

The Aspect of Religious History: Law and Promise; Law and Freedom (*VNTTh* 163–73). Baur reiterates the point that, when the fulfillment arrives, the function of the law is superseded. Already in the promise to Abraham faith stands above the law. The law is a facilitator, standing between promise and fulfillment: it is the mediator, the teacher, the disciplinarian. But God himself is the unity of promise and fulfillment. Paul finds the prototype of law and freedom expressed in Abraham's relationship to his two sons, Ishmael and Isaac. Their mothers represent two religious dispensations. The slave woman Hagar, the mother of Ishmael, is the present-day Jerusalem, and the free woman Sarah, the mother of Isaac, is the heavenly Jerusalem above. Although Paul sees in Christianity something solely supernatural, as God's direct dispensation, he nevertheless strives to grasp it in historical terms. When the Apostle says (Galatians 4:4–6) that God sent his Son, born of a woman, born under the law, he means that "God placed him wholly within the historical development in which the one period passes over into the other... Christianity is not merely something that entered into humanity from without, but is instead a stage of the religious development, a stage that emerged from an inner principle immanent to humanity. Christianity is spirit's advance to the freedom of self-consciousness, in the period when that free spirit can first appear, when it has overcome dependency and bondage." Here Paulinism is interpreted with Hegelian categories, and indeed Baur sees a connection between the Apostle and the speculative philosopher.[16] The consciousness of freedom arises within Judaism itself and does not at this stage come from the Greeks.

Spirit and Faith, Love, Works (*VNTTh* 174–82). Spirit as the principle determining a human being's entire orientation is the principle of Christian consciousness. Faith relates to spirit as form relates to content. What is merely still an external relationship (being *counted* as righteous) has become a truly inner relationship through the mediation of the Spirit, in which God, as the Spirit of Christ, indwells human beings – a relation of spirit to the Spirit. The human spirit, as the principle of subjective consciousness, comes together in oneness with its objective ground, the Spirit of God, as the Spirit of Christ. Faith passes over into love, which is the sum and substance of the law.

At this point Baur makes a surprising turn. He says that the Old Testament does not consist merely of legal precepts and regulations. It too recognizes the need for divine grace and forgiveness. It knows how to distinguish the externality of legalistic acts from inward disposition as what gives humans true moral worth before God. "The Old Testament already mitigates the harshness in how the Apostle relates Judaism, as law, to Christianity." Who can deny that in the Old Testament too "it was possible to have not merely the condemnatory verdict of the law but also the peace of a heart reconciled with God? So 'works of the law' is a purely theoretical concept abstracted from the Old Testament." The antithesis between works of the law and faith is cancelled out; each of them is a subjective condition without which it is not possible to be declared righteous. Faith, as a vital inward disposition, must be active in works. Paul's abstract antithesis between Judaism and Christianity becomes a relative antithesis as soon as it is applied to the concrete circumstances of actual life. Works and faith together constitute the essential nature of piety – the disposition or moral quality apart from which a human being cannot be justified before God. The two propositions of

16 Speculative philosophy thematizes the double mirroring of objectivity by subjectivity and of subjectivity by objectivity – a mirroring with its roots partly in the Pauline theology of the reflected light of glory and perhaps ultimately in the Jewish view of the speculum (see below, n. 17).

being declared righteous by faith or by works must counterbalance each other in practical life. Works are not "works of the law" but simply moral conduct as such. Anyone who does what is right is acceptable to God.

Christology

Paul's christology (*VNTTh* 186–99) is a Spirit-christology that stresses Christ's humanity, not his objective divinity (no divine Logos comprises his personal nature). Although he is human like Adam, and although psychical and spiritual elements are equally substantial components of human nature, in Christ the spiritual element is the essential thing. "The Lord is the Spirit" (2 Corinthians 3:17). The Apostle links the essential being of spirit with the substance of light, a luminous character, a radiance, a splendor of glory. Christ as the Spirit is the Lord of Glory. He is essentially spirit and light, the reflected light of God, a "speculum that shines"[17] – again, a deeply Jewish concept. This reflecting shining Spirit is the live-giving principle operative within humanity.

Paul, unlike later New Testament writers, never calls Christ God in the absolute sense, as creator of the world. He emphasizes God's absolute transcendence or sublimity (*Erhabenheit*[18]), definitely subordinates Christ to God, and expressly calls Christ a human being. He does not distinguish a divine nature from a human nature since he refers to Christ allegorically as a "spiritual rock" (the rock that followed the Israelites, 1 Corinthians 10:3–4), which as such depicts a whole human person. Of course, for the Apostle, Christ introduces a new principle into humanity that far exceeds the bounds of the Old Testament revelation. All the antitheses by which Paul delineates the new covenant from the old come together in the thesis that the Lord is the Spirit, and where the Spirit of the Lord is, there is freedom. This is a lofty conception of the person of Christ, but he is a human,

---

17 See Elliot R. Wolfson, *Through a Speculum That Shines: Vision and Imagination in Medieval Jewish Mysticism* (Princeton: Princeton University Press, 1994): Moses, unlike the other prophets, saw "through a speculum that shines" (26). Christ *is* the speculum that shines: "No veil lies over his face as it did in Moses' case... God, as the creator of light, shines in our hearts ... in order to make clearly known the light of glory streaming forth from the face of Jesus Christ, as it once did from the face of Moses. Christ himself is the image of God, and just as God's light of glory is mirrored in him, this light of glory therefore is mirrored again in his gospel ... He is the reflected light of God, and so too the same light is said to spread out from him over all of humankind" (Baur, *VNTTh* 187–8).

18 The term used by Hegel to characterize the Jewish religion.

not a divine person; he is a spiritually infused human person. As such, is he not intrinsically conceivable from a Jewish point of view?

Pauline theology is couched in categories that are still essentially Jewish even as it transcends Judaism. The teaching of Jesus sets forth a qualitative reform of Judaism with a focus on moral conscience, religious righteousness, the inwardness of God's kingdom, and the humanity of the messianic figure. Baur struggled to find an appropriate balance between continuity and novelty, identity and difference, in describing Christianity's relationship to Judaism in this earliest phase of its history. The influence of this aspect of his New Testament studies is difficult to trace because for the most part it was ignored or stereotyped by subsequent scholars. But the issues that Baur examined so carefully in the lectures on New Testament theology continue to be relevant today.

Bibliography

Baur, Ferdinand Christian. "Die Christuspartei in der korinthischen Gemeinde, der Gegensatz des petrinischen und paulinischen Christenthums in der ältesten Kirche, der Apostel Petrus in Rom." *Tübinger Zeitschrift für Theologie* 5.4 (1831): 61–206.

Baur, Ferdinand Christian. *Paulus, der Apostel Jesu Christi: Sein Leben und Wirken, seine Briefe und seine Lehre*. 1st edition. Stuttgart: Becher und Müller, 1845; 2nd edition, ed. Eduard Zeller, 2 vols. Leipzig: Fues's Verlag, 1866–67. (*Paul the Apostle of Jesus Christ, His Life and Works, His Epistles and Teachings*. Trans. from the 2nd edition by Allan Menzies, 2 vols. London and Edinburgh: Williams & Norgate, 1873–75).

Baur, Ferdinand Christian. *Das Christenthum und die christliche Kirche der drei ersten Jahrhunderte*. 1st edition. Tübingen: L. F. Fues, 1853; 2nd edition 1860; 3rd edition identical with 2nd, published under the title *Kirchengeschichte der drei ersten Jahrhunderte*, 1863. (*The Church History of the First Three Centuries*. Trans. from the 3rd edition, ed. by Allan Menzies, 2 vols. London and Edinburgh: Williams & Norgate, 1878–79).

Baur, Ferdinand Christian. Vorlesungen über neutestamentliche Theologie. Ed. Ferdinand Friedrich Baur. Leipzig: Fues's Verlag, 1864.

Carleton Paget, James. "The Reception of Baur in Britain." *Ferdinand Christian Baur und die Geschichte des frühen Christentums*. Ed. Martin Bauspiess, Christoph Landmesser, and David Lincicum. Tübingen: Mohr Siebeck, 2014. 380–386.

Davies, W. D. *Paul and Rabbinic Judaism: Some Rabbinic Elements in Pauline Theology*. 4th edition. Philadelphia: Fortress Press, 1980.

Gerdmar, Anders. "Baur and the Creation of the Judaism-Hellenism Dichotomy." *Ferdinand Christian Baur und die Geschichte des frühen Christentums*. Ed. Martin Bauspiess, Christoph Landmesser, and David Lincicum. Tübingen: Mohr Siebeck, 2014. 107–128.

Hegel, Georg Wilhelm Friedrich. *Lectures on the Philosophy of World History*, vol. 1. Ed. and trans. Robert F. Brown and Peter C. Hodgson. Oxford: Clarendon Press, 2011.

Kelley, Shawn. *Racializing Jesus: Race, Ideology and the Formation of Modern Biblical Scholarship*. London and New York: Routledge, 2002.
Landmesser, Christof. "Ferdinand Christian Baur als Paulus-Interpret. Die Geschichte, das Absolute und die Freiheit." *Ferdinand Christian Baur und die Geschichte des frühen Christentums*. Ed. Martin Bauspiess, Christoph Landmesser, and David Lincicum. Tübingen: Mohr Siebeck, 2014. 161–194.
Tillich, Paul. "Kairos." *The Protestant Era*. Trans. James Luther Adams. Chicago: University of Chicago Press, 1948. 32–51.
Wolfson, Elliot R. *Through a Speculum That Shines: Vision and Imagination in Medieval Jewish Mysticism*. Princeton: Princeton University Press, 1994.

Ivan Kalmar

4 Jews, Cousins Of Arabs: Orientalism, Race, Nation, And Pan-Nation In The Long Nineteenth Century

In the western world, attitudes towards Jews and Muslims historically stem from the fact that the West is by definition of Christian heritage. Judaism and Islam, the other Abrahamic religions, share with Christianity considerable theological similarities, many of them the result of mutual contact and of the influence on all three of Hellenism. The Christian and Muslim-dominated worlds have been neighbors, with some Christians living among Muslims, some Muslims living among Christians, and Jews living among both. In short, Christians, Muslims, and Jews are closely related by the facts of theology and geography. This should guarantee a certain continuity to the history of the relationship among them, including a continuity in how they imagine one another.

The relationship among Christians, Jews, and Muslims lends itself to different strategic triangulations: Jews and Muslims against Christians, Muslims and Christians against Jews, or Jews and Christians against Muslims.[1] Today the dictates of the Israel-Palestine conflict, with most Muslims on the Palestinian side and most Jews as well as large numbers of Christians on the Israeli, unsurprisingly encourage discourses of a "Judeo-Christian tradition," a post-World-War II idea born of a combination of Christian guilt about the Holocaust and western, including Jewish, support for the Zionist project. But in earlier times – I am speaking of centuries going back perhaps to the very beginning of Islam – Jews were associated in the Christian mind with Muslims. Certainly, when it comes to the long nineteenth century, a "Judeo-Muslim tradition" would have made at least as much sense to western Christians, including the scholars among them, as a "Judeo-Christian tradition." One of my goals is to show that it would also have made sense to most western, modernizing, or to use that common misnomer, "assimilated" Jews. It would have made sense, we will see, because it was strategic. "Self-orientalizing" Jews wished to increase the symbolic capital of being Jewish by hitching the Jewish image to that of the Orient. For they took the imagined "Orient" at its face value, as a place of great spiritual, not to say sexual, allure.

---

1 I owe the thought expressed in this sentence to Susannah Heschel's intervention at the Workshop on Antisemitism and Islamophobia, University of Oxford, June 15, 2015.

Let us not pretend that scholars have been immune to the overall strategies of the communities they belong to. In the long nineteenth century, many Christian and Jewish scholars in the West emphasized commonalities between Muslims and Jews. Today the reaction by academics of all three heritages tends to be very cautious. Identifying the many historical conjunctions at which the potential for linking Jew and Muslim was NOT realized, some stop there and reject any joint study at all. Those of us who do choose to study representations of Jew and Muslim together certainly have an agenda: recognizing that each has been imagined through similar language and imagery should, we hope, battle mutual intolerance and extremism.

Fortunately, as I hope to show, this personal preference to seek similarities in the western representation of Muslims and Jews is, in spite of many extremely important differences, bolstered by an overwhelming array of facts. When Edward Said mused that orientalism was a "strange, secret sharer of Western anti-Semitism,"[2] he revealed nothing new about the facts. What was new, rather, was that those facts had become a secret. For the evidence that everyone in the West, Jew or gentile, considered Jews to be an oriental people in the long nineteenth century is absolutely overwhelming.

In addition to demonstrating this fact, I would also like to examine some of the lessons the archive may hold for current debates about the notions of race and racialization. When it comes to the notion of the "Semite," but also more generally, "race" and "nation" are in my view too readily equated by some scholars. In fact, it may be profitable to keep them apart, at least in our case, and even to introduce an intermediate term, the "pan-nation." "Semite," like "Aryan," are pan-national groupings based on linguistic kinship relations uncovered by that shock troops of long-nineteenth-century scholarship, the philologists. Thus, after a description of the facts, I will argue for the inclusion in debates on racialization of a clear distinction between nation and race, and of the pan-nation in between.

Moorish Style Synagogues

To look at those facts, let us begin with September 5, 1844, when the cheerful congregants of the Israelite House of God in Hamburg gathered to consecrate their newly built temple. Together, men and women, boys and girls, intoned a

2 Edward W. Said, *Orientalism* (New York: Verso, 1978).

hymn specially composed for the occasion. *Ost und Westen, schön verbunden*, they sang, "East and West, beautifully united." [3]

Undoubtedly, many of these Jewish citizens knew of the *West-East Diwan*, wherein the widely adored Wolfgang Goethe, inspired by the Persian poet Hafez, included the following verse,

Gottes ist der Orient!
Gottes ist der Occident!
Nord- und südliches Gelände
Ruht im Frieden seiner Hände.

God's is the East!
God's is the West!
Northerly and southerly lands
Rest peacefully in His hands. [4]

"God's is the West, God's is the East" is a paraphrased passage from the Qur'an. The *surat al-Baqarah* adds, "Wherever you go, the presence of God is there."[5] Goethe attaches to this theological message a special geopolitical and cultural meaning. Goethe's *Diwan* is an example of the desire to unite Orient and Occident, meaning the lands of Islam and of Christianity, but also the ancient spirituality of the East and the modern civilization of the West. This was a romantic goal that would later expand further east to include the spiritual traditions of first Hindu, Buddhist, and Zoroastrian India and then, lastly, of Chinese and Japanese mystic Buddhism.

In 1844, it was this ideal that the Hamburg Jews were responding to in their own, specifically Jewish, way. Whether or not they individually remembered Goethe's work, they like many other Germans shared in its spirit. Beautifully binding together East and West was something that many people, Jewish or not, thought that Jews could do.

---

3 See Krinsky, Carol Herselle, *Synagogues of Europe: Architecture, History, Meaning* (Cambridge, MA: MIT Press, 1985), 298.

4 Goethe, *Ostwestlicher Diwan:* "Moganni Nameh – Buch des Sängers, Talismane." Johann Wolfgang Goethe, *Sämtliche Werke, Briefe, Tagebücher und Gespräche*, ed. Karl Eibl, vol. 3, 1 (Berlin: Deutscher Klassiker-Verlag, 1987), 307. The lines were written in 1815 and first published in 1819, then republished in an altered edition of the *Diwan* in 1827 (http://freiburger-anthologie.ub.uni-freiburg.de/fa/fa.pl?cmd=gedichte&sub=show&add=&id=1205&spalten=1&noheader=1, accessed on July 8, 2015).

5 Surat *al-Baqra* ("The Cow"), Quran 2:115.

Was this self-orientalization? Yes, it was – as long as we accept that Jews were orientalized by others before they were orientalized by themselves; and as long as we keep in mind that this self-orientalization, like orientalization in general, was often felt to be praise rather than denigration. Self-orientalization was not in any way the same thing as self-hatred. The Hamburg Jews imagined their East-West hybridity with pride.

They were certainly not alone. A good decade before the Israelite Temple was built in Hamburg, it appears that the Bavarian government ordered that new synagogues in the Kingdom be built in an oriental style.[6] By the nineteen sixties, so-called Moorish Style synagogues stood throughout most of the modernizing Jewish world, in liberal and what we would now call modern Orthodox German-speaking communities in and outside Germany and Austria, including the United States. Soon the German-speakers were to be imitated by forward-looking Jews from England to Russia.

The Cincinnati synagogue known as the Rabbi Wise Temple today, built in 1862, is still believed to have the tallest minarets in the United States. Its large entrance door IS reminiscent of great mosques like that of Isfahan. It is worth noting that the synagogues of Moorish Spain were not well known at the time, and to the extent that Moorish buildings inspired the so-called Moorish style synagogues, the prime example was the Alhambra of Grenada. But there were no minarets or, to refer to another common feature of these synagogues, no domes, in either Muslim or Jewish Spain. In fact, Spain was not the inspiration for Moorish-style synagogues. Contemporary documents seldom refer to the so-called Golden Age of the Jews in Spain but much more often refer to the perceived kinship between Jews and Arabs. In fact, the style was originally more often referred to as "Arabian" rather than "Moorish."

Characteristic is the commentary by Ludwig Förster, the architect of the much imitated Dohany Street Synagogue in Budapest and a slightly earlier attempt in Vienna Leopoldstadt. Regarding the Viennese synagogue, completed in 1858, Förster said that architects must "choose, when building and Israelite Temple, those architectural forms that have been used by oriental ethnic groups that are related to the Israelite people, and in particular the Arabs, and thereby in general to allow the introduction of only such modifications that are occasioned by the climate and by new discoveries in the art of building."[7] Förster was a Viennese

6 See Ivan Davidson Kalmar. „Moorish Style: Orientalism, the Jews, and Synagogue Architecture," *Jewish Social Studies: History, Culture, and Society* 7.3 (2011), 68–100.

7 Förster, Ludwig, «Das israelitische Bethaus in der Wiener Vorstadt Leopoldstadt,» *Allgemeine Bauzeitung* (1859), 14.

gentile, and his sentiment was often shared by the non-Jewish building authorities. In 1872, the Accademia dell'Arte of Florence after researching German precedents more or less forced the local Jews to build their large new *tempio israelitico* in an "Arab style."[8] However, Jewish communities often agreed quite happily. The number of Jewish architects building Moorish style synagogues increased steadily. One was Marco Treves, the main architect of the Florence *tempio,* who would also build the Moorish style synagogue of Vercelli.[9]

In reality these synagogues were very modern and western in terms of construction technique and overall structure. The oriental elements were confined to decoration. Indeed the oriental style often served to surreptitiously import church-like elements, a process that Orthodox Jews and some Christians heavily objected to. The Cincinnati as well as the Budapest temples like many other, less famous ones, had two minarets, not one like most mosques. The two towers were reminiscent of the two steeples common on larger churches. The domes, introduced ostensibly on an Arabian model, happened to be slightly Orientalized versions of church cupolas. There was stained glass and an organ, played on Shabbat preferably by a renowned gentile musician. But the liturgical music developed for cantor and organ by Jewish composers often emphasized, or even invented, elements in the Jewish musical tradition that resembled the elements of the chants of the East. This marriage of East and West expressed perfectly the idea of Jews as an oriental people, cousins of Arabs, which – while always contested – captured the imagination of many Jews in the long nineteenth century.

How did the modern, even so-called assimilated Ashkenazi Jews of the long nineteenth century come to be seen as racial cousins of the Arabs, the people of Muhammad and Islam? Why did they accept this ascription and were proud of it? Why does all this seem odd today? And what would be the best analytical or theoretical framework to account for it?

---

8 *Reale Accademia delle Arti del Disegno in Firenze* to the President of the Council of the Israelite Community of Firenze, December 5, 1872. Archives of the Jewish Community of Florence. See Ivan Kalmar, "The Israelite Temple of Florence: The Struggle for a Jewish Space and Style in Nineteenth and Twentieth Century Europe," in: *Religious Architecture: The Anthropological Perspective,* ed. Oskar Verkaaik (Chicago: University of Chicago Press).

9 See, Kalmar, "The Israelite Temple of Florence."

Terminology

To answer these questions, let us begin with some terminology and a note on language and geography.

The *Orient* in this context is essentially Muslim-dominated North Africa and West Asia. This heartland of Islam was long the focus of what Europeans and Americans meant by the Orient. So when we speak of orientalizing the Jews we mean likening them to Muslims.

The *long nineteenth century*, as Eric Hobsbawm delimited it, lasted from 1789 to 1914, but of course he was not suggesting that these dates marked sharp transitions. The orientalization of the Jews began, much earlier, though as I shall soon have a chance to show, Jewish *self*-orientalization almost fits into the Hobsbawmian boundaries, though the archive requires an extension to 1933 or may be even 1948.

The dominant language of both the orientalization and the self-orientalization of the Jews was German. This has to do with the nature of German orientalist scholarship, which as Suzanne Marchand showed had a strong theological preoccupation with the Bible seen as an oriental document. It also has to do with the leading position that German-speaking Jews occupied in the liberal and Reform movements of the long nineteenth century. When I say German-speaking, I am not thinking only of Germany. In Budapest many and in Prague almost all Jews spoke German as their first language, and most of those who migrated to America from there reckoned themselves German Jews. But even in St. Petersburg and Odessa, in Warsaw and in Moscow, acculturated Jews spoke German as an important second language. They looked down upon the Yiddish spoken by many of the Orthodox and Hassidic Jews, who were referred to as *Ostjuden*, meaning "Eastern Jews." Most of the *Ostjuden* lived in the European East, in the Russian Empire including Russian-ruled Poland, and in eastern Austria-Hungary. But *Ostjude* was more of a cultural than a geographic term. Yiddish speaking, Orthodox Jews were referred to as *Ostjuden* even in the West. In English Franz Boas, the German-born father of American anthropology, translated the term as "East European Hebrews," and considered them a distinctive physical type, separate from western Jews like himself.

The paradox that is very important to remember is that it was western, modernizing Jews who often became enthusiastic about their racial affinity with the Orient. The more insular *Ostjuden* either never heard of the concept or opposed its expressions. As for the "real" oriental Jews, that is the Jews of the Orient, of North Africa and West Asia, orientalization did not significantly impact them in the long nineteenth century. It did become relevant once many *mizrahim* or oriental Jews moved to Israel, but that important fact is beyond the focal period of this essay.

Orientalizing the Jews

It is almost a truism today, yet it is only partly true, that the Orient represented to the long nineteenth century West the essential Other. It is also only partly true that, as Gil Anidjar showed, Jews and Arabs (the latter being an ethnic metonym for Muslims) are varieties of a common figure of the Christian West's enemy.[10] Otherness and animosity are not the only relations that define the imaginative construction of the Orient, or of Jews and Muslims, in the West. In the long nineteenth century, Christian theologians and philologists imagined Judaism as an oriental religion, and this judgment was accepted by their Jewish colleagues as well as by the general Jewish and gentile public. Christianity itself was therefore seen, through its Jewish origins, as a religion with oriental roots. The Orient was not only the Other but also the Mother of Christianity.

Christians often respected their oriental heritage but saw it as superseded by the coming of Christ. They saw both Jews and Muslims as stubbornly clinging to an oriental version of monotheism. It is this attitude that made it possible for Christians at different times in the three religions' history to imagine Islam as a throwback to Judaism[11] and, in the long nineteenth century, to imagine Jews as racial relatives of Muslim Arabs.

We find some parallels in the artistic representation of male biblical Jews and living Muslims at least as early as thirteenth century Tuscan art. Both were depicted wearing a specific kind of head scarf. This was replaced in the late fourteenth century, as the power of the Ottoman Turks became palpable in Europe, with a turban on the Turkish model. This convention spread throughout Latin

10 Gil Anidjar, *The Jew, the Arab: A History of the Enemy* (Stanford, CA: Stanford University Press, 2003).

11 Jeremy Cohen, "The Muslim Connection: On the Changing Role of the Jew in High Medieval Theology," in: *From Witness to Witchcraft: Jews and Judaism in Medieval Christian Thought*, ed. Jeremy Cohen (Wiesbaden: Harrassowitz, 1996), 141–162; Suzanne Conklin Akbari, "Placing the Jews in Late Medieval English Literature," in: *Orientalism and the Jews*, ed. Ivan Davidson Kalmar and Derek J. Penslar (Hanover, NH: University Press of New England, 2005), 32–50.

Christendom. It can still be seen followed in some church art and nativity scenes today.[12]

Renaissance scholars were interested in both Hebrew and Arabic philosophical texts, although their focus was often on translations of and commentaries on ancient Greek philosophy. The understanding of the Bible as an oriental text did not develop substantially until the seventeenth century, when it became common in centers of learning such as Oxford and Leiden. The Leiden Arabist Albert Schultens counseled the use of the Arabic language for elucidating biblical Hebrew.

In England, the term "orientalism" appears to have been invented in the context of researching the poetic imagination of the Hebrews, which was thought not only to have created the language of the Bible, but also influenced that of the ancient Greeks. To my knowledge, the first occurrence of the term "orientalism" in English was the *Essay on Pope's Odyssey* published in 1726, by Joseph Spence (1699–1768). This is how one of Spence's characters comments on a sentence from Homer:

> *"Of the sun being perished out of Heaven, and of darkness rushing over the Earth!"* (...) This whole prophetical vision ... is the *True Sublime;* and in particular, gives us an higher *Orientalism* than we meet with in any other part of Homer's writings.

Spence bases his comments here on the then common assumption that Homer knew the Bible. Later in the eighteenth century biblical criticism that resorted to the philology of non-Hebrew languages of the Orient included the work of Robert Lowth in England. Lowth collaborated with scholars at the University of Göttingen, such as Johann David Michaelis.

Michaelis in turn was the teacher of Johann Gottfried Eichhorn, who is credited with being one of the founders of the so-called new biblical criticism. The philologists who belonged to this school were often trained in Arabic as well as Hebrew.

The philologers were in dialogue with the philosophers. Among the latter, Georg Hegel is the most worthy of mention. Hegel's monumental *Philosophy of History* was based on a reading of a vast corpus of philological work. To Hegel Judaism and Islam were both typical religions of the western Orient, forming a transition from the more purely oriental religions of India and China to the Chris-

---

12 Ivan Davidson Kalmar. „Jesus Did Not Wear a Turban: Orientalism, the Jews, and Christian Art," in: *Orientalism and the Jews*, ed. Ivan Davidson Kalmar and Derek J. Penslar, 3–31.

tian West.[13] Hegel's Islam cannot be understood without Hegel's Judaism, as it was to him only a late mutation of the Jewish religious principle. To Hegel the Jewish mission was exhausted with the incarnation of Christ. Judaism should have disappeared at that point. But not only did it not disappear; its religious principle even produced a delayed reaction, an anomalous upsurge of *Begeisterung*, a belated swan song of energy, and that was Islam.

Hegel's technical analysis need not detain us here. Suffice it to note that Judaism and Islam represented to him a highly developed form of religion, but not as high as Christianity. He called both Judaism and Islam "Arabian" religions and judged that the Arabian – later to be called Semitic – *Geist* or spirit was not capable of proceeding to the next stage. Protestant Christianity, the end of the history of religions, could only be produced by the Germanic *Volksgeist* or ethnic/national/racial spirit.

Although Hegel's scheme is clearly a partially secular equivalent of Christian supersessionism, it is probably a mistake to think that he meant to disparage Jews and Muslims. His final stage of religion crucially depended on the helping hand of the "Arabian" spirit to bring it to fruition. This was probably thought by Hegel to be a great merit.

Appreciation of the value of ancient Israel could not fail to have consequences for attitudes towards living Jews. Hegel was a supporter of legal equality for Jews. The movement for Jewish emancipation was initiated by gentile thinkers, such as Wilhelm Dohm, who agreed that living Jews were currently a morally corrupt lot, given to usury and communal selfishness, but recognized the noble character of ancient Israel. They believed that doing away with the legal disabilities of the modern Jews could return them to that former state of glory. Jewish emancipation was, in other words, a project of national restoration. Some even favored accomplishing that end by restoring a Jewish state; that is, by returning the Jews to the Orient, a long standing dream among some streaks of Protestantism.

Not everyone, however, was necessarily appreciative about oriental character, whether seen in Arabs or Jews. The dubious merit of formulating the features of a common Semitic spirit belonged to the French orientalist, writer, and philosopher, Ernest Renan. Ever fond of contrarian opinions, Renan shocked Christians and Jews alike by suggesting that the Semites, whom he called by that name, were unimaginative people incapable of creating genuine mythology. Monotheism was the product of the desert where Renan, probably thinking of Muhammad more

---

13 Michel Hulin, *Hegel et l'orient : suivi de la traduction annotée d'un essai de Hegel sur la Bhagavad – Gîtâ* (Paris: Librairie philosophique J. Vrin, 1979), 133.

than of Moses, thought that Semitic religion originated. Rich myths are not born in such a stark environment, but in the forests inhabited by multiple gods.

Although Renan eventually insisted that living Jews were no longer to be equated with their ancient forebears, his attack on the philosemitic link between oriental religion and modern Judaism was enough for leading Jewish scholars like Haim Steinthal and Daniel Chwolson[14] to react with shock and to polemicize vehemently.

Jewish Self-Orientalization

Many, though certainly not all, Jews – such as the worshippers gathered in Moorish style synagogues – responded to the gentile orientalization of themselves by espousing it themselves, and by protecting the symbolic capital of the "good" Orient against criticisms such as Renan's. Their response was strategic. In the eighteen-seventies, the West's imperial project was clearly running into resistance by the natives, including many Muslims and Arabs. In tandem, the always ambiguous and contested image of the Orient was increasingly acquiring pronounced negative characteristics, opposing the backward Orient to the progressive West (it is this period that Said's work focused on). Jews had been seduced into self-orientalization when orientalism still appeared, at least on the surface, to be admiring towards the East. As negative elements which later became more obvious, self-orientalization required a defensive twist of the Jews. It made them into vocal defenders of the imagined Orient as the equal of the West.

It was in the earlier, more pro-oriental mood of the early and mid nineteenth century that Jewish attachment to the Orient was famously articulated by Benjamin Disraeli. He was not only a brilliantly successful politician and Queen Victoria's favorite Prime Minister, but also a prolific and widely read author. Technically and perhaps in his own way religiously, it is true, Disraeli was not a Jew but a Christian, since he had been taken to the baptismal font by his parents when he was still a young boy. But he freely referred to himself as a Jew, as did his contemporaries. There is a famous apocryphal story that, when in 1835 O'Connell, the powerful Irish parliamentarian, attacked his Jewish ancestry, Disraeli replied without hesitation: "Yes, I am a Jew, and when the ancestors of the right honor-

14 Daniel Abramovich Chwolson, *Die Semitischen Völker, Versuch einer Charakteristik.* (Berlin: F. Duncker, 1872); H. Steinthal, "Zur Charakteristik der semitischen Völker," *Zeitschrift für Völkerpsychologie und Sprachwissenschaft* 1. Reprinted in: Über Juden und Judentum, Vorträge und Aufsätze, ed. Gustav Karpeles (Berlin: M. Poppelauer, 1906), 91–104.

able gentleman were brutal savages in an unknown island, mine were priests in the temple of Solomon." Though it may be untrue, the episode accords well with the spirit of Disraeli's novels such as *Tancred*, published in 1847, where he wrote of "some flat-nosed Frank, full of bustle and puffed-up with self-conceit (a race spawned perhaps in the morasses of some Northern forest hardly yet cleared.)"[15] The *chutzpah* is ratcheted up as he, in contrast, speaks of the Jews.

Disraeli's proud self-orientalization was probably aided by the fact that he was of Sephardi rather than Ashkenazi descent. His appearance only added to the exotic impression he made on the average Englishman: he had large dark eyes and his hair fell about his olive-colored face in large black, un-English curls. "A little black Jew, and a very Arab one," the phrase Jacques Derrida would use to describe himself, also applied to Disraeli.[16] If the Jew in general was, in the western imagination, almost white but not quite, Disraeli was even less white than the rest.

But it was not only the Sephardim but all Jews that he describes in *Tancred* as an "Arabian tribe," while the Arabs are "only Jews upon horseback." Together, Arab and Jew are depicted as a favored race destined to receive divine revelation. When a character in *Tancred* says, with the author's obvious approval, that "God never spoke except to an Arab," he means of course that Moses, the Prophets of Israel, Jesus, and Mohammed were all Arabs. Disraeli fancied himself a descendant of what, certainly in God's mind, was the world's best stock.

As I have mentioned, however, not all Jews and not all Gentiles took on the habit of orientalizing the Jewish people. I am not aware of anyone of importance who actively opposed it, but some of the important debates about the so-called "Jewish Question" ignored the Orient altogether. In 1789, when the debate about emancipating Jews as equal citizens first came up in the revolutionary National Assembly in France, the agenda included at the same emancipating actors and executioners. I do not wish to deny the permanence of the racial and religious elements in the contemporary image of the Jews, and I will come back to that issue later. But we must recognize that there was in the Middle Ages and continuing to our own day an occupational and economic quasi-definition of the "Jew." This associated the Jew with money. In anti-Jewish imagery Jesus' disciple suggestively named Judas, betrays the Savior of Humanity for silver coins. In the middle ages and in modern times, the Jew was portrayed as a moneylender and trader. Like professional acting, engaging in finance was not then the celebrity

---

15 Benjamin Disraeli, *Tancred* (London: R. Brimley, 1904), 233.

16 Jacques Derrida, *"Circumfession,"* in: *Jacques Derrida*, ed. Geoffrey Bennington and Jacques Derrida (Chicago: University of Chicago Press, 1993), 58/F57.

occupation that it has become. It was thought to be more like hanging people: a necessary activity but one that morally pollutes its practitioners. Something like selling cell phones today.

There was no question of religious or ethnic/racial identity for Count Tonnerre, who defended Jewish emancipation on condition that Jews are given rights as individuals and not as a "nation": a typically French sentiment echoed later by Napoleon. The attitude also permeated the thinking of many Jewish political thinkers of the socialist to the liberal stripe, throughout the long nineteenth century. They expected Jewish citizens to benefit not from a recognition of corporate rights but from a relegation of religious distinction from the political to the private sphere.

Karl Marx was one of them. Like Disraeli, Marx was routinely considered an ethnic Jew in spite of his childhood baptism extorted by family ambitions. However, he does not touch on Jewish race at all, or the Orient, in his famous or infamous 1844 essay on the Jewish Question. He sets the religious Jew almost contemptuously aside and like a good anthropologists prefers to look at the real, every day Jew of *Alltagjude,* whom he defines almost entirely by his financial activities. Religion like race was for Marx a kind of a red herring, or a smoke screen that covered up the historical importance of social class.

Marx was heard and responded to by his fellow correspondent at the *Neue Rheinische Zeitung,* Moses Hess. In *Rome and Jerusalem*, published in 1862, Hess decided to stand Marx on his head when he declaimed, "The race struggle is primary; the class struggle is secondary."[17] Now those who battled in Hess's "race struggle" were the Aryans and the Semites. His "Rome" and Jerusalem" were mere metaphors for these two "races." On the other hand, when the Italian *risorgimento* politician, David Levi, spoke (some 20 years later) of the fight between Rome and Jerusalem, he meant an actual event in ancient history. It was, he said, the struggle of "a handful of men who in the name of nationality opposed their existence against the entire Roman world."[18]

It was an oriental nationality Levi's Israelites fought for, against an occidental Roman Emprie. Levi's discourse, like Hess', is permeated with binary oppositions like the following: "The Occident investigates, experiments, decomposes

---

17 *„Der Rassenkampf ist das Ursprüngliche, der Klassenkampf das Sekundäre."* Moses Hess, *Rom und Jerusalem, die letzte Nationalitätsfrage; Briefe und Noten* (Prague, n. d.), 211 (Epilogue, section V).

18 ... *in nome della nazionalità, contrastano la loro esistenza contro tutto il mondo Romano.* David Levi, *Il Profeta, o La Passione di un Popolo. I. L'Oriente* (Torino, 1884), xxiv.

and recomposes matter in order to discover its laws. The Orient ... is the anxious work of humanity managing its God.[19]

Martin Buber takes us into the twentieth century, but his language is strongly reminiscent of David Levi's. "The great complex of Oriental nations," Buber wrote, "can be shown to be one entity ..."[20] The psychological characteristics of such nations are those of the "motor type" (*motorischer Mensch*) and contrast with the characterstics of the "sensory type" (*sensorischer Mensch*), typified by the peoples of the West. The Occidental, sensory type regards the world as an inventory of items seen as relatively independent of each other and of the beholder. In this type of human being, the senses are "separated from each other and from the undifferentiated base of organic life." They are under the influence of sight, the most independent and objective among them.[21] The Oriental is adverse to separating either the objects of perception or the senses through which they are perceived. "He is aware less of the multifarious existence of things in repose than of their processes and relationships. (...) "To motor-type man, the world appears as limitless motion, flowing through him." Consequently, "He views the world, naturally and primarily, as something happening to him; he senses rather than perceives it, for he is gripped by and permeated by this world, which, detachedly, confronts the Occidental."[22]

A Viennese-born German-speaker who grew up in now Ukrainian L'viv, Buber idealized the *Ostjude,* contrary to the prevailing mood at the time. And he developed a form of Zionism that meant to foster the oriental connection to the Arabs, to the point where after his move to Palestine he tried to work towards a binational state.

The number of examples of Jewish self-orientalization could be multiplied almost *ad infinitum*. But I hope the ones I mentioned suffice to drive home the point that Jewish self-orientalization was extremely common even if not universal, and that it was meant to praise rather than to denigrate the Jews and their racial relationship with Arabs.

---

19 *"L'Occidente indaga, esperimenta, scompone e ricompone la materia per iscoprirne le leggi. L'Oriente, come dice un storico, è il travaglio affannoso della umanita' in gestione del suo Dio."* Levi, *Il Profeta*, viii.

20 Martin Buber, "The Spirit of the Orient and Judaism," in: *On Judaism*, ed. Nahum N. Glazer (New York: Schocken 1967), 56.

21 *ibid.*, 58.

22 *ibid.*, 59.

Analytical Paradigms

How can we understand this odd fact of Semitic allegiance among Jews, in the overall context of the long nineteenth century and the imperialist project?

One approach has been to discuss the Jews as a colonized people. Susannah Heschel, for example, has written about Abraham Geiger as engaging in colonial revolt.[23] It must be admitted, however, that no western Jewish population found themselves colonized by a foreign power in the same way as, for example, the Moroccans or Tunisians did. There may be many comparisons, but essentially the Jews of the West were colonized metaphorically at best, rather than literally. Indeed, the Zionist settlers in Palestine and now in the West Bank have notoriously been termed colonizers. Derek Penslar has dealt very well with this complex and controversial issue.[24]

Another way to connect western Jews and the colonies is not by claiming that the Jews themselves were either colonizers or colonized, but to suggest that the way they were treated in the West became a template for treating populations in the colonies.

I have mentioned earlier the tendency to read Islam as a revived Judaism, which characterized western Christian attitudes to Islam from the beginning. But such a transfer of identification also occurred with respect to the colonial populations. Ulrike Brunotte has examined how the Puritan settlers of America found lost tribes of Israel, and the process was repeated for centuries in other places.[25] Tudor Parfitt showed how lost Jews were found in a large number of colonies.[26] Jonathan Boyarin has suggested that ways of dealing with the Jews as the West's internal Other were exported to dealing with the Other external to the West: Muslims in the areas targeted by western imperialism, but even the far

---

23 An anachronistic but perhaps telling comparison would be between the western Jews in the long nineteenth century making inroads into academia and the liberal professions, and similar successful efforts by South Asian immigrants more recently, including people responsible for much of the progress in colonial and postcolonial studies.

24 Derek Penslar, "Zionism, Colonialism and Postcolonialism," *Journal of Israeli History* 20.2–3 (2011), 84–98.

25 Ulrike Brunotte, "'The Jewes did Indianize; or the Indians doe Judaize': Philo-Semitism and anti-Judaism as Media of Colonial Transfer in Seventeenth-Century New England," paper presented at the *International Workshop on Colonialism, Orientalism, and the Jews: The Role of Gender and Postcolonial Studies Approaches*, University of Antwerp, June 24–26, 2015.

26 Tudor Parfitt, *The Lost Tribes of Israel: The History of a Myth* (London: Weidenfeld & Nicolson, 2002) and "The Use of the Jew in Colonial Discourse," in: *Orientalism and the Jews*, ed. Kalmar and Penslar.

away American Indians, even in the great majority of cases when they were not imagined as lost Jews.

Boyarin's focus was on early imperialism, but Amir Mufti suggested that the Jewish example also worked for colonial policy in the long nineteenth century and beyond, all the way to the independence and partition of India.[27] Mufti's analysis has great merit. He proposes that the Jewish Question established the Jews of Europe as a prototypical minority. Then, he suggests, the Jewish Question inspired European thinking about minorities in the colonies. Such thinking led to partition as a solution, both within and outside Europe. Zionism was a kind of radical partition, a sundering apart of the Jews from Europe. It led to the partition of Palestine between them and the Arabs. Next this experience was applied in British India to create India and Pakistan.

In spite of the many strengths of Mufti's book, however, he fails to mention that minoritization and partition were processes that were applied across Europe and the Middle East in many other cases. In most cases, these processes hardly seem to be affected by the so-called Jewish Question, which rather seems to be affected by them. Rather, they were the result of nation building on the ethnic principle, or what came to be known as the "self-determination of peoples" and is now a right enshrined in the Charter of the United Nations. Minoritization and partition were generally a side effect of this kind of nation building, when populations who did not belong to the so-called state-forming nation, including Jews, found themselves defined as internal outsiders.

The Jewish revival that was expressed in the Moorish style synagogue and elsewhere as a Semitic revival, was connected to other national revivals. Italians, Germans, and Hungarians were first to build ethnically defined states. The Slavic nations of central Europe had to wait for their triumph until the end of World War I. The idea of the self-determination of peoples became useful to the western powers at the end of World War I, which saw the defeat of two multinational empires: the Austro-Hungarian and the Ottoman.

Race, Nation, Pan-Nation

This notion of the state-forming nation or people requires us to explore the notions of race, nation, and pan-nation. Recent scholarship has been moving away from

---

27 Amir Mufti, *Enlightenment in the colony: the Jewish question and the crisis of postcolonial culture* (Princeton, NJ: Princeton University Press, 2007).

an essentialist definition of "race" that privileges physiognomy and especially skin color. There are other criteria on which a group can be racialized.[28] These include religion, as the Jewish case abundantly illustrates. Race can be seen as imagined common descent; that is a group is imagined as if they had the same ancestors, and those ancestors can be characterized by physiognomy as well as by things like religion.

Such a flexible definition of race as imagined common descent does not differentiate between race and the ethnic *Volk*. Some scholars might not mind this. They may wish to deliberately ignore the difference between race and nation; I myself have done so in the past.[29] On second thought, however, the distinction is actually very important.

It is true that what defines a group called a race and what defines a group called a nation may in certain circumstances be the same things, including when that defining criterion is religion. It is also true that there has always been in ordinary usage a slippage between the terms "race" and "nation." The Jews, for one, have often been called both.

However, I would like to consider here not the content of the terms "race" and "nation," which is famously flexible, but rather their use. And I note that races have never been held as deserving of a state, while nations, also known in this context as "peoples," are thought to be entitled to national self-determination. Nation or *Volk* is potentially a state-forming subject, while a race is not. On the other hand, as Hannah Arendt suggested, race was the "ideological weapon for imperialistic politics." [30] While the discourse of Nation is the ideological scaffolding of the nation-state, the discourse of race is the ideological scaffolding of Empire.

Of course, it must be remembered that, in the long nineteenth century, discourses of Empire and Nation were connected. Each colonizing nation saw itself as spearheading the colonizing mission of the West as a whole, which was racialized as the white man's burden. New nation states dreamed of a colonial mission, though none could compete with England or France. "Reunited" Germany and Italy actually acquired colonies in Africa. Czechoslovakia had to be content by annexing Carpatho-Ukraine and sending anthropologists to Central America.

28 See, for example, Robert Bernasconi, "Critical Philosophy of Race," in: *Routledge Companion to Phenomenology*, ed. Sebastian Luft and Søren Overgaard (New York: Routledge), 551–62.

29 Ivan Davidson Kalmar, "Race By Grace: Race and Religion, the Secular State, and the Construction of 'Jew' and 'Arab,'" in: *Jews Color Race: Rethinking Jewish Identities*, ed. Efraim Sicher (London: Berghahn Press, 2013), 482–509.

30 Hannah Arendt, *The Origins of Totalitarianism* (New York, N.Y.: Harcourt Brace Jovanovich, 1973), 160.

As I have already intimated, the scientific support for the notion of nation was created by the philologists. It was also the philologists who pointed to a link between the Nation and wider quasi-racial relationships.

These enthusiasts for the lost past helped European populations to define themselves on the basis of ancestral language, even if it was no longer spoken much by the elites. German nationalists railed against the use of French by the nobility. Some Czech nationalists had to learn their "own" language from scratch, as they had grown up speaking German. Finns had to embrace Finnish and give up Swedish. This logic defined Jews as a nation with Hebrew as its tongue, even though few Jews spoke it.

The philological definition of nation, however, took place in a broader framework. Philologists did not only uncover ancient relationships between dialects that they then grouped together as the languages of nations. They went above and beyond that, positing linguistic relationships that spanned huge expanses of the Earth, ultimately helping to draw the family tree of Man. Annie McClintock has shown how the notion of the Family of Man supported an imperialist discourse of superiority and inferiority among nations.[31] In the linguistic family tree of Man, the mightiest branch was the Indo-European, also known as Indo-German, Indo-Aryan, and Aryan. It branched out into such language families as the Indic, the Iranian, and in Europe of course the Romance, the Slavic, and the Germanic.

The Semitic language family, generally considered close to the Aryan, included most prominently Hebrew and Arabic. The Hebrews – in many ways the prototypical Nation of the biblical heritage – came to be seen as relatives of the Arabs, fellow "Semites" from the Orient. The notion of reviving the Hebrew language became inherently connected to the fantasies of reviving a Jewish commonwealth in Palestine, which have already been mentioned.

Though most Zionists were not self-orientalizing Jews, many were. Orientalization as Semites facilitated the conception of creating a homeland for the Jewish minority in the Orient. The Viennese architect Wilhelm Stiassny, who built many Moorish style synagogues, had a whole blueprint for creating a Jewish city in the Holy Land or, as he put it, a "neighboring country" (*Nebenland*) in the Orient.[32] Of

---

31 Annie McClintock, *Imperial Leather: Race, Gender, and Sexuality in the Colonial Contest* (New York: Routledge, 1995).

32 Wilhelm Stiassny, *Anlage einer Kolonie im Heiligen Lande oder in einem seiner Nebenländer* (Vienna: Jüdischer Kolonisations-Verein in Wien, 1909). (Pamphlet in the collection of the Jewish Museum of Vienna.)

course, such a move was only possible in the historical circumstances under the aegis of one or another colonial power.

Philologically defined nationalist movements often saw themselves as the local expression of the whole pan-nation's revival. German nationalism, in Hegel and Fichte already, was meant to restore the glories of the Aryan but especially the Germanic peoples. For Hegel, the *Volksgeist* that would take religion to its highest, Protestant, stage was not German or *deutsch*, but Germanic or *germanisch*. From this perspective, the creation of a German nation-state was to invigorate the Germanic spirit from America to the German settlements in Russia.

In Russia in the meantime, a rising pan-Slavic spirit tended to support Russifying policies within the Empire, but was also strategically invoked to bolster the state-forming claims of Slavic-speaking separatists in Austria and Hungary, which came to fruition under the protection of the victorious western powers through the creation of Czechoslovakia and Yugoslavia.[33]

In short, German nationalists spoke in the name of the Germanic peoples as a whole. Czech or Bulgarian nationalists saw their goals as empowering to all Slavs. And Jews who dreamed of a Jewish homeland in the biblical Holy Land thought that through their own revival they would be helping their Arab cousins.

Although for the most part the hope to benefit the Arabs was but a way to make Jews feel better about settling in an Arab-majority land, there were some important exceptions, when self-orientalizing Jews did see themselves as championing a rising Orient against the declining West. (That the West was in decline was a widely held perception, the best known works claiming this being Houston Chamberlain's *Foundations of the Nineteenth Century*, published in 1899, and Oswald Spengler's *The Decline of the West*, published in two volumes between 1918 and 1923.)

The group around Martin Buber was one of the most important among those who advocated a Jewish espousal of the values of the Orient, but there were others. The rabbi of the Moorish style Jerusalem Street congregation in Prague, to which Kafka's family seems to have belonged, was even more radical than Buber. Rabbi Aladar Deutsch wrote that a fight between the East and West had already begun. The "smallest of the fighters proved himself the strongest. He had enough spirit to quickly see through the hollowness and the weakness of Western culture,

---

33 This linguistic-nationalist policy was in concert with the pan-Slavic rhetoric of the Austro-Hungarian Slavs themselves, and for Russia represented a change from when they had supported the independence of Slavic Bulgaria and non-Slavic Romania from the Ottoman Empire. For in that case, they had argued in terms of Eastern Orthodox, not Slavic solidarity.

(...) and he organized the resistance to it." This unnamed "fighter" are the Zionists. Deutsch sees them as the vanguard of a great oriental revolt:

> A small fragment of the old Orient had given its old virtues, which had never decayed, a new life, in order to sweep away the Lie. The Orient is moving, it is beginning the fight with a small maneuver against the falseness of the West ... The Orient as the old site of spiritually infused Semitism (*Semitentum*) will, recognizing the spiritual emptiness and cowardice of the Aryan so-called culture force back the Aryan where he belongs.[34]

That this fight is not exclusively that of the Jews is made clear in the next paragraph, which demands

> ... the unification of the whole Family of Sem and the preservation of the purity of their cultures and principles.[35]

Such self-orientalizing sabre-rattling should not be mistaken for an anticolonial stance, though. Nowhere does Deutsch, or Buber, for that matter, suggest an alliance of oriental equals against the western colonial powers. On the contrary, from Disraeli to Herzl and beyond, restoring the Jewish nation in the Orient imagined one or another western power, or at times the Ottomans, as its protectors and guarantors.

In this curious and round-about way, the orientalization and self-orientalization of the West's Jews through a "return" to the Orient, lead to their final occidentalization as the agents of western power in the Orient.

To be sure, the powerful forces of racialization and ethnicization, of orientalization and self-orientalization, are ones that we are as scholars attributing to the actions of Jews in the long nineteenth century. They were not necessarily their own conscious concern. They simply followed intuitively strategies meant to gain prestige for themselves as individuals or as a group, or in many cases to defend themselves against discrimination and worse.

As far as they were concerned, in 1844 the Jews of Hamburg were bringing the exotic wisdom and glory of the East to the West. The Jews settling in the Land of

---

34 Typescript, Jewish Museum, ch. 9, 144. Jewish Museum of Prague, Deutsch archive. The typescript text is not signed, and I am going by the attribution given to it by the Jewish Museum. Deutsch was made the head of the Jewish community of Bohemia and Moravia under German occupation. He may conceivably have been forced to produce this text for purposes of German anti-Jewish propaganda. However, even if its radicalism is uncommon, his self-orientalist Zionism is not. Here as elsewhere Jewish and gentile orientalization of the Jews depend very closely on each other, though they are never identical.

35 *ibid.*, 144.

Israel, on the other hand, were bringing the achievements of the West to the East. Fatefully, the Arab cousins failed to see the beauty in this very specific union of Orient and Occident.

Bibliography

Akbari, Suzanne Conklin. "Placing the Jews in Late Medieval English Literature." *Orientalism and the Jews*. Ed. Ivan Davidson Kalmar and Derek J. Penslar. Hanover, NH: University Press of New England, 2005. 32–50.

Anidjar, Gil. *The Jew, the Arab: A History of the Enemy*. Stanford, CA: Stanford University Press, 2003.

Arendt, Hannah. *The Origins of Totalitarianism.* New York, N.Y.: Harcourt Brace Jovanovich, 1973.

Bernasconi, Robert. "Critical Philosophy of Race." *Routledge Companion to Phenomenology.* Ed. Sebastian Luft and Søren Overgaard. New York: Routledge, 551–62, 2011.

Brunotte, Ulrike. "'The Jewes did Indianize; or the Indians doe Judaize': Philo-Semitism and anti-Judaism as Media of Colonial Transfer in Seventeenth-Century New England." Paper presented at the *International Workshop on Colonialism, Orientalism, and the Jews: The Role of Gender and Postcolonial Studies Approaches*, University of Antwerp, June 24–26, 2015.

Buber, Martin. "The Spirit of the Orient and Judaism." *On Judaism*. Ed. Nahum N. Glazer. New York: Schocken, 1967.

Chwolson, Daniel Abramovich. *Die Semitischen Völker, Versuch einer Charakteristik.* Berlin: F. Duncker, 1872.

Cohen, Jeremy. "The Muslim Connection: On the Changing Role of the Jew in High Medieval Theology." *From Witness to Witchcraft: Jews and Judaism in Medieval Christian Thought.* Ed. Jeremy Cohen. Wiesbaden: Harrassowitz, 1996. 141–162.

Derrida, Jacques. "Circumfession." *Jacques Derrida.* Ed. Geoffrey Bennington and Jacques Derrida. Chicago: University of Chicago Press, 1993. 58/F57.

Disraeli, Benjamin. *Tancred.* London: R. Brimley, 1904.

Förster, Ludwig. „Das israelitische Bethaus in der Wiener Vorstadt Leopoldstadt." *Allgemeine Bauzeitung* (1859): 14.

Goethe, Johann Wolfgang von. *Ostwestlicher Diwan:* "Moganni Nameh – Buch des Sängers, Talismane." *Sämtliche Werke, Briefe, Tagebücher und Gespräche.* Ed. Karl Eibl, vol. 3, 1. Berlin: Deutscher Klassiker-Verlag, 1987, 307.

Hess, Moses. *Rom und Jerusalem, die letzte Nationalitätsfrage; Briefe und Noten.* Prague, n.d.

Hulin, Michel. *Hegel et l'orient: suivi de la traduction annotée d'un essai de Hegel sur la Bhagavad – Gîtâ*. Paris: Librairie philosophique J. Vrin, 1979.

Kalmar, Ivan Davidson. "The Israelite Temple of Florence: The Struggle for a Jewish Space and Style in Nineteenth and Twentieth Century Europe." *Religious Architecture: The Anthropological Perspective.* Ed. Oskar Verkaaik. Chicago: University of Chicago Press, 2013. 171–184.

Kalmar, Ivan Davidson. "Jesus Did Not Wear a Turban: Orientalism, the Jews, and Christian Art." *Orientalism and the Jews* . Ed. Ivan Davidson Kalmar and Derek J. Penslar. Hanover, NH: University Press of New England, 2005. 3–31.

Kalmar, Ivan Davidson. "Moorish Style: Orientalism, the Jews, and Synagogue Architecture." *Jewish Social Studies: History, Culture, and Society* 7.3 (2011): 68–100.

Kalmar, Ivan Davidson "Race By Grace: Race and Religion, the Secular State, and the Construction of 'Jew' and 'Arab." *Jews Color Race: Rethinking Jewish Identities.* Ed. Efraim Sicher. London: Berghahn Press, 2013. 482–509.

Krinsky, Carol Herselle. *Synagogues of Europe: Architecture, History, Meaning.* Cambridge, MA: MIT Press, 1985.

Levi, David. *Il Profeta, o La Passione di un Popolo. I. L'Oriente.* Torino, 1884.

McClintock, Annie. *Imperial Leather: Race, Gender, and Sexuality in the Colonial Contest.* New York: Routledge, 1995.

Mufti, Amir. *Enlightenment in the colony: the Jewish question and the crisis of postcolonial culture.* Princeton, NJ: Princeton University Press, 2007.

Parfitt, Tudor. *The Lost Tribes of Israel: The History of a Myth.* London: Weidenfeld & Nicolson, 2002.

Parfitt, Tudor. "The Use of the Jew in Colonial Discourse." *Orientalism and the Jews.* Ed. Ivan Davidson Kalmar and Derek J. Penslar. Hanover, NH: University Press of New England, 2005. 51–67.

Penslar, Derek J."Zionism, Colonialism and Postcolonialism." *Journal of Israeli History* 20.2–3 (2011): 84–98.

Said, Edward W. *Orientalism.* New York: Verso, 1978.

Steinthal, H. "Zur Charakteristik der semitischen Völker," *Zeitschrift für Völkerpsychologie und Sprachwissenschaft*, vol. 1. Reprinted in Über Juden und Judentum, Vorträge und Aufsätze. Ed. Gustav Karpeles. Berlin: M. Poppelauer, 1906. 91–104.

Stiassny, Wilhelm. *Anlage einer Kolonie im Heiligen Lande oder in einem seiner Nebenländer.* Vienna: Jüdischer Kolonisations-Verein in Wien, 1909. (Pamphlet in the collection of the Jewish Museum of Vienna.)

Noah B. Strote

5 Sources of Christian-Jewish Cooperation in Early Cold War Germany

> "A people that has a bad concept of God also has a bad state, a bad government, and bad laws."
>
> G.W.F. Hegel, *Lectures on the Philosophy of Religion* (1831)

The phrase "Judeo-Christian," with its neo-classical prefix, rarely appears in German historical literature or in daily German speech. Its absence can be traced to the very invention of the term in early nineteenth-century Europe. Whereas English-, French-, Spanish-, and Italian-speaking writers used "Judeo-Christian" to refer to the ancient followers of Jesus who practiced Mosaic Law, German-speaking scholars preferred the term "Jew Christians" (*Judenchristen*). The German philologist Friedrich Nietzsche traced the development of "Jewish-Christian" (*jüdisch-christlich*), not "Judeo-Christian," morality in his famous *Genealogy of Morals*. Still today, one will not hear the term "Judeo-Christian" in public discussions about Germany's cultural heritage. Instead, one finds reference to "Christian-Jewish values," or the "Christian *and* Jewish roots" of Germany and Europe, or, perhaps, the "Jewish-Christian tradition." By failing to subordinate the Judaic to the Christian, the German language perhaps better maintains the memory of the two belief systems' distinctiveness. Indeed, it could be argued that German intellectuals have written more about the historical *divide* between Judaism and Christianity than any other group in the modern period.

Since the Second World War and the Nazi genocide of Europe's Jews, however, Germans have been more apt to emphasize the commonalities between Christians and Jews. The language of "Christian-Jewish Cooperation" and "Brotherhood," which emerged in the 1950s and forms the object of analysis in this chapter, has served a number of functions in the postwar world. Of course, a new emphasis on partnership and inclusion helped restore the reputation of discredited individuals and institutions, indeed, the reputation of a discredited nation. It also helped pluralize German culture and clear the path for the inclusion of other religious groups in society, such as Muslims, even though – as recent debates have clearly shown – the role of Islam in the public celebration of German cultural "cooperation" is anything but uncontroversial.

While the following pages will touch upon some of the integrational and potentially exclusionary functions of Christian-Jewish cooperation, the main focus will be on the *moral legitimacy* it bestowed on the young Federal Republic

(West Germany) during the early Cold War, and in particular, on the neo-liberal form of economy developed there during the so-called "economic miracle" of the 1950s. There is already a large literature on reconciliation, memory, and interfaith dialogue in this period of German history, as well as substantied scholarship on the economic policies of the Federal Republic's government, but the nexus between these two has never been explored.[1] This is surprising, given that historians of nineteenth- and twentieth-century antisemitism have often linked the "Jewish question" to the problem of liberal political economy. It is perhaps part of a larger tendency among scholars of postwar Christian-Jewish relations to focus on the psychology of traumatic memory rather than on the context of The Cold War. It is true that after the Second World War, interfaith dialogue in Germany cannot be analyzed separately from Holocaust consciousness. But neither can it be decontextualized from efforts to create a new kind of postwar economy – a so-called "social market economy" – in which inter-faith cooperation would be just one component in better "human relations" and social harmony in general.

Prejudice costs money; it is unproductive and limits the marketplace. That was an observation made in 1957 by Carl Zietlow, the American Methodist pastor whom the U.S. Military Government had sent a decade earlier to facilitate the creation of the first Society of Christian-Jewish Cooperation in occupied Germany. Zietlow, a regional director of a branch of the National Conference of Christians and Jews, estimated that the price of prejudice amounted to about "thirty billion dollars a year in wasted manpower, production, and morale."[2] He could have added that racism and bigotry also incurred tolls on the *moral legitimacy* of a free-competition economy in the global struggle for hearts and minds against socialism. Throughout the 1950s, the Soviet Russian government had been committing considerable resources (perhaps even the bulk of its anti-Western propaganda) to the dissemination of facts about past and present racism in the United States and its new military ally, the Federal Republic of Germany. The existence

---

1 For some of the recent studies see Steven Schroeder, *To Forget It All and Begin Anew: Reconciliation in Occupied Germany, 1944–1954* (Toronto: University of Toronto, 2013); Esther Braunwarth, *Interkulturelle Kooperation in Deutschland am Beispiel der Gesellschaften für Christlich-Jüdische Zusammenarbeit* (Munich: Herbert Utz, 2011); Norbert Frei, *Adenauer's Germany and the Nazi Past*, trans. Joel Golb (New York: Columbia, 2002); Jeffrey Herf, *Divided Memory: The Nazi Past in the Two Germanys* (Cambridge, MA: Harvard University Press, 1997); Frank Stern, *The Whitewashing of the Yellow Badge: Antisemitism and Philosemitism in Postwar Germany* (New York: Oxford University Press, 1992). None of these works, however, treats the "Jewish problem" in postwar German in context with the economic problem.

2 "Christians, Jews Form Organization," *Lockport, N.Y. Union Sun & Journal* (14 February 1957), 7.

of prejudice diminished the reputation of the Western system throughout the rest of the world.[3]

From its very beginnings, Christian-Jewish cooperation in Germany was transnational and trans-Atlantic. Therefore, its story can only be told with reference to both North American and Western European sources.

1 Inter-faith cooperation as value system of the social market economy

One crucial piece of evidence for the argument that Christian-Jewish cooperation in Germany was a byproduct of Cold War competition is the timing of its emergence. In the immediate aftermath of the Second World War, many church leaders condemned Nazi antisemitism, but there was no institutional movement toward inter-faith dialogue. In October 1945, the Council of the Protestant Church in Germany (EKD) released a "Declaration of Guilt," for having failed to resist the Nazi regime more actively, but no specific reference was made to Judaism, the Jews, or Christian responsibility to reconcile with Jewish groups.[4] It was only in April 1948 that the EKD issued its first message specifically on the "Jewish Question."[5] It was also in that year, in early July, that a group of Catholics, Protestants, and Jews founded the first Society for Christian-Jewish Cooperation in Munich, located in the U.S. Zone of occupation. Karl Thieme, a close observer of these developments, wrote in retrospect that the year 1948 inaugurated a "new phase in Christian-Jewish cooperation" for "those countries in Europe west of the Iron Curtain," with church leaders in what become the Federal Republic at its vanguard.[6] It was also the year that historians agree marked the beginning of the struggle between U.S. and the Soviet Union known as the Cold War.

Once the movement for Christian-Jewish cooperation began, it gained momentum quickly. Individual chapters of the Societies for Christian-Jewish Cooperation opened in other major cities. After Munich, lay leaders gathered in

---

3 See Mary L. Dudziak, *Cold War Civil Rights: Race and the Image of American Democracy* (Princeton, NJ: Princeton University Press, 2000).
4 See Matthew Hockenos, *A Church Divided: German Protestants Confront the Nazi Past* (Bloomington: Indiana University Press, 2004), chapter 4.
5 "A Message Concerning the Jewish Question" (1948), trans. World Council of Churches, in *The Relationship of the Church to the Jewish People* (Geneva: WCC Publications, 1964), 48–62.
6 Karl Thieme, "Eine neue Phase christich-jüdischer Zusammenarbeit," *Judaica* 7, no. 3 (1951), 234–235.

Wiesbaden, Freiburg, Stuttgart, Nuremberg, and Frankfurt.[7] Josef Brandlmeier, the founding director of the Munich Society, reported to the U.S. Military Government (OMGUS) in early 1949 that his chapter was rapidly gaining membership, attracting prominent business and union leaders and winning the praise of local "authorities" for having brought together Christians and Jews "for the first time after the Nazis took over the power [sic].[8] By September of that year, there were enough individual Societies and members to justify the creation of an umbrella "Coordinating Council" (based in Frankfurt), whose president would be none other than the recently appointed President of the Federal Republic, Theodor Heuss. The Societies thus stand among the founding institutions of the postwar liberal-democratic German state. They have also shown lasting power. In 2015, there are roughly eighty-three chapters throughout reunited Germany, totaling more than 20,000 official members.

The organizational and financial impetus for the creation of the Societies was originally American. This is not to claim that Christians and Jews in Germany would not have formed cooperative institutions had it not been for the prolonged U.S. military occupation. But the founding document in the history of the movement is a letter from U.S. Military Governor Lucius Clay to the Presbyterian Reverend Everett Clinchy, president of both the National Conference of Christians and Jews in New York and the new International Council of Christians and Jews based in Geneva, sent in August 1947. In the letter, Clay threw his support behind Clinchy's offer to assist in "ameliorating the group tensions in Germany" through the establishment of "local councils of Catholics, Protestants and Jews."[9] After Clinchy voyaged personally to the U.S. Zone to establish initial contacts among Germans, OMGUS installed a full-time liaison from the National Conference named Carl Zietlow in March 1948. Zietlow helped organize the men and women who opened the first Society for Christian-Jewish Cooperation in Munich three months later, in June 1948.

The interwar origins of the National Conference of Christians and Jews in the U.S. are shrouded in legends accumulated over the years. Contrary to the standard narrative, which holds that Christians and Jews came together in the late 1920s to combat racism and Protestant nativism, the organization was actually a reaction to the growth of the socialist movement in American cities during and

---

7 Josef Foschepoth, *Im Schatten der Vergangenheit. Die Anfänge der Gesellschaft für Christlich-Jüdische Zusammenarbeit* (Göttingen: Vandenhoeck & Ruprecht, 1993), 75–79.

8 Joseph Brandlmeier, Activity Report for OMGUS, February 1949, National Archives, College Park, MD, RG 260, Box 162.

9 Lucius Clay to Everett Clinchy, 16 August 1947, National Archives, RG 260, Box 162.

after the First World War.[10] In his path-breaking research on the National Conference and the beginnings of Judeo-Christian discourse in the U.S., the historian Benny Kraut showed that, fear of the social consequences of the "un-churching" of Americans drove several large Christian groups to unite their forces – and even extend their hands to non-Christian religious organizations – for the sake of promoting the salutary effects of religion on liberal-capitalist society. "The liberty which flows from the obedience to the will of God is the only secure basis upon which free American institutions can be perpetuated," read the first joint statement signed by Christian groups and the Central Conference of American Rabbis in 1919.[11] Alfred Williams Anthony, President of the Home Mission Council of the ecumenical Federal Council of Churches of Christ in America (and the central figure in the ultimate foundation of the National Conference of Christians and Jews), expressed concern in 1921 that "Socialism, really a religion now to many of its advocates, has assumed threatening aspects": "Townships have been found which are reverting to paganism, because in our sectarian zeal we have left them open to dissension and strife. [...] Large groups of workers have been reported who, because cut off from the humanizing influences of Christian society, nurture convictions inimical to all forms of orderly government."[12] According to Anthony, hatred among the confessions bred disillusionment with religion in general and prepared the ground first for atheism, and then anarchism and communism. It is true that the National Conference, when it finally formed in 1928, opposed the Ku Klux Klan with its traveling "tolerance trios" of priests, ministers, and rabbis. However, while its leaders ever since have celebrated the anti-racist identity of the organization, they have suppressed the memory of its anti-Socialist roots.

As is well known, widespread collaboration between Christians and Jews and the notion of a "Judeo-Christian" – as opposed to simply Protestant – civil religion in the U.S. were products of the Second World War. Under the presidency of Everett Clinchy, the National Conference led a massive home-front campaign to contrast a deeply religious yet *diverse* "American way of life" with the allegedly

10 These origin myths are repeated in Esther Braunwarth, *Interkulturelle Kooperation in Deutschland*, 6–7, and most other references to the Societies.

11 Quoted in Benny Kraut, "Towards the Establishment of the National Conference of Christians and Jews: The Tenuous Road to Religious Goodwill in the 1920s," *American Jewish History* 77 (1988), 388–412.

12 Alfred Williams Anthony, "The Whole Home Front," *The Herald of Gospel Liberty* (11 August 1921), 776–777. Anthony helped form the Federal Council of Churches of Christ Committee on Goodwill Between Jews and Christians in 1923. Kraut argued that it was Jewish suspicions of Christian missionizing within the Committee on Goodwill that led to the creation of the Conference of Christians and Jews.

godless totalitarianism of Nazism.[13] The campaign for "brotherhood" between Protestantism, Catholicism, and Judaism was so extensive that some authors even felt the need to remind American readers about the religions' incommensurability, as the German-Jewish émigré Trude Weiss-Rosmarin did in her *Judaism and Christianity: The Differences* (1943).[14] The pluralist philosopher Alain Locke, a convert to the Bahá'í faith, regarded the prolific Christian-Jewish dialogue that was taking place during the war as a first step toward inclusion of "the Muslim and Oriental fronts," which he argued was "equally if not more important for spiritual rapprochement on a world scale."[15] Locke's hopes were not realized in the subsequent years – rare attempts to articulate a "Christian-Islamic," "Judeo-Christian-Islamic," or even more expansive "world" civilization consistently failed – but the celebration of "Judeo-Christian values" and "Judeo-Christian civilization" became a fixture of American civil religion in the early years of the Cold War.[16]

When Clinchy approached General Clay after the war to involve the National Conference in German democratization programs, the proposal fit nicely into the Military Government's broader policy of (literally) rebuilding Christian religious life in Germany. From the earliest days of the occupation, Clay had briefed his officers that OMGUS was interested in seeing the church structures rise again. Military personnel were to avoid requisitioning church property; they were to attempt to return church property confiscated by the Nazi government to local ecclesiastical bodies for use as schools and churches; and they were to facilitate the convening of Catholic, Protestant, and especially ecumenical Church confer-

---

13 Kevin Schultz, *Tri-Faith America: How Catholics and Jews Held America to Its Protestant Promise* (New York: Oxford, 2011), 58.

14 Trude Weiss-Rosmarin, *Judaism and Christianity: The Differences* (New York: Jewish Book Club, 1943).

15 Alain Locke, "Lessons in World Crisis," in *The Bahá'í World: A Biennial International Record*, vol. 9 (1945), 746.

16 For excellent studies on the birth of Judeo-Christian civil religion, see Wendy Wall, *Inventing the "American Way": The Politics of Consensus from the New Deal to the Civil Rights Movement* (New York: Oxford, 2008); Mark Silk, "The Protestant Problem(s) of American Jewry," in *The Protestant-Jewish Conundrum*, ed. Jonathan Frankel and Ezra Mendelsohn (New York: Oxford, 2010), 126–141; K. Healan Gaston, "The Genesis of America's Judeo-Christian Moment: Secularism, Totalitarianism, and the Redefinition of Democracy" (Ph.D. Dissertation, U.C. Berkeley, 2008); Douglas Hartmann, Xuefeng Zhang, and William Wischstadt, "One (Multicultural) Nation Under God? Changing Uses and Meanings of the Term 'Judeo-Christian' in the American Media," *Journal of Media and Religion* 4, no. 4 (2005), 207–234; Deborah Dash Moore, "Jewish GIs and the Creation of the Judeo-Christian Tradition," *Religion and American Culture* 8, no 1 (1998), 31–53; and Mark Silk, "Notes on the Judeo-Christian Tradition in America," *American Quarterly* 36 (1984), 65–85.

ences, which were considered essential to the orderly revival of German life.[17] In a report from around 1947, the chief of the Religious Affairs Branch of OMGUS wrote, "While it is not the aim of Military Government to interfere in the internal affairs of the Churches, they are encouraged to drop centuries old [sic] antagonisms and to cooperate in many fields," noting that the ecumenical movement was especially strong in Bavaria. This was to be supported, he claimed, because it "means the Churches are united in their opposition to totalitarianism, not split by bitter religious quarrels."[18]

U.S. occupation officers partnered with German leaders who shared their mission. Clinchy's first influential partner in establishing local councils for Christian-Jewish Cooperation was Munich's mayor Karl Scharnagl, who at first glance looked like a typical Bavarian Catholic politician of the pre-Nazi mold.[19] After the war, Scharnagl had helped create a new Bavarian party, the ecumenical Christian Social Union (CSU), gaining him the praise of future chancellor Konrad Adenauer, who told him that "only this planned concentration of all forces with a Christian and democratic basis can protect us from the dangers emanating from the East."[20] Like Adenauer, Scharnagl was known to make comments to the effect that only a return to Christian education could truly "de-Nazify" the German population and turn them from antisemitism and other prejudice. For them, Christian-Jewish cooperation was important to regain a decent national image as they attempted to integrate into a Western alliance against the Soviet Union.[21]

However, to consider the early history of Christian-Jewish cooperation purely in terms of anti-communism would present a picture that neglects the larger political-economic platform of the founders. Munich's mayor provides a case in point. Scharnagl, about whom little has been written, was at the time of Clinchy's visit engaged in an internal struggle between two wings of the Christian political

---

17 Report, "The Christian Churches in Germany," undated (probably 1945 or 1946), National Archives, RG 260, Box 158.

18 Brief prepared by James M. Eagen, undated (probably late 1946 or early 1947), National Archives RG 260, Box 158.

19 By this I mean skeptical of the centralizing and secularizing tendencies of the Social Democratic supporters of the Weimar Republic, but also critical of National Socialism. Karl Scharnagl's brother Anton Scharnagl was high clergy in the Catholic Church and had been one of the outspoken critics of the racial and economic nationalism of Hitler. See Anton Scharnagl, *Die völkische Weltanschauung und wir Katholiken* (Munich: Huber, 1932).

20 Konrad Adenauer to Karl Scharnagl, 21 August 1945, in *Adenauer Briefe 1945–1947*, ed. Rudolf Morsey and Hans-Peter Schwarz (Berlin: Siedler, 1983), 77–79.

21 This is main narrative told by the first historian of the Societies, Josef Foschepoth, *Im Schatten der Vergangenheit.*

party he had helped found: a struggle from which his engagement against antisemitism cannot be separated. He had just become a member of the Popular Economic Working Community for Bavaria, part of a circle advocating on behalf of consumer good manufacturers who pressed for the abolition of the price controls still in effect all over Germany. This free-market wing of the CSU was opposed by the party's protectionist agricultural wing.[22] (It was a familiar position for Scharnagl: in the Weimar years, when he had also been mayor of Munich, he had been instrumental in securing American loans for Munich business-owners and among the founding members of the Munich branch of the Rotary Club, an American organization that promoted free trade, friendly relations, and rejected economic nationalism.[23]) Furthermore, Scharnagl struggled with the culturally conservative members his party. He had provoked a small scandal after being photographed bathing nude in the company of men and women.[24]

Bavarians at the time faced a food crisis, like the rest of occupied Germany – but unlike the other regions, Jews were again at the center of political controversy. Bavaria housed the majority of the nearly 200,000 Jews from Eastern Europe (mainly Poland) who had survived genocide and tragically found themselves in the country of their recent oppressors, in Occupation-run "Displaced Persons camps" as they waited for transit papers to Palestine or the United States. The Jewish DPs in Bavaria received provisions from American NGOs and thus often gained access to goods that were otherwise unavailable on the tightly controlled German consumer market, selling them at unregulated prices and without permit.[25] That practice had spawned outrage among some Bavarian politicians who wanted to protect local farmers (many of whom, incidentally, were also hoarding food to sell at black-market prices). In June 1947, the entire cabinet of ministers in the Bavarian government had met specifically to discuss the influx of Eastern European Jews. Complaints were lodged against their involvement in the black market and fears were announced that hatred against Jews was approaching previously unknown levels. Surveys conducted by Military Government in the U.S. Zone confirmed the growth of antisemitic sentiment among the local population that year.[26]

---

22 Bernhard Löffler, *Soziale Marktwirtschaft und administrative Praxis* (Franz Steiner), 284–85, 492–93.

23 See Brendan M. Goff, "The Heartland Abroad: The Rotary Club's Mission of Civil Internationalism" (Ph.D. Dissertation, University of Michigan, 2008).

24 "Auf die Spitze getrieben. Scharnagl nachkend," *Der Spiegel* (9 August 1947).

25 See Atina Grossmann, *Jews, Germans, and Allies* (Princeton, NJ: Princeton University Press, 2007), 221.

26 See Anthony Kauders, *Democratization and the Jews: Munich, 1945–1965* (Lincoln: University of Nebraska Press, 2004); Michael Brenner, *After the Holocaust: Rebuilding Jewish Lives in Post-*

The so-called "black market" – being, essentially, a *free market* emerging alongside, and subverting, a regulated one – was both prompting antisemitism *and* provoking economic nationalism, providing grist especially among agriculturalists to increase controls on trade and protect local estates. Scharnagl and his free-market wing of the CSU, which included party chairman Josef Müller, both supported the proposals of Ludwig Erhard, who was calling for the abolition of all price controls in his new position as director of the money and credit section of the new Bizonal Economic Council.[27] Erhard had briefly served as the minister of economics in Bavaria after the war, but had left in part because of his unpopularity with the CSU's agricultural wing. In the same month that Erhard joined the Bizonal Economic Council – October of 1947 – Scharnagl helped found a Committee for the Fight Against Antisemitism in Munich.

Was it mere coincidence, too, that the Munich Society for Christian-Jewish Cooperation (which developed out of the Committee) was founded just weeks after Erhard successfully banned ninety percent of price controls in June of 1948?[28] At its founding in 1948, Scharnagl became the Society's first Catholic chairman, along with the philosopher Ernst Lichtenstein (Protestant) and the medical doctor Julius Spanier (Jewish). But already in the spring of 1949, during a visit to the United States, Scharnagl made an insensitive comment about Jewish DPs and was forced to resign his chairmanship.[29] Evidently, Scharnagl did not advocate amity and cooperation between Christians and Jews for humanitarian or conciliatory reasons alone, but as part of a larger moral-economic program of postwar Christian liberalism.[30]

---

war Germany (Princeton, NJ: Princeton University Press, 1997); and Constantin Goschler, "The Attitude towards Jews in Bavaria after the Second World War," in Robert Moeller, ed., *West Germany under Construction: Politics, Society, and Culture in the Adenauer Era* (Ann Arbor: University of Michigan Press, 1997), 231–250.

27 Müller had in fact been instrumental in helping Erhard to his position in the Economic Council in October 1947. See Alf Mintzel, *Geschichte der CSU* (Opladen: Westdeutscher Verlag, 1977), 245.

28 On the role of the CDU and CSU in the economic reforms of June 1948, see For a recent recognition of the importance of the Catholic Church within the Economics Council, Christian Glossner, *Making of the German Post-war Economy* (New York: I.B. Taurus, 2010), especially 80–106.

29 The relevant portion of the interview is reproduced in Ellen Latzin, *Lernen von Amerika? Das US-Kulturaustauschprogramm für Bayern und seine Absolventen* (Stuttgart: Franz Steiner, 2005), 249.

30 A similar story postwar story might be told for Catholic liberals in France around this time. For its pre-history, see Joël Sabban, "La genèse de la 'morale judéo-chrétienne'. Étude sur l'origine d'une expression dans le monde intellectuel français," *Revue de l'histoire des religions* 1 (2012), 85–118.

The same can be said for many other founding personalities of Christian-Jewish cooperation in West Germany. Franz Böhm, the Protestant co-founder and first director of the Frankfurt Society for Christian-Jewish Cooperation – recognized by his biographer as "one of the most prominent representatives of reconciliation between Jews and Christians in the postwar years" – also launched his fight against antisemitism as part of a struggle for which he was much more famous: the neo-liberal transformation of the economy.[31] An expert in business law at the universities of Freiburg and Jena during the Nazi years, Böhm developed a moral-economic theory according to which it was incumbent upon the state to protect what he and his associates considered the categorical imperative of free internal economic competition. When Böhm's book was published in 1937, its tenets collided violently with the Nazi regime's transition to a command economy.[32] That same year, Böhm was sacked, ostensibly for having privately criticized racial policy, but more likely for his public opposition to economic interventionism.[33] After the war, Böhm led the academic crusade against price regulation, cartels, and monopolies as editor of the country's primary neo-liberal journal, *ORDO*. In addition, he was appointed by Chancellor Adenauer to be the Federal Republic's chief negotiator for a reparations deal with Israel for Germany's crimes against the Jews.[34] For Böhm, the role of the state in a neo-liberal order must be more than the night-watchman of old *laisser-faire* liberalism; it must take an active role

---

31 Traugott Roser, *Protestantismus und Soziale Marktwirtschaft. Eine Studie am Beispiel Franz Böhms* (Berlin: Lit, 1996), 148.

32 Franz Böhm, *Die Ordnung der Wirtschaft als geschichtliche Aufgabe und rechtsschöpferische Leistung* (Stuttgart: Kohlhammer, 1937). For a contextualization of this work as one of the key texts of what became known as ORDO- or neo-liberalism after the war, see Ralf Ptak, "Neoliberalism in Germany: Revisiting the Ordoliberal Foundations of the Social Market Economy," in *The Road from Mount Pèlerin: The Making of the Neoliberal Thought Collective*, eds. Philip Mirowski and Dieter Plehwe (Cambridge, MA: Harvard University Press, 2009), 118. Böhm relied heavily on the work of Walter Eucken, whose arguments for free competition were based on Kantian moral categories as well as Protestant religious values.

33 The oral order to dismiss Böhm cited both "reasons of worldview and political economy." Hans Albrecht Grüninger to the minister for Volksbildung in Thüringen, 4 May 1937, in Franz Böhm Papers, Sankt Augustin, Archiv für Christlich-Demokratische Politik, Konrad-Adenauer-Stiftung 01-200, 003/1.

34 He became editor of *ORDO* after Walter Eucken died in 1948. The copious literature on Böhm has failed to make the explicit connection between the two spheres of his work. See Niels Hansen, *Franz Böhm mit Ricarda Huch: Zwei wahre Patrioten* (Düsseldorf: Droste, 2009); Jan Tumlir, "Franz Böhm and the Development of Economic-Constitutional Analysis," in *German Liberals and the Social Market Economy*, eds. Alan Peacock and Hans Willgerodt (London: Macmillan, 1989), 125–178; Hans Otto Lenel, "The Life and World of Franz Böhm," *European Journal of Law and Economics* 3 (1996), 301–307.

in promoting the (Kantian and Christian) *morality* of free and fair competition. The same went for the Jews: the old liberal state simply protected Jews physical safety, whereas the neo-liberal state would actively combat the kind of religious and racial prejudice that hinders the moral behavior of its citizens.

The first director of the Munich Society, the Catholic businessman Josef Brandlmeier, began his career in the late Weimar years with an appeal to shrink the state's role in welfare for the sick, unemployed, and homeless and return the majority of such duties to the country's religious organizations.[35] The first Protestant chair of the Berlin Society, also founded in 1949, was Joachim Tiburtius, the author of the postwar tract *The Christian Order of the Economy*, which became what one economist called "a kind of economic Magna Charta of the CDU."[36] It posited the necessity of a free-competition market economy, but empowered the state to "decide on parameters of enterprise and apportionment in agriculture," thereby endowing competition with "moral norms."[37] As longtime city-senator in Berlin in the 1950s, Tiburtius became a staunch defender of free enterprise in the island of West Berlin surrounded by the communist East German state. Theodor Heuss, who presided over the Coordinating Council of the Societies for Christian-Jewish Cooperation, was also the chairman of the pro-market Free Democratic Party and a key supporter of Erhard's liberalization.

A concern for political economy even motivated the figure in the Societies whose role was supposedly devoted to purely religious affairs. Karl Thieme, a Protestant-raised convert to Catholicism who had returned after the war from emigration in Switzerland, became the Coordinating Council's "adviser for religious affairs" in 1949. Thieme's work combating antisemitism and pressuring the Catholic hierarchy to revise its anti-Jewish liturgy has become well known, largely thanks to the path-breaking research of the historian John Connelly,[38] but few have appreciated Thieme in light of his moral-economic program during this time. Planning for Germany's future during the war, Thieme wrote to his new friend, the neo-liberal economist Wilhelm Röpke, about his intention "to help create the preconditions for an alliance of Catholics and liberals" after seeing "with horror

---

35 Josef Brandlmeier, *Die Caritas innerhalb der Wohlfahrtspflege und ihre volkswirtschaftliche Bedeutung in Deutschland, unter besonderer Berücksichtigung bayerischer Verhältnisse* (Freiburg: Caritasdruckerei, 1931).

36 Wilhelm Hasenack, "Joachim Tiburtius 70 Jahre alt," *Betriebswirtschaftliche Forschung und Praxis* 11 (1959), 548.

37 Joachim Tiburtius, *Christliche Wirtschaftsordnung. Ihre Wurzeln und ihr Inhalt* (Berlin: Union Verlag, 1947), 82.

38 John Connelly, *From Enemy to Brother: The Revolution in Catholic Teaching on the Jews* (Cambridge, MA: Harvard University Press, 2012).

how widely the delusion of planned economy has intruded into so-called 'liberal' and also Catholic circles."[39] The book Thieme was writing, entitled *Destiny of the Germans* (1945) was a screed against the Prussian tradition of centralized state socialism.[40] Likewise, Thieme's postwar collaborator on Christian-Jewish interfaith dialogue, Gertrud Luckner, had begun her career in the late 1930s with an unpublished dissertation in economics at Freiburg with the neo-liberal scholar Bernhard Pfister, on a topic that implicitly criticized state socialism and praised voluntarism in a free-competition economy.[41]

Wilhelm Röpke's famous postwar tract, *The German Question* (1946) – though not explicitly about Christian-Jewish relations – offered an illuminating perspective on the relationship between neo-liberalism and the Jews. Like his fellow neo-liberal economists, Röpke argued that Germany's "pathological" descent into self-destruction began with its turn toward economic nationalism in the late-nineteenth century.[42] He saw antisemitism as the consequence of anti-marketism: as the creation of a false enemy that ostensibly threatens the national economic body and justifies self-enclosure. This could only be healed, he argued, through a return to competition-based market relations. But Röpke, like many involved in Christian-Jewish reconciliation after the war, also placed a *cultural* precondition on the long-term health of the nation. He believed that German liberals themselves, including German Jews, had been responsible for the recent inability to defend the religious values *upon which the values of free competition were based*. He mourned the contributions of secular German Jews to the obsolescence and "using up" of Christianity, "a development whose ultimate

39 Karl Thieme to Wilhelm Röpke, 8 February 1943, Karl Thieme Papers, ED 163/67, Institut für Zeitgeschichte, Munich. Thieme wrote that he was "intending to open with a fundamental general offensive within Aristotelian-Thomistic philosophy *against* corporativism and *for* the principle of self-administration [...]." The correspondence began when Thieme sent Röpke a copy of his manuscript *Das Schicksal der Deutschen*, and Röpke responded that it was the "weightiest and most illuminative" of all the things he had read after following all the literature on the German question both inside and outside Germany. Wilhelm Röpke to Karl Thieme, 3 August 1942, Karl Thieme Papers, ED 163/67.

40 Karl Thieme, *Das Schicksal der Deutschen* (Basel: Kober, 1945).

41 Gertrud Luckner, *Die Selbsthilfe der Arbeitslosen in England und Wales auf Grund der englischen Wirtschafts- und Ideengeschichte* (Ph.D. Dissertation, Freiburg, 1938). Pfister was part, with Franz Böhm, of the Freiburg Circle around Walter Eucken. Luckner published the *Freiburger Rundbriefe* with Thieme after the war.

42 See for example Alexander Rüstow, "General Sociological Causes of the Economic Disintegration and Possibilities of Reconstruction," in Wilhelm Röpke, *International Economic Disintegration* (London: William Hodge and Company, 1942), 267–283.

consequences," he wrote, "produced so appalling a catastrophe for Jewry."[43] In other words, Röpke suggested that both Christians and Jews who had fallen from their respective faiths needed to recognize the importance of Christian *cultural* institutions for the maintenance of free *economic and political* institutions.[44]

2 The Christian demand for Jewish cooperation

To be regarded as legitimate, the complementarity of neo-liberal economics and Christian cultural conservatism that Röpke described – and that most founders of the Christian-Jewish movement explicitly or implicitly advocated – required recognition from Jews themselves. That demand for Jewish support explains the remarkable popularity of the returning German Jewish émigré Hans-Joachim Schoeps, whom the Bavarian cultural minister appointed in 1947 to teach history of religion and ethical culture at the University of Erlangen near Nuremberg.[45] Schoeps was one of roughly 15,000 German Jews who had either survived underground or returned from abroad after what had already been a small minority before the war. The majority of his family had been killed in the Nazi genocide.[46]

43 Wilhelm Röpke, *The German Question*, trans. E.W. Dickes (Leicester: Blackfriars, 1946), 164 fn. 9.

44 In early 1948, Röpke gave an interview to the journalist Erik von Kuehnelt-Leddihn complaining about those "leftist" officials in OMGUS – it was clear that he meant the German-Jewish émigré Fritz Karsen – who still wished to eviscerate Catholic public schools in Bavaria and instead impose a secular American-style unified school system on the U.S. Zone. "These Jacobins are opposed to the very roots of our culture and civilization," Röpke said, "and they persecute those institutions of learning which are Western, Christian and humanistic with almost the same hatred as the Nazis did." Erik von Kuehnelt-Leddihn, "American Blunders in Germany. Professor Roepke speaks," *Catholic World* (August 1948), 400–401.

45 He gained his teaching appointement as Extraordinariat in 1947 and Ordinariat in 1950. For introductions to Schoeps's role in postwar Germany see Michael Brenner, "Jüdische Geistesgeschichte zwischen Exil und Heimkehr: Hans-Joachim Schoeps im Kontext der Wissenschaft des Judentums," in Monika Boll and Raphael Gross, *"Ich staune, dass Sie in dieser Luft atmen können": jüdische Intellektuelle in Deutschland nach 1945* (Frankfurt am Main: Fischer, 2013), 21- 39; Gideon Botsch, ed., *Wider den Zeitgeist: Studien zum Leben und Werk von Hans-Joachim Schoeps* (Hildesheim: Olms, 2009); Gary Lease, "Hans-Joachim Schoeps settles in Germany after eight years of exile in Sweden," in *Yale Companion to Jewish Writing and Thought in German Culture, 1096–1996*, eds. Sander Gilman and Jack Zipes (New Haven, CT: Yale University Press, 1997), 655–661.

46 On the tragic story of Schoeps's parents see Astrid Mehmel, "Ich richte nun an Sie die grosse Bitte, eine zweckdienliche Eingabe in dieser Sache zu machen…," *Zeitschrift für Religions- und Geistesgeschichte* 52, no. 1 (2000), 38–46.

Through his many books, articles, and lectures – one of his first classes at Erlangen registered 600 students – Schoeps became, for a while at least, the country's best-known spokesperson for the German-Jewish cultural heritage. In early 1949, he joined the religious committee of the Munich Society for Christian-Jewish Cooperation and was the only Jewish scholar to give an address at the first major conference on Christian-Jewish relations that year.

Why Schoeps? Part of the answer to that question lies in his activities during the later years of the National Socialist regime. Schoeps had spent the war years in Sweden after emigrating from Germany in duress in late 1938. (His preferred place of exile had actually been the U.S., but the New School's Alvin Johnson – who was arranging employment for many other prestigious émigré academics – could not find a seminary or divinity school that would employ him, despite the support of the Jewish historian Salo Baron. Baron suggested that Schoeps's Judaism, heavily inflected by the Protestant theology of Karl Barth, might have been too radical even for Reform circles.[47]) He had secured a position at the University of Uppsala through the help of the Protestant theologians Anton Fridrichsen and Gösta Lindeskog, opponents of the German Christian attempts to remove the Hebrew Bible and other Jewish elements from Christian scripture. Without teaching responsibilities, Schoeps spent his days in a fully equipped German-language library preparing the books on early Christianity for which he would eventually gain academic tenure back in his homeland. Most importantly, he argued in his journalistic work that only a re-embrace of true Christian values would be able to turn German youth away from the prejudice of their parents' generation. He rejected the idea that young people had been brainwashed by racist education. "The church's knowledge can find fruitful ground among the young if the church can find the right words," he wrote in a Swedish-language publication just after the war.[48] "Despite all that has happened," he told Karl Barth in a letter, he had "no more yearning wish than to return to Germany," to fulfill the task he felt "as anti-Nazi and Jew" to "be of service to the education of German academic youth."[49]

German Jews who had known Schoeps since the Weimar years, such as Leo Baeck and Gershom Scholem, expressed either deep gratitude or baffled amaze-

---

47 See the relevant correspondence in Karl O. Paetel Papers, Box 6, German and Jewish Intellectual Émigré Collection, State University of New York at Albany.

48 Hans-Joachim Schoeps (pseud. Joachim Frank), *Vad skall det bli av tyskarna?* (Stockholm: Rabén & Sjögren, 1944), 79–92, 111–114. I am grateful to my colleague Walter Jackson, of blessed memory, for his help with the Swedish text.

49 Hans-Joachim Schoeps to Karl Barth, 25 September 1945, and also 8 April 1946, reprinted in *Menora* (1991), 128–129.

ment (or both) when informed of Schoeps's commitment to inter-faith relations and the rebuilding of the Christian churches in post-genocidal Germany.[50] It was unclear to many Jewish observers what, if anything, survivors might gain from such collaborations, especially when the work involved physical and psychological hardship. In his first year back, Schoeps slept in a room at a Jewish nursing home in Frankfurt, the only place he could find with central heating during the frigid winter of early 1947. He relied on friends abroad to send him basic amenities like food and paper.[51] The first regular employment he obtained was with a Protestant relief organization in Stuttgart whose members wanted to come to terms with their guilt for having failed to answer the question, "Cain, where is your brother Abel?"[52] When Schoeps moved to Bavaria to take his university professorship, he joined the tiny Jewish community there, but an impression soon developed that he might be more interested in rebuilding Christian life than he was in reconstituting Judaism in Germany.[53]

It is easy to see Schoeps – and by extension, the tiny minority of other German Jews involved in the early efforts at Christian-Jewish cooperation after the war – as an "alibi" for those Germans who sought to turn the page on their own involvement in National Socialism. Schoeps's personal papers at Berlin's State Library are littered with letters from old youth movement friends who wanted him, as a "full Jew," to write letters of character reference for their denazification hearings.[54] It is also true that some Christians might have used Schoeps for broader exculpatory purposes, citing his continued love for Germany's cultural heritage as proof that National Socialism had been an aberration of the nation's true spirit. Many of Schoeps's students in Erlangen later attested that it was an inspiring gesture for the younger generation of Germans to see a Jewish intellectual returning to his homeland, despite the resolution of the Jewish World Congress that Jews should "never again live on the blood-stained ground of Germany."[55] Indeed, scholars have estimated that less than five percent of surviving German Jewish émigrés

---

50 Leo Baeck wrote to Schoeps with great anticipation for the "abundance of tasks and plans" that lay ahead of him upon his impending return in November 1946. Leo Baeck to Hans-Joachim Schoeps, 15 November 1946, Ordner 97, Hans-Joachim Schoeps Papers, Staatsbibliothek Berlin.
51 Hans-Joachim Schoeps to Heinz Frank, dated December 1947, Ordner 108, Schoeps Papers.
52 Hans-Joachim Schoeps to Margarete Susman, 6 August 1946, Margarete Susman Papers, 88.11.920, Literaturarchiv Marbach.
53 Hans Lamm to Hans-Joachim Schoeps, 9 December 1948, Schoeps Papers, Ordner 109.
54 See Ordner 97, Schoeps Papers.
55 World Jewish Congress, "Germany," in *Resolutions Adopted by the Second Plenary Assembly of the World Jewish Congress, Montreaux, Switzerland, June 27-July 6, 1948* (London: Odhams Press, 1948), 7.

ever returned after the war.[56] This scarcity inflated the value of each individual Jew who did make the trip back. "As a Jewish German I stand in solidarity with other decent Germans," Schoeps told listeners at the first conference for Christian-Jewish relations in 1949, "whereby their decency is not dependent on the decision of the denazification court."[57] Such olive branches could appear as a Jewish blessing for the controversial German plan to amnesty former Nazis who seemed to have "subjectively atoned" (as Germany's first chancellor, Konrad Adenauer, put it).[58] Some occupation authorities in the U.S. Zone falsely suspected Schoeps of having held sympathy for the Nazis, not only because of his nationalist writings, but also due to his frequent postwar contact with figures who had been involved with the Hitler regime.[59]

On a deeper level, Schoeps's and other Jews' participation in the Christian-Jewish cooperation movement served a larger, moral-economic purpose. Historians have taken little note of the fact that the official title of the aforementioned conference, held in the Munich Town Hall, was "Congress for Better Human Relations" (*Kongress für bessere menschliche Beziehungen)*, an explicit reference to the "human relations" movement among American employers.[60] That year, the National Conference of Christians and Jews co-sponsored a pamphlet released by the directors of Johnson & Johnson, Libbey-Owens-Ford Glass Company, the EBASCO engineering consultant company, Radio Corporation of America, Macy's, and other large business-owners articulating the moral basis for a *humane capitalism* – one that would protect private property but reject *laissez-faire* Manchesterism, one that would convince restive workers that they did

---

56 The exact number is difficult to ascertain because of the age-old difficulty in defining and measuring Jewish identity. See Marita Krauss, *Heimkehr in ein fremdes Land* (München: Beck, 2001).

57 Quoted in the report on the meeting of 30 May 1949, "Gottlosigkeit. Feind der Christen und Juden," *Abendzeitung* (31 May 1949). His co-panelists at the conference included the Protestant theologian Rudolf Bultmann, who had offered no public critique of the regime during the Nazi years, and the Catholic professor Michael Schmaus, who had even lauded the similarities in Catholic and National Socialist worldview in 1933.

58 Konrad Adenauer, "Erste Regierungserklärung" from 20 September 1949, in *Reden 1917–1967*, ed. Hans-Peter Schwarz (Stuttgart: Deutsche Verlagsanstalt, 1975), 163.

59 On Schoeps's nationalism see Carl Rheins, "Deutscher Vortrupp, Gefolgschaft deutscher Juden 1933–1935," *Leo Baeck Institute Year Book* 26 (1981), 207–229; John von Houten Dippel, *Bound upon a Wheel of Fire* (New York: Basic Books, 1996); and Richard Faber, *Deutschbewusstes Judentum und jüdischbewusstes Deutschtum: der historische und politische Theologe Hans-Joachim Schoeps* (Würzburg: Königshausen und Neumann, 2008).

60 Knud Knudsen, ed., *Welt ohne Hass. Führende Wissenschaftler aller Fakultäten nehmen Stellung zu brennenden deutschen Problemen* (Berlin: Christian Verlag, 1950).

not have to turn all the way to communism just because they sought economic justice. "If we accept the brotherhood of man under God, important conclusions follow," wrote Robert W. Johnson, one of the principal authors. "Men must judge their conduct, not merely in terms of personal gain or convenience but also as right or wrong. Service to society, as well as to personal interest, becomes important. Teamwork and cooperation follow."[61] In fact, one of the first publications of the Coordinating Council was a translation of that publication.[62] Just as Christians and Jews were to recognize each others' inherent worth, employers and workers needed to recognize each others' dignity if the economic system of free competition was not to lose moral legitimacy and collapse into class warfare.

Dignity and worth did not mean equality. Schoeps was willing to accept for Judaism a junior partnership role – a role given linguistic expression in the phrase "Judeo-Christian" – as long as Christians recognized the legitimacy of Jewish existence and the moral duty to protect it.

In theological terms, Schoeps's theory revolved around an idea of "two covenants," a concept he summarized at the conference in 1949. True inter-faith partnership, he argued, demanded Christian recognition of "the truth of the Jewish knowledge of God," renunciation of the centuries-long "belief in the obduracy of the Jews," and "abandonment by the church of its mission among the Jews." He noted that such developments would in turn necessitate a fundamental revision of the Pauline "thesis of the annulled 'old' and fulfilled 'new' covenant" contained in Romans 9–11, the historically foundational text for the Christian stance on the Jews. In his prolific work on early Christianity, Schoeps attempted to show that the Christian apostle Paul – whose writings formed the intellectual basis of the Christian scripture – had badly erred in his description of the Israelites and Jewish tradition. Whereas Paul proclaimed that the strict rules composing Mosaic Law constituted the essence of the (allegedly outdated) Jewish tradition, Schoeps argued that it was the *revelation* of the Ten Commandments at Sinai and the faith it demanded it that provided Judaism with its beating heart.[63] Christian-Jewish reconciliation would therefore be dependent on Christian disavowal of that original misunderstanding that falsely opposed "Jewish law" to "Christian faith."

61 *Human Relations in Modern Business: A Guide for Action sponsored by American Business Leaders* (New York: Prentice-Hall, 1949), 4.

62 *Human Relations im Wirtschaftsleben von heute*, trans. U. Gruber and J. Ph. Kopeitko and supervised by Bernhard Pfister, introduction to the German edition by John Franklin Cronin (Bad Nauheim: Christian Verlag, 1952).

63 Schoeps, *Paulus. Die Theologie des Apostels im Lichte der jüdischen Religionsgeschichte* (Tübingen: Mohr, 1959).

Conversely, Schoeps argued, Jews would have to recognize that a new truth had been revealed with the birth of Christianity. "It cannot be a matter of indifference to Jews whether a man is a Christian or a non-Christian," Schoeps wrote. "With Franz Rosenzweig, I would even go so far as to declare that perhaps no Gentile can come to God the Father otherwise than through Jesus Christ." Though "we cannot recognize Yeshuah ha-Nozri as the Christ, i.e., as the Messiah for Israel [...], we are [...] prepared to recognize that, in some way which we do not understand, a Messianic significance for non-Jewish mankind is attached to this man."[64]

To German-speaking audiences, Schoeps was best known for his popular histories of the Prussian Kingdom, especially *The Other Prussia*, which went through multiple editions after its first publication in 1952. Like other "other Germany" narratives, these bestsellers attempted to rehabilitate Germans' historical sense of self by moving past their reputation of militarism and genocide and remembering the "good" values of duty, obedience, order, austerity, industriousness, and Christian tolerance for religious minorities. Schoeps told the story of those founders of the ill-fated Conservative Party who, in opposition to Bismarck's power politics, argued that the laws and institutions of a state must have sanction from a power higher than man. These Conservatives had supported the protection of individual and social freedoms not simply for expediency's sake, *but because they were Christian.*[65] In the climax of the book, Schoeps pointed out the paradox and supreme irony that this Conservative tradition, so infamous for its antisemitic prejudices, was actually *Jewish* in spirit: like the monarchy described in the Hebrew Bible, the state and all its laws must have divine sanction to be considered morally legitimate.[66]

In the early part of the 1950s, Schoeps was connected to a trans-Atlantic network of conservative authors who were similarly worried about the cultural and institutional preconditions for what might be called the sustainability of liberal democracy. The young writer Irving Kristol, a great admirer of Schoeps's writings, recruited him to write articles for *Commentary*, the magazine published

---

64 Hans-Joachim Schoeps, "A Religious Bridge between Jew and Christian: Shall We Recognize Two Covenants?" *Commentary* 9 (1950), 129–31. The essay was essentially an English version of Schoeps, "Probleme der christlich-jüdische Verständigung," in *Welt ohne Hass*, 70–80.

65 Schoeps pointed out that in Ludwig von Gerlach's eyes, a "republic, too, could be a legitimate authority which is conscious of its divine mandate," as long as it served "its function in representing and guarding law as the expression of divine will." Hans-Joachim Schoeps, *Das andere Preussen* (Stuttgart: F. Vorwerk, 1952), esp. 1–50. The quotation is from p. 15.

66 Ibid., 59.

by the American Jewish Committee.[67] Kristol and many of the contributors there were arguing that Christianity and Judaism formed the bedrock of values upon which a free and moral society must be based. Two of the magazine's most famous occasional contributors – Protestant theologian Reinhold Niebuhr and the Jewish sociologist Will Herberg – joined hands in the early 1950s to embrace the dual covenant theology Schoeps espoused.[68] Erik von Kuehnelt-Leddihn, the Austrian-born European correspondent for the conservative journal *National Review* (and a formative influence on its founder William F. Buckley), wrote to Schoeps in 1953 to say that conservatives on both sides of the ocean were united by their "theism, the faith in a personal God that pulls us into responsibility," and, in this belief, "synagogue and church form a primary factor."[69]

In the mid-1950s, to have contacts with Schoeps became something of a liability for the trans-Atlantic network of liberal conservatives because of his widely ridiculed attempt to revive monarchy in Germany through a campaign for Louis Ferdinand, the would-be heir to the Prussian throne. Though a poll conducted by the political magazine *Der Spiegel* found in 1954 that over half of Germans over sixty supported a return to monarchy, it also showed that less than a quarter of those under forty-four supported it.[70] The aspiring conservative lawyer Ernst-Wolfgang Böckenförde, who was in his mid-twenties – and was otherwise sympathetic to the idea that Christian values must underpin a free German order – told Schoeps in a letter that conservative institutions such as monarchy and the church needed to be continuous in order to survive. Unlike in England, in Germany the crown had not existed for more than thirty years.[71] The historian and political commen-

67 Irving Kristol to Hans-Joachim Schoeps, 7 April 1949, Ordner 110, Schoeps Papers. Schoeps wrote two articles for *Commentary* in 1950 and 1953.

68 See Hyrum Lewis, "Sacralizing the Right: William F. Buckley Jr., Whittaker Chambers, Will Herberg, and the Transformation of Intellectual Conservatism, 1945–1964" (Ph.D. Dissertation, USC, 2007), 162. In his landmark book *Protestant, Catholic, Jew*, Herberg announced that the conservation of Christianity and Judaism was crucial not only for the anti-communist struggle (which was "organized as an interfaith venture"), but also for the inculcation of values that would underpin good laws for protecting workers and tempering the marketplace. Will Herberg, *Protestant, Catholic Jew: An Essay in American Religious Sociology* (Garden City, NY: Anchor Books, 1955).

69 Erik Kuehnelt-Leddihn to Hans-Joachim Schoeps, 13 January 1953, Schoeps Papers, Ordner 102. See further Erik Kuehnelt-Leddihn, *Liberty or Equality: The Challenge of Our Time* (Caldwell, ID: Caxton, 1952). See also Erik Kuehnelt-Leddihn, *Christians and Jews Get Together* (National Conference of Christians and Jews, 1948), 1–8.

70 See "Die Ehre Preussens," *Der Spiegel* (3 March 1954), 6–10.

71 Ernst-Wolfgang Böckenförde to Hans-Joachim Schoeps, 5 September 1954, Ordner 203, Schoeps Papers.

tator Helga Grebing, who was the same age as Böckenförde but significantly to the left, knew her generation and trusted that Schoeps's whole campaign would die simply from "absurdity."[72] Schoeps himself eventually saw the writing on the wall and withdrew his plans, though he would never renounce his belief that a benevolent and religiously founded monarchy was a superior form of state to the democratic republic.

Schoeps's practical plans were eccentric and untimely, but the motivating conservative ideals behind them spoke to relevant problems of postwar political philosophy and political economy. Kuehnelt-Leddihn explained to a U.S. audience that monarchy appealed to as many Central Europeans as it did because modern democratic states "control the private lives of the 'citizens' to a far greater extent than the monarchs of the past would ever have dared to regulate the doings of their 'subjects.'"[73] In a German-language article in 1956 entitled "Neo-Conservatism and Neo-Liberalism," Kuehnelt-Leddihn wrote that "true" (or "neo") liberals must cooperate with "true" (or "neo") conservatives. "Old liberals," he argued, had advocated liberty so strongly that they ended up creating a rootless system of plutocracy and exploitation, while "old conservatives" had sought so strenuously to preserve the past that they had been willing to enlist the support of dictators. In reality, true liberals and true conservatives "can and should *complement one another*." Liberals needed conservatives to help preserve the values upon which liberalism was presumably based.[74]

Schoeps's books remained bestsellers into the late 1950s because of West Germany's geopolitical competition with East Germany. While the East German Democratic Republic could not claim superiority in the economic realm – the West German GDP was growing faster than any other country in the world, and many East Germans were sneaking over the border to live and work there – it *could* easily attack the moral foundation of the Federal Republic. In 1956, in an attempt to delegitimize the Adenauer regime's claim to lead a future German reunification, the East German government launched a massive, multi-year propaganda campaign revealing the number of suspected war criminals and "Jew murderers" in high positions of West German society, both in government and especially in big business.[75] The number of likely perpetrators living unperturbed in the West

72 Helga Grebing, "Kritik an Demokratie," *Staat – Erziehung – Gesellschaft* 1, no. 1 (1956), 16.
73 Erik von Kuehnelt-Leddihn, *Liberty or Equality: The Challenge of Our Time*, ed. John Hughes (Caldwell, ID: Caxton, 1952), 280–281.
74 Erik von Kuehnelt-Leddihn, "Neukonservatismus und Neuliberalismus," *Neues Abendland* (1956), esp. 121–127.
75 See the many brochures distributed by the Committee for German Unity formed by the East German government, such as *Bundesrepublik – Paradies für Kriegsverbrecher* (Berlin Ost: Auss-

was indeed large (though it was probably also significant in the East). Those West Germans eager to shore up the moral legitimacy of the Federal Republic, such as the media magnate Axel Springer, argued that it was not only the West's prosperous order of free competition that would make life more livable for Jews in Germany, but most importantly, its attachment to *Christian values* of freedom and tolerance that would overcome Germany's antisemitic past.[76] Schoeps became one of Springer's close friends and a frequent contributor to his many publications. Indeed, one cannot comprehend why the years after 1957 saw a spike in the level of public discussion about the fate of Jews in Germany without understanding the West German media war with the East.

By the end of the decade, "Christian-Jewish Cooperation" had become an entrenched institution of education in the Federal Republic. The number of local chapters under the auspices of the Coordinating Council of the Societies had increased to thirty, from only four a decade earlier. The Coordinating Council held regular conferences for educators about methods for teaching antisemitism and the Nazi past in schools. When a wave of antisemitic defacements appeared on West German synagogues and cemeteries during Christmas week of December 1959 and January 1960, the Federal Republic's Christian Democratic regime could react immediately with a policy that utilized the educational resources already developed by the Societies. The CDU responded to the spate of antisemitism by devoting more resources to civic education, Brotherhood Week, and other programs aiming to counteract the "prejudices still living in a few young heads," as the CDU Minister of the Interior Gerhard Schröder put it.[77]

The presumptive successor to Adenauer's chancellorship, the CDU-affiliated Ludwig Erhard, revealed the deeper structure of Christian-Jewish cooperation in Cold War Germany when he made his own statements about antisemitism in the wake of the 1959/1960 disturbances. In the subsequent years, Erhard consistently referenced the German Jewish identity of his beloved teacher, the neo-liberal Franz Oppenheimer, as a representative of the valuable ideas that had been

---

chuss für Deutsche Einheit, 1956), *Antisemitismus in der Bundesrepublik* (Berlin Ost: Ausschuss für Deutsche Einheit, 1956), *Judenmörder und Kriegsverbrecher an den Hebeln der Macht* (Berlin Ost: Ausschuss für Deutsche Einheit, 1956). For further context see Manfred Wilke, *The Path to the Berlin Wall*, trans. Sophie Perl (New York: Berghahn, 2014), especially chapter five.

76 On Springer and the Jews more generally see *Bild dir Dein Volk!*, eds. Dmitrij Belkin and Raphael Gross (Göttingen: Wallstein, 2012), and Hans-Peter Schwarz, *Axel Springer* (Berlin: Propyläen, 2008), 250–270.

77 Gerhard Schröder in an interview of early 1960, quoted in Torsten Oppelland, *Gerhard Schröder* (Düsseldorf: Droste, 2002), 324–325.

lost under National Socialism.[78] Oppenheimer had supervised Erhard's doctoral dissertation at the University of Frankfurt in the early 1930s, and was known to have interpreted the rise of antisemitism in those years as a "crisis of capitalism." Oppenheimer taught that antisemitism was a result of modern nationalism, which itself was the result of economic rivalry between super-large capitalist monopolies competing for the world market. The only solution, he believed, was to forge a world economic system in which monopolies could be eliminated and *actual free competition* in domestic and international trade could emerge. Only then, he believed, would nationalism, and thus antisemitism, subside.[79] Erhard had attempted to create such an order in postwar Germany as economics minister under Adenauer, with his battle against price controls and his successful fight for an anti-cartel law.

These multiple contexts have not, for the most part, been considered by historians of the postwar period. But neither can they be left out of a European story that traces the genealogy of Christian-Jewish cooperation or "Judeo-Christian amity," as it was known elsewhere in continental Western Europe. As Karl Thieme noted long ago, Christians in Germany were not unique in the Brotherhood movement that took place in all the countries west of the Iron Curtain. Germans did, however, stand at its vanguard – not only because the crimes against the Jews had been so great there, but more significantly, because the propaganda war against the Communists there was so fierce.

Given the miniscule number of Jews in the Federal Republic, the movement for Christian-Jewish cooperation in early Cold War Germany was a primarily Christian affair. For many of those Christians involved, it was surely an opportunity to close the books on a bankrupted history of accommodation with fascism. For the few German Jews who participated, the movement perhaps presented the possibility of shedding once and for all the old reputation of "Judeo-Bolshevism" that had been so prevalent in the first half of the century.[80] But most of all, Christian-Jewish cooperation served a political function. It provided a moral comple-

---

78 See for example Ludwig Erhard's speech on Oppenheimer's centenary in 1964, in *Wirken und Reden* (Ludwigsburg: Hoch, 1966), 365–373. On Erhard's appropriation of Oppenheimer's legacy for the neo-liberal camp in Germany, see Dieter Haselbach, "Franz Oppenheimer's Theory of Capitalism and of a Third Path," in Peter Koslowski, ed., *The Theory of Capitalism in the German Economic Tradition: Historism, Ordo-Liberalism, Critical Theory, Solidarism* (Heidelberg: Springer, 2000), 81–83.

79 Franz Oppenheimer, "Zur Weltlage der Juden im 20. Jahrhundert," *Jahrbuch für jüdische Geschichte und Literatur* (1931), 29–55.

80 See Paul Hanebrink, *A Spectre Haunting Europe: The Idea of Judeo-Bolshevism in Twentieth-Century Europe* (Harvard University Press, forthcoming).

ment to the neo-liberal economy, which by itself had no means of self-legitimation and was at the time coming under heavy attack.

Bibliography

Adenauer, Konrad. "Erste Regierungserklärung, 20 September 1949." *Reden 1917–1967*. Ed. Hans-Peter Schwarz. Stuttgart: Deutsche Verlagsanstalt, 1975. 153–169).
Adenauer, Konrad. "Karl Scharnagl, 21 August 1945." *Adenauer Briefe 1945–1947*. Ed. Rudolf Morsey and Hans-Peter Schwarz. Berlin: Siedler, 1983. 77–79.
Anthony, Alfred Williams. "The Whole Home Front." *The Herald of Gospel Liberty* (11 August 1921): 776–777.
Belkin, Dmitrij, and Raphael Gross, eds. *Bild dir Dein Volk!* Göttingen: Wallstein, 2012.
Botsch, Gideon, ed. *Wider den Zeitgeist: Studien zum Leben und Werk von Hans-Joachim Schoeps*. Hildesheim: Olms, 2009.
Böhm, Franz. *Die Ordnung der Wirtschaft als geschichtliche Aufgabe und rechtsschöpferische Leistung*. Stuttgart: Kohlhammer, 1937.
Brandlmeier, Josef. *Die Caritas innerhalb der Wohlfahrtspflege und ihre volkswirtschaftliche Bedeutung in Deutschland, unter besonderer Berücksichtigung bayerischer Verhältnisse*. Freiburg: Caritasdruckerei, 1931.
Braunwarth, Esther. *Interkulturelle Kooperation in Deutschland am Beispiel der Gesellschaften für Christlich-Jüdische Zusammenarbeit*. Munich: Herbert Utz, 2011.
Brenner, Michael. *After the Holocaust: Rebuilding Jewish Lives in Postwar Germany*. Princeton, NJ: Princeton University Press, 1997.
Brenner, Michael. "Jüdische Geistesgeschichte zwischen Exil und Heimkehr: Hans-Joachim Schoeps im Kontext der Wissenschaft des Judentums." *"Ich staune, dass Sie in dieser Luft atmen können": jüdische Intellektuelle in Deutschland nach 1945*. Ed. Monika Boll and Raphael Gross. Frankfurt am Main: Fischer, 2013. 21- 39.
Bulliet, Richard. *The Case for Islamo-Christian Civilization*. New York, NY: Columbia University Press, 2004.
Connelly, John. *From Enemy to Brother: The Revolution in Catholic Teaching on the Jews*. Cambridge, MA: Harvard University Press, 2012.
Council of the Protestant Church in Germany (EKD). "A Message Concerning the Jewish Question" (1948). *The Relationship of the Church to the Jewish People*. Trans. World Council of Churches. Geneva: WCC Publications, 1964. 48–62
Cronin, John Francis et al. *Human Relations im Wirtschaftsleben von heute*. Trans. Ursula Gruber and Johannes Ph. Kopeitko, supervised by Bernhard Pfister, introduction to the German edition by John Franklin Cronin. Bad Nauheim: Christian Verlag, 1952.
Dudziak, Mary L. *Cold War Civil Rights: Race and the Image of American Democracy*. Princeton, NJ: Princeton University Press, 2000.
Erhard, Ludwig. *Wirken und Reden*. Ludwigsburg: Hoch, 1966.
Faber, Richard. *Deutschbewusstes Judentum und jüdischbewusstes Deutschtum: der historische und politische Theologe Hans-Joachim Schoeps*. Würzburg: Königshausen und Neumann, 2008.

Foschepoth, Josef. *Im Schatten der Vergangenheit. Die Anfänge der Gesellschaft für Christlich-Jüdische Zusammenarbeit*. Göttingen: Vandenhoeck & Ruprecht, 1993.
Frei, Norbert. *Adenauer's Germany and the Nazi Past*. Trans. Joel Golb. New York: Columbia, 2002.
Gaston, K. Healan. "The Genesis of America's Judeo-Christian Moment: Secularism, Totalitarianism, and the Redefinition of Democracy." Ph.D. Dissertation, U.C. Berkeley, 2008.
Glossner, Christian. *Making of the German Post-war Economy*. New York: I.B. Taurus, 2010.
Goff, Brendan M. "The Heartland Abroad: The Rotary Club's Mission of Civil Internationalism." Ph.D. Dissertation, University of Michigan, 2008.
Goschler, Constantin. "The Attitude towards Jews in Bavaria after the Second World War." *West Germany under Construction: Politics, Society, and Culture in the Adenauer Era*. Ed. Robert Moeller. Ann Arbor: University of Michigan Press, 1997. 231–250.
Grebing, Helga. "Kritik an Demokratie." *Staat – Erziehung – Gesellschaft* 1.1 (1956): 16. 15–24.
Grossmann, Atina. *Jews, Germans, and Allies*. Princeton, NJ: Princeton University Press, 2007.
Hanebrink, Paul. *A Spectre Haunting Europe: The Idea of Judeo-Bolshevism in Twentieth-Century Europe*. Cambridge, MA: Harvard University Press, forthcoming.
Hansen, Niels. *Franz Böhm mit Ricarda Huch: Zwei wahre Patrioten*. Düsseldorf: Droste, 2009.
Hartmann, Douglas, Xuefeng Zhang, and William Wischstadt. "One (Multicultural) Nation Under God? Changing Uses and Meanings of the Term 'Judeo-Christian' in the American Media." *Journal of Media and Religion* 4.4 (2005): 207–234.
Haselbach, Dieter. "Franz Oppenheimer's Theory of Capitalism and of a Third Path." *The Theory of Capitalism in the German Economic Tradition: Historism, Ordo-Liberalism, Critical Theory, Solidarism*. Ed. Peter Koslowski. Heidelberg: Springer, 2000. 81–83.
Hasenack, Wilhelm. "Joachim Tiburtius 70 Jahre alt." *Betriebswirtschaftliche Forschung und Praxis* 11 (1959): 545–549.
Herberg, Will. *Protestant, Catholic Jew: An Essay in American Religious Sociology*. Garden City, NY: Anchor Books, 1955.
Herf, Jeffrey. *Divided Memory: The Nazi Past in the Two Germanys*. Cambridge, MA: Harvard University Press, 1997.
Hockenos, Matthew. *A Church Divided: German Protestants Confront the Nazi Past*. Bloomington: Indiana University Press, 2004.
Houten Dippel, John von. *Bound upon a Wheel of Fire*. New York: Basic Books, 1996.
Johnson, Robert W. *Human Relations in Modern Business: A Guide for Action sponsored by American Business Leaders*. New York: Prentice-Hall, 1949.
Kauders, Anthony. *Democratization and the Jews: Munich, 1945–1965*. Lincoln: University of Nebraska Press, 2004.
Knudsen, Knud, ed. *Welt ohne Hass. Führende Wissenschaftler aller Fakultäten nehmen Stellung zu brennenden deutschen Problemen*. Berlin: Christian Verlag, 1950.
Krauss, Marita. *Heimkehr in ein fremdes Land*. München: Beck, 2001.
Kraut, Benny. "Towards the Establishment of the National Conference of Christians and Jews: The Tenuous Road to Religious Goodwill in the 1920s." *American Jewish History* 77 (1988): 388–412.
Kuehnelt-Leddihn, Erik von. *Christians and Jews Get Together* (National Conference of Christians and Jews, 1948), 1–8.
Kuehnelt-Leddihn, Erik von. "American Blunders in Germany. Professor Roepke speaks." *Catholic World* (August 1948): 400–401.

Kuehnelt-Leddihn, Erik von. *Liberty or Equality: The Challenge of Our Time.* Ed. John Hughes. Caldwell, ID: Caxton, 1952.
Kuehnelt-Leddihn, Erik von. "Neukonservatismus und Neuliberalismus." *Neues Abendland* (1956): esp. 121–127.
Latzin, Ellen. *Lernen von Amerika? Das US-Kulturaustauschprogramm für Bayern und seine Absolventen.* Stuttgart: Franz Steiner, 2005.
Lease, Gary. "Hans-Joachim Schoeps settles in Germany after eight years of exile in Sweden." *Yale Companion to Jewish Writing and Thought in German Culture, 1096–1996.* Ed. Sander Gilman and Jack Zipes. New Haven, CT: Yale University Press, 1997. 655–661.
Lenel, Hans Otto. "The Life and World of Franz Böhm." *European Journal of Law and Economics* 3 (1996): 301–307.
Lewis, Hyrum. "Sacralizing the Right: William F. Buckley Jr., Whittaker Chambers, Will Herberg, and the Transformation of Intellectual Conservatism, 1945–1964." Ph.D. Dissertation, USC, 2007.
Locke, Alain. "Lessons in World Crisis." *The Bahá'í World: A Biennial International Record*, vol. 9 (1945), 746.
Löffler, Bernhard. *Soziale Marktwirtschaft und administrative Praxis.* Stuttgart: Franz Steiner, 2002.
Luckner, Gertrud. "Die Selbsthilfe der Arbeitslosen in England und Wales auf Grund der englischen Wirtschafts- und Ideengeschichte." Ph.D. Dissertation, Freiburg, 1938.
Mehmel, Astrid. "Ich richte nun an Sie die grosse Bitte, eine zweckdienliche Eingabe in dieser Sache zu machen..." *Zeitschrift für Religions- und Geistesgeschichte* 52.1 (2000): 38–46.
Mintzel, Alf. *Geschichte der CSU.* Opladen: Westdeutscher Verlag, 1977.
Moore, Deborah Dash. "Jewish GIs and the Creation of the Judeo-Christian Tradition." *Religion and American Culture* 8.1 (1998): 31–53.
Oppelland, Torsten. *Gerhard Schröder.* Düsseldorf: Droste, 2002.
Oppenheimer, Franz. "Zur Weltlage der Juden im 20. Jahrhundert." *Jahrbuch für jüdische Geschichte und Literatur* (1931): 29–55.
Ptak, Ralf. "Neoliberalism in Germany: Revisiting the Ordoliberal Foundations of the Social Market Economy." *The Road from Mount Pèlerin: The Making of the Neoliberal Thought Collective.* Ed. Philip Mirowski and Dieter Plehwe. Cambridge, MA: Harvard University Press, 2009: 98–138.
Rheins, Carl. "Deutscher Vortrupp, Gefolgschaft deutscher Juden 1933–1935." *Leo Baeck Institute Year Book* 26 (1981): 207–229.
Roser, Traugott. *Protestantismus und Soziale Marktwirtschaft. Eine Studie am Beispiel Franz Böhms.* Berlin: Lit, 1996.
Röpke, Wilhelm. *The German Question.* Trans. E.W. Dickes. Leicester: Blackfriars, 1946.
Rüstow, Alexander. "General Sociological Causes of the Economic Disintegration and Possibilities of Reconstruction." *International Economic Disintegration.* Ed. Wilhelm Röpke. London: William Hodge and Company, 1942. 267–283.
Sabban, Joël. "La genèse de la 'morale judéo-chrétienne'. Étude sur l'origine d'une expression dans le monde intellectuel français." *Revue de l'histoire des religions* 1 (2012): 85–118.
Scharnagl, Anton. *Die völkische Weltanschauung und wir Katholiken.* Munich: Huber, 1932.
Scharnagl, "Auf die Spitze getrieben. Scharnagl nachkend." *Der Spiegel* (9 August 1947).
Schoeps, Hans-Joachim. *Vad skall det bli av tyskarna?* Stockholm: Rabén & Sjögren, 1944.
Schoeps, Hans-Joachim. "Gottlosigkeit. Feind der Christen und Juden." *Abendzeitung* (31 May 1949).

Schoeps, Hans-Joachim. "A Religious Bridge between Jew and Christian: Shall We Recognize Two Covenants?" *Commentary* 9 (1950): 129–31.

Schoeps, Hans-Joachim. *Das andere Preussen* . Stuttgart: F. Vorwerk, 1952.

Schoeps, Hans-Joachim. *Paulus. Die Theologie des Apostels im Lichte der jüdischen Religionsgeschichte*. Mohr (Siebeck) Tübingen, 1959.

Schroeder, Steven. *To Forget It All and Begin Anew: Reconciliation in Occupied Germany, 1944–1954*. Toronto: University of Toronto, 2013.

Schultz, Kevin. *Tri-Faith America: How Catholics and Jews Held America to Its Protestant Promise*. New York: Oxford, 2011.

Schwarz, Hans-Peter. *Axel Springer*. Berlin: Propyläen, 2008.

Silk, Mark. "Notes on the Judeo-Christian Tradition in America." *American Quarterly* 36 (1984): 65–85.

Silk, Mark. "The Protestant Problem(s) of American Jewry." *The Protestant-Jewish Conundrum*. Ed. Jonathan Frankel and Ezra Mendelsohn. New York: Oxford, 2010. 126–141.

Stern, Frank. *The Whitewashing of the Yellow Badge: Antisemitism and Philosemitism in Postwar Germany*. New York: Oxford University Press, 1992.

Thieme, Karl. *Das Schicksal der Deutschen*. Basel: Kober, 1945.

Thieme, Karl. "Eine neue Phase christich-jüdischer Zusammenarbeit." *Judaica* 7.3 (1951): 234–235.

Tibi, Bassam. *Islam in Global Politics: Conflict and Cross-Civilizational Bridging*. Abingdon: Routledge, 2012.

Tiburtius, Joachim. *Christliche Wirtschaftsordnung. Ihre Wurzeln und ihr Inhalt*. Berlin: Union Verlag, 1947.

Tumlir, Jan. "Franz Böhm and the Development of Economic-Constitutional Analysis." *German Liberals and the Social Market Economy*. Ed. Alan Peacock and Hans Willgerodt. London: Macmillan, 1989. 125–178.

Wall, Wendy. *Inventing the "American Way": The Politics of Consensus from the New Deal to the Civil Rights Movement*. New York: Oxford, 2008.

Weiss-Rosmarin, Trude. *Judaism and Christianity: The Differences*. New York: Jewish Book Club, 1943.

Wilke, Manfred. *The Path to the Berlin Wall*. Trans. Sophie Perl. New York: Berghahn, 2014.

World Jewish Congress. "Germany." *Resolutions Adopted by the Second Plenary Assembly of the World Jewish Congress, Montreaux, Switzerland, June 27-July 6, 1948*. London: Odhams Press, 1948. Box A19 Folder 5 – no actual page number, its an archive : http://collections.americanjewisharchives.org/ms/ms0361/ms0361.html#series1

Zietlow, Carl F. "Christians, Jews Form Organization." *Lockport, N.Y. Union Sun & Journal* (14 February 1957), 7. http://fultonhistory.com/Newspaper%2018/Lockport%20NY%20Union%20Sun%20Journal/Lockport%20NY%20Union%20Sun%20Journal%201957/Lockport%20NY%20Union%20Sun%20Journal%201957 %20-%200535.pdf

Part 2: **Theology and Philosophy**

Emmanuel Nathan

6 Two Pauls, Three Opinions: The Jewish Paul between Law and Love

The Apostle Paul, writing in the 50s of the Common Era, is actually the earliest of Christian writers, if Christian indeed he was. Pamela Eisenbaum, a Jewish scholar of Paul's letters, is quite adamant that he was not a Christian.[1] Her position is reflective of the current scholarly emphasis on Paul's Jewishness, something that has become a commonplace in biblical studies of Paul for at least 40 years now, when the preceding wave in scholarship, taking seriously the Jewishness of Jesus, had already taken root. In fact, nowadays it is hard to imagine biblical studies ever having disputed the Jewishness of Jesus or Paul. But the sad fact is that the conceptual and methodological shift that was needed for this to happen only took place in the latter half of the 20th century, and I shall briefly trace that shift in the first part of this contribution.

My question in this contribution, however, is whether the 'Jewish' Paul that is now taken for granted does not in fact cover up an even more fundamental debate that continues to linger. As a Jesus-believing Jew, Paul the apostle has been an ideological battleground in biblical studies to identify the origins of the so-called 'Parting of the Ways' between Judaism and Christianity. That is to say, Paul's personal encounter with Christ has been used to crystallize that moment in time (if there was indeed *one* moment) when a Jewish sect became its own religion. While the current landscape of biblical studies on Paul has now an amazing range of varieties on 'the Jewish Paul' to offer, I shall argue in the second part of this contribution that this range, when taken as a spectrum, reveals two opposing ends: on the one, a 'Torah observant' Paul who clings resolutely to Judaism and its commandments; on the other, a 'liberal' Paul whose mysticism breaks free of religious constraints. This to me suggests a continuing struggle in biblical studies to situate Paul the apostle between 'Law' and 'Love',[2] and in so doing, Paul comes

---

1 Pamela Eisenbaum, *Paul Was Not a Christian: The Original Message of a Misunderstood Apostle* (New York: HarperCollins, 2009).

2 An interpretive framework of Judaism representing law and Christianity love occurs very early on in Christian collective memory. The Gospel of John (dated roughly to sometime in the 90s of the Common Era) already contains in its prologue, "The law indeed was given through Moses; grace and truth came through Jesus Christ" (Jn 1:17 [all biblical quotations in English from the New Revised Standard Version]). In this way the Fourth Gospel sets up an opposition between Moses, representing the Law, and Jesus, representing not just grace and truth, but more

to represent that hyphen in the so-called signifier of 'Judeo-Christian'.[3] But how justified is such an assumption? To delve into these and other questions, let me first commence by indicating the conceptual and methodological shifts that have taken place in studies of Paul and his letters over the past 50 years.

From Paul the Christian ...

Paul's contribution to Christian theology can hardly be underestimated. It is in fact no exaggeration to say that for many he, and not Jesus, was the real founder of Christianity as a religion. Gerd Lüdemann, a modern exponent of such a view words it thus: "The new religion required a doctrinal unity and the authority to enforce it; that in turn called for vision (and perhaps *a* vision) and the supreme self-assuredness to insist on its truth; and those, of course, were the spark and the fuel which powered the immense missionary effort that made Paul the founder of Christianity."[4]

To see Paul as the founder of Christianity, though, is really to deal with an established problem in Pauline studies: the question of Paul and Judaism.[5] This is more traditionally known as the 'problem of Paul and the Law', that is to say, Paul who saw the Law as a stumbling-block to faith in Christ. So the question of Paul and Judaism should really be understood here as Paul *versus* Judaism, as antithetical opposites, or to put it in German Lutheran terms, the opposition between *Gesetz und Evangelium*. This binary opposition sees an unbridgeable gap between two spheres of influence, the Law (Judaism) and the Gospel (Christianity). What is needed to move from one to the other is a clean break. So, while in such a view

---

importantly, love. Jesus, the new law-giver, institutes a new commandment, "I give you a new commandment, that you love one another. Just as I have loved you, you also should love one another" (Jn 13:34). Yet my contribution will show that this pattern of law versus love is actually superimposed upon Paul's understanding of his Jewishness by the much later Lutheran interpretive framework of *Gesetz und Evangelium* (law and gospel).

3 Jean-François Lyotard and Eberhard Gruber, *The Hyphen. Between Judaism and Christianity*, Philosophy and Literary Theory (New York: Humanity Books, 1993). And, indeed, as Pascal-Anne Brault and Michael Naas, point out in the "Translator's Foreword," viii: "For depending on which side of the hyphen one is standing on, almost everything appears – or can be read – differently."

4 Gerd Lüdemann, *Paul: The Founder of Christianity* (Amherst, NY: Prometheus Books, 2002) 215.

5 See, for instance, "Paul, the Law and Judaism: The Collapse of a Theological Consensus," in Frank Thielman, *Paul and the Law: A Contextual Approach* (Downers Grove: InterVarsity, 1994) 14–47.

it is conceded that Paul *was* Jewish,[6] the emphasis is rather on Paul having found new meaning in Christ.[7] Paul's writings, then, are read to measure the distance between Paul's new religion (Christianity) and his former religion, Judaism. His letters are therefore the writings of a Christian, someone who realized the futility of the Law to save (from sin). Paul thus converted (this was the transitional break that was required) to a new religion. This new religion was one in which righteousness is now freely granted to everyone, Jew and Gentile, through faith in Christ. This position has represented the standard view of Paul in German (mostly Protestant) biblical scholarship.[8]

While Lüdemann points out the influence of Friedrich Nietzsche on his understanding of Paul as the founder of Christianity,[9] most biblical scholars

---

6 Consider Paul's letter to the Galatians where he boasts of his *former life in Judaism*: "You have heard, no doubt, of my earlier life in Judaism. I was violently persecuting the church of God and was trying to destroy it." (Gal 1:13).

7 Here a proof-text would be from Paul's letter to the Philippians: "More than that, I regard everything as loss because of the surpassing value of knowing Christ Jesus my Lord. For his sake I have suffered the loss of all things, and I regard them as rubbish, in order that I may gain Christ" (Phil 3:8).

8 The constraints of this contribution prevent me from fully entering into *why* this has represented the standard German view in Pauline scholarship, but the 'New Perspective on Paul' (which I shall shortly discuss), has been quite clear in stating that anti-Judaism (stretching back to Luther) has definitely been a factor here. So, for instance, James D.G. Dunn, "The Justice of God: A Renewed Perspective on Justification by Faith," *JTS* 43 (1992) 1–22, here p. 5: "Unfortunately, however, the further corollary was drawn: that Judaism was the antithesis of Christianity, what Paul had been saved from. Such a view, of course, had been prominent in Christianity at least since the Epistle of Barnabas, and fitted well with the strong strand of anti-semitism which so disfigured Christianity's attitude to Jews and Judaism in the Middle Ages, an attitude which Luther himself expressed in characteristic forthrightness in his infamous *On the Jews and Their Lies* (*Von den Jüden und iren Lügen*). Tragically, however, it reinforced Christian suspicion, not to say hatred of Judaism, which was to reach its horrific outworking in the Holocaust. In scholarly circles the idea that Judaism was the antithesis of Christianity was expressed well through the middle of this century in the depiction of Judaism as simply the precursor of Christianity: so that *pre*-Christian Judaism was simply '*late* Judaism' (where this left the Judaism of the next nineteen centuries was a question not even considered)." Cf. also Tania Oldenhage, *Parables for Our Time: Rereading New Testament Scholarship after the Holocaust* (Oxford: Oxford University Press, 2002).

9 Lüdemann, *Paul: The Founder of Christianity*, 227: "I would like to draw the reader's attention again to Nietzsche, whose analysis has greatly helped me to understand Paul as the founder of Christianity." This is then followed by a quote from Nietzsche's *The Dawn* sec. 68, where Paul is credited with both launching Christianity and removing it from its Jewish roots. It is interesting to note that other contributions in this volume have also picked up on Nietzsche's influence on the question of a Judeo-Christian tradition.

would more readily admit the role of Ferdinand Christian Baur, whose antithesis of 'Petrinism' and 'Paulinism' has influenced the way biblical scholars have viewed the emergence of early Christianity.[10] Baur argued that the clash between the Jewish-centered Petrine and the Gentile-centered Pauline parties represented the real crucible from which Christianity was born. Paulinism gave Christianity its inner, spiritual and universal dimensions. By contrast, Petrine Christianity's attachment to the formal, external and the particular would be the reason why Jewish Christianity ultimately disappeared. When the gospel spread among the Gentiles, it was because Pauline Christianity had broken free of the constraints of an ethnically particular mission targeted only at Jews.

It should also not be forgotten that Baur relied on Hegelian categories. Jewish particularism was antithetically opposed to the pluralism on offer within the Roman empire. The happy synthesis, Christianity, represented all that was best of both worlds. Baur's model also served confessional ends within his own 19th century German context. Petrine and Pauline Christianity reflected the differences between Catholicism and Protestantism. As such, it remained a dominant paradigm in Protestant scholarship and the subsequent revisions to the model in the late 19th and early 20th centuries by such figures as Joseph Barber Lightfoot, Abrecht Ritschl, or the *Religionsgeschichtliche Schule* (the History of Religions school), did little to remove the basic dualistic scheme or the perception of the nascent Church as 'early Catholicism'.[11] But all of that would change in the latter part of the 20th century.

… to Paul the Jesus-believing Jew

A new way of understanding Paul arrived in the second half of the 20th century. This was in no small part because of the tragedy of the Shoah and the systemic

---

10 Ferdinand Christian Baur, "Die Christuspartei in der Korinthischen Gemeinde, der Gegensatz des petrinischen und paulinischen Christentums in der ältesten Kircher, der Apostel Petrus in Rom," *TZTh* 5 (1831) 61–206, and then further developed in *Das Christenthum und die christliche Kirche der drei ersten Jahrhunderte* (1853). See also Robert Morgan, "The Significance of 'Paulinism'," *Paul and Paulinism: Essays in Honour of C.K. Barrett,* ed. M.D. Hooker and S.G. Wilson (London: SPCK, 1982) 320–338.

11 See James D.G. Dunn, *The Partings of the Ways Between Christianity and Judaism and their Significance for the Character of Christianity* (London: SCM Press; Philadelphia: Trinity Press International, 1991) 1–17 for an overview of the trends in modern biblical scholarship with regard to the origins of earliest Christianity.

failure within biblical studies to treasure the Jewish roots of Christianity.[12] A first step towards rectifying this problem in Pauline studies was to dismantle the centuries of interpretive layers that had been superimposed onto the historical Paul. In what would become a seminal article,[13] Krister Stendahl argued that it was actually Luther's introspective search for salvific grace, concentrating on the individual's relation to God, which had been read back into the mind of Paul, ignoring the apostle's more social concerns of relations between Jews and Gentiles that had been made possible in Christ. Similarly, Paul's critique of a Jewish legalistic 'works-righteousness' was really a reflection of Luther's own battle against the Church's reliance on paid-for indulgences.

Stendahl's article came to greater recognition in a 1976 reprint,[14] a year before another prominent figure, Ed Sanders, published a monumental work that highlighted the deleterious effects of reconstructing Judaism from Paul's rhetorical presentation of it in his epistles.[15] The legalistic caricature of Judaism that emerges from an unbridgeable gulf between Law and Gospel is responsible for viewing Rabbinic Judaism as *Spätjudentum*, 'late Judaism', implying that after the dawn of Christianity nothing further of serious note occurs in surviving Judaism. Refuting this, Sanders set out to show that Judaism is an equally grace-filled religion by virtue of 'covenantal nomism', the notion that God elects Israel into his covenant as an act of grace ('getting in') while Israel obeys the commandments ('staying in') to remain faithful to that covenant.[16] While this is a huge advance upon the previous paradigm that saw Paul leaving behind a legalistic Judaism, Sanders' presentation of Judaism looks oddly like a form of Christianity without Christ.[17] And, in fact, when pressed as to why Paul still chose to break with

---

12 Cf. Jules Isaac, *The Teaching of Contempt: Christian Roots of Anti-Semitism* (New York: Holt, Rinehart and Winston, 1964).

13 Krister Stendahl, "The Apostle Paul and the Introspective Conscience of the West," *HTR* 56 (1963) 199–215.

14 Reprinted in *id.*, *Paul Among Jews and Gentiles and Other Essays* (Philadelphia: Fortress, 1976) 78–96.

15 Ed Parish Sanders, *Paul and Palestinian Judaism: A Comparison of Patterns of Religion* (London: SCM Press, 1977).

16 *Ibid.*, 75: "Briefly put, covenantal nomism is the view that one's place in God's plan is established on the basis of the covenant and that the covenant requires as the proper response of man his obedience to its commandments, while providing means of atonement for transgression."

17 Clearly articulated by Pamela Eisenbaum in "Paul, Polemics, and the Problem of Essentialism," *Biblical Interpretation* 13.3 (2005) 224–238, p. 236: "What is not helpful, however, is the quest for the essence of Judaism. Whether this essence is negative as in the traditional model (legalism), or whether it is positive as in the New Perspective (covenantal nomism), Judaism still ends up looking like a form of Christianity without Christ."

such a grace-filled Judaism, Sanders could say nothing more than that it simply was not Christianity.[18] In this way, Sanders ended up reintroducing a pattern of Paul *versus* Judaism, and remains indebted to the interpretive framework of two (Lutheran) spheres of influence, Law and Gospel.

Sanders's legacy was further taken up by James Dunn who proposed a 'new perspective on Paul'.[19] Dunn saw himself in broad agreement with Sanders's *Paul and Palestinian Judaism*, but there was one crucial difference. Dunn claimed that Paul's problem with Judaism was that its ritual identity markers (food laws, circumcision, Sabbath observance) were functioning as ethnic 'badges of covenant membership,' denoting privileged ethnicity and nation status. "*Covenant* works had become too closely identified as *Jewish* observances, *covenant* righteousness, as *national righteousness*."[20] Dunn's Paul, unlike Sanders's, continues to stay within the Jewish covenant, but advocates that this covenant should be broadened to also include Gentile members without need of ethnic identity markers. Within this new perspective, Paul is no longer divorced from Judaism since the 'the Parting of the Ways' between Judaism and Christianity would only occur a century later, after the Bar Kokhba Revolt of 132–135 CE.[21]

With the recovery of Paul's Jewishness over the past 50 years (similar in trend to the rehabilitation of the Jewishness of Jesus[22]), biblical scholarship of Paul's letters has advanced towards situating the theological content of his writings within a matrix of Paul's relationship to late Second Temple Judaism. These strides have run parallel to advances made in the field of early Judaism, aided by the discovery and publication of the Dead Sea Scrolls, the flourishing diversity of

---

18 Sanders, *Paul and Palestinian Judaism*, 552: "In short, *this is what Paul finds wrong in Judaism: it is not Christianity*." Sanders later clarified this position by saying that Paul attacked viewing observance of the law as a sign and condition of favoured status. E.P. Sanders, *Paul, the Law and the Jewish People* (Philadelphia: Fortress, 1983) 45–48.

19 James D.G. Dunn, "The New Perspective on Paul," *BJRL* 65 (1983) 95–122. See also the collected essays in *id.*, *The New Perspective on Paul: Collected Essays*, WUNT I/185 (Tübingen: Mohr Siebeck, 2005).

20 Dunn, "The New Perspective on Paul," 114 (emphasis his).

21 This became Dunn's central contention in *The Partings of the Ways Between Christianity and Judaism and their Significance for the Character of Christianity*. That argument (from 1991) has since been challenged by the contributors in *The Ways That Never Parted: Jews and Christians in Late Antiquity and the Early Middle Ages*, ed. Adam H. Becker and Annette Yoshiko Reed, Texts and Studies in Ancient Judaism 95 (Tübingen: Mohr Siebeck, 2003) who argue for a slower process and a much later date to an eventual parting of ways.

22 For example, Geza Vermes, *Jesus the Jew: A Historian's Reading of the Gospels* (London: Collins, 1973), building on the legacy of such towering figures as Abraham Geiger, Jules Isaac, Martin Buber and Samuel Sandmel before him.

Jewish Studies programs, and the explosion of interest in pursuing cross-disciplinary research projects.

The success of this paradigm shift can hardly be underestimated. Put simply, within the space of a decade of scholarship (the mid-1970s to the mid-1980s), Paul went from being a Christian to a Jew. There was now no longer talk of his 'conversion', but instead his 'calling'. The Law was no longer futile for Paul. In fact, Paul was Torah-observant. Instead of righteousness (or, to put it more, strongly, justification through God's free grace) being the center of Paul's gospel, the main goal of Paul's mission was to extend to the Gentiles entry into the Jewish family, which they could obtain through faith in Christ. And yet. The question of Paul and Judaism really being about Paul *versus* Judaism still haunts this 'new perspective on Paul'. Whereas before Paul's perceived problem with Judaism was its legalism, now it was its ethnocentrism. Paul now comes across as finding Judaism, with all its practices, just a little too particular (too Jewish?) to successfully peddle alongside his gospel in the marketplaces of the Roman Empire.

Aware of this residual binary dichotomy, the last 15 years has witnessed alternative perspectives that attempt to move beyond this no-longer new perspective on Paul.[23] The question has no longer become that of Paul *and* Judaism, since that still presumes Paul leaves Judaism behind eventually. One should rather simply speak of Paul's Judaism, without any qualifiers.[24] So it is Paul's continuing Judaism, both before and after his encounter with Christ, which defines these recent endeavors in Pauline scholarship. To return to Pamela Eisenbaum, "belief in Jesus does not make Paul a Christian".[25] His entire gospel, apostolic ministry, and writings were in fact irreducible aspects of Paul's Judaism.

23 The key players in this have been helpfully outlined by Magnus Zetterholm in "Beyond the New Perspective," *Approaches to Paul: A Student's Guide to Recent Scholarship* (Minneapolis, MN: Fortress, 2009) 127–163. Zetterholm also lists many other approaches to Paul (in his chapter, "Breaking Boundaries," 195–224), including those by recent philosophers, most notably Agamben, Badiou and Žižek, who I will not be treating in this contribution (since they are dealt with in Gesine Palmer's contribution to this volume).

24 Mark D. Nanos, "Rethinking the 'Paul and Judaism' Paradigm: Why Not 'Paul's Judaism'," May 28, 2008 online version available at: http://www.marknanos.com/Paul%27sJudaism-5-28-08.pdf (accessed June 11, 2015).

25 Eisenbaum, "Paul, Polemics, and the Problem of Essentialism," 232. Eisenbaum uses this label to categorize scholars who do not compromise on Paul's Jewish identity. Within this group she lists Mark Nanos, Neil Elliott, Paula Fredriksen, Lloyd Gaston, Krister Stendahl, Stan Stowers (and also Nils Dahl and W.D. Davies). As a survey article she does not include herself in this list, but it is clear from her article and its conclusion that her sympathies lie with this group, and that this article laid the groundwork for her later book, *Paul Was Not a Christian*. See also now the latest volume along these lines: Mark D. Nanos and Magnus Zetterholm (eds.), *Paul within*

In order to understand just how radical this latest trend in Pauline studies is, it is worthwhile to pause briefly and consider that only a century prior (towards the end of the 19th century) Paul was understood as the great Hellenizer of Judaism.[26] As a Diaspora Jew deeply influenced by the Hellenistic world, Paul 'invented' Christianity in order to fully assimilate Judaism into the Greek mainstream. In this manner (primitive) particularity gave way to (enlightened) universalism. At the beginning of the 21st century, however, a complete reversal has taken place: Paul never intended to universalize Judaism. In advocating that his Gentile followers abandon worship to native gods, Paul was no different than his rivals who were also engaging in 'Judaizing the nations', the type of proselytizing action that the pagans of Paul's time would have understood as leading straight to Judaism.[27]

So it appears that within the span of a century, we have managed to achieve a complete overhaul in how we view Paul and Judaism.[28] It is perhaps worth mentioning that among the latest advocates of such a move are Jewish scholars of early Christianity, among them Mark Nanos, Pamela Eisenbaum, and Paula Fredriksen, to name just a few. First of all, and positively, this indicates how much the field of Pauline studies has opened up to accommodate scholars from different backgrounds, and particularly from the Jewish fold that 19th century Protestant scholarship was only too happy to shun. It also indicates, equally positively, the 'reversal of the gaze' that Susannah Heschel highlighted when discussing Abraham Geiger's Jewish Jesus.[29] I shall return to this insight a little later, but for now I want to focus upon two, equally Jewish, portrayals of Paul that go to the heart, I think, of the continuing struggle in Pauline studies to situate the Apostle between 'Law' and 'Love'.

Judaism: Restoring the First-Century Context to the Apostle (Minneapolis, MN: Fortress, 2015) with contributions from Nanos, Zetterholm, Caroline Johnson Hodge, Paula Fredriksen, Neil Elliott, Kathy Ehrensperger and Terence Donaldson.

26 Indebted of course to F.C. Baur, but also taken on by such Jewish scholars as Heinrich Graetz and, by extension, the movement of *Wissenschaft des Judentums*.

27 Such is the claim of Paula Fredriksen, "Judaizing the Nations: The Ritual Demands of Paul's Gospel," in *Paul's Jewish Matrix*, ed. Thomas G. Casey and Justin Taylor, Bible in Dialogue 2 (Rome: Gregorian and Biblical Press, 2011) 327–354.

28 It should be noted that this has not gone without challenge. Magnus Zetterholm devotes a whole chapter surveying the robust (Protestant) rebuttals that have been mounted: "In Defense of Protestantism," *Approaches to Paul*, 165–193.

29 Susannah Heschel, *Abraham Geiger and the Jewish Jesus* (Chicago: Chicago University Press, 1998).

Will the real Jewish Paul please stand up?

As an example of the current enthusiasm for the Jewish Paul, I would like to take a recently published collection of thematic papers on Paul's Second Letter to the Corinthians against the backdrop of Late Second Temple Judaism.[30] I do so because the focus of that volume was not directly Paul's Jewish identity. Nonetheless, his Jewish identity is assumed by all the contributors of the volume and never called into question. That already indicates how mainstream the question of Paul's Jewish identity has become within the guild of biblical scholarship that it need no longer be questioned, but instead can be used to investigate further lines of inquiry.

At the same time, though, because Paul's Jewish identity goes unquestioned, it tends to cover up the plurality of perspectives that are currently held regarding Paul's Judaism. One of the contributors, Joshua Schwartz, captures that sense of plasticity well: "While Paul's Jewish background might be well established, he has been associated with almost every type of ancient Judaism from Hellenistic to Qumranic to Pharasaic, Hellenistic or otherwise, and to later rabbinic. Based on our discussion above on Jewish identity, we might perhaps suggest that he be located in 'Second Temple Judaism', although from our discussion above it should also be clear that there really was no such thing. We can then suggest perhaps that it would be better to place him within the array of Second Temple *Judaisms*".[31]

From Paul the rabbi ...

Within that impressive array, though, two clear positions emerge as polar opposites of one another and I shall deal with each in turn. The first could be termed the 'halakhic' proto-rabbinic Paul advocated in this case by Ze'ev Safrai and Peter Tomson.[32] Their lengthy article deals with understanding the Jewish background to a financial collection that Paul was requesting of his Corinthian community

30 Reimund Bieringer et al., eds., *Second Corinthians in the Perspective of Late Second Temple Judaism*, CRINT 14 (Leiden: Brill, 2014).
31 Joshua Schwartz, "Methodological Remarks on 'Jewish' Identity: Jews, Jewish Christians and Prolegomena on Pauline Judaism," in *Second Corinthians in the Perspective of Late Second Temple Judaism*, 36–58, here p. 56 (emphasis his).
32 Ze'ev Safrai and Peter J. Tomson, "Paul's 'Collection for the Saints' (2 Cor 8-9) and Financial Support of Leaders in Early Christianity and Judaism," in *Second Corinthians in the Perspective of Late Second Temple Judaism*, 132–220.

in support of whom he terms 'the saints' (the community of Jesus followers in Jerusalem). This investigation leads in turn to understanding the antecedents to a salaried leadership in early Christianity and early rabbinic Judaism. The details of their analysis need not detain us here, but I shall summarize some salient features of their methodology.

First of all, Safrai and Tomson situate Paul's collection within a matrix of early Christian and Jewish literature, that is to say, Paul's letter (in this case the section of 2 Cor 8-9) is analyzed alongside literature from the New Testament, the apostolic fathers, Jewish apocalyptic sources (like Daniel and Enoch), and early rabbinic sources (Tannaic and Amoraic literature). That is to say, positively, that Paul is read comparatively to contemporaneous literature existing at the time, without maintaining an anachronistic confessional divide between them. Such a comparative exercise makes it possible for Safrai and Tomson to conclude that "[t]he debate regarding payment for spiritual leaders appears in both traditions, although the Jewish material is far greater because of the sheer quantity of sources."[33]

Second, because Paul is placed along this chronological continuum of early Christian and Jewish literature, his request for a collection for the 'saints' can be seen to be exceptional to Paul and his communities since no similar case could be found among Jewish communities.[34] At the same time, to the larger question of a salaried leadership, where Paul had assumed the right to financial support elsewhere in the Corinthian letters (1 Cor 9:4-10), Paul can be seen to build upon existing Jewish tradition that would anticipate later developments in rabbinic Judaism by at least a century and a half.[35] That being said, Paul's model of financial support for spiritual leaders was never adopted in the same way by the Tannaim (the earliest rabbis of the Common Era); in fact, they opposed an institutionalized and professional leadership on ideological grounds, and only in the Amoraic period (from the 3rd century CE onwards) was there a gradual shift towards a salaried leadership.

Third, there is a marked absence of material from the Graeco-Roman world. Safrai and Tomson argue that "the Graeco-Roman world was not familiar with the phenomenon of holy men, certainly not as a social group. Nor was the system of

---

33 *Ibid.*, 215.

34 *Ibid.*, 216: "Our main subject is Paul's collection for the 'saints'. We found no institution in the Jewish community, and as mentioned, in earliest Christianity it also remained exceptional because it did not accord with the general policy on supoort for teachers."

35 *Ibid.*, 215: "Through the doing of Paul, however, the early Church attained within a generation or two what took the Jewish community all five generations of the Tannaic period, and even then only partially in the Land of Israel."

paying salaries or giving donations to leaders familiar. As we have observed, the elite fulfilled the task of leading and administering society voluntarily, though they often used these positions to enrich themselves. Nor was the Roman world familiar with personal payments to priests. Needless to say, support for a group of leaders living in a distant and supposedly holy province was not common in the Roman world. In short, Paul did not borrow the model for the system he established from the Roman world."[36] As such, although Paul was unique in developing this system of financial support for spiritual leaders, he is nonetheless seen to be more in line with Jewish traditions and ethos which predate him and which he in turn also anticipates of the later rabbis after him. In this sense Paul is 'proto-rabbinic' and almost attuned, *avant la lettre*, to later halakhic discussions on receiving a salary for teaching Torah.[37]

Safrai and Tomson are not alone in seeing both the uniqueness of Paul's contributions and his indebtedness to – almost aptitude for – what would become established rabbinic principles. Daniel Schwartz, examining another issue in Paul's letter to the Romans (the question of food laws and ritual impurity in Rom 14), similarly compares Paul's writings to other Jewish writings. Quite naturally, towards the end of his argument, Schwartz turns to Pharisaic proto-rabbinic literature since it too deals with questions of food laws and ritual impurity. Schwartz's concluding contention is that Paul's stance in Rom 14 "reflects what was common for Diaspora and Pharisaic-rabbinic Jews".[38] The 'halakhic' proto-rabbinic Paul represents, therefore, the 'legal' pole of the spectrum that the Jewish Paul spans between law and love.

---

36 *Ibid.*, 178–179.

37 *Ibid.*, 217: "A minority opinion in this [Tannaitic] literature, however, allows for support being given to wandering Tora scholars. We get the impression that this was the loophole utilized by Paul." I should caution that the lack of Graeco-Roman material on the issue of holy men and salaried leadership may not actually be the case but simply be because Safrai and Tomson's primary focus was on early Jewish and Christian sources.

38 Daniel R. Schwartz, "'Someone who Considers Something to Be Impure – For Him it Is Impure' (Rom 14:14): Good Manners or Law?," in *Paul's Jewish Matrix*, 293–309, here p. 309. I chose this example because Schwartz's paper was given in the same year (2009) as Safrai and Tomson's paper, yet delivered at another, although thematically related, conference examining Paul's letters within a larger Jewish matrix and context.

… to Paul the mystic

On the other end of that pole resides the visionary and mystical Paul. Christopher Morray-Jones explored Paul's report of an ascent into paradise recorded in 2 Cor 12.[39] He did so in order to trace what influence Jewish apocalyptic and visionary-mystical traditions had on Paul. What is interesting is that, unlike Safrai and Tomson, who were able to situate Paul's appeal for financial support on a chronological continuum of evolving Jewish views, but also isolate those elements that were unique to Paul, Morray-Jones saw only a striking resemblance between Paul's account of an ascent into paradise and the later rabbinic accounts of Akiva who entered *pardes* along with three others (the Jewish mystical literature known as the *Hekhalot* and *Merkava* texts). So strong is the resemblance for Morray-Jones that he makes his central claim: "We know from the context in which Paul's account is set that he based his claim to possess the authority of an apostle on this vision. We must therefore conclude that merkava mysticism was central to his religious practice and experience, and that it profoundly shaped his understanding of his calling and apostolic role."[40]

Morray-Jones is not alone in his enthusiasm for the mystical Paul. He readily admits his reliance on the work of Alan Segal and Albert Schweitzer before him.[41] It was Albert Schweitzer, a Lutheran, who questioned the Lutheran insistence on righteousness as the center of Paul's gospel. Instead, Schweitzer argued that for Paul what mattered was being 'in Christ', which Schweitzer understood to mean as participating in a mystical union with Christ. Equating mysticism with apocalypticism, Morray-Jones has made the case for studying early Jewish mysticism on the premise that early Christianity originated as an apocalyptic movement within Judaism.[42] From another angle, roughly at the same time of Morray-Jones' work

---

39 Christopher R.A. Morray-Jones, "The Ascent into Paradise (2 Cor 12:1-12): Paul's *Merkava* Vision and Apostolic Call," in *Second Corinthians in the Perspective of Late Second Temple Judaism*, 245–285.

40 *Ibid.*, 282.

41 Alan F. Segal, *Paul the Convert: The Apostolate and Apostasy of Saul the Pharisee* (New Haven, CT: Yale University Press, 1990). Albert Schweitzer, *Die Mystik des Apostels Paulus* (1930) repr. with Introduction by W.G. Kümmel (Tübingen: Mohr Siebeck, 1981). It is perhaps interesting to speculate here on the influence that F.C. Baur would have had on Albert Schweitzer.

42 Christopher Rowland and Christopher R.A. Morray-Jones, *The Mystery of God: Early Jewish Mysticism and the New Testament*, CRINT 12 (Leiden: Brill, 2009).

on Jewish mysticism and the New Testament, Paul's mystical experiences were being investigated as ecstatic experiences with insights from neurobiology.[43]

What was interesting about the published volume of papers on Second Corinthians is that here we had two articles, reading different parts of the same epistle, and drawing on different portraits of Paul's Jewish experiences. First of all, for both papers, the issue was no longer *whether* Paul continued being Jewish; that much was a given. The question has now instead become: what *kind* of Jew was Paul? I have argued that for the one it was Paul the rabbi, for the other Paul the mystic. One might say that Paul's epistle itself offers that spectral range since he boasts of his Jewish credentials in 2 Cor 11:22-24[44] and then speaks of being caught up to the third heaven in the very next chapter (2 Cor 12;2). But it also reflects recent scholarly trends and I believe it actually says something about the continuing struggle in Pauline studies of where to place Paul between 'Law' and 'Love'.

In fact, my reservation to Morray-Jones' reading of Paul as a Jewish mystic,[45] is that Morray-Jones all too easily (but unconsciously) slips into the well-known distinction between 'prophet' and 'priest', the opposition that the sociologist Max Weber introduced between charisma and ritual, revolution and institution.[46] Paul

---

43 Cf. Colleen Shantz, *Paul in Ecstasy: The Neurobiology of the Apostle's Life and Thought* (Cambridge: Cambridge University Press, 2009).

44 2 Cor 11:22-24: "Are they Hebrews? So am I. Are they Israelites? So am I. Are they descendants of Abraham? So am I. Are they ministers of Christ? I am talking like a madman – I am a better one: with far greater labors, far more imprisonments, with countless floggings, and often near death. Five times I have received from the Jews the forty lashes minus one." Cf. also Phil 3:4-6: "If anyone else has reason to be confident in the flesh, I have more: circumcised on the eighth day, a member of the people of Israel, of the tribe of Benjamin, a Hebrew born of Hebrews; as to the law, a Pharisee; as to zeal, a persecutor of the church; as to righteousness under the law, blameless."

45 Another, more technical, objection I have to reading Paul as a mystic in Second Corinthians is that I wonder whether this would really have been effective with Paul's Corinthian recipients. In light of the charges brought against Paul that his gospel was veiled (cf. 2 Cor 4:3), what would Paul have to gain by highlighting such an individual esoteric experience? He had already charged his opponents with being "peddlers of God's word" (2:17). In what way would Paul be different? Furthermore, while one cannot entirely discount that Paul may have had mystical leanings, he also maintains a certain reserve. In 2 Cor 11:13 he polemically demonizes the super/pseudo apostles for disguising themselves as true apostles of Christ, thus highlighting that Paul was all too aware of the dangers of false transformation. On this, see Edith M. Humphrey, "Ambivalent Apocalypse: Apocalyptic Rhetoric and Intertextuality in 2 Corinthians," *The Intertexture of Apocalyptic Discourse in the New Testament*, ed. Duane F. Watson, SBLSS 14 (Atlanta: SBL, 2002) 113–135, p.125 n.18.

46 Max Weber, *The Theory of Social and Economic Organization*, trans. A.R. Anderson and Talcott Parsons 1947 [German original 1922] (New York: Simon and Schuster, 1964) 358–372 (the relevant sections on charisma and charismatic authority). See also, Max Weber, "The Prophet,"

the visionary, the ecstatic mystic, is given access to secret and direct revelations that liberate him from the strictures of his former life in the Law. For Morray-Jones, Paul is less the Pharisaic proto-rabbinic forerunner of the later halakhists, but rather a direct heir to such charismatic prophets as Moses, Isaiah, Jeremiah and Ezekiel, all of whom were privy to revelations, divine mysteries and audiences. The problem with this is that Morray-Jones has unknowingly reintroduced the binary opposition that has been so hard to shake when treating aspects of Paul's Jewish experiences.

I have argued thus far that there is a continuing struggle in biblical studies to situate Paul the Jew, artificially I might add, between 'law' and 'love'. The 'Torah observant' Paul who clings resolutely to Judaism and its commandments, or the 'liberal' Paul whose mysticism breaks free of religious constraints, both represent two ends of that artificial spectrum. But, to me, the *mystical* variant hides a dangerous potential of which many of its proponents seem not to be aware.[47] For, to then maintain that Christianity emerged out of this mystical/apocalyptic/charismatic seedbed, no matter how Jewish, only implies that what did not become Christianity was its ritualistic and legalistic shell that of course forms the core of rabbinic Judaism. Christianity is thus Jewish, but an evolved form of Judaism. Rabbinic Judaism and, by extension, every form of contemporary Judaism, is at best a mere shadow of enlightened Christianity. If, as I mentioned at the start of this contribution, Paul the apostle represents that hyphen in the so-called signifier of 'Judeo-Christian', only one conclusion is sadly clear: the 'Judeo' exists only to the extent that it ends up becoming 'Christian'. To mimic the words of E.P. Sanders when explaining why Paul left Judaism: what is wrong with Judaism is that it is not Christianity.[48]

---

in *The Sociology of Religion* (1963) 46–59 [German original 1922]; reprinted in *Prophecy in Israel: Search an Identity*, ed. David L. Petersen, (Philadelphia: Fortress; London: SPCK, 1987) 99–111.

47 I might even press the point further and speculate on a residual (even if unconscious) anti-Judaism in the same way that Marianne Moyaert in her contribution to this volume will speak of 'latent anti-Judaism'. That is to say, an anti-Judaism that goes unnoticed because it has seeped into patterns of thinking deep within Christian collective consciousness.

48 I am reproducing the quote again here for the sake of emphasis. Sanders, *Paul and Palestinian Judaism*, 552: "In short, *this is what Paul finds wrong in Judaism: it is not Christianity*."

Gazing back: A concluding reflection

I mentioned that I would return to the reversal of the gaze that Susannah Heschel speaks of at the start of *Abraham Geiger and the Jewish Jesus*. Heschel describes Geiger's portrait of the Jewish Jesus very much as a subaltern revolt, of object refusing any longer to be objectified; that is to say, a scenario of the Jew no longer content to be the object of fascination and study by non-Jews, but now him/herself looking back and offering a critical glance and voice in return.

Coupled with this critical reversal of the gaze is an awareness of the constructions we as interpreters make of our subjects. Returning to Paul, the biblical scholar Margaret Mitchell has remarked: "There is a Paul for everyone to be had, or rather carefully constructed here. And each Paul governs certain types of readings of his letters."[49] Along similar lines, Daniel Boyarin has stated, "Viewing Paul through the lens of Galatians, and especially through Galatians 3:28-29, the baptismal declaration of the new humanity of no difference, constructs a particular Pauline object, a different Paul from the one constructed by reading Paul through 1 Corinthians, Romans, or 1 Thessalonians."[50]

Daniel Langton has recently collected an impressive array of Jewish constructions of Paul.[51] In his book, Langton examines multiple Jewish views on the apostle Paul from the realms of religion, art, literature, philosophy and psychoanalysis. What emerges is a fascinating mosaic of a growing and diffuse Jewish interest in Paul during the modern period (thus from the 18th Century onwards). Paul is normally perceived as a person traditionally shunned by Judaism for having betrayed his faith. Yet it is precisely this notion of a traditional Jewish antipathy to Paul that Langton sets out to question. What is even more interesting about Langton's analysis is that modern Jewish treatments of the apostle Paul actually reflect deeper underlying concerns within the community about the nature of Jewish authenticity amidst growing self-assurance, acceptance, and emancipation in European Christian societies. The Jewish interest in Paul is only

---

49 Margaret M. Mitchell, *The Heavenly Trumpet: John Chrysostom and the Art of Pauline Interpretation* (Tübingen: Mohr Siebeck, 2000) 432.

50 Daniel Boyarin, *A Radical Jew: Paul and the Politics of Identity* (Berkeley, CA: University of California Press, 1994) 5. It is perhaps interesting to note that Boyarin's own reading of Paul in *A Radical Jew* is deeply sympathetic to Baur's reading of Paul as a universalizing critique of Jewish particularity.

51 Daniel R. Langton, *The Apostle Paul in the Jewish Imagination: A Study in Modern Jewish-Christian Relations* (Cambridge: Cambridge University Press, 2010). For a brief overview, see my review of this book in *Relegere: Studies in Religion and Reception* (2012) 222–229.

marginally interested in him as a historical person, and more interested in how he exemplifies issues of identity, changing religious practice, politics, etc.

The canvas on which Langton has chosen to display the many constructions of Paul is vast, from the inner to the outer reaches of the Jewish cultural imagination. Vast as this may seem, there is an immediate advantage to condensing and collating the discussion in the way that Langton has: it answers directly to the puzzlement that some Christian biblical scholars experience when faced with Jewish scholars' simultaneous uncovering of Paul's authentic Jewishness and continued rejection of his theology.[52] That is because these Christian scholars are not sufficiently aware that what they consider to be the so-called 'Jewish reclamation of Paul' is actually only part of a wider series of continuing Jewish constructions of Paul, not all of them in harmony with one another.[53] Christian biblical scholars could stand to learn from this for, although key proponents of the so-called 'New Perspective on Paul' (Krister Stendahl, E.P. Sanders and James Dunn) called attention to the 'Lutheran' construction of Paul, biblical schol-

52 "Despite all the energy expended by Jewish scholars to uncover Paul's authentic Jewishness and to approach him positively and appreciatively, it is all the more remarkable that his theology is rejected *in toto*." Donald A. Hagner, "Paul in Modern Jewish Thought," in *Pauline Studies: Essays Presented to F.F. Bruce*, ed. Donald A. Hagner and Murray J. Harris (Exeter: Paternoster, 1980) 143–165, here p. 158. More recently: "Perhaps the reason why there will never be a Jewish 'reclamation' of Paul is because, in Helmut Koester's words, Paul was trying to 'accomplish the impossible'. [...] While some may want to find in Paul a gateway to reconciliation, in Jewish eyes, Paul is perhaps destined to remain a heretic worst or anti-hero at best." Michael Bird and Preston Sprinkle, "Jewish Interpretation of Paul in the Last Thirty Years."*Currents in Biblical Research* 6.3 (2008) 355–376, here p. 372. Daniel Langton's *The Apostle Paul in the Jewish Imagination* provides a far richer panoply of Jewish perspectives on Paul beyond simply that of heretic and/or anti-hero.

53 Analysing the study of Paul from the perspective of contemporary Jewish-Christian relations and dialogue, Michael Peppard arrives at a similar observation: "There is thus no essential quality of Jewishness in Jewish scholarly conclusions about the New Testament. What has changed significantly, rather, is the pervasive awareness among both Jews and Gentiles of living, theologizing, and writing against the horizon of the Shoah. [...] These facts refine theological thinking about the foundational texts of Jewish-Christian relations. In short, the emergence of diverse, elitely trained Jewish New Testament scholars has brought new focus to the types of questions being asked, broadened the set of Jewish *comparanda* from antiquity, sensitized Christians to the reception of their scholarship by Jews, and thus invigorated a field of study – without manufacturing predetermined results." Michael Peppard, *Theological Studies* 76 (2015) 260–279, here p. 273. Peppard's article is far more accepting of the Jewish diversity of opinions on Paul than the Christian scholars mentioned in the previous footnote.

ars still seem to nourish the optimistic view that their own studies of Paul are untouched by any such constructivist tendencies.[54]

Christian biblical scholars tend to be interested in identifying the precise kind of Jew that Paul was, and they do so – as I have tried to argue – by locating him somewhere along the spectrum between law and love. Jewish scholars, on the other hand, if they are interested in Paul at all, are unencumbered by such constraints. The proverbial phenomenon of 'two Jews, three opinions,' wittily captures the diversity one finds in Jewish treatments of Paul. Yet this difference in perspective continues to distinguish Jewish and Christian approaches to Paul, even when that difference sometimes appears no greater than the breadth of a hyphen.

Bibliography

Baur, Ferdinand Christian. "Die Christuspartei in der Korinthischen Gemeinde, der Gegensatz des petrinischen und paulinischen Christentums in der ältesten Kircher, der Apostel Petrus in Rom." *TZTh* 5 (1831): 61–206.

Baur, Ferdinand Christian. *Das Christenthum und die christliche Kirche der drei ersten Jahrhunderte*. Tübingen: Fues, 1853.

Becker, Adam H. and Annette Yoshiko Reed, eds. *The Ways That Never Parted: Jews and Christians in Late Antiquity and the Early Middle Ages*. Texts and Studies in Ancient Judaism 95. Tübingen: Mohr Siebeck, 2003.

Bieringer, Reimund and Didier Pollefeyt. "Prologue: Wrestling with the Jewish Paul," *Paul and Judaism: Crosscurrents in Pauline Exegesis and Jewish-Christian Relations*, Ed. Reimund Bieringer and Didier Pollefeyt. LNTS 463. London: T&T Clark, 2012. 1–14.

Bieringer, Reimund et al., eds. *Second Corinthians in the Perspective of Late Second Temple Judaism*. CRINT 14. Leiden: Brill, 2014.

Bird, Michael and Preston Sprinkle. "Jewish Interpretation of Paul in the Last Thirty Years." *Currents in Biblical Research* 6.3 (2008): 355–376.

Boyarin, Daniel. *A Radical Jew: Paul and the Politics of Identity*. Berkeley, CA: University of California Press, 1994.

Dunn, James D.G. "The New Perspective on Paul." *BJRL* 65 (1983): 95–122.

54 But there have also been Christian scholars who have honestly called attention to this and reflected upon the ramifications of such kinds of Pauline exegesis for Christian self-understanding, soteriology and, indeed, Christian-Jewish relations. See for example: Reimund Bieringer and Didier Pollefeyt, "Prologue: Wrestling with the Jewish Paul," *Paul and Judaism: Crosscurrents in Pauline Exegesis and Jewish-Christian* Relations, ed. Reimund Bieringer and Didier Pollefeyt, LNTS 463 (London: T&T Clark, 2012) 1–14.

Dunn, James D.G. *The Partings of the Ways Between Christianity and Judaism and their Significance for the Character of Christianity*. London: SCM Press; Philadelphia: Trinity Press International, 1991. 1–17.

Dunn, James D.G. "The Justice of God: A Renewed Perspective on Justification by Faith." *JTS* 43 (1992): 1–22.

Dunn, James D.G. *The New Perspective on Paul: Collected Essays*. WUNT I/185. Tübingen: Mohr Siebeck, 2005.

Eisenbaum, Pamela. "Paul, Polemics, and the Problem of Essentialism." *Biblical Interpretation* 13.3 (2005): 224–238.

Eisenbaum, Pamela. *Paul Was Not a Christian: The Original Message of a Misunderstood Apostle*. New York: HarperCollins, 2009.

Fredriksen, Paula. "Judaizing the Nations: The Ritual Demands of Paul's Gospel." *Paul's Jewish Matrix*. Ed. Thomas G. Casey and Justin Taylor. Bible in Dialogue 2. Rome: Gregorian and Biblical Press, 2011. 327–354.

Hagner, Donald A. "Paul in Modern Jewish Thought." *Pauline Studies: Essays Presented to F.F. Bruce*. Ed. Donald A. Hagner and Murray J. Harris. Exeter: Paternoster, 1980. 143–165.

Heschel, Susannah. *Abraham Geiger and the Jewish Jesus*. Chicago: Chicago University Press, 1998.

Humphrey, Edith M. "Ambivalent Apocalypse: Apocalyptic Rhetoric and Intertextuality in 2 Corinthians." *The Intertexture of Apocalyptic Discourse in the New Testament*. Ed. Duane F. Watson. SBLSS 14. Atlanta: SBL, 2002. 113–135.

Isaac, Jules. *The Teaching of Contempt: Christian Roots of Anti-Semitism*. New York: Holt, Rinehart and Winston, 1964.

Langton, Daniel R. *The Apostle Paul in the Jewish Imagination: A Study in Modern Jewish-Christian Relations*. Cambridge: Cambridge University Press, 2010.

Luther, Martin. *On the Jews and Their Lies* (*Von den Jüden und iren Lügen*). Wittenberg, 1543.

Lüdemann, Gerd. *Paul: The Founder of Christianity*. Amherst, NY: Prometheus Books, 2002.

Lyotard, Jean-François and Eberhard Gruber. *The Hyphen. Between Judaism and Christianity*. Trans. Pascal-Anne Brault and Michael Naas. Philosophy and Literary Theory. New York: Humanity Books, 1993.

Mitchell, Margaret M. *The Heavenly Trumpet: John Chrysostom and the Art of Pauline Interpretation*. Tübingen: Mohr Siebeck, 2000.

Morgan, Robert. "The Significance of 'Paulinism'." *Paul and Paulinism: Essays in Honour of C.K. Barrett*. Ed. M.D. Hooker and S.G. Wilson. London: SPCK, 1982. 320–338.

Morray-Jones, Christopher R.A. "The Ascent into Paradise (2 Cor 12:1-12): Paul's *Merkava* Vision and Apostolic Call." *Second Corinthians in the Perspective of Late Second Temple Judaism*. Ed. Reimund Bieringer et al. CRINT 14. Leiden: Brill, 2014. 245–285.

Nanos, Mark D. "Rethinking the 'Paul and Judaism' Paradigm: Why Not 'Paul's Judaism'." May 28, 2008. Online version available at: http://www.marknanos.com/Paul%27sJudaism-5-28-08.pdf (accessed June 11, 2015).

Nanos, Mark D. and Magnus Zetterholm (eds.). *Paul within Judaism: Restoring the First-Century Context to the Apostle*. Minneapolis, MN: Fortress, 2015.

Nathan, Emmanuel. "Review of *The Apostle Paul in the Jewish Imagination: A Study in Modern Jewish-Christian Relations*, by Daniel R. Langton." *Relegere: Studies in Religion and Reception* (2012): 222–229.

Oldenhage, Tania. *Parables for Our Time: Rereading New Testament Scholarship after the Holocaust*. Oxford: Oxford University Press, 2002.

Peppard, Michael. *Theological Studies* 76 (2015): 260–279.
Rowland, Christopher and Christopher R.A. Morray-Jones. *The Mystery of God: Early Jewish Mysticism and the New Testament.* CRINT 12. Leiden: Brill, 2009.
Safrai, Ze'ev and Peter J. Tomson. "Paul's 'Collection for the Saints' (2 Cor 8-9) and Financial Support of Leaders in Early Christianity and Judaism." *Second Corinthians in the Perspective of Late Second Temple Judaism.* Ed. Reimund Bieringer et al. CRINT 14. Leiden: Brill, 2014. 132–220.
Sanders, Ed Parish. *Paul and Palestinian Judaism: A Comparison of Patterns of Religion.* London: SCM Press, 1977.
Sanders, Ed Parish. *Paul, the Law and the Jewish People.* Philadelphia: Fortress, 1983.
Schwartz, Daniel R. "'Someone who Considers Something to Be Impure – For Him it Is Impure' (Rom 14:14): Good Manners or Law?" *Paul's Jewish Matrix.* Ed. Thomas G. Casey and Justin Taylor. Bible in Dialogue 2. Rome: Gregorian and Biblical Press, 2011. 293–309.
Schwartz, Joshua. "Methodological Remarks on 'Jewish' Identity: Jews, Jewish Christians and Prolegomena on Pauline Judaism." *Second Corinthians in the Perspective of Late Second Temple Judaism.* Ed. Reimund Bieringer et al. CRINT 14. Leiden: Brill, 2014. 36–58.
Schweitzer, Albert. *Die Mystik des Apostels Paulus* (1930). Repr. with Introduction by W.G. Kümmel. Tübingen: Mohr Siebeck, 1981.
Segal, Alan F. *Paul the Convert: The Apostolate and Apostasy of Saul the Pharisee.* New Haven, CT: Yale University Press, 1990.
Shantz, Colleen. *Paul in Ecstasy: The Neurobiology of the Apostle's Life and Thought.* Cambridge: Cambridge University Press, 2009.
Stendahl, Krister. "The Apostle Paul and the Introspective Conscience of the West." *HTR* 56 (1963): 199–215. (Reprinted in *id., Paul Among Jews and Gentiles and Other Essays.* Philadelphia: Fortress, 1976. 78–96.)
Thielman, Frank. "Paul, the Law and Judaism: The Collapse of a Theological Consensus." *Paul and the Law: A Contextual Approach.* Downers Grove: InterVarsity, 1994. 14–47.
Vermes, Geza. *Jesus the Jew: A Historian's Reading of the Gospels.* London: Collins, 1973.
Weber, Max. *The Theory of Social and Economic Organization.* Trans. A.R. Anderson and Talcott Parsons 1947 [German original 1922]. New York: Simon and Schuster, 1964.
Weber, Max. "The Prophet." *The Sociology of Religion* (1963): 46–59 [German original 1922]. (Reprinted in *Prophecy in Israel: Search an Identity.* Ed. David L. Petersen. Philadelphia: Fortress; London: SPCK, 1987. 99–111.)
Zetterholm, Magnus. *Approaches to Paul: A Student's Guide to Recent Scholarship.* Minneapolis, MN: Fortress, 2009.

Gesine Palmer

7 Antinomianism Reloaded – Or: The Dialectics of the New Paulinism

0 Wasted Centuries?

The centuries following the great upheavals of the European enlightenment saw Christianity and its churches ever more exhausted and depleted. Even when they were able to exercise great social influence, they paid for such success by being cut off in substance from intellectual elites, not least from the thinkers considered "avant-garde." Christian theology has been unable to counterbalance this loss, even as "belief" and religions have gained considerable popularity in the decades that have witnessed the "return of religions" to the political stage (though not really to intellectual debate). The several Christianities share this fate with most other religious systems, despite there always having been "believing" or "pious" or "practicing" philosophers, scholars, scientists, poets, and artists in all cultures. The creative and innovative individual typically struggled her way to substantial production, through freeing herself from the entanglements of a more or less religious upbringing. Lately, however, enlightenment and its reasoning have come to seem fatigued; indeed, we see young people reaching for authoritarian and aggressive forms of religious dogmatism that typically make little sense to anyone educated in the manner of my generation or of their immediate predecessors. Moreover, attempts to revive something called "Judeo-Christianity" – imagined as a kind of common ground upon which to strengthen our common morals in the face of a common enemy – still seem comparatively helpless, especially as responses to the challenges posed by a terrifying presence of totalitarian Islamism.

Recently, however, noted thinkers of the avant-garde have not only joined the endeavor, but have been generally outspoken about the political visions governing this attempt. Assuming that it is the philosophical drive alone which has set such outstanding theorists as Giorgio Agamben, Slavoj Zizek, and Alain Badiou to work on the apostle Paul, a puzzling observation emerges: in light of the vibrant theories delivered by the New Paulinians, one could suppose that the results of centuries of theological thought, especially of the Protestant type, would have been relegated to the waste bin. At the same time, however, whatever progress Christian theologians have made, in the wake of the Shoah, towards addressing Christian arrogance and aggressiveness towards Jews and Judaism seems once again to be overtaken by a wave of neo-Paulinian antinomianism, which seeks and finds its enemy in the same place it has been "found" throughout the centuries of Christian antisemitism: in Jewish law. Yet, the key witnesses invoked by the new Paulinian philosophers are German Jews, in particular Walter Benjamin (Agamben) and Franz Rosenzweig (Santner on Badiou). In this essay, I wish to illuminate certain fundamental elements of the dialectics involved in this problem.

1 Universalism Again?

Alain Badiou presents Paul as a fighter for a "new" universalism. Classical modern theory had been so fond of universalism, with its secularized Protestant immediate relationship between the individual and the universal, that it tended to disregard the meaning of particular cultures. Postmodern theories, in their search for the facets of cultural identities, tended instead to charge Western universalistic concepts with being little more than ideological coverings of Western imperialism. But in the face of terrifying violence wrought in the name of and for the sake of particular cultures, how can one argue against obvious violations of human rights, not least when the concept of human rights is no longer considered to hold universal validity?

This question has led universalistic ideas to reemerge in circles and debates that seemed to have foregone such ideas in the wake of postcolonial discourses. Zizek debates Paul in three books, yet does so in order to defend an "absolute" that has become "fragile." Likewise, if Agamben proceeds from his concept of *homo sacer* to a Paulinian reading of Walter Benjamin or a Benjaminian reading of Paul, it seems that he intends this as a reframing of the conditions for a universal "freedom of the subject."[1] Badiou, in turning his attention to Paul, dedicates substantial reasoning to the relationship between the individual and the universality of the new spirit. Unlike in earlier moments, however, these thinkers intend to be more circumspect. Beginning with the doubts that Hannah Arendt raised via her influential notion of the "right to have rights," philosophers now seem bothered by the right to exclude, a right that is integral and essential to every group identity. The right to have rights has always been grounded in the fact of

1 The problem appears throughout his commentary on *Romans* as an examination of the conditions that could free a speaking subject from the criticized normativity of the law, Giorgio Agamben, *The Time That Remains: A Commentary on the Letter to the Romans,* translated by Patricia Dailey, Stanford 2005, passim.

belonging or not belonging to a particular community – with that community organizing the mutual recognition of rights in the respective other. Interestingly, the leading figures among those defending a new, all-inclusive universalism with a new Paulinism are not only male, but also from generally secularized Catholic backgrounds. Moreover, this seems to nicely complement a secularized Jewish perspective that considers itself rooted in some universalized idea of exile.

The debate over how universal notions in their relation to ideas or real things can possibly exist, especially in the field of ethics and law, is at least as old as the dispute between Plato and the Sophists. The question as to what exactly early Christianity added to this question is a complex matter. There were Platonist and sophist tendencies in both early Judaism and early Christianity; among the Jewish sages Platonists became a minority, whereas they were a majority among the Christians. Christian culture has, to this day, considered itself the more universal part of "Judeo-Christianity." It assumed that its basic notions mirrored an independent and universal reality and that its ethical demands were valid for everybody.[2]

With Kantian philosophy and the Enlightenment, the idea of a universal ethics was sharpened by both the categorical imperative and the firm conviction that there is a normative rationality of its own order, which we must imagine as being ruled by the destination of each individual for moral autonomy. However, when Kant, in his later works, wrote quite disconcertingly about foreign races, it had obviously not occurred to him that such assertions violated his own principles. Nor would he have failed to be extremely disturbed by Horkheimer's and Adorno's *Dialectic of Enlightenment*. What could be wrong with including all of humanity in the great project of fulfilling its destiny and making its way ever closer to reasonable and autonomous ways of life? And how could reason and enlightenment be blamed for human failings and shortcomings?

Now, after everything that has been leveled against the idea of universal morals, the third universalism of the new Paulinians tries to get it right.

---

2 Cf. Daniel Boyarin, "Paul Among the Antiphilosophers; or Saul Among the Sophists," in: John D. Caputo / Linda Martin Alcoff (Eds.), *St. Paul among the Philosophers*, Indiana University Press 2009, 109–141.

2 Tales of Incarnation and Love

When Paul wrote the seven letters to his communities – letters that remain foundational texts of Christian culture – these communities, like most of the Jewish communities in the Mediterranean region, were living in a social environment that seemed to have little interest in the individual, save the ruler or the wise man. Such a person was thought to be incarnation of the *nomos* – or of the *logos.*[3] A political body, if imagined as a human body, needed to have a spirit or a soul to coordinate its limbs and functions. In republican times the law, with its institutions, was the proper candidate for this connecting entity. When political structures turned to monarchy, the spirits of the monarch were ascribed the same function. This imagery was an omnipresent background to the self-perception of people and cultures in Hellenistic late antiquity, when Judaism and Christianity emerged. As Daniel Boyarin has detailed, the first centuries after the crucifixion of Jesus of Nazareth saw myriad sorts of religious systems. These included Jews who did not believe that Jesus was the messiah but who maintained a full-fledged theology, in which the logos was incarnated in some Messiah to come; other Jews believed that Jesus was indeed the Messiah, but did not dwell upon issues like justification or incarnation. And there were gentiles who were interested in certain aspects of Jewish tales, wisdoms, and institutions.[4]

As concerns the law, we can say that, at the time, almost all societies or ethnic groups shared a common structural problem. Each was organized around a particular tradition, albeit one overruled by Roman law. The various *nomoi* sometimes clashed, and usually could rely on the Roman habit of allowing for or even "inventing"[5] something like *patrioi nomoi* or *mos maiorum* for the various peoples, so long as they did not disturb Roman rule. This concept was formally universalistic and materially particularistic, and, for a while, was quite effective. A community could generally govern itself by its own traditions; however, as concerned questions of imperial relevance, Roman law applied. In general, conflicts

3 Erwin R. Goodenough, „The Political Philosophy of Hellenistic Kingship", YCS 1 (1928) 53–102. I have utilized this fine article in the chapter "*Corpus imperii* und *corpus Christi*. Überlegungen zur Entpolitisierung des Gesetzesbegriffs" of my *Ein Freispruch für Paulus. John Tolands Theorie des Judenchristentums*, Berlin 1996, 118–133.

4 Cf. Daniel Boyarin, *Border Lines. The Partition of Judaeo-Christianity*, Philadelphia 2004, especially Chapter 5, "The Jewish Life of the Logos: Logos Theology in Pre- and Pararabbinic Judaism," 112–127.

5 Cf. Hans G. Kippenberg in his *Die vorderasiatischen Erlösungsreligionen in ihrem Zusammenhang mit der antiken Stadtherrschaft. Heidelberger Max-Weber-Vorlesungen 1988*, Frankfurt a. M. 1991, 487–499.

of loyalty could become a creative force, especially if the "imposed" law afforded more liberties than the *patrioi nomoi.*[6] Such conflicts became even more widespread when the law, or even the spirit, was thought of as being embodied in a single exemplary individual who was to be worshipped.

Paul was unquestionably not just brilliant but also someone who adopted an abstract approach to problems. He describes himself as having been an activist in favor of traditional and rather strict Jewish groups; he sought to retrieve "apostates" by authoritarian means, until he was, as he reports in his letter to the Galatians, struck by a visionary insight that changed his life. From that moment on, the story of Jesus afforded him a mode of engagement that both fit into the scheme of the exemplary individual as well as transcended all other pretenders to that purpose, including the unembodied, abstract laws of "Greeks and Jews" alike (and certainly those of the Romans). Any worldly ruler purporting to be the embodiment of the law or the spirit would necessarily be exposed and convicted of being merely another failed human being. Yet what if God himself were the logos and incarnated on earth? Such were the ideas that early Christians circulated among themselves.[7]

The consequences for these new communities and for the individuals organizing within them were intensely debated.[8] Their respective laws appeared to lose importance, and Paul's statement in Gal 3,28, in which he seems to deny relevance to various major distinctions by which we live as social beings, has time and again been interpreted as a manifesto of Christian inclusivism and universalism. The Jews, who remained as a Jewish "rest" after the historical victory of Christianity in the Roman empire, now gathered around what Christians considered excessively "legalist" interpretations of Hebrew tradition which the rabbis had developed in contradistinction to the Christian communities. From the beginning

---

6 Today, one need not go far to witness similar phenomena in the conflicts of migrant populations in Western cities.

7 An interesting interpretation of the deutero-Paulinian letter to the Ephesians with respect to Christ transcending the earthly ruler is found in Eberhard Faust, *Pax Christi et Pax Caesaris.* Frigourg 1998. This work, though it shares problems of more conservative strains of Protestant theology in the latter's traditional contempt for the particular Jewish law, is useful in understanding the political-ideological environment of the Paulinian problem. Badiou, in his work on Paul, draws sharp distinction between, on one hand, the theology of the logos as developed in the Gospel of John and, on the other, Paul's "diagonal" thought which maintains equal distance from both the (Greek) logos and the (Jewish) prophets. This helps Badiou to do away with anti-Judaism, which he dismisses as a disturbing by-product of antinomianism, cf. Alain Badiou, *Paulus. Die Begründung des Universalismus*, München 2002, 83.

8 Literature about who they were is found in works by Brigitte Kahl, Gerd Theissen, Wayne A. Meeks, and their followers.

of the Christian rise to power, the Jews knew the flipside of Christian universalism. Persecutions of Jews, who were identified with Judas, were hardly limited to springtime, when Christians celebrated the passion of Christ.[9] The structural problem has since become well known: as Guy G. Stroumsa has noted, "*While ethnic or religious particularism tends to turn rather fast into exclusivism that ignores or despises outsiders, ecumenical inclusivism entails the illegitimization of the other's existence, and hence generates tensions and violent intolerance.*"[10]

Zizek, in his piece on love without mercy (the German translation is entitled *Die gnadenlose Liebe*) draws further upon the problem. Whereas the Jewish claim of having a special relationship to the universal God (a relationship based upon the Jews being elected by God) allows for non-Jews – the unelected – to live as they like, Christian universalism tends to exclude the unbeliever from the very notion of humanity.[11] Once Zizek admits this, however, he proceeds to find other and much better ways in Christian *agape*. Love beyond grace or without mercy – that seems to be a discovery in the texts of Paul, which can still render both Paul's texts and Christianity relevant. One might initially think, especially based on the commentary on the book's back cover, that Zizek argues, in Lacanian terms, basically the same things as everyone else writing in this vein: namely, that the Christ event, no matter how sophisticated, sets the individual free. But free of what? Even if Zizek as well as Badiou dismiss as fable the story of God, who sacrificed his son in order to pay for humanity's sins,[12] the dogma of justification by faith rather than by law still seems to function as an "empowerment" of the individual against legal or otherwise ethical restrictions. However, in these new readings, legal restrictions themselves are specified as an "automatism of desire," stipulated by the law itself, as is typically developed in Lacanian interpretations of Romans 7.7–25. In short: verses 7.7–10 are read as a brief recapitulation of emotional development from "innocent" childhood, in which neither

---

9 Cf. the interesting conclusions drawn by Hermann Levin Goldschmidt, "Heilvoller Verrat: Besinnung auf Judas," in Herrmann Levin Goldschmidt, *Werkausgabe in neun Bänden*, ed. Willi Goetschel, Vienna 2014, 211–233. The penchant for identifying Jews and Judaism is still present in Germany. For example, during the 2008 elections, posters for the Left Party politician Gregor Gysi, whom many Berliners identified as "Jewish," were defaced with anti-Jewish graffiti. In my neighbourhood in Berlin Schöneberg I saw "Judas" written on his posters.

10 Guy G. Stroumsa, "Early Christianity as a Radical Religion," in: *Concepts of the Other in Near Eastern Religions*, ed. b. I. Alon u. a., Jerusalem 1994, 173–193; 191.

11 Cf. Slavoj Zizek, *Die gnadenlose Liebe*, Frankfurt a. M. 2001, 176.

12 Badiou actually begins his discourse by explaining why he is engaging himself in a discussion of Paul despite the latter's story being a fable, Alain Badiou, *Paulus*, München 2002, 11ff and passim.

death nor desire occurs on the screen of the unconscious – but the "nomos," as it steps in and points to the objects of desire, arouses desire in the very moment it comes to forbid desire.[13] The specifics vary from here, though in any case the law is like a knife[14] that splits a premature inner unity – first *inside* each human soul, putting law and desire (with their incarnated automatism as sin) on the negative side, and the emerging believer, who is true to "the event," on the positive side. In psychoanalytic language: the law is the father.[15] And the Christ event reveals the son – who is supposed to bring about a spirit of universal freedom and love in a special way.

In considering the (Jewish) father of psychoanalysis – namely, Sigmund Freud, who saw himself as being in a paternal position and explained antisemitism against the background of the father-son conflict – it makes perfect sense to take a closer look at this relation.

3 The Law Won't Come. It Won't Even Give You a Call[16]

Considering the semantic background of late antiquity, we can perhaps assume the following: there is a hope, underlying the hope for an incarnated liberator, that presents itself as fulfilled in the story of Christ,[17] but only as anticipated in rabbinical or later Jewish messianism. It is the yearning for an incarnated law, or "the father." This is more than a banal statement if one considers the imbalance prevailing (in a very old and hence recurring pattern) in postmodern theories of "Jewish law." These theories, in addressing, often with great complexity and

---

13 Alain Badiou, *Paulus,* München 2002, 150 ff. Zizek claims to intend the return to the "founding symbolic structure" of Christianity – which is certainly less outspoken yet amounts to the same disinterest in the story itself, cf. Slavoj Zizek, *Die gnadelnose Liebe,* Frankfurt a. M. 2001, 10.

14 Giorgio Agamben instead combines the "knife" metaphor with the messianic, drawing on both Benjamin's text about the cut of Apelles and the Rosenzweigian idea of Judaism as the only entity that founds itself on the establishing of ever more rests of the rest (a word on which rests the title of Agamben's book on Paul), cf. Giorgio Agamben, *Die Zeit, die bleibt (Il tempo che resta. Un comment alla* Lettera ai Romani), 2000, 62 ff.

15 Badiou is especially explicit on this point. And his Paul is, of course, the "son" or the one who opens a discourse of the son. Cf. Badiou, *Paulus*, 105–121.

16 This title quotes Shalom Chanoch's famous song "Mashiach Lo Ba." I transfer this story of failed expectations from the Messiah to the law without repeating the quotations and interpretations of Kafka's narration "Vor dem Gesetz" in this context.

17 As Freud explained in his *Der Mann Moses und die monotheistische Religion.*

sophistication, the symbolic consequences of the "Christ event" or some other, more abstract messianism, employ notions of the law or the "Jewish law" that are usually deficient or even colloquial. They fail to do justice to the real historical development as figured by recent scholarship (that of Boyarin, for example), nor do they accord with the general sociological observation that a "muted" group must contend with more challenges to its survival under the rule of a dominant group than does the latter. It is more probable that a group whose symbolic order survives long-term oppression will, in terms of intellectual sophistication, outgrow the dominant group than vice versa.

To be clear: this may have applied in the meantime to Christianity as well – at least somewhat, at least in some niches, at least where some inner space of freedom was retained.[18] And insofar as substantial Christian thinking has become a minority phenomenon, it may have improved considerably lately. This is probably the case with the new Paulinians. Making good use of generally secular psychoanalytic thinking, the new Paulinians have produced magisterial reflections on how the soul can be conceived. The common assumption is that of a universal need to believe.[19] But whereas classical psychoanalytic theory (and the Frankfurt School's accompanying negative dialectic) would state and respect the need, yet avoid believing that the need is fulfilled simply because it should be, a Lacanian impulse to defend a symbolic order will press forth to positively establish a symbolic order and to maintain close, loyal contact with this order even in case of severe disappointment.[20] It seems plausible that this shift in "intellectual

---

18 The stress on the inner space is important. When elites under pressure deploy severity against their dependents in the inner circle so as to survive, sophistication suffers. But when they are able to preserve a space for humour, art, and education, thereby respecting the individual in their inner circles, minorities have good chances to surpass the majority in terms of wit, originality, education, and mental discipline.

19 One of the few women who seem to take significant interest in Paulinian psychology is Julia Kristeva – another Lacanian philosopher and psychoanalyst, and another secularized Catholic. She states that the need to believe is a universal characteristic of every human soul: "I am trying to explain that all religions, each in its way throughout history, are being founded on a universal need to believe, which is pre-religious and appears to be an anthropological fact. Everybody has experienced it in their childhood in relation to the mother or the father. The need to trust, the need to be recognized, this need belongs to all of us. It becomes a desire or an experience, but it is always there." See http://www.deutschlandradiokultur.de/das-beduerfnis-zu-glauben.954.de.html?dram:article_id=146098 (in German).

20 Zizek, for example, considers the Adornian attitude a dead-end and proposes two possible exits: the Habermasian approach of communicative theory, in which the "reliable" consists in the rules of fair dealing and negotiating the common truth; and the Lacanian approach of the outlined subject that exists only insofar as it has denied itself (cf. Zizek, *Gnadenlose Liebe*, 124).

fashion" is linked to a change in the historical moment: immediately following the Shoah theoretical thinking sought to be true to the destructive shock of that event, and there followed a post-traumatic desire for "healing." Some thinkers now seek to regain what seemed to have been lost in the disaster.

Hence, Agamben states that Christianity has a Kafkaesque universe of mercy, just as Judaism has its Kafkaesque universe of law.[21] But this Kafkaesque character is a subsequent flaw, which has no justification in Paul's original letters, with their pure messianism. In Gal 2,4, Agamben finds "an experience of pure word" that creates a "freedom of the subject"; this freedom allows for grace and vitality between human beings, beyond the nomos of denotative relations. Agamben describes freedom as that which emerges from pure acts of belief, as something that becomes lost in dogmatic claims concerning the content of belief.[22]

Badiou further specifies the achievement of Paul's notion of justification, speaking of a split in the subject. He sees in this a preformation of what Freud would describe as the unconscious – and discerns in its description, and subsequent acceptance of the inner split, a sustainable empowerment of the "son." The "father" who is always particular (as embodied in the "cosmic" law of the Greeks or the "moral" law of the Jews) retreats; the universal son takes his place, unrestricted by legal definitions of the "objects" of his automatism of desire. For Badiou, the inner space gained by this act helps the subject to meet unorthodox decisions and to establish independent judgment.

Zizek criticizes Badiou for not being genuinely political, in that the latter proposes to identify and explain the event only after it has occurred.[23] Zizek repeatedly draws upon Lacan's ideas about the function of the intervening father in the development of desire and even fulfilled love in everyday life (as described in Lacan's *Encore*); he renders Christianity the "best religion," stating that the Jewish position is uncanny because of its excessive self-reduction to the symbolic "without the phantasmatic screen." According to Zizek's rhetorical questions, Jews suffer, due to the situation of exile, from the lack of a silent "root" and must therefore minutely specify everything in their legalistic discourse (*Die gnadenlose Liebe*, 161). Thus Jews have no inner identity that could be both interrupted yet at the same time secured by a father or a law that would represent the father. And

---

I suggest elsewhere to instead return to Hermann Cohen and to consider Habermas as one possible branch of his theory, without ignoring what Lacanian analysis, deconstruction, and feminism have to contribute.

21 Agamben, *Kommentar*, 137.

22 Agamben, *Kommentar*, 150 f.

23 Zizek, *Gnadenlose Liebe*, 158 f.

where there is no ear there can be no real call, however often the rules (which are written somewhere) are repeated.

This is only a glimpse into what these new Paulinians have in common. Each dismisses belief in the gospel's and Paul's "fable," in order to make (in general, psychoanalytic) sense of the act of believing. Each seeks to explain and then "sew" (in German: "vernähen") the traumatic split within the individual, which is so crucial both for the life of desire as well as for every moral judgment not guided by the tempting equation between law and sin, between the super-ego and the objects it denotes – and each does so in strange contradistinction to what he terms the Jewish law. Messianism remains that part of Judaism that is acceptable to Christians and to those who, though they no longer consider themselves Christian in any traditional way, still try to use the Christian heritage. To this effect, they would blame institutionalized Christianity for legalism, together with what they dislike in Jewish Law as well as in the ever stronger "juridification" of everyday life (Agamben). In fact, each of these thinkers seems to be tempted by imagery of the "innocent" childlike life that would be regained once the human soul undergoes the psychoanalytically conceived (and essentially traumatic) process of triangulation and interiorization of morality. Yet the father never arrives, and a law that is as abstract as it appears in Paul's reduced formula "thou shalt not covet" may be less than functional in establishing anything more than the basic foundations of an independent and universal human soul, to whose development the Oedipal "no" is indeed crucial.

4 Options

Franz Rosenzweig, whose observations that Judaism "reproduces itself by subtraction and the building of ever new rests alone" now seem so important to the New Paulinians (particularly Zizek), had no illusions about the close connection between antinomianism and antisemitism. Nor was he tempted to reduce the law to a body of soulless rules, or to flat, abstract imperatives such as "Thou shalt not covet." Clearly, his thoughts about the intimate relation between ideas of the father and ideas of the law were not especially far from later psychoanalytic thinking. Remarkably, when Rosenstock-Huessy quoted John 14,6 to him, Rosenzweig simply agreed, noting that "Nobody will get to the father, if not through Jesus." But he added: "Except for the Jews, as they are already there."[24]

This is entirely in line with Rosenzweig's other gestures of "staying" in Judaism by refusing conversion to Christianity, and of what I call anti-conversion: an active move of regaining, for Judaism, a positive force, which Christians had previously blamed on or projected onto a negative instance (or force). It is being the exception – and hence of often being in the position of what Agamben developed as the *homo sacer* – of Christian and European universalism that proves to be Judaism's crucial contribution to a new universalism. For Rosenzweig, however, it was this time a respected contribution. Today's moment could have been another opportunity. It could have been an enriching opening, but, given the approach of the new Paulinians, it looks to have been yet another missed engagement. This hardly seems to be the fault of the Jewish philosophers involved. Neither Arendt, who saw in Zionism a gesture of weariness concerning the "privilege" of being the chosen people, nor Rosenzweig, who, in his *Star of Redemption*, constructed an inner conversion of notions and feelings, nor even Cohen, who not only defended Jewish law but suggested utilizing its structures so as to establish a new ethical foundation of the humanities, can be blamed for not having endeavored to contribute a respectively Jewish part to thinking universalism anew. If they were not in any case "explicitly" or "positively" or "religiously" Jewish, they had this in common with their Christian counterparts who were no longer 'positive believers' either. And, as concerns establishing dialogue as a method and accepting that the other will always remain the other, they were undoubtedly the forerunners not only in philosophy but in theology and in psychology. It was Derrida, another Jewish thinker, who abstained from taking the universal as a given, and spoke instead about the "universalizable" *in* a tradition, thereby allowing for difference and differance between the Jewish and the Christian as well as between the individuals in between.

Whether it was Rosenzweig or Goldschmidt, Cohen or Ben Chorin, Benjamin or Levinas or Scholem, the Jewish side was traditionally burdened with the heavier load of the "muted group" or the minority. In order to perform among the

---

24 This passage of his letters has been quoted abundantly in Rosenzweig scholarship: „Das Christentum erkennt den Gott des Judentums an, nicht als Gott aber als den ‚Vater Jesu Christi' ... Was Christus und seine Kirche in der Welt bedeuten, darüber sind wir einig: es kommt niemand zum Vater denn durch ihn [Johannes 14/6]. Es kommt niemand zum Vater – anders aber wenn einer nicht mehr zum Vater zu kommen braucht, weil er schon bei ihm ist. Und dies ist nun der Fall des Volkes Israel." (GS I, 133). For an accessible and profound introduction cf. Wolfdietrich Schmied-Kowarzik, Franz Rosenzweigs Stern der Erlösung, https://kobra.bibliothek.uni-kassel.de/bitstream/urn:nbn:de:hebis:34-2008092224023/4/RosenzweigsStern.html.txt.

majority Christians, who already had their own respective difficult methods of constructing, deconstructing, and reconstructing the relevant universal notion of how the soul functions, Jewish thinkers had to make much ado about method. But perhaps these Jewish thinkers' hidden method for all this and for what they were writing was as simple and as smart as that of the rabbis: that is, that you should not even try to compete with those who build grand systems from within their own self-set conditions. Such projects bear the insignia of a worldly power that you, in your defensive minority position, will rarely if ever be able to access or to retain. In order to endure, you must resort to nomadic ways: collect what you have, and pass it on, if you can; fix your times and learn your texts and keep them in play; and if you happen to have an hour of peace, write what comes to mind. Moreover: teach your children well; teach them to question and to listen carefully; and encourage them to speak in their own way.

This is somewhat less than the complicated systems of the new Paulinians and their Lacanian rooting. Zizek's observation that Judaism lacks "rooting" of the Christian philosopher's kind may have a grain of truth. But with its "rooting" distorted or hidden, rabbinic tradition is much more than the flat legalism that Christians have always seen in it. The pre- and post-Paulinian Jewish individual can establish an inner space of consciousness even without the dialectics so crucial to this development for Christians. The Jew, in other words, is already there. If you wish to know how much soul and inner space Jewish thought definitely has, read the second part of the second book of the *Star of Redemption*. But, please, neither abolish nor baptize this precious piece of Jewish literature!

5 Conclusion, Sobriety Style

The attempt to regain meaning and relevance for "Western values" by winning back the strength of "Judeo-Christianity" takes as many forms as there are authors involved. It has become a matter of Western self-defense against an Islamist movement run amok, as well as against authoritarian and collectivist ideologies from across the world, to develop Judeo-Christianity as an inner dialogue between the two asymmetric theological spaces that the hyphen conjoins. Yet I am surely not the first to be bothered by two problems here. First, the "Western" apology tends to glorify its own roots of individual freedom, even as it develops a tendency to sacrifice these roots in order to build a common resort that can stand against "the other," be it Islamism as such, communism, or whatever formerly communist regimes such as those in China or Russia have become. Here, the new integration of Judaism into the "community of values" comes with the price of serious deprecation of the other, who, be it Muslims, radical Zionists, or communists, stands outside the new space of common values. A community of values that does not even respect those outside it will likely suffer deterioration in its capacity to attract or even convince.[25]

In contrast, the second problem is that critics of these phenomena, especially of what some have termed a "bedfellowship" of Christians and Jews against Muslims, are almost cripplingly reluctant to defend the real achievements of Judeo-Christianity. These critics tend to (naïvely) give credit to what are in fact nothing more than elementary authoritarian or reactionary forces in the other, whose spiritual and cultural qualities they seek to accommodate within themselves (albeit only so as to lean upon someone who offers an alternative to capitalist disaster). And as soon as this occurs, antinomianism and its central consequence, antisemitism, are never distant, including when people try to build their revolutionary subject on the apostle Paul, the founding father of Christian theology.

Against these two extremes, it may be a common desire for universal human rights, rather than the rivalry between Rosenzweigian "New Thinking" and Neo-Paulinian "New Spirit," that truly aids Judeo-Christianity to be as good as its best intentions: this would include being both open towards other cultures yet also firm when it comes to defending its freedom for every individual – freedom that it has worked so hard to gain.

Bibliography

Agamben, Giorgio. *The Time That Remains: A Commentary on the Letter to the Romans*. Trans. Patricia Dailey. Stanford: Stanford University Press 2005.

Agamben, Giorgio. *Die Zeit, die bleibt. Ein Kommentar zum Römerbrief (Il tempo che resta. Un comment alla* Lettera ai Romani). Trans. Davide Giuriato. Frankfurt am Main (Suhrkamp) 2000.

Badiou, Alain. *Paulus. Die Begründung des Universalismus*. Trans. Heinz Jatho. München, Sequenzia 2002.

Boyarin, Daniel. *Border Lines. The Partition of Judaeo-Christianity.* Philadelphia: Penn 2004.

Boyarin, Daniel. "Paul Among the Antiphilosophers; or Saul Among the Sophists." *St. Paul among the Philosophers*. Ed. John D. Caputo and Linda Martin Alcoff. Indiana: Indiana University Press, 2009. 109–141.

25 As Martha Nussbaum demonstrates throughout her *The New Religious Intolerance* (2012), this would also explicitly go against the philosophies and theologies of the founding fathers of this community of values.

Faust, Eberhard. *Pax Christi et Pax Caesaris.* Frigourg: Vandenhoek und Ruprecht, 1993.
Freud. *Der Mann Moses und die monotheistische Religion.* Sigmund Freud Studienausgabe, Bd. 9, Fragen der Gesellschaft/Ursprünge der Religion, Frankfurt am Main, Fischer 2000, 455–581.
Goldschmidt, Hermann Levin. “Heilvoller Verrat: Besinnung auf Judas.” *Werkausgabe in neun Bänden.* Ed. Willi Goetschel. Vienna: Passagen 2014. 211–233.
Goodenough, Erwin R. “The Political Philosophy of Hellenistic Kingship.” *YCS* 1 (1928): 53–102.
Kippenberg, Hans G. *Die vorderasiatischen Erlösungsreligionen in ihrem Zusammenhang mit der antiken Stadtherrschaft. Heidelberger Max-Weber-Vorlesungen 1988.* Frankfurt a. M.: Suhrkamp, 1991.
Kristeva, Julia. *Dieses unglaubliche Bedürfnis zu glauben,* Trans. Eva zum Winkel, Gießen, Psychosozial-Verlag, 2015.
Nussbaum, Martha. *The New Religious Intolerance*, Boston/Mass., Harvard University Press, 2012.
Palmer, Gesine. “*Corpus imperii* und *corpus Christi*. Überlegungen zur Entpolitisierung des Gesetzesbegriffs”. *Ein Freispruch für Paulus. John Tolands Theorie des Judenchristentums.* Berlin: Verlag Institut für Kirche und Judentum 1996. 118–133.
Schmied-Kowarzik, Wolfdietrich and Franz Rosenzweig. “Stern der Erlösung. ” https://kobra.bibliothek.uni-kassel.de/bitstream/urn:nbn:de:hebis:34-2008092224023/4/RosenzweigsStern.html.txt, accessed 12/4/2014.
Stroumsa, Guy G. “Early Christianity as a Radical Religion.” *Concepts of the Other in Near Eastern Religions*. Ed. I. Alon et al. Jerusalem: Brill 1994. 173–193.
Zizek, Slavoj. *Die gnadenlose Liebe.* Frankfurt a. M.: Suhrkamp 2001.
http://www.deutschlandradiokultur.de/das-beduerfnis-zu-glauben.954.de.html?dram:article_id=146098 (in German), accessed 12/4/2014.

Marianne Moyaert

8 Christianizing Judaism? On the Problem of Christian Seder Meals

The meaning of the term 'Judeo-Christian' partly depends upon the context in which it is used. I write this contribution as a Roman Catholic theologian *after the Second Vatican Council* (held from 1962 to 1965 and henceforth in this contribution referred to as 'Vatican II'). My considerations revolve around the theological significance of the Judeo-Christian tradition with a specific focus on its importance for the dialogue between 'Judaism' and 'Christianity' *in a post- Shoah era.*[1] I shall commence by pointing out how the term 'Judeo-Christian' symbolizes a dramatic change in the relations between the Roman Catholic Church and the Jewish people.[2] From a Catholic perspective, the hyphen between Judaism and Christianity expresses a retrieval of the Jewish roots of Christian tradition, which were denied for close to two thousand years, even to the point of their erasure. After Vatican II and the promulgation of *Nostra Aetate* (the Declaration on the Relation of the Church to non-Christian Religions), Catholic theologians began to realize that one cannot understand Christianity without Judaism.[3]

---

1 When discussing the Judeo-Christian tradition(s), Catholic theologians who locate themselves after the Shoah and after Vatican II will testify to their sincere intention to move beyond two thousand years of anti-Jewish theologies which emphasized the discontinuity between Judaism and Christianity. They realize that Christian anti-Judaism constituted the soil in which Nazism could take root and ultimately led to the destruction of two-thirds of European Jews. This realization shapes theology. Catholic theologian Johannes Baptist Metz states that no theology can be done without asking what it means in light of the Shoah. Our theological language before and after the Shoah cannot be the same, and the symbolic and real violence done to Jews necessitates a reconsideration of Christian tradition. See Johannes Baptist Metz, *The Emergent Church* (New York: Crossroad, 1981) 28.

2 Certainly one could also analyze the way this term functions in Protestant theological circles, and to be fair, generally speaking Protestant churches (the World Council of Churches especially) were much faster in addressing questions about Christian-Jewish relations than the Roman Catholic Church.

3 See John M. Oesterreicher, *The Rediscovery of Judaism: A Re-examination of the Conciliar Statement on the Jews* (Orange: Seton Hall University, 1971); Edward W. Bristow, *No Religion is an Island: The Nostra Aetate Dialogues* (New York: Fordham University Press, 1998); Neville Lamdan and Alberto Melloni, *Nostra Aetate: Origins, Promulgation, Impact on Jewish-Catholic Relations.*

Acknowledgment: I would like to express my sincere gratitude to Ruth Langer for helping me find the relevant sources dealing with the liturgical dimension of Christian-Jewish encounters.

In the aftermath of the Council, Catholics grew accustomed to speaking about the Judeo-Christian tradition, thereby at once recognizing the continuity between both traditions. Scholarly research began to reveal the complex history of the parting of the ways between the two traditions. At a grassroots level, several initiatives were taken to stimulate the dialogue between Jews and Catholics, and to establish friendly relations between both communities. The changed attitude of the Church vis-à-vis the Synagogue also found its expression in the liturgical realm. In the years after Vatican II, some Catholics have started to adopt certain ritual practices, which Jesus (and his followers) presumably observed. The celebration of some form of the Jewish Passover Seder in particular is becoming more popular.[4] The primary goal of such celebration is to imitate as closely as possible Jesus and his disciples during the Last Supper, as well as learn to appreciate the Jewish origins of the Eucharist. This ritual cross-over can be seen as a concrete expression of Judeo-Christianity. I will argue that this specific form of *cross-riting* brings to the surface some problems related to the notion of the *Judeo-Christian tradition*, which are not sufficiently thought through by theologians who locate themselves after the Shoah and after Vatican II. That is to say, emphasis on the Judeo-Christian tradition is meant to express *Christian* appreciation for the bond between the two traditions. Yet its usage may also indicate the difficulty in recognizing Judaism as a self-sufficient and independent religion. To put it more strongly: its usage may even indicate a form of latent anti-Judaism.[5]

Proceedings of the International Conference Jerusalem, 30 October – 1 November, 2005 (Münster: Lit, 2005); Marianne Moyaert and Didier Pollefeyt, *Never Revoked: Nostra Aetate as Ongoing Challenge for Jewish-Christian Dialogue*, Louvain Theological and Pastoral Monographs, 40 (Leuven: Peeters, 2010); Anthony Cernera, *Examining Nostra Aetate after 40 Years: Catholic-Jewish Relations in our Time* (Fairfield: Sacred Heart University Press, 2007); Gavin D'Costa, *Vatican II: Catholic Teachings on Jews and Muslims* (Oxford: Oxford University Press, 2014).

4 Protestants preceded Catholics in this liturgical turn to Judaism, a finding that should give us reason to pause. According to Frank Senn, "It is not a surprise that Christian observance of Passover began in the Reformed Tradition (although they have also been observed in Roman Catholic and Lutheran parishes). The chief characteristic of the Zwinglian/Reformed/Puritan spirituality has been a historical criticism which attempts to peel away the layers of tradition in order to get at and therefore be able to experience the original event. The celebration of the Lord's Supper thus became a reenactment of the Last Supper so as to be put in mind of Christ's sacrifice for our redemption." Frank Senn, "Should Christians Celebrate the Passover," in: Paul F. Bradshaw and Lawrence A. Hoffman (eds.), *Passover and Easter: The Symbolic Structuring of Sacred Seasons* (Notre Dame: University of Notre Dame Press, 1999) 183–205, here p. 197.

5 Jewish scholars are traditionally more critical of what they call the Judeo-Christian myth. It is regarded as a 20th century construct, manufactured for political reasons (e.g., American reaction against Nazism and/or Communism). However, the notion was probably first used in the 19th century in Europe (France and Germany especially). The Dreyfus-case seems to have played a

I shall structure my argument as follows in three parts. In the first part of this contribution, I dwell upon a theological (anti-Jewish) tradition that emphasized the discontinuity between Judaism and Christianity. Second, I articulate the shift that the Second Vatican Council (and *Nostra Aetate*) brought to Catholic theologies of Judaism and how the notion of *the Jewish-Christian tradition* in this theological context was, and continues to, be an expression of appreciation for the Jewish roots of Christian tradition. Third, I will then turn to the contemporary practice of Catholics who re-enact Jesus' Last supper by celebrating Jewish Seder meals. However sincerely intended, I will argue that this liturgical expression of 'Judeo-Christianity' is problematic from a historical point of view (did Jesus actually celebrate Seder?), from a religious-ethical point of view (is it appropriate for Catholics to appropriate the rituals of Jewish tradition?), and from a reconciliatory perspective (will Christian Seders contribute to reconciliation between Christian and Jewish communities?).

1 Christian Theologies of Discontinuity and the Forgetfulness of Jesus' Jewishness

For the greatest part of its history, Christianity did not succeed in positively accepting its Jewish origins, and only until recently the dominant Christian theological discourse was one of highlighting the *discontinuity* between both traditions. The cross of Jesus, his salvific suffering, death and resurrection definitively cancelled out Israel's hopes. The Church developed her own self-understanding as people of God and heir to God's promises by denying Israel a lasting place in God's plan of salvation. This resulted in so-called replacement or supersessionist theolo-

key role in its emergence. Both defenders of Dreyfus and anti-Dreyfusards used the term. The former used it in the sense of a common Western tradition of values, to which both Judaism and Christianity laid the foundation. The latter group used it when speaking of a common conspiracy of Judaism, Protestantism and Free Masonry. The notion was also used in a negative way by philosophers like Voltaire and Nietzsche. In any case, Jewish scholars point out that Christians are more eager to embrace this term, whereas Jews are more reluctant to do so, because it does not do justice to the history of both traditions with all its divisiveness and conflict. It is in effect a denial of the tradition of *contra Iudaeos*. For a critique of the Judeo-Christian tradition see Mark Silk, "Notes on the Judeo-Christian Tradition in America, "American Quarterly 36 (1984) 66–85; Arthur Cohen, *The Myth of the Judeo-Christian Tradition* (New York: Harper and Row, 1957); Jacob Neusner, *Jews and Christians: The Myth of a Common Tradition* (London and Philadelphia: SCM Press and Trinity Press International, 1991).

gies.[6] That is to say, the Church is the New People of God, which has replaced Israel, the Old People of God. This replacement entails an abrogation of the first covenant between God and Israel.[7] There exist various kinds of supersessionism.[8]

According to one version, Israel's replacement by the Church is a divine punishment. Because they missed the time of their visitation by God and refused to embrace the gracious gift of salvation offered them in Christ, God has turned away from Israel and has revoked his promises to them. Israel is no longer his beloved people. According to some theologies, the Jewish people is even cursed by God. The Church, on the other hand, has accepted Jesus Christ, the Messiah, and has welcomed his message about the Kingdom to come and is therefore called the New People of God. We find this sort of punitive supersessionism common among the early Church Fathers.[9] In its most objectionable form it contains the charge of deicide,[10] the accusation that the Jewish people is collectively responsible for the death of Jesus, the Son of God. As a result of this collective responsibility, Jews henceforward bear the mark of Cain, which, for many Christians throughout history, became an excuse to mistreat Jews. If Abel's blood cursed Cain, then Christ's blood has cursed the Jewish people.[11] When asked about the continuing reason for the existence of Israel after the Jewish No to Jesus, the answer is twofold. The continuing existence of Israel is first of all meant as proof to Christians that Jews deserve to be subjugated. What is more, they are testimony to the Christians through their own scriptures that Jesus has come to fulfill the messianic prophecies.

Another type of supersessionist theology emphasizes instead how God's divine plans for the salvation of humanity once had an important part for Israel

---

6 Supersessionism comes from the Latin *supersedere* (to sit upon). It refers to the theological claim that the Church has replaced Israel as God's people.

7 See Marianne Moyaert and Didier Pollefeyt, "Israel and the Church: Fulfillment beyond Supersessionism?" in: Marianne Moyaert and Didier Pollefeyt (eds.), *Nostra Aetate as Ongoing Challenge for Jewish-Christian Dialogue*, Louvain Theological and Pastoral Monographs, 40 (Leuven: Peeters, 2010) 159–183.

8 Michael Vlach, *The Church as a Replacement of Israel: An Analysis of Supersessionism*, Edition Israelogie (EDIS) 2 (Frankfurt: Peter Lang, 2009a).

9 Michael Vlach, "Various Forms of Replacement Theology," *The Master's Seminary Journal* 20 (2009b) 5769.

10 In his homily, *Peri Pascha*, Melito of Sardis (2nd century) formulated the charge of deicide charge, namely, that Israel killed God. For a thoroughgoing study, see Alistair Stewart-Sykes, *The Lamb's High Feast: Melito, Peri Pascha and the Quartodeciman Paschal Liturgy at Sardis* (Leiden: Brill, 1998).

11 Lisa A. Unterseher, *The Mark of Cain and the Jews: Augustine's Theology of Jews and Judaism*, Early Christian Studies 9 (Piscataway, NJ: Gorgias Press, 2009) 55.

to play, but that this role has now expired, because God decided that physical, "Carnal" Israel (1 Cor 10:18) was to be replaced by the spiritual Church. Kendall Soulen rightly points out that

> according to this view God's covenant with Israel was carnal, since it was transmitted by carnal means (natural descent from the patriarchs) and since it focused on carnal goods (posterity, prosperity, and land). In contrast the Church is spiritual, since its membership is conferred by faith and not by natural descent, and since it focuses on spiritual goods such as salvation form sin and eternal life. According to this second version of supersessionism, God elected Israel as a kind of 'dry run' on His way to the Church, like a sculptor who first molds a design in clay before committing it to marble. Once the spiritual Church appears, carnal Israel becomes obsolete. Like the clay model, it can be set aside and even destroyed since the reality that it once prefigured is now present.[12]

The implication of this theology is that there is no longer any place for Israel in God's plan of salvation. Israel's role in the history of revelation and redemption has been written out of the world's script forever.

At the heart of many replacement theologies, and the quotation from Soulen above already alludes to this, is an antithesis between the carnal and the spiritual. Carnal Israel with its Mosaic covenant of the Law became associated with the flesh (earthly desires), but also with the particular, and the transient. The Church, with Christ as its founder, came to be associated with the spiritual, the universal and the eternal. As Christians divinized Jesus and began to see the Jewish people as enemies of the Church, they also came to spiritualize Jesus' Jewishness (de-judaization of Jesus), removing him from any dependence on the legalism and ritualism of Judaism. Jesus was the Christ *in spite of* the fact that he was Jewish, rather than because of it. Thus the history of Christianity implied emancipation from Judaism: The Church distanced herself from the Mosaic Law, abandoned Jewish practices (such as circumcision) and posited a clear distinction between the elevated spiritual Church of belief and the mundane, carnal Israel of ritual observance.[13]

This emancipation manifested itself in various ways. I shall note here how that emancipation affected Christian views of the Passover, given that I shall

---

12 Kendall Soulen, "Israel and the Church," in: Tikva Frymer-Kensky, David Novak, Michael Signer, David Sandmel (eds.), *Christianity in Jewish Terms* (Boulder, Westview, 2000) 167–174, here pp. 171–172.

13 The fiercest attempts to de-judaize Christ, Paul, and the first Christian communities were undertaken by 19th and 20th century German Christian theologians. Their goal was to turn Jesus into an Aryan Christ. See Susannah Heschel, *The Aryan Jesus: Christian Theologians and the Bible in Nazi Germany* (Maryknoll: Orbis, 2010).

develop later on in this contribution.[14] Early on in the Christian tradition Christ came to be compared to the Passover lamb that was slaughtered as a sign of the liberation from slavery, a comparison also expressed in the statement by John the Baptist at the beginning of John's gospel: "Behold the lamb of God, who takes away the sin of the world" (Jn 1:29; cf. Isa. 53:7). This comparison was later picked up and further developed by several Church Fathers. We can refer to Melito of Sardis (2nd Century) who claims that Jesus is the true Paschal sheep:

> Once, the slaying of the sheep was precious, but it is worthless now because of the life of the Lord; the death of the sheep was precious, but it is worthless now because of the salvation of the Lord; the blood of the sheep was precious, but it is worthless now because of the Spirit of the Lord; a speechless lamb was precious, but it is worthless now because of the spotless Son; the temple below was precious, but it is worthless now because of the Christ above ... [15]

Justin Martyr too develops this theme in his dialogue with Trypho, where he tries to convince the Jew Trypho of the fact that Jesus fulfills the Hebrew prophecies.[16] He connects Jesus' sacrificial death with Isaiah's prophecy about the suffering servant: "The Passover, indeed was Christ, who was later sacrificed, as Isaiah foretold, when he said, *He was led as a sheep to the slaughter* (Isa. 53: 7)...Now, just *as the blood of the Passover saved those who were in Egypt, so also the blood of Christ* shall rescue from death all those who have believed in him" (111. 3). The Passover theme also reappears in the writings of Athanasius, patriarch of Alexandria (295–373), who wrote his Festal Letters to caution the Christians of Alexandria against the Passover festivities. For Athanasius the Jewish Passover was but a shadow of the real Passover as established by Christ's sacrificial offering for all humanity. If the Jewish Passover brings redemption to a particular ethnic group, Christ's sacrificial death promises salvation for all. Athanasius accuses the Jewish people for not having understood the true spiritual meaning of Passover, for they are still attached to animal sacrifice, their particular people, and antiquated covenant:

---

14 Namely, an examination of Christians celebrating Seder meals as a liturgical expression of their Judeo-Christian heritage.

15 Quoted in Baruch M. Bokser, *The Origins of the Seder: the Passover Rite and Early Rabbinic Judaism* (Berkeley: Berkeley University of California Press, 1984) 27.

16 See Marianne Moyaert, "Who is the Suffering Servant? A Comparative Theological Reading of Isaiah 53 after the Shoah," in: Michelle Voss Roberts (ed.), *Comparative Theology: Insights for Systematic Theological Reflection* (New York: Fordham Press) [2016].

> Now, however, that the devil, that tyrant against the whole world, is slain, we do not approach a temporal feast, my beloved, but an eternal and heavenly. Not in shadows do we shew it forth, but we come to it in truth. For they being filled with the flesh of a dumb lamb, accomplished the feast, and having anointed their door-posts with the blood, implored aid against the destroyer. But now we, eating of the Word of the Father, and having the lintels of our hearts sealed with the blood of the New Testament, acknowledge the grace given us from the Saviour, who said, 'Behold, I have given unto you to tread upon serpents and scorpions, and over all the power of the enemy.' For no more does death reign; but instead of death henceforth is life, since our Lord said, 'I am the life;' so that everything is filled with joy and gladness; as it is written, 'The Lord reigneth, let the earth rejoice.'[17]

History has shown that theologies are not innocent, but impact the way Christians relate to their fellow human beings, in this case their Jewish neighbors. One need only take the Christian Holy Week as an example. The week commemorates of Christ's sacrificial death on Good Friday, followed by his descent into hell on Holy Saturday, culminating in his glorious resurrection on Easter Sunday. While Holy Week became the pivot of the Church's liturgical year, for Jews it was all too often an unholy week of terror. It was the time when, from the Middle Ages onwards, Christians not only celebrated the death and resurrection of Christ, but also recalled the 'deadly role' the Jews played in Christ's death. On Good Friday many priests incited their parishioners with hatred against the Jews for their deicide. This charge was sometimes also staged with processions and passion plays,[18] supplemented with libels against the Jews.[19] Spontaneous and semi-organized pogroms often resulted from this.[20] As a consequence, Frank Senn explains "[the] Passover of the Jews has been celebrated many times during

---

17 Philip Schaff (ed.), *Nicene and Post-Nicene Fathers.* Second Series, vol IV: Athanasius: Select Works and Letters (New York: Cosimo, 2007), 516.

18 Consider the Oberammergau plays. See Philip A. Cunningham, "Oberammergau: A Case Study of Passion Plays," in Philip A. Cunningham (ed.), *Pondering the Passion. What's at Stake for Christians and Jews?* (Oxford: Rowman and Littlefield, 2004); Mary C. Boys, *Redeeming our Sacred Story* (New York: Paulist Press, 2013) Chapter 5.

19 One of these myths was that Jews had kidnapped a Christian child, crucified him and stabbed him to use his blood into the unleavened bread they needed for their Passover ritual. Another charge was that of the desecration of the Eucharistic host. Israel J. Yuval explains that "the charge of host desecration is an extension of the blood libel, since it followed from the doctrine of transubstantiation that Jews no longer needed real flesh and blood Christians; they could simply stab the host." Israel Y. Yuval, "Easter and Passover as Early Jewish-Christian Dialogue," in: Paul Bradshaw and Lawrence A. Hoffman (eds.), *Passover and Easter. Origin and History to Modern Times,* Two Liturgical Traditions vol. 5 (Notre Dame: University of Notre Dame Press, 1999) 98–124.

20 Mitchell B. Merback, *Pilgrimage and Pogrom: Violence, Memory and Visual Culture at the Host-Miracle Shrines of Germany and Austria* (Chicago: University of Chicago Press, 2012); Bar-

nights of terror. It has not only been a festival of liberation but a festival of fear."[21] I need not go over this history in these pages. Allow me simply to remark that, as a result of this terrible chapter in Christian-Jewish encounters, it should be no surprise that symbolic practices connecting Passover and Easter can evoke strong emotional responses from Jewish communities. Some of these historical events have become deeply rooted in their collective memories. This will be something to return to later in this contribution, especially when considering Catholic attempts at reconciliation with Jews.

2 The Judeo-Christian Tradition and Its Theological Significance

The Declaration *Nostra Aetate* issued by the Second Vatican Council on October 28, 1965, on 'the relationship of the Church to non-Christian religions' marks a revolutionary "milestone"[22] in the history of Christian- (and specifically, Catholic-) Jewish relations. Of special importance is the fourth and longest paragraph which deals with the attitude of the Catholic Church towards the Jews. This paragraph represents a turning-point and can even be considered a breakthrough moment; the document breaks with a centuries-old history of anti-Jewish violence resting upon supersessionist theological convictions that the Jewish people was accursed because of 'its' rejection of Christ.[23] Now the Council aimed at a

---

bara Newman, "The Passion of the Jews of Prague: The Pogrom of 1389 and the Lessons of a Medieval Parody," *Church History* 81:1 (March 2012) 1–26.

21 Frank Senn, "Should Christians Celebrate the Passover?" 200.

22 Commission for Religious Relations with the Jews, *Guidelines and Suggestions for Implementing the Conciliar Declaration 'Nostra Aetate' (n.4).*

23 Two remarks are important. First of all, even though the Shoah is often – and rightfully so – seen as the dramatic catalyst needed to enable a theological change of heart in the Church's relationship to the Jews, it is important to note that there were Catholic pioneers (often in dialogue with Jewish people) who already before the world wars tried to bring about a new understanding of Judaism and the Jews. See e.g., Léon Bloy (1846–1917), Charles Péguy (1873–1914), and Raïssa Maritain (1883–1960). Second, when we look at the preparatory phase of the Council, a phase in which an effort was made to consult the bishops from all over the world, it cannot be denied that Jewish-Christian relations were not an immediate and pressing concern for the Church. The question of the relation between the Church and the Jewish people clearly did not occupy the minds of the bishops as it is absent from the advice and suggestions from the bishops. If it had not been for Pope John XXIII, Cardinal Bea and Jules Isaac, *Nostra Aetate* would not have come into being. Anti-Jewish theologies were so deeply engrained that the Church even after the Shoah

fundamental rethinking of the image of the Jews that had prevailed until then in the Church and that had been disseminated through preaching, catechesis, the liturgy, art and popular culture.

First, the bond between Judaism and Christianity is now emphasized. The Church in *Nostra Aetate* also recognizes that "her faith and her election are found already among the Patriarchs, Moses and the prophets." Next, the text confirms that God first concluded a covenant with Israel, the people who received the revelation of the Old Testament. Further on we read of "the root of that well-cultivated olive tree onto which have been grafted the wild shoots, the Gentiles", referring once again to the bond between Judaism and Christianity. The document next turns its attention to the fact that Jesus, Mary, the first apostles and many of the first disciples sprang from the Jewish people, to whom "the glory and the covenants and the law and the worship and the promises" belong. The fact that many Jews did not accept Jesus does not take away the fact that the Jews are still dear to God and that God "does not repent of the gifts He makes or of the calls He issues." It is very important that *Nostra Aetate* explicitly states with regard to the death of Christ that "what happened in His passion cannot be charged against all the Jews, without distinction, then alive, nor against the Jews of today". This is a rejection of the accusation of 'deicide' that had so often been levelled against the Jewish people throughout history leading to violence against the Jews. The document condemns every form of persecution arising from anti-Semitism.

With the promulgation of *Nostra Aetate*, the Church tried to move beyond two thousand years of anti-Jewish sentiments and actions, and now officially stated that the way forward was through Catholic-Jewish dialogue. Scholarly research that could help in coming to a better theological understanding of the relations between Israel and the Church (exegesis, historical studies, archaeology, etc.) also received a boost. The story that began to emerge and continues to emerge to this day is much more complex than the theological narrative of discontinuity (between the flesh and the spirit; the Law and Christ; Synagogue and Church) that 'we' have been constructing for centuries; the story that emerges is not a pleasant one; yes, it is marked by prejudices, stereotyping, exclusion and violence. But research also shows that the Jewish roots of Christianity (however hard we tried in the past) cannot be erased. We have learned that Jesus, his family and friends

---

struggled to formulate a new and more appreciative theological language to talk about the Jewish people. As John Connely points out in his historical work, the Church needed outsiders (Jews, Protestants) and newcomers (converts) to help her renew her theology of Judaism. John Connely, *From Enemy to Brother: The Revolution in Catholic Teaching on the Jews 1933–1965* (Cambridge: Cambridge University Press, 2012).

were observant Jews who were faithful to the Law, that Paul cannot be understood apart from his Jewish heritage, and that the first followers of Jews should not be called Christians, but Christ following Jews.[24] The "parting of the ways"[25] was a gradual process with many stages that in fact lasted quite long (until the 4th to the 5th century the boundaries of Jewish and Christian communities were somewhat porous). We have also learned that the antithesis between the vengeful God of the Old Testament and the God of love of the New Testament is theologically indefensible, and that there is much more continuity between Jewish and Christians values, norms, and practices than we ever dared to imagine.

When theologians use the term 'the Judeo-Christian tradition', I take them as expressing all of the above, realizing that not only have we rediscovered that God always remains faithful to his promises and that he has more than one blessing to give, but also that by reading Christianity through Jewish eyes, we may discover and rediscover forgotten truths that may help us come to a better understanding of God's plan of salvation. Thus many Catholics have come to understand themselves as Judeo-Christian, because so much of their own tradition stems from Judaism. The term 'Judeo-Christian' announces the dawn of a dialogical age with new life-giving possibilities for the Church and the Jewish people. Pointing to the bond between both traditions through a simple signifier, the hyphen in 'Judeo-Christian' represents now a bond that is unique and cannot be broken. That little hyphen carries with it the expectation that the days of theological anti-Judaism are over and that finally Jews and Catholics can try to make sense of one another in new ways.[26] With that comes a new theological challenge: how do you at the same time recognize that God has never taken back his promises to Israel and that their covenant was never revoked, while still maintaining the

---

24 The so-called rediscovery of the Jewish roots of Christianity was already initiated by Jewish scholars in the 19th century, but at that time strongly opposed and even rejected by Christian scholars. The Jewish scholar Abraham Geiger was one of the most influential Jewish historians, who wrote on the Jewish background of Jesus. See Susannah Heschel, "Jewish Studies as Counterhistory," in: David Biale, Michael Galchinsky and Susannah Heschel (eds.), *Insider/Outsider. American Jews and Multiculturalism* (Berkeley and Los Angeles, University of California Press, 1998).

25 Adam H. Becker and Annette Y. Reed (eds.), *The Ways that Never Parted: Jews and Christians in Late Antiquity and the Early Middle Ages* (Tübingen: Mohr Siebeck, 2003); Daniel Boyarin, *Border Lines: the Partition of Judeo-Christianity* (Philadelphia: University of Pennsylvania, 2004); James. D.G. Dunn, *Jews and Christians: The Parting of the Ways A.D. 70 to 135* (Grand Rapids: Eerdmans, 1992).

26 It is interesting to note that the Holy See's Commission for Religious Relations with the Jews, established by Pope Paul VI on 22 October 22 1974, works closely together with the Pontifical Commission for Promoting Christian Unity.

Christian belief that Jesus fulfills the Hebrew prophecies? The tension between both claims remains unresolved to this day, and probably explains in part why it is sometimes difficult for Catholics to come to terms with Judaism as a living tradition that does not seem to need Christianity.

3 The ambiguity of Catholics celebrating Seder meals

The rediscovery of the Jewishness of Jesus, and more broadly speaking the Jewish origins of Christianity, has also found its way into the liturgical domain. It has led to the realization that many Christian celebrations have roots in the Hebrew scriptures and Jewish symbolic practices. Ritual scholars, historians, and especially exegetes are now all trying to make sense of the complex liturgical history of Judaism and Christianity. They explore how the liturgy of Jewish communities influenced the liturgy of emerging Christian communities, and how it happened that Christian anti-Jewish polemics entered into the language of ritual.[27] This research contributes to a better understanding of the complex process of the parting of the ways, and helps to nuance the antithesis between Carnal Israel and the Spiritual Church.[28] It also forces the Church to confront some of the more dark pages of her history, e.g. anti-Jewish sermons that target Jewish ritual practices and festivities, as well as libels revolving around alleged Jewish anti-Christian symbolic practices.[29]

---

27 This, to my mind, is also an important correction to the misrepresentation of Judaism as a religion primarily of the book.

28 See for example, Ruth Langer, "The Liturgical Parting(s) of the Ways: A Preliminary Foray," in David A. Pitt et.al. (eds.), *A Living Tradition: On the Intersection of Liturgical History and Pastoral Practice*, (Collegeville: Liturgical Press, 2012) 43–58.

29 As is the case with scholarly research on the Jewish roots of Christianity *in general*, pioneers already started to explore the Jewish origins of Christian liturgy during the 19th and early 20th century. In her article on this topic "A New Horizon for Liturgy," Mary Christine Athans mentions that "[i]n 1893 the Jewish scholar Kaufmann Kohler published an article titled "Ueber die Ursprünge und Grundformen der synagogalen Liturgie" (About the Origins and Basic Forms of Synagogal Liturgy) (Kohler, 441–451; 489–497). He called attention to Christian interpolations added to Jewish prayers in the *Apostolic Constitutions*, books 7 and 8, which dealt with liturgical material derived from Jewish blessings (Ryan, 10). In 1905, Edmund von der Goltz compared the Jewish table prayers with the prayers in the *Didache*, in the *Apostolic Constitutions*, book 8, and in the older Greek *anaphoras* (eucharistic prayers). One of the prolific writers was German lay liturgist Anton Baumstark. In 1923, he wrote "Das Erbe der Synagoge" (The Heritage of the

These scholarly explorations into the Jewish roots of Christianity should be regarded as laying the groundwork for changes in Catholic liturgical traditions, which for centuries were plagued by anti-Jewish symbolism. The Church realizes that to really change Christian-Jewish relations after the Shoah and contribute to reconciliation between both communities, she has to disseminate the rediscovery of the Jewish origins of Christian tradition on a large scale. This extends itself to Catholic rituals in her liturgical tradition.[30] After the Council, several initiatives were taken to that end. The Vatican issued recommendations on how to present the Jews during her liturgies, the prayer for Jews recited on Good Friday[31] was reformulated, and blessings over bread and wine (resembling the ancient Jewish Hebrew Table blessings) were introduced.[32] What we are encountering here is the liturgical expression of the Judeo-Christian tradition.

My focus in this contribution, however, is not on official liturgical initiatives, but rather on what may be called a paraliturgy, i.e. a liturgy outside the normally approved Catholic rites and liturgies. More specifically, I wish to further explore the epiphenomenon of Catholics celebrating a Jewish Seder meal as part of their Holy Week ceremonies. Though this practice is not authorized (nor has it been officially rejected) by the Roman Catholic Church, it is becoming more popular in certain Catholic milieux. Usually such celebration happens on Maundy Thursday, the evening when Jesus gathered with his disciples to have his last supper before he was betrayed by Judas and captured by the Roman authorities. The assumption is that "Christian observance of this ritual meal celebrates not only our tra-

---

Synagogue) (12–21). He insisted that the synagogue be taken into consideration for an understanding of Christian worship. W.O.E. Oesterley's volume *The Jewish Background of the Christian Liturgy* (1925) was widely read. Frank Gavin's study *The Jewish Antecedents of the Christian Sacraments* (1928, reprinted in 1969) discussed the *berakah* (Hebrew blessing) as a source of the eucharistic prayer (59–98), The discovery of the ruins of both a synagogue and a house-church at Dura-Europos during excavations in modern Syria in 1932 brought excitement and perspective from archeologists to the study of both Jewish and Christian liturgy (Chiat and Mauck, 73–75)." See Mary Christine Athans, "A New Horizon for Liturgy," online article; http://www.jcrelations.net/Judaism_and_Catholic_Prayer.235.0.html (accessed 29 June 2015).

30 Matthew Myer Boulton, "Supersession or Subsession? Exodus Typology, the Christian Eucharist and the Jewish Passover Meal," *Scottish Journal of Theology* 66 (2013) 18–29.

31 On the Good Friday Prayer, see "Israel and the Church: Fulfillment Beyond Supersessionism?" with Didier Pollefeyt, in Marianne Moyaert and Didier Pollefeyt (eds.), *Never Revoked: Nostra Aetate as Ongoing Challenge for Jewish-Christian Dialogue*, Louvain Theological and Pastoral Monographs, 40 (Leuven: Peeters, 2010) 159–183.

32 Commission for the Relation with the Jews, *On the Correct Way to Present the Jews and Judaism in Preaching and Catechesis in the Roman Catholic Church*, 1985; www.vatican.va (accessed 30 June 2015).

dition of Christ's last supper but our own Jewish heritage which provided the context for Jesus' institution at the last supper."[33] What is more, many Catholics are convinced that this form of cross-riting is one way to expresses appreciation for Judaism as the soil in which Christianity took root.[34] It may even contribute to the reconciliatory process that was started during the Second Vatican Council. As Eugene Fisher explains:

> Because the seder, when properly done, communicates so effectively the essential narrative 'framing' of Jewish history and Jewish self-identity as a people, this can have a very positive impact on Catholic understanding of and respect for Judaism. Likewise, as the Council reminded Catholics, Jesus lived and died as a pious Jew of his time. So the seder can give Catholics a very necessary sense of the religious context within which Jesus taught.[35]

However well-intended, though, we should ask if Catholics ought to celebrate Seder meals. Is it appropriate for them to replicate this ritual that is so central to Jewish self-understanding?[36] Does this ritual reenactment of the 'hyphen' not take the Judeo-Christian continuity one step too far? We should ask if this cross-riting does justice to the theological uniqueness of both traditions and, connected with that, Catholics should ask if they are not at risk of Christianizing Judaism once again. When that happens, the term *Judeo-Christian* becomes very problematic.[37]

To come to a nuanced evaluation of Christian Seder meals, I begin by asking the following question. Seeing that one of the reasons why Catholics want to celebrate Seder meals is because it would help them to better understand the Jewish

---

33 Catholic Activity: The Seder Meal as a Christian Home Celebration: Preparing and Celebrating the Holy Thursday Meal; https://www.catholicculture.org/culture/liturgicalyear/activities/view.cfm?id=544 (accessed 30 June 2015).

34 This practice of Christians celebrating Seder meals as part of the Holy Week celebrations is not authorized by the Roman Catholic Church nor has it been officially rejected. It can be regarded as a sort of para-liturgy, which is a liturgy that happens outside of the normally approved Catholic rites and liturgies.

35 Eugene J. Fisher, "Seders in Catholic Parishes," *Sh'ma: Journal of Jewish Ideas* 29 (1999) 4–5.

36 It seems that Jewish voices are divided on this topic. Many Jews are highly critical of this phenomenon. However, some would support Christians celebrating Seder meals. Rabbi Klenicki even wrote a Haggadah for Christians. An important qualification of Klenicki's Haggadah is that it is intended for Christians celebrating the Seder meal with Jewish friends, i.e. as guests of the Jewish other. Rabbi Leon Klenicki/Myra Cohen Klenicki, *The Passover Celebration: a Haggadah Prepared for the Seder*, Introduction by Gabe Huck, Chicago: Liturgical Training Publications, 1980.

37 Clearly there are Jews who do not reject the possibility of Christians celebrating Seder meals. Some of the guidelines for Christian Seder meals have even been prepared in discussion with Jewish consultants.

roots of Christianity and would bring them closer to the Jewish Jesus, we must ask if this makes sense, *historically speaking*. What does historical evidence say about Jesus' Last Supper being a Seder meal? We must ask if in the first Century, before the destruction of the Temple, the custom existed to gather on the first night of Passover to enjoy a ceremonial meal with a fixed order of symbolic practices (Seder) and the ritual relating of the Exodus narrative (Haggadah).[38]

3.1 Historical questions

Passover is an eight day feast, which commemorates the liberation of Israel from Egypt (the Exodus).[39] This feast is inaugurated by a Seder meal, which is (usually) celebrated as a home ritual with family and friends. There is ritual food (which is not all to be eaten), songs, wine and prayer. As far as I can tell, most guidelines for Catholics celebrating a Seder (the ritualized meal that follows a fixed order) try to follow traditional Jewish ritual guidelines as written down in a Haggadah.[40] The Exodus from Egypt is recounted as a story about liberation from slavery and this story is ritually reenacted in and through the various symbols. There will be songs and prayers, lighting of candles, blessings, washing of hands and ritual food: the boiled egg, unleavened bread (*matzah*), the shank bone (reminding one of the sacrificed lamb), the salty water (that symbolizes the tears of affliction), the green herbs, *charoset* (a mixture of apple, almonds and, wine that points to the mortar the Israelite slaves used in construction), *maror* – the bitter herbs (as a reminder of the bitterness of slavery), four cups of wine (and an extra cup for Elijah), and the search for the *Afikoman* (the hidden piece of unleavened bread).

---

38 Joel Marcus, "Passover and Last supper Revisited," *New Testament Studies* 59 (2013) 303–324, here p. 304.

39 "The roots of the festival are found in Exodus 12, in which God instructs the Israelites to sacrifice a lamb at twilight on the 14th day of the Jewish month of Nisan, before the sun sets (Exodus 12:18). That night the Israelites are to eat the lamb with unleavened bread and bitter herbs. The lamb's blood should be swabbed on their doorposts as a sign. God, seeing the sign, will then "pass over" the houses of the Israelites (Exodus 12:13), while smiting the Egyptians with the tenth plague, the killing of the first-born sons. Exodus 12 commands the Israelites to repeat this practice every year, performing the sacrifice during the day and then consuming it after the sun has set." Jonathan Klawans, "Was Jesus' Last Supper a Passover Meal?" *Bible Review* 17 (2001) 24–33. *The article was first republished in Bible History Daily in October 2012*. Available online at: http://www.biblicalarchaeology.org/daily/people-cultures-in-the-bible/jesus-historical-jesus/was-jesus-last-supper-a-seder/(accessed 2 July 2015).

40 See https://www.catholicculture.org/culture/liturgicalyear/activities/view.cfm?id=544 (accessed 2 July 2015).

Catholics want to observe this Jewish ritual, which they believe was already in place at Jesus' time.[41] They want to share in an experience of Jesus and stay as close as possible to what he did. All of this, however, hinges upon the assumption that Jesus actually celebrated a Seder meal that closely resembles the one that exists today. Commenting on this phenomenon, Jonathan Klawans acknowledges that "in these times of ecumenism and general good feeling between Catholics and Jews, many people seem to find it reassuring to think that communion and the Passover Seder are historically related." However, he continues, "history is often more complex and perhaps a little less comforting than we might hope. We must be careful not to let our emotions get the better of us when we are searching for history."[42] We do not actually know if what Catholics have come to call the 'Last Supper' was a Seder meal as it is known today.[43]

---

41 Sometimes Catholics celebrate the Seder as dinner at home in the presence of their family. More often, however, they are invited to celebrate this special evening with their church community with a priest as the leader of the Seder meal. In the latter case the celebration usually does not happen in the Parish Church but elsewhere, e.g. a cafeteria. The presence of the priest, as the leader of the evening, tends to give the Seder meal a solemn nature as if it were a consecrated meal, which differs considerably from the joyous event Seder meals are meant to be according to Jewish traditions. This already points to the fact that even when Catholics are intent on staying faithful to the Jewishness of Seder meals (because they want to imitate Jesus more closely as he prepared for the cross and because they want to recognize the Jewish roots Christian liturgy), the meaning of the ritual of course changes, since the participants who are not Jewish bring their own Christian interpretations to the table and, willingly or not, redescribe the event. I shall return to this point a bit later.

42 Klawans, "Was Jesus' Last Supper a Seder?"

43 'Last' in the sense that there were no more earthly suppers to follow, but also in the sense that during his earthly life Jesus shared many meals with his disciples on a regular basis. Characteristic of Jesus' earthly life is that he regularly accepted invitations for "dinner." Jesus travelled around with his disciples without any fixed abode (Luke 9:58) and was therefore "dependent" to a certain extent on the hospitality of others. Aside from John's gospel, the other gospel writers relate that Jesus was a guest of Pharisees, sinners, and tax collectors. These stories refer to memories about the historical Jesus. Luke writes how Jesus accepted the invitation of a Pharisee three times (Luke 7:36-50; 11:37-52; 14:1-24). Levi, a tax collector, held a large banquet for Jesus. Jesus was reproached for being "a glutton and a drunkard, a friend of tax collectors and 'sinners'" (Matthew 11:19; cf. Luke 7:34). This image of Jesus is also confirmed in the gospel of Mark and is the reason why Raymond Collins gave Jesus the title of *The Man Who Came to Dinner* (Collins 2005: 172). But Jesus is not only a guest in the houses of others. He also takes on the role of host: "Blessed is the man who will eat at the feast in the kingdom of God" (Luke 14:15). In this invitation Jesus recalls the vision of Isaiah, which tells of a messianic banquet that God will give for all people on Mount Zion (Wildberger 1977: 373).

According to some scholars, it is possible to identify the Last supper as a Seder meal.[44] They argue that Jesus and his disciples ate together at Passover (see Luke 22) and point to the parallels between Jesus' Last Supper and a Seder meal: there is a sacrifice that is prepared in advance, there is wine and bread, blessings are said, Jesus teaches, and the evening ends with a closing hymn. These are all elements, which make it plausible to conclude that Jesus' Last Supper was a Passover meal.[45]

Most scholars, however, seem to argue against identifying the Last Supper and the Passover meal. They first of all point out that the key symbols of the Passover meal – the lamb and bitter herbs – were absent during Jesus' Last Supper; that the elements present – wine, bread and blessings – are actually part of any Jewish ritual meal (and we know Jesus partook in many of these). More importantly, however, they argue against identifying Jesus' Last Supper with a Seder meal because the latter, with its fixed order and accompanying Haggadah, only began to develop as a distinctive religious response to the crisis caused by the destruction of the Temple (70 CE).[46] The destruction of the Temple caused the Jewish community to formulate a "liturgical alternative to the old sacrificial rite, addressing simultaneously the difficult question of how to celebrate a festival of redemption in an age of foreign domination and oppression."[47] In any case, the Passover rituals before and after the destruction of the Temple differ dramatically.

In Jesus' time, Passover was one of the pilgrimage festivals revolving around the Temple and sacrifice. To celebrate Passover, Jews would have embarked on a journey to Jerusalem where they would sacrifice a lamb. This lamb recalls the lambs that were sacrificed by the Jews on the eve of their flight from Egypt. The blood of these lambs was used to mark the doorposts so that the angel of death

44 See for example Joel Marcus, "Passover and Last Supper Revisited," *New Testament Studies* 59 (2013) 303–324.

45 Joel Marcus follows this line of thought. He states that "all three Synoptic Gospels portray Jesus' Last Supper as a Passover meal and show him ritually distributing matzah and wine to his disciples at this meal and interpreting these elements symbolically and in sacrificial terms ('my body [given for you]...my blood shed on behalf of many'). Moreover, at least two out of the three Synoptics link the 'cup word' with the covenant established by Moses in the exodus when they show Jesus Echoing Exod 24.8, 'Behold the blood of the covenant...'" Joel Marcus, "Passover and Last Supper Revisited," *New Testament Studies* 59 (2013) 303–324, here pp. 312–313.

46 Lawrence A. Hoffman, "The Passover Meal in Jewish Tradition," in: Paul Bradshaw and Lawrence A. Hoffman (eds.), *Passover and Easter. Origin and History to Modern Times*, Two Liturgical Traditions vol. 5 (Notre Dame: University Of Notre Dame Press, 1999) 9–26, here p. 10.

47 Israel Y. Yuval, "Easter and Passover as Early Jewish-Christian Dialogue," in: Paul Bradshaw and Lawrence A. Hoffman (eds.), *Passover and Easter. Origin and History to Modern Times*, Two Liturgical Traditions vol. 5 (Notre Dame: University Of Notre Dame Press, 1999) 98–124, here p. 98.

would pass over their houses and spare their firstborn. The sacrificial aspect of the Passover meal – something which Christian theologies would later connect with Jesus' sacrificial death reenacted in the Eucharist – was central to pre-rabbinic Passover celebrations. We know that Jesus, as an observant Jew, participated in these festivities, together with his family (see Luke 2:41-42).

It was this way of celebrating Passover that changed radically after the destruction of the Temple, which was both a political and religious disaster (in Hebrew, a *churban*). The sacrifice of the lambs at the Temple became impossible, and in response to this impossibility Jewish communities began to develop a domestic ritual, which we now know as a Seder meal. The earliest account of this ritual with its fixed order and Haggadah can be found in the Mishnah Pesahim (chapter 10), edited around 200 CE. According to Baruch Bokser, the account of the Seder meal in the Mishnah is part of the "the general early rabbinic reinterpretation of cultic rites and legitimization of extra-Temple means of religious expression."[48]

Though we do not know the precise type of meal that Jesus' Last Supper was, we can say that "there is virtually no ground to assume that Jesus would have practised the rituals described in later rabbinic literature."[49] In brief, the Seder meal was *never part of a shared Judeo-Christian tradition* in the first place. As a consequence, celebrating a Christian Seder meal will, for one, not help to be closer to Jesus during his last evening, nor will it help to better understand the Jewish origins of the Eucharist.

3.2 Is it appropriate for Catholics to celebrate Seder meals?

In light of the above historical evidence, we need to ask if it is appropriate for Catholics to replicate this ritual that is so obviously at the heart of Jewish self-understanding. To my mind, the answer to this question should be no; I would even argue that despite all good intentions Catholics celebrating Seder meals bear testimony to the problem of what Daniel Joslyn-Siemiatkoski calls latent anti-Judaism.[50] Let me elaborate on this.

48 Baruch M. Bokser, *The Origins of the Seder: The Passover Rite and Early Rabbinic Literature*, 4.
49 Joshua Kulp, "The Origins of the Seder and the Haggadah," *CBR* 4 (2005) 109–134, here p. 113.
50 Daniel Joslyn-Siemiatkoski, "Comparative Theology and the Status of Judaism: Hegemony and Reversals," in: Francis Clooney (ed.), *The New Comparative Theology: Interreligious Insights from the Next Generation* (London: T&T Clark, 2010) 88–108.

Anti-Judaic discourse is complex; it is not merely a surface problem that can be easily removed through some uncomplicated and straightforward measures. Supersessionist theology was for centuries an undisputed element of Christian doctrine in both the Western and Eastern churches. For two thousand years, Christianity cultivated an anti-Jewish polemic, traces of which can already be found in the gospels. That polemic was pursued by various Church Fathers and imprinted itself upon the collective memory of Christian 'civilization' through liturgy, prayer, sermons, but also through art, sculptures, illuminated manuscripts, popular culture, theater, and music.[51] Far from it being merely a surface issue, anti-Jewish discourse has seeped deeply to the core of Christian culture. History teaches us that these theologies were translated into concrete political actions, e.g. the marginalization, exclusion, expulsion and even killing of Jews. They are part of the collective memory of Christian identity; as a result, anti-Jewish biases often go unnoticed because they are so pervasive. Vatican II therefore undoubtedly initiated an important change in Catholic-Jewish relations that was affirmed in many post-conciliar initiatives. However, it will probably take more than a couple of decades of dialogue to really move beyond anti-Jewish patterns of thought, which have penetrated the pores of Christian thinking. In what follows, I will argue that Christian Seders are an expression of such latent anti-Judaism. This shows itself in a twofold manner: (1) in the very assumption that the ritual celebrated in Jewish communities today resembles the ritual celebrated by Jesus and his disciples; (2) in the way Catholics in celebrating the Seder meal treat this Jewish ritual as a resource to enhance Christian self-understanding without much concern for its meaning for contemporary Jewish communities.

(1) For most of Christian history, the Church seemed to believe that Judaism, because it 'failed' to recognize Jesus as the prophesied Messiah, lost its reason for existence. Moreover, the general assumption was that Judaism, after the destruction of the Second Temple by the Romans and the expulsion from Jerusalem, had come to an end. It still existed, but no longer developed.[52] These theological assumptions made it difficult, if not impossible, for the Church to recognize Judaism as a vibrant tradition, with its own symbolic practices and textual hermeneutics. Judaism *after the coming of Christ* (and the destruction of the Temple)

---

51 J. Boonstra et al., *Antisemitism. A History Portrayed* (Amsterdam: Anne Frank Foundation, 1993). See also, Emmanuel Nathan, "Memories of the Veil: The Covenantal Contrasts in Christian-Jewish Encounter," in: P. Carstens, N.P. Lemche & T.B. Hasselbalch (eds.), *Cultural Memory in Biblical Exegesis* (Piscataway, NJ: Gorgias Press, 2013) 343–365.
52 See Rochelle L. Millen, "Land, Nature and Judaism: Post-Holocaust Reflections," in: Didier Pollefeyt (ed.), *Holocaust and Nature* (Münster: Lit, 2013) 86–104, here p. 91.

was viewed as an anachronism. There was no provision within Christianity to reckon with further developments within living Judaism. Rabbinic Judaism brought about the replacement of: Temple by Synagogue, sacrificial ceremonies by study, prayer and home rituals, and the *Kohen* (priest) by the Rabbi. On the contrary, for Christianity Judaism had become a relic, something that belonged to the past, its meaning frozen in time. I see traces of this line of reasoning in the practice of Christian Seders.

The ritual guidelines on which most Catholic communities (and the same goes for Protestant communities) seem to rely are rather traditional.[53] This Christian tendency to stay close to the orthodox Jewish ritual guidelines is inspired by a longing to be authentic, to preserve the integrity of the Jewish ritual and thus to *affectively* reenact what they understand Jesus did at the eve before his death, and what Christians think Jews have continued to do throughout their history. Apart from this reasoning being historically incorrect, we are confronted here with a more problematic assumption, namely that *today's Jewish tradition is more or less the same as that to which Jesus adhered*. The assumption that we can basically project a ritual celebrated in the 21st century by (more traditional) Jewish communities into 1st century Palestinian Judaism amounts to saying *once more* that Judaism is an almost ahistoric tradition frozen in time. There is no acknowledgment of how Jewish self-understanding developed after the fall of the Temple, of rabbinic Judaism, the centrality of the Mishnah and Talmud, of the different geographical contexts in which Judaism took root, the differences between Sephardic and Ashkenazi Judaism, the build-up of dramatic events it was confronted with, e.g. the pogroms, the expulsion from Spain, the Shoah, and the State of Israel, the different strands in modern Judaism (Orthodox, Conservative, Reform, etc.). All of that can simply be put between brackets, because the Judaism of today is the same as the Judaism of yesterday (so the thinking goes), and that is why Catholics can just take a ritual of contemporary Judaism and project it back into Jesus' time.

(2) Catholics celebrating Seder meals engage in a practice known as *cultural appropriation*. Cultural appropriation points to the phenomenon of one cultural group adopting artefacts, symbols, rituals, etc. from another cultural group with the additional qualification of a power imbalance between both groups. Because of this power imbalance, both groups do not have equal access to each other's cultural resources. Those in power can decide what to take or not and, what is more, they also control the meaning ascribed to the adopted artefact, symbol, ritual, etc. Often the culture being taken from finds itself in a situation of margin-

53 https://www.catholicculture.org/culture/liturgicalyear/activities/view.cfm?id=544; http://www.crivoice.org/seder.html; https://www.wf-f.org/Seder.html (accessed 2 July 2015).

alization or oppression. Due to this power imbalance, we do not speak about a mere cultural exchange as would be the case between cultural groups that relate in a more or less symmetrical way, but rather about wrongful cultural appropriation, which can cause harm or offense. Cultural appropriation is especially problematic when it involves the adoption of a symbolic practice that is central to the identity of the culture to which it belongs. Its problematic character is often hidden under the guise of being a homage or a token of deep respect.

When Catholics celebrate a Seder meal and claim that this is also a manner of expressing their deep reverence for Judaism, they overlook the historical power imbalance between Catholics and Jews and the violence that sprang from it. For centuries Jews suffered under the colonial power of a "violent European dominated Christianity."[54] Christians were in control; they were the majority religion supported and enhanced by the political system. Jews were at best tolerated. Often, however, they were socially excluded, persecuted, and sometimes killed. Generally speaking, Jewish tradition was incorporated into a Christian hegemonic framework: Christianity as the fulfillment of Jewish prophecies, the Church as the replacement of Israel, the wandering Jew as visible sign of God's punishment contrasted with God's eternal love for the followers of Christ. Through this binary structure, Judaism was always the negative counter-part of Christianity. In this process Jewish self-understanding was distorted, Jews were harmed in their right to self-definition: "[they] were depicted either as witnesses of opponents of a victorious Christianity but always as representatives of disputed principles, never as subjects of their own self-defined historical narratives."[55] Jews became Christ-killers, host-desecrators, a cursed people, etc. And it was these negative anti-Jewish depictions that were ritually staged during Holy Week. Too often the Jewish people have had to celebrate their Passover in fear of what Christians might do to them.

In light of this reality, Catholics celebrating a Seder meal are guilty of cultural appropriation (not of cultural exchange, and certainly not of rediscovering the Jewish roots of Christianity). It is a form of trespassing: they take and redefine a ritual practice that belongs to the heart of the religious life of Jewish tradition, which they have oppressed for centuries. Once again Christians are in control: a Jewish ritual is used to enhance Christian tradition without much concern for what that ritual means for Jewish communities today. Since Jews are typically not

---

54 Marc H. Ellis, "After The Holocaust and Israel: On Liturgy and the Postcolonial (Jewish) Prophetic in the New Diaspora," in: Claudio Carvalhaes (ed.), *Liturgy in Postcolonial Perspectives: Only One is Holy* (New York: Palgrave Macmillan, 2015) 45–70, here p. 50.

55 Susannah Heschel, "Jewish Studies as Counterhistory," 105.

present during such Christians Seders, once again Christians are writing Jews out of their own story. In the following, I want to press this issue further by highlighting the parts from the Haggadah that Catholics, in their desire to be 'authentic', decide *not* to tell when they celebrate a Seder meal.

3.3 The Story not Told and How it Affects Reconciliation

The affective dimension of Catholics celebrating Seder meals is obvious: the ritual and dramatic reenactment of the Last Supper (as a Seder meal) would put them in closer touch with Jesus and his disciples during their last night together. They desire to retrace the origins of the Christian movement, and through imitation to affectively remember what once happened.[56] This practice of cross-riting is also meant to exhale a spirit of dialogue and reconciliation. If Catholics, during the process of the parting of the ways, redefined Jewish ritual practices in a supersessionist framework (discontinuity), then by celebrating the Seder they give liturgical expression to the renewed bond between both traditions (continuity).

To me it seems, however, that Catholics who partake in this form of cross-riting as an effort to redress the violent history of Christian-Jewish relations, try to *go back to a time when 'we' were all Jews.* Would it be too far-fetched to suggest that Catholic Seders symbolize a desire to return to innocence, before the parting of the ways and before anti-Jewish violence? It is an expression of a Judeo-Christian bond, before rivalry, polemics and the imbalance of power. Celebrating a Seder meal, Catholics can *pretend (make believe and play act) to share with Jesus (the Jew) and his disciples the Jewish experience of oppression and liberation.* In doing so, Catholics seem to be saying *your experience was Jesus' experience and his experience is our experience*, and that is why we can, and will, celebrate this Seder meal.

This return to innocence, however, is not all that innocent. The speaker's benefit of this ritual act enables Catholics to look away from the fact that *they did not share* the Jewish experience(s) of oppression, but were rather complicit in Jewish suffering throughout most of Church history. Catholics are able to look away from and confront their complicity in Jewish suffering, because they actually control the way a Catholic Seder meal is celebrated and how it is enacted, because there are no Jews present at this ritual. Even though they try to stay as faithful to the traditional Jewish ritual, in effect Catholics do decide how they tell the Passover story, what they include and exclude. This becomes obvious when

56 Frank Senn, "Should Christians Celebrate the Passover?" 195–197.

we turn to the way Jewish communities celebrate Seder meals today and ask what part Catholics decide not to celebrate.

In Jewish tradition, the Seder meal is not just a commemoration of a past event, the emphasis is rather on the present. Even if the Seder meal with all its symbolic practices enables a ritual reiteration and reenactment, its meaning cannot be reduced to that of remembrance; it is an active retelling, for it is said "In every generation each individual is bound to regard himself as if he had gone forth from Egypt personally." Jews are called upon to make Passover personal and contemporary. They have to live through the events of the Exodus as a contemporary event. The Passover night was a night of fear and terror, before it brought liberation and redemption. These events did not happen in some far away past, they continue to happen now. Jews celebrating the Seder meal are involved in a process of "personal identification in the here and now". Carole Balin explains that "[e]ach participant is adjured to breathe new life into the Haggadah, and Jews have done so by imbuing its pages with the ideas and concerns of their age. Thus each printed Haggadah serves as a barometer of sorts – registering fluctuations and gauging the mood of a particular Jewish community in its unique time and place in history."[57] That is why it happens that new symbols and practices are added to recontextualize and reactualize Passover, and these new symbols and practices reflect the concerns of contemporary Jewish communities.

Today there exist numerous Haggadoth which guide Jews in the process of re-presenting and reliving the dual experience of slavery and redemption. This testifies to the fact that Jewish ritual traditions continue to develop to this day in an ongoing process of recontextualization. As Debra Nusbaum-Cohen explains "[t]he central Exodus story is re-told, with specific symbolic foods, but around that there is plenty of room – which we Jews have long filled – for a multiplicity of interpretations."[58] In contemporary Judaism, both the Shoah and the establishment of the State of Israel especially have been given a prominent place in shaping the Haggadah. There exist numerous Haggadoth relating the exodus narrative in connection to the Shoah. Sometimes the oppression during the Shoah is connected to the redemption experienced in the erection of the state Israel, as a safe haven for Jews. As Carole Balin explains: "Given its central and characteristic theme of servitude-redemption – a movement from degradation to glory – the

57 Carole B. Balin, "The Modern Transformation of the Ancient Passover Haggadah," in: Paul Bradshaw and Lawrence A. Hoffman (eds.), *Passover and Easter. Origin and History to Modern Times*, Two Liturgical Traditions vol. 5 (Notre Dame: University Of Notre Dame Press, 1999) 189–213, here p. 189.

58 Debra Nusbaum-Cohen, "Christianizing the Passover Seder," *Sh'ma* 20 (1999) 1–2, here p. 1.

Haggadah has proved to be an ideal setting for proclaiming such a linkage. The traditional Haggadah retells the tragedy of Egyptian bondage *and* the *connected* divine deliverance of the People Israel; modern Haggadahs use it also to retell, in sequence, the tragedy of the Holocaust (modern-day servitude) *and* the Jews' connected triumph, again in the Land, this time by the founding there of the State Israel (modern-day redemption)."[59]

This story, however, is not being told, reflected upon, nor celebrated in Catholic Seders, which prefer to go back to an 'innocent shared past' (which was never really shared in the first place). Catholics prefer a ritual enactment of the Judeo-Christian tradition which does not oblige them to confront the part they have played in two thousand years of anti-Judaism and in the Shoah.[60] They prefer an innocent past in which they can share Jesus' Jewish experience of Passover. This, however will not bring reconciliation. The latter asks for confrontation with the past, recognition of the hegemonic tendencies of Christianity and the acceptance to no longer write Jews out from their story. *Rewriting* that Jewish story, then, is certainly *not* the solution.

Conclusion

I began this contribution by partly coming to the rescue of the notion of a Judeo-Christian tradition. Recognizing the Jewish background of the Christian tradition, theologians have started to reread Jesus' life, the history of the early Christian communities, the gospels and the Pauline letters through Jewish eyes.[61] This has not only lead to a fuller and more nuanced understanding of Christianity, but also to the formulation of a theological alternative for anti-Jewish superses-

---

59 Carole B. Balin, "The Modern Transformation of the Ancient Passover Haggadah," 199.

60 Although a distinction can (and should) be made between Christian anti-Judaism and Nazi anti-Semitism, it is clear that the Nazi ideology could never have infiltrated the heart of European civilization in the way that it did without the long history of Christian anti-Jewish views and anti-Jewish acts of violence that resulted. It goes without saying that Christian anti-Judaism quite simply constituted the soil in which Nazism could take root and ultimately led to the destruction of two-thirds of European Jews.

61 See for example John Shelby Spong, *Liberating the Gospels: Reading the Bible with Jewish Eyes: Freeing Jesus from 2000 Years of Misunderstanding* (San Francisco, CA: HarperSanFrancisco, 1996); Beatrice Bruteau, *Jesus through Jewish Eyes: Rabbis and Scholars Engage an Ancient Brother in a New Conversation* (Maryknoll: Orbis Books, 2001); James H. Charlesworth (ed.), *Jesus' Jewishness: Exploring the Place of Jesus within Early Judaism* (New York: The American Interfaith Institute Crossroad, 1991).

sionist theologies that had been dominant throughout most of Christian history.[62] Despite all the critical considerations I have listed in my contribution, I would still want to emphasize all the good this notion has brought to Christian-Jewish relations. In light of two thousand years of Christian anti-Judaism and the tragedy of Nazi anti-Semitism, the commitment of the Catholic Church, since Vatican II, to dialogue and reconciliation, should not be discarded. The recognition of the Jewish roots of Christianity is unmistakably an expression of appreciation. The one-sided story of discontinuity, which practically erased the Jewish origins of Christian tradition is being corrected; the continuity between both traditions symbolized in the notion Judeo-Christianity is now being affirmed.

Nevertheless, the notion of a Judeo-Christian tradition has its limits, which the practice of Christian Seder meals makes amply clear. First of all, the notion of 'Judeo-Christian' seems to be appreciative of Judaism to the extent that Christianity *originated from Judaism*. Judaism is recognized as the soil in which Christianity took root, but less as a living tradition that continued to develop. From a Christian perspective, the focus on the Jewish roots of Christian tradition is both understandable and important. But the notion of a Judeo-Christian tradition runs the risk of *only appreciating Judaism* in so far as it contributes to the Christian storyline. It may even lead to out-narrating the Jews from that storyline. Catholic Seders are an extreme example thereof.

Second, the notion of a Judeo-Christian tradition seems to express a rather harmonious bond between both traditions that covers up the historical reality of anti-Jewish violence. It avoids the difficult question of asking how Christians were involved in causing Jewish suffering. It is an embrace that is made too easily, and for that reason it is suspicious. Here too, Catholic Seders are examples, since they create the 'illusion' of a shared Jewish experience (Jesus' Last Supper as a Seder meal celebrating Passover), which distorts the reality that for centuries Jews celebrated Passover in fear. To skip over this history and to return to an innocent time (Jesus celebrating a Seder meal), is offensive and will not contribute to reconciliation.

Third, I would argue that when it comes to celebrating Seder meals, Catholics should uphold the principle of theology after the Shoah: namely, that such overtures should be dialogical and happen in the presence of the Jewish other. In view of centuries of power imbalances and Christian anti-Jewish violence, it

---

62 See also subsequent documents *Guidelines and Suggestions for Implementing the Conciliar Declaration Nostra Aetate* (1974); *Notes on the Correct Way to Present the Jews and Judaism in Preaching and Catechesis* (1985); *We Remember: A Reflection on the Shoah* (1998); Pontifical Biblical Commission, *The Jewish People and Their Sacred Scriptures in the Christian Bible* (2001).

would only be right that Catholics accept the fact that the Passover Seder is a dynamic Jewish ritual still celebrated by Jews today. If Catholics are to partake in this ritual, it should be as guests entering into the ritual realm of the Jewish other. Though (minor) adjustments may be made because of the presence of guests, usually the liturgical standards of the home (Jewish) tradition will be followed. The aim of this form of cross-riting will then not be to recreate Jesus' Last Supper, but rather a deep learning from Judaism as it exists nowadays and continues to develop in response to contemporary challenges.

Bibliography

Athans, Mary Christine. "A New Horizon for Liturgy." Online article; http://www.jcrelations.net/Judaism_and_Catholic_Prayer.235.0.html (accessed 29 June 2015).

Balin, Carole B. "The Modern Transformation of the Ancient Passover Haggadah." *Passover and Easter. Origin and History to Modern Times*. Ed. Paul Bradshaw and Lawrence A. Hoffman. Two Liturgical Traditions 5. Notre Dame: University of Notre Dame Press, 1999. 189–213.

Becker, Adam H. and Annette Y. Reed, eds. *The Ways that Never Parted: Jews and Christians in Late Antiquity and the Early Middle Ages*. Tübingen: Mohr Siebeck, 2003.

Bokser, Baruch M. *The Origins of the Seder: the Passover Rite and Early Rabbinic Judaism*. Berkeley: Berkeley University of California Press, 1984.

Boonstra, J. et al. *Antisemitism. A History Portrayed.* Amsterdam: Anne Frank Foundation, 1993.

Boulton, Matthew Myer. "Supersession or Subsession? Exodus Typology, the Christian Eucharist and the Jewish Passover Meal." *Scottish Journal of Theology* 66 (2013): 18–29.

Boys, Mary C. *Redeeming our Sacred Story.* New York: Paulist Press, 2013.

Boyarin, Daniel. *Border Lines: the Partition of Judeo-Christianity*. Philadelphia: University of Pennsylvania, 2004.

Bristow, Edward W. *No Religion is an Island: The Nostra Aetate Dialogues.* New York: Fordham University Press, 1998.

Bruteau, Beatrice. *Jesus through Jewish Eyes: Rabbis and Scholars Engage an Ancient Brother in a New Conversation*. Maryknoll: Orbis Books, 2001.

Cernera, Anthony. *Examining Nostra Aetate after 40 Years: Catholic-Jewish Relations in our Time*. Fairfield: Sacred Heart University Press, 2007.

Charlesworth, James H., ed. *Jesus' Jewishness: Exploring the Place of Jesus within Early Judaism*. New York: The American Interfaith Institute Crossroad, 1991.

Cohen, Arthur. *The Myth of the Judeo-Christian Tradition*. New York: Harper and Row, 1957.

Pontifical Commission for Religious Relations with the Jews. *Guidelines and Suggestions for Implementing the Conciliar Declaration 'Nostra Aetate' (n.4)*. 1965; http://www.vatican.va/roman_curia/pontifical_councils/chrstuni/relations-jews-docs/rc_pc_chrstuni_doc_19741201_nostra-aetate_en.html (accessed 15 August, 2015).

Pontifical Commission for Religious Relations with the Jews. *On the Correct Way to Present the Jews and Judaism in Preaching and Catechesis in the Roman(Catholic Church*, 1985. http://www.vatican.va/roman_curia/pontifical_councils/chrstuni/relations-jews-docs/rc_pc_chrstuni_doc_19820306_jews-judaism_en.html (accessed 30 June 2015).

O'Collins, Raymond. *The Man Who Came to Dinner*, in Reimund Bieringer, Gilbert Van Belle & Joseph Verheyden (ed.), *Luke and his Readers.* Festschrift Adelbert Denaux (BETL, 182), Leuven:Peeters, 2005, 151-172.
Connely, John. *From Enemy to Brother: The Revolution in Catholic Teaching on the Jews 1933–1965.* Cambridge: Cambridge University Press, 2012.
Cunningham, Philip A. "Oberammergau: A Case Study of Passion Plays." *Pondering the Passion. What's at Stake for Christians and Jews?* Ed. Philip A. Cunningham. Oxford: Rowman and Littlefield, 2004.
D'Costa, Gavin. *Vatican II: Catholic Teachings on Jews and Muslims.* Oxford: Oxford University Press, 2014.
Dunn, James. D.G. *Jews and Christians: The Parting of the Ways A.D. 70 to 135.* Grand Rapids: Eerdmans, 1992.
Ellis, Marc H. "After The Holocaust and Israel: On Liturgy and the Postcolonial (Jewish) Prophetic in the New Diaspora." *Liturgy in Postcolonial Perspectives: Only One is Holy.* Ed. Claudio Carvalhaes. New York: Palgrave Macmillan, 2015. 45–70.
Fisher, Eugene J. "Seders in Catholic Parishes." *Sh'ma: Journal of Jewish Ideas* 29 (1999): 4–5.
Heschel, Susannah. "Jewish Studies as Counterhistory." *Insider/Outsider. American Jews and Multiculturalism.* Ed. David Biale, Michael Galchinsky, and Susannah Heschel. Berkeley, University of California Press, 1998. 102–104.
Heschel, Susannah. *The Aryan Jesus: Christian Theologians and the Bible in Nazi Germany.* Maryknoll: Orbis, 2010.
Hoffman, Lawrence A. "The Passover Meal in Jewish Tradition." *Passover and Easter. Origin and History to Modern Times.* Ed. Paul Bradshaw and Lawrence A. Hoffman. Two Liturgical Traditions 5. Notre Dame: University of Notre Dame Press, 1999. 9–26.
Joslyn-Siemiatkoski, Daniel. "Comparative Theology and the Status of Judaism: Hegemony and Reversals." *The New Comparative Theology: Interreligious Insights from the Next Generation.* Ed. Francis Clooney. London: T&T Clark, 2010. 88–108.
Klawans, Jonathan. "Was Jesus' Last Supper a Passover Meal?" *Bible Review* 17 (2001): 24–33. Republished in *Bible History Daily in October*, 2012. http://www.biblicalarchaeology.org/daily/people-cultures-in-the-bible/jesus-historical-jesus/was-jesus-last-supper-a-seder/ (accessed 2 July 2015).
Klenicki, Rabbi Leon and Myra Cohen Klenicki. *The Passover Celebration: a Haggadah Prepared for the Seder.* Introduction by Gabe Huck. Chicago: Liturgical Training Publications, 1980.
Kulp, Joshua. "The Origins of the Seder and the Haggadah." *CBR* 4 (2005): 109–134.
Lamdan, Neville and Alberto Melloni. *Nostra Aetate: Origins, Promulgation, Impact on Jewish-Catholic Relations. Proceedings of the International Conference Jerusalem, 30 October – 1 November, 2005.* Münster: Lit, 2005.
Langer, Ruth. "The Liturgical Parting(s) of the Ways: A Preliminary Foray." *A Living Tradition: On the Intersection of Liturgical History and Pastoral Practice.* Ed. David A. Pitt et. al. Collegeville: Liturgical Press, 2012. 43–58.
Marcus, Joel. "Passover and Last Supper Revisited." *New Testament Studies* 59 (2013): 303–324.
Merback, Mitchell B. *Pilgrimage and Pogrom: Violence, Memory and Visual Culture at the Host-Miracle Shrines of Germany and Austria.* Chicago: University of Chicago Press, 2012.
Metz, Johannes Baptist. *The Emergent Church.* New York: Crossroad, 1981.
Millen, Rochelle L. "Land, Nature and Judaism: Post-Holocaust Reflections." *Holocaust and Nature.* Ed. Didier Pollefeyt. Münster: Lit, 2013. 86–104.

Moyaert, Marianne. "Who is the Suffering Servant? A Comparative Theological Reading of Isaiah 53 after the Shoah." *Comparative Theology: Insights for Systematic Theological Reflection*. Ed. Michelle Voss Roberts. New York: Fordham Press, forthcoming.

Moyaert, Marianne and Didier Pollefeyt. "Israel and the Church: Fulfillment beyond Supersessionism?" *Never Revoked: Nostra Aetate as Ongoing Challenge for Jewish-Christian Dialogue*. Ed. Marianne Moyaert and Didier Pollefeyt. Louvain Theological and Pastoral Monographs 40. Leuven: Peeters, 2010. 159–183.

Moyaert, Marianne and Didier Pollefeyt, eds. *Never Revoked: Nostra Aetate as Ongoing Challenge for Jewish-Christian Dialogue*. Louvain Theological and Pastoral Monographs 40. Leuven: Peeters, 2010.

Nathan, Emmanuel. "Memories of the Veil: The Covenantal Contrasts in Christian-Jewish Encounter." *Cultural Memory in Biblical Exegesis*. Ed. P. Carstens, N.P. Lemche, and T.B. Hasselbalch. Piscataway, NJ: Gorgias Press, 2013. 343–365.

Neusner, Jacob. *Jews and Christians: The Myth of a Common Tradition*. London: SCM Press; Philadelphia: Trinity Press International, 1991.

Newman, Barbara. "The Passion of the Jews of Prague: The Pogrom of 1389 and the Lessons of a Medieval Parody." *Church History* 81.1 (March 2012): 1–26.

Nussbaum-Cohen, Debra. "Christianizing the Passover Seder." *Sh'ma: Journal of Jewish Ideas* 20 (1999): 1–2.

Oesterreicher, John M. *The Rediscovery of Judaism: A Re-examination of the Conciliar Statement on the Jews*. Orange: Seton Hall University, 1971.

Schaff, Phikip (ed.), *Nicene and Post-Nicene Fathers*. Second Series, vol IV: Athanasius: Select Works and Letters. New York: Cosimo, 2007.

Senn, Frank. "Should Christians Celebrate the Passover." *Passover and Easter: The Symbolic Structuring of Sacred Seasons*. Ed. Paul F. Bradshaw and Lawrence A. Hoffman. Notre Dame: University of Notre Dame Press, 1999. 183–205.

Silk, Mark. "Notes on the Judeo-Christian Tradition in America." *American Quarterly* 36 (1984): 66–85.

Soulen, Kendall. "Israel and the Church." *Christianity in Jewish Terms*. Ed. Tikva Frymer-Kensky, David Novak, Michael Signer, and David Sandmel. Boulder: Westview, 2000. 167–174.

Spong, John Shelby. *Liberating the Gospels: Reading the Bible with Jewish Eyes: Freeing Jesus from 2000 Years of Misunderstanding*. San Francisco, CA: HarperSanFrancisco, 1996.

Stewart-Sykes, Alistair. *The Lamb's High Feast: Melito, Peri Pascha and the Quartodeciman Paschal Liturgy at Sardis*. Leiden: Brill, 1998.

Unterseher, Lisa A. *The Mark of Cain and the Jews: Augustine's Theology of Jews and Judaism*. Early Christian Studies 9. Piscataway, NJ: Gorgias Press, 2009.

Vlach, Michael. *The Church as a Replacement of Israel: An Analysis of Supersessionism*. Edition Israelogie (EDIS) 2. Frankfurt: Peter Lang, 2009a.

Vlach, Michael. "Various Forms of Replacement Theology." *The Master's Seminary Journal* 20 (2009b): 5769.

Wildberger, Hans "*Das Freudenmahl auf dem Zion. Erwägungen zu Jes. 25,6–8,* " *Theologische Zeitschrift* 33 (1977) 373–383.

Yuval, Israel Y. "Easter and Passover as Early Jewish-Christian Dialogue." *Passover and Easter. Origin and History to Modern Times*. Ed. Paul Bradshaw and Lawrence A. Hoffman. Two Liturgical Traditions 5. Notre Dame: University of Notre Dame Press, 1999. 98–124.

Christoph Schmidt

9 Rethinking the Modern Canon of Judaism – Christianity – Modernity in Light of the Post-Secular Relation

I

The debate between Jürgen Habermas and Cardinal Josef Ratzinger in Munich in 2004 on a new post-secular relation between secular society and religion beyond mutual delegitimization[1] can be read as a demand for an alternative reconstruction of the classical enlightened canon of modernity. This canon, created at the end of the 18th century by Gotthold Ephraim Lessing, was supposed to represent the history of freedom in the diachronic succession of Judaism, Christianity and its fulfillment in modern enlightened culture. The coming realm of freedom was supposed to be the political realization of the Christian religious hope for the kingdom of God. Thus modernity created a specific eschatological form of political theology whose claim to be the fulfillment and dissolution of Christianity resembled all too markedly the classical Christian claim, namely, to be the eschatological fulfillment and dissolution of Judaism. Religion in this form was always already dissolved as the secular truth and thus was not a possible partner for dialogue.

I shall argue that the post-secular relation between modern secular society and religion not only presupposes another form of canonic succession of Judaism, Christianity and Modernity beyond this double eschatological mechanism, but also turns against any attempt at total detachment of these elements from each other in the various strategies of a (post) modern Gnosis, typical for Adolph

1 J. Habermas, "On the Relations Between the Secular Liberal State and Religion. Pope Benedict XVI: Prepolitical Moral Foundations of a Free Republic," in: H. de Vries and L. Sullivan, *Political Theologies. Public Religions in a Post-Secular Word*, New York, 2006. The problem of the modern canon is not only due to the debate on post-secularity, but it has become necessary today because of the new Neo Gnostic tendency to dismiss with the Old Testament, articulated by: N. Slenczka, "Die Kirche und das Alte Testament," in: *Marburger Jahrbuch für Theologie* XXV (2013).

von Harnack,[2] Eric Voegelin[3] and Hans Blumenberg.[4] By redefining the relation between secularity and religion, the "post-secular" thus opens the horizon for a different constitution of the enlightened canon beyond political eschatology and political Gnosis, which both affects and is influenced by modern Judaism. Modernity is thus the third player in the challenge to rethink the relation between Judaism and Christianity.

In a first step the Habermas–Ratzinger debate will be presented in a short summary (1). An analysis of the specific eschatological mechanism determining enlightened political theology will follow (2), in order to explain the logic of the modern canon between this eschatological mechanism and the effects of orthodox refusal against this mechanism. (3) The reconstruction of the Gnostic response to the crisis of modernity and its canon (4) will serve as the point of departure for the different forms of reconstruction of a post-secular and open type of modern canonicity (5) creating a balance between diachronic succession and synchronic dialogue.

II

The German philosopher Jürgen Habermas had already considered the necessity of a "*critique of pure secular reason*" some years before the famous debate with Cardinal Ratzinger. In 2001 he pointed to the double threat of a radical naturalizing of the mind and a process of dissolution of social relations, arguing in favor of a post-secular culture which would do justice to the continued existence of religious communities in an ever more secular world.[5] By referring to Kant's "Religion within the Boundaries of Reason alone" (1793) he offered a formula which allowed for the coexistence of a religious world view and modern autonomy: "God remains only a 'God of free men', as long as we do not even up the absolute difference between Creator and creature. (...) This Creator, because he is the God of Creation and Redemption, does not have to operate according to natural laws or according to the rules of a code like a technician. The voice of God which calls men into life communicates from the beginning with a universe which is morally

2 A. von Harnack, *Marcion. Das Evangelium vom fremden Gott*, Leipzig 1921.
3 E. Voegelin, *The New Science of Politics. An Introduction*, Chicago 1952.
4 H. Blumenberg, *The Legitimacy of the Modern Age*, Massachusetts 1985.
5 Jürgen Habermas, *Glauben und Wissen, Dankesrede für den Friedenspreis des deutschen Buchhandels*, 2001, in http://www.glasnost.de/docs01/011014habermas.html.

sensitive."[6] Although Habermas, in the Munich debate three years later, seemed to be concerned primarily about any attempt to question the autonomous foundations of secular society,[7] he nevertheless considered the possibility of a crisis of this society, which, due to globalization of the market and a progressing atomization of the citizens, would no longer be able to reproduce the value system it relies on, namely, its most important value: solidarity. He returned then to the demand for a post-secular design of modern culture, including the religious attitude, the acceptance of modern science and the premises of the constitution, together with a new secular attitude towards religion which has kept these values alive over the centuries. This new attitude, however, would demand a correction of the classical enlightened attitude towards religion which tended to delegitimize the metaphysical concept of its truth. "In Post-secular society, the realization that the modernization of public consciousness takes hold of and reflexively alters religious as well as secular mentalities in staggered phases is gaining acceptance. If together they understand the secularization of society to be a complementary learning process, both sides can, for cognitive reasons, take seriously each other's contributions to controversial themes in the public sphere."[8]

This *post-secular* understanding thus developed by the major representative of modern enlightened critical theory pleaded for a new attitude of both secular society and religion, beyond the classical strategies of mutual de-legitimization.

In fact, Habermas did not have to wait for the ecclesial response, since the church had basically formulated its response 40 years before, in Vatican II. "Libertas non datur sine veritate" was the formula promoted by Cardinal Woytila at

---

6 Ibid., 7.

7 J. Habermas, "On the Relation Between the Secular Liberal State and Religion," in: H. de Vries and L. Sullivan, *Political Theologies*, New York 2006, 254: "From this it does not follow that the liberal state is incapable of reproducing its motivational preconditions out of its own secular resources. Of course, the motives for citizens' participation in political opinion- and will-formation draw upon ethical conceptions of life as well as cultural forms of life. But democratic practices develop their own political dynamic."

8 J. Habermas, "On the Relations Between the Secular Liberal State and Religion," *Political Theologies*,258. Habermas returns to many of these motives in his lecture: "Politics and Religion," published in: F.W. Graf and H. Meier: *Politik und Religion – Zur Diagnose der Gegenwart*, München 2013. The mutual acceptance between secular culture and religion is not only defined as an achievement of true universalist enlightenment (293). In this essay he adds a short description of the ritual as the binding force of social solidarity and its history, in order to redefine the modern separation between knowledge and belief as a condition for this universalist enlightenment. Still, belief seems to be anchored in ritual and thus offers a special version of social bond and solidarity.

the time which reflected a specific "*critique of pure dogmatic belief.*"[9] This critique demanded the end of the church's resistance to the idea of modern secular freedom in the name of dogmatic truth. The modern church expressed its regret for having fought, in the name of dogmatic truth, against the emergence of a secular society of freedom; however, it reminded this modern society in return that liberty without a clear value orientation – Libertas sine veritate – would be at a dangerous loss – the very loss, which Habermas seems to have complained about and which brought him to a new appreciation of religion and church!

Cardinal Ratzinger developed this position of the Church vis a vis modern secular society in light of natural law and the tradition of Thomas Aquinas as a universal value basis transcending the autonomous framework of human societies: "Natural Law – especially in the Catholic Church – remains the topos with which the Church, in conversation with secular society as well as with other communities of faith, appeals to a shared reason and searches for the foundations of a communication about the ethical principles of the law in a secular, pluralistic society."[10] Despite their differences on the question concerning the necessity for pre-political foundations of the political sphere and despite their different points of departure, the debate in Munich in 2004 between Habermas and Cardinal Ratzinger seemed to lead to an interesting consensus between these two representatives concerning the legitimacy of the secular and the religious way of life, and the dialogical modes of the post-secular relation. After all, it was Libertas (Liberty) which served as the very principle of a new pragmatic kind of communicative action between secular society and the church. This "Post-secular relation" would be founded on a mutual need and a necessary critique of each other presupposing these differences and the basic dissent between faith and reason.

It is not the place here to elaborate on these underlying differences and the later responses from each of the partners to the outcome of this debate. Instead I shall give an account of the specific form of enlightened political theology and its eschatological mechanism which was part of the very formation of modern secular society and its canon.

---

9 See W. Kasper, *Wahrheit und Freiheit. Die Erklärung der Religionsfreiheit des II. Vatikanischen Konzils*, Heidelberg 1988, 26. For an excellent account of the transformation of the Church before and after Vatican II, see E. Boeckenfoerde, *Staat, Gesellschaft, Kirche*, Freiburg 1982.
10 "Pope Benedict XVI: Prepolitical Moral Foundations of a Free Republic", in: H. de Vries and L. Sullivan, *Political Theologies:* Public Religions in a Post-Secular World, New York 2006, 265.

III

From the beginning the Enlightenment was characterized by an inherent ambivalence between its idea of a secular culture of freedom and autonomy and its messianic concept of politics, such that the borders between secular and religious society, state and church, between political and religious authority were dissolved in the idea of a society as the third realm of freedom or redemption from domination. Gotthold Ephraim Lessing used an apocalyptic rhetoric when he described the age of 18th-century enlightenment, emancipation and autonomy as the age of the Holy Spirit, which would represent the true practical reason beyond the political powers and the principal of domination.[11] The detachment from orthodox and dogmatic religion led Lessing to an adoption of what he considered to be the true Christian messianic message, in which freedom and love were the foundations for a political theology dedicated to the new ideal society to be erected as the realization of the kingdom of God here and now. The enlightened subject – after having fettered the serpent of sin – would thus "do the good, (only) because it is the good," i.e., because he/she rationally understood the meaning of goodness and would act according to this rational understanding. Lessing's formula was clearly meant as an antithesis to St. Paul's famous short description of the existential situation of the sinful Ego in the Epistle to the Romans (7:19): "For the Good that I would I do not: but the evil which I would not, I do." In the third realm of freedom sin would be thus overcome, and the heavenly Jerusalem would be established by all enlightened and illuminated rational human beings as the ideal human society of freedom.

The ambivalence of the enlightened concept of a political theology between a detachment from religion and its messianic implementation also determined Immanuel Kant's "Religion within the borders of Reason alone" from 1793,[12] even if Kant was a bit more careful as to the enthusiastic possibilities of a radical emancipation from sin as described by Lessing. Human nature was, after all, characterized by "radical evil" which would demand an eternal battle between the realm

---

11 G.E. Lessing, "Die Erziehung des Menschengeschlechts," in: *Lessings Werke* II, Berlin 1961, Paragraphs 85 to 88, 995 ff. On the idea of the Third Reich in modern historiography, see H. Grundmann, *Studien* über *Joachim von Floris*, Leipzig 1927; H. de Lubac, *Le Drame de l'humanisme athee*, Paris 1945; K. Löwith, *Meaning in History*, Chicago 1949. On the present debate on secularity and religion, see: T. Asad, *Formations of the Secular: Christianity, Islam, Modernity*, Stanford 2003; C. Taylor, *A Secular Age*, Harvard 2007; J. Casanova, *Rethinking Secularity. A Global Perspective*, www.iasc-culture.org.

12 I. Kant, *Die Religion innerhalb der Grenzen der blossen Vernunft*, in: W. Weischedel, *Werkausgabe* VIII, Frankfurt/Main 1982.

of goodness and the realm of evil, pointing only to an infinite march of humanity towards the true invisible church as the true kingdom of God.[13]

But this basic messianic claim of enlightenment and its political theology to realize the messianic goal through reasonable action would not only determine the fundamental ambivalence between the secular and the religious; it would – in spite of its rhetoric of tolerance – in fact neutralize the traditional orthodox religion through a rather intolerant gesture, since the enlightened religion of political reason defined itself as the rational and only true interpretation of this religion.

IV

On the basis of this eschatological vision of the ideal society as the Christian kingdom of God, the Enlightenment period created its famous vision of past and history as the Trinitarian succession of three ages, namely, the age of the Father, the Son and the Holy Spirit represented by Judaism, Christianity and enlightened Modernity,[14] which would not only determine Hegel's and the Young Hegelians' concept of history. Long before this enlightened historiography of the three realms culminating in a third realm of messianic fulfillment was totally distorted by the National Socialist apocalypse of the Third Reich,[15] it served as the messianic framework within which enlightened modernity created its own canon. Instead of the *binary* canon of the Christian biblical canon, enlightened culture created a *ternary* canon; this canon included both the Old and New Testaments and the modern enlightened Testament of freedom and emancipation. It is precisely here that the modern canon revealed itself as a repetition of the Christian messianic self-understanding now turned against orthodox Christianity itself. In the same way that Christianity interpreted itself as the messianic fulfillment of

13 Ibid. The first chapter describes "the inhabitation of the radical evil in human nature" which is to be overcome in the ongoing battle leading to the final "victory of the good principle over the evil one and the erection of the kingdom of God on earth" described in the third Chapter.

14 See footnote 11. In addition: J. Taubes, *Abendländische Eschatologie*, München 1991; E. Bloch, *Das Prinzip Hoffnung*, Frankfurt/Main, 1954, 195; J. Moltmann, „Theologie im Projekt der Moderne“, in: id., *Gott im Projekt der modernen Welt. Beiträge zur öffentlichen Relevanz der Theologie*, Gütersloh 1997.

15 Moeller Van den Bruck, *Das dritte Reich*, Hamburg 1923 which served as the basis for the National Socialists' adoption of the concept. See E. Voegelin's commentary, in: *The New Science of Politics*, Chicago 1953, 113.

Judaism, enlightened culture saw itself now as the messianic fulfillment or Hegelian "Aufhebung" of Christianity.

In fact, Hegel's philosophy of religion was not only a dialectical reformulation of Lessing's canon of enlightenment suspending Judaism as one of its stages and culminating in the modern state as the eschatological fulfillment of the "absolute religion" of Christianity.[16] His historical–teleological reconstruction of the genesis of the spirit as free and self-conscious subjectivity would influence Ferdinand Christian Baur's historical turn of Protestant theology as well as the radical versions of the young Hegelians Ludwig Feuerbach and Karl Marx. Hegel's idea of subjectivity liberating itself in the course of history served, in Ferdinand Christian Baur's "Christianity and the Christian Church,"[17] as the paradigm for an explanation of the transformation of legalistic and particularistic Judaism into the universal ethical form of subjectivity in Christianity, which Baur described in Hegelian terms as the "absolute religion." When Baur adopted Hegel's philosophy of religion, in order to explain the supreme Christian idea of freedom as the culmination of human culture, the leftist Hegelians radicalized and secularized Hegel's philosophy of religion in political forms of Christian eschatology while adopting the same attitude towards Judaism as a prefiguration of absolute religion, but in fact they were much more dismissive.[18]

It was a Jewish philosopher and student of Kant, Saul Ascher, who, already in his polemical text "Eisenmenger der Zweite" from 1794,[19] pointed to this Enlightenment tendency, which he saw represented by Kant and (in an openly anti-Semitic version) by Fichte, not only creating a reduplication of the Christian

---

16 G.F.W. Hegel, „Vorlesungen über die Philosophie der Religion," in: *Werke in zwanzig Bänden, Band 17. III. Teil: Die absolute Religion*, Frankfurt/Main 1975, 185 ff.

17 F.C. Baur, *Das Christentum und die christliche Kirche der ersten drei Jahrhunderte*, Tübingen 1853, 5: „Als allgemeine Form des religiösen Bewusstseins erscheint das Christentum darin, dass es die übrigen Religionen mehr und mehr zurückdrängt, in sich auflöst und sich selbst über sie zur allgemeinsten Religion in der Welt aufgeschwungen hat, es ist somit jenen Religionen gegenüber die absolute. Like Hegel Baur identifies Jewish and Greek religion as legitimate, but uncomplete prefigurations of the absolute religion of Christianity. This tendency is supported by Baur's reliance on F.D.E. Schleiermacher's Über *die Religion – Reden an die Gebildeten unter ihren Verächtern*, first published in 1799, Hamburg 2004. But Baur obviously preferred Hegel's idea of prefiguration on Schleiermacher's attitude towards Judaism, which was harsh and dismissive, as he wrote that "Judaism was for long a dead religion, and those who still wear its color, sit actually mourning next to a unperishable mummy" (159).

18 L. Feuerbach, „Das Wesen des Christentums, „ Vol. V of L. Feuerbach, *Gesammelte Werke*, Berlin 1979, see 218–219. K. Marx: *„Zur Judenfrage,"* in: Marx and Engels, *Werke*, Vol. I, Berlin 1976, 347–377.

19 S. Ascher, *Eisenmenger der Zweite, 4 Flugschriften, 1794*, Berlin 1991.

messianic strategy of suspension. He saw that enlightened modernity was in fact on the way towards radicalizing the Christian attitude towards Judaism when it claimed that Judaism, because of its legalistic character, was not capable of a rational messianic adoption. "The Jewish faith is supposed to be grounded in its original institution only on statuary laws, serving as the constitution of the state. But it is certain that the author is thinking here not of the original constitution of Judaism. Judaism did not have an original constitution, but it was (...) regulative. I could claim the same thing from Christianity, that only after a long time of a regulative existence it became statuary law."[20] Thus Saul Ascher pointed to a sincere problem when he radically questioned the idea of the modern canon being built only on the Christian messianic paradigm, since it not only suspended Judaism but in fact excluded it from the new paradigm of modern culture. His critique was meant as an insistence on the messianic integration of Judaism in the political-ethical project of the Enlightenment.

Modernity created its canon then not only as a double messianic suspension, but potentially as the realization and suspension of Christianity alone, while discrediting Judaism as a whole for not being "secularizable," i.e., not being able to be secularized.

From the perspective of this retrospective organization of history as a ternary canon, the problem of modern enlightened political theology becomes radically transparent. There could be no doubt that the Enlightenment could never rely on the recognition of Christian orthodoxy, as the Christian religion could never be accepted by Jewish orthodox religion, owing to the former's messianic claim to be the latter's fulfillment. Thus for the first time both religions found themselves in a situation of a "*forced messianic adoption*," which they could respond to only in an act of what I would like to call "*orthodox rejection*."

V

Against the principle of messianic suspension never accepted by the religion being suspended, both philosophers and theologians of secular culture have demanded a reformulation of the relation between secular modernity and religion within the Christian context. They urged for a disentanglement of the messianic synthesis and synonymy of politics and religion as constructed in Enlightenment political philosophy. The experience with political totalitarianism, culminating in state

20 Ibid., 57.

terror and the creation of concentration camps for the supposed ultimate enemy of race or class, led Erik Voegelin, in the early 1950s, and Hans Blumenberg, in the late 1960s, to the conclusion that both the quest for an absolute messianic knowledge and absolute messianic action in history were nothing but reinventions of a Gnostic form of an absolutism of thought and politics – but from opposite perspectives. The impossibility to realize the absolute messianic goal, Voegelin concluded, had to lead to the formation of radical modernities which compensated the idea of the liquidation of sin and evil through the construction of an absolute enemy – the enemy of class or race, who represented the evil principle precisely because he prevented the realization of the ultimate Telos of history. Political Gnosis was thus the reappearance of the antiquated dualism of the good and bad god in the disguise of the perfect human being and the absolute enemy.

To avoid the catastrophic potentials of modernity, Eric Voegelin, in his book "The new Science of Politics" from 1952,[21] radically dismissed the messianic ambivalence of modernity as Gnostic and sought to return to the classical order of the two realms created by St. Augustine in his famous "De Civitate Dei." "St. Augustine distinguished between a profane sphere of history in which empires rise and fall and a sacred history which culminates in the appearance of Christ and the establishment of the church. He, furthermore, imbedded sacred history in a transcendental history of the Civitas Dei which includes the events of the angelic sphere as well as the transcendental eternal Sabbath. Only transcendental history, including the earthly pilgrimage of the church, has direction toward its eschatological fulfillment. Profane history, on the other hand, has no such direction; it is waiting for the end; its present mode of being is that of a saeculum senescens, of an age that grows old."[22] Modernity, which Voegelin interpreted as a heretical Gnostic distortion of orthodox dogmatic theology, without any differentiations between enlightenment and totalitarianism, was thus not only rejected in its messianic claims, but had in fact become radically illegitimate.

Against this Gnostification of modernity, Hans Blumenberg, in his "Legitimacy of the Modern Age" from 1966,[23] could recognize only a new form of the classical de-legitimization of modernity through theology. This led him to the opposite accusation, namely, that it was in fact theology itself that had the tendency to become a radical Gnosticism and that Modernity was the result of a radical overcoming of Gnosis and of all theology. We do not have to enter the virtuosic argument of Blumenberg, but he claimed that basically every theology

---

21 E. Voegelin, *The New Science of Politics. An Introduction*, Chicago 1952.
22 Ibid., 118.
23 H. Blumenberg, *Legitimacy of the Modern Age*, Massachusetts 1985.

which understood its own concept of god had to think this concept precisely in the way that radical Scotism tended to do, namely, as being potentially not only "beyond being" and "beyond reason" but also "beyond goodness." A real infinite God could not only change the rules of his creation at any given moment, he could also create a bad world if he wished to. "The God who places no constraints on Himself, who cannot be committed to any consequence following from his manifestation, makes time into a dimension of utter uncertainty. This affects not only the identity of the subject, the presence of which at any given moment does not guarantee it any future, but also the persistence of the world, whose radical contingency can transform it, from one moment to the next, from existence into mere appearance, from reality to nothingness."[24] Against such an *absolute epistemological emergency case*, modernity had to radically defend itself via the Cartesian retreat into the realm of rational certainty and safety of the "ego cogito." "The model of the trains of thought induced in this situation stands before us in Descartes' Meditations as the reduction of the process of doubt to the gaining of a new absolute fundament in the cogito ergo sum."[25] Blumenberg wished to de-activate all possible derivations of Modernity from theology in order to avoid a totalitarianism from taking possession of it. Modernity was legitimate in itself and so did not need theological legitimization, certainly not the kind of legitimization emerging from the enlightened modes of political theology. Blumenberg was convinced that theology in the context of modernity could function only as a Trojan horse, which in the dark night of a crisis of the legitimacy of the modern age would free all the forgotten theological partisans and absolutist ideologists in order to destroy the city of modernity!

Thus Blumenberg responded to Voegelin's de-legitimization with a counter de-legitimization. Each claimed in the end that the other was a hidden Gnostic and each pleaded for a radical detachment of religion from secular society. Beyond the confusions and eschatological mechanisms of modern political theology religion should now remain just orthodox, while secular society should finally truly secularize its secularity, in order to liberate it from all its secret religious and eschatological "left-overs." The crisis of modern political messianic

24 Ibid., 161–162.

25 Ibid., 178. Blumenberg in fact reads Luther's famous formula: Non potest Deus naturaliter velle Deum esse Deum, immo vellet se ipse esse Deum et Deum non esse Deum (Man cannot truly want God to be God, but he himself wants to be God and that God is not God) as an indication for the modern secular mind. This is of course a quite violent reading of Luther's dictum, since through it Luther wanted to explain the basic sinful nature of man dependent on grace!

theology would find its resolution then – according to Voegelin and Blumenberg – in a total dismissal of the modern canon.

VI

In fact, this Gnostic aspect of late modernity had much deeper roots in a certain type of Protestant theology. Thus it seems to be no accident that Blumenberg, throughout his argument of the modern "overcoming" of Gnosis, leant heavily on the Protestant theologian Adolph von Harnack. This Protestant theologian had shown that canonic Christian reliance on the double canon of the Old and New testaments could be understood only as a defense against the Gnostic, namely, the Marcionite tendency demanding elimination of all traces of the Jewish Old Testament; at the same time, in his book on Marcion from 1921, he wished to adopt this very Marcionite Gnosis as the essential expression of true Protestant Christianity which could indeed dispense then with its Jewish origins in the Old Testament. The essence of a true and pure Christianity did not need – after 1900 years – any legitimization through Judaism; the Gospel of Jesus and the New Testament had no need of the Jewish Theology of the law. "So the question of the Old Testament, as Marcion once put and decided it, stands still today before the Protestant Christianity. The rest of Christianity will certainly overhear it, because it is not capable to give the right answer. But Protestantism is able to and can give this answer all the more, because the terrible dilemma which Marcion had to face, has been removed. He had to reject the Old Testament as a wrong and heretical book, in order to secure the pure gospel. But today there is no talk about rejection, rather the uniqueness and meaning of this book (the prophets) will be recognized everywhere, when it has lost its canonical authority, which it does not earn."[26]

Indeed, both Harnack and Blumenberg seemed to adopt a similar strategy of purification of their essential "gospel," which aimed at a strong resistance to all historical derivations from the former paradigm. The true Protestant Christianity was all too similar to Blumenberg's pure and true essence of modernity.

The Gnostic paradigm thus not only had its modern prehistory; it also concerned all three elements of the modern canon – Judaism, Christianity and Modernity. As a radical rejection of messianic adoption it left the three elements totally detached from each other. Modernity stood on its own when it created its new

26 A. von Harnack, *Marcion. Das Evangelium vom fremden Gott. Eine Monographie zur Geschichte der Grundlegung der katholischen Kirche*, Leipzig 1921, 254–255.

form of autonomous subjectivity. Christianity was thus expelled in order to return to its original dogmatic faith and binary canon, just as Judaism was dismissed by modern Protestant Christianity – in the same way it had been eschatologically adopted before – without being consulted.

Let us now have a short look at three different responses to the breakdown of the modern canon: a Jewish, a Christian and a modernist enlightened response. Each turns against the Gnostic strategies of a radical detachment of the canonic elements from each other; likewise, each strives for a post-messianic reformulation of the modern canon, a canon which would allow for another diachronic succession of these elements beyond eschatological suspension, orthodox resistance and Gnostic detachment.

VII

It is worthwhile to recall that the first sharp protest against Gnostic modernity, namely, against Harnack's program to detach Protestant Christianity from Judaism, was articulated by Jewish theologians! Leo Baeck, Martin Buber and Franz Rosenzweig, to name just the most famous of these Jewish theologians, strongly protested against the canonic Secessio Judaica[27] proposed by Adolph von Harnack. No doubt, this protest had political origins as well. It seemed clear that the detachment of Christian theology from its Jewish roots would have political implications for the Jewish presence in modern German culture, which was dominated by Protestant Christianity. Harnack aimed in fact at a kind of new double canon of the New Testament and modern liberal Culture as the political theological fundament for the Wilhelminian imperial Germany; this double canon not only excluded the Jewish Old testament, but also rejected the classical Catholic reliance on the double canon of both the Old and the New Testament. Harnack after all played – according to the famous jibe from Franz Overbeck – the role of the "theological hairdresser of the imperial wig!" But these Jewish theologians, especially those who were involved in or influenced by or simply rejected the project of liberal theology with its philological historical critique and anti-dogmatic attitude, obviously not only sensed the political danger which seemed to be

27 "Secessio Judaica" was the title of a book written by one of the founders of the German youth movement and later professional antisemite Hans Blüher, *Secessio Judaica. Philosophische Grundlegung der deutschen Situation, des Judentums und der antisemitischen Bewegung*, Berlin 1921. In 1931 he summarized his opinions in the thesis of a Jewish revolt against Christian culture. H. Blüher, *Die Erhebung Israels gegen die christlichen Güter*, Hamburg 1931.

greater than the messianic suspension through Christianity; they also recognized that Judaism had become part of a canon it had always rejected in its religious essence. When Leo Baeck wrote his little book on the "Gospel as a document from the Jewish history of belief" in 1938, the process of real "Secessio Judaica," of separation, exclusion and destruction, had long since begun. Still, even in this moment of catastrophe, Baeck wished to remind the reader that "Jesus was a Jew among Jews,"[28] whom Jewish history and thought should not ignore nor forget. But even if Christianity had changed and developed the original Jewish belief "of" Jesus into a specific belief "in" Jesus, it had adopted and kept – against Marcion's and Harnack's Gnosis – the double canon: "The right belief, the healthy teaching demanded the canon. They demanded the Bible, which could reside next to the Bible of the Jews."[29] Unlike Buber, who, in his book on the "Two ways of Belief," accused the apostle Paul not only of turning the Jewish belief "of" Jesus into the dogmatic belief "in" Jesus, but of opening the gates of Gnosis and anti-Judaism,[30] Baeck noted Paul's insistence in the Epistle to the Romans (chapters 9–11) that the Christians' belief should always be grounded in the Jewish roots.

Yet Franz Rosenzweig had already summarized this relation, in his "Star of Redemption"[31] from 1921, as a direct response to Adolph von Harnack's Gnosis. After the collapse of liberal theology Rosenzweig gave a formula for a canonic relation from the Jewish point of view as a kind of official and legitimate liaison between Judaism and Christianity. He wished to remind the Christian of the fact that the Dogmatic Christ, although conceived of as two – human and divine – natures, was indeed grounded in the concrete life of the Jewish Jesus, a fact that the Greek metaphysical tradition of Patristic theology tended to forget.

"But the historical Jesus, precisely the Jesus Christ of the Dogma, does not stand on a pedestal, he really moves in the market place of life and urges life, to

28 L. Baeck, *Das Evangelium als Urkunde der jüdischen Glaubensgeschichte*, Berlin 1938, 70.
29 Ibid., 54.
30 See M. Buber, " Zwei Glaubensweisen, " in: *Schriften zur Philosophie*, Heidelberg 1962, 755 ff.
31 F. Rosenzweig, *Der Stern der Erlösung*, 2nd edition 1930, Frankfurt/Main 1988. Many motives of Rosenzweig's conception of the two ways are prefigured in his correspondence with his friend Eugen Rosenstock. See: E. Rosenstock-Huessy, *Judaism Despite Christianity. The 1916 Wartime Correspondence Between Eugen Rosenstock-Huessey and Franz Rosenzweig*, Chicago 2011. Rosenzweig is entirely uninterested in joining the liberal idyll which is supposed to replace the enmities between the two canonic paradigms. Au contraire, he wants to rethink the canonic relation in light of the mutual enmity of the partners as a dual path to truth. In one letter Rosenzweig even reminds his converted friend that "to put it in a popular way: that we have crucified Christ and, believe me, would do it again every time, we alone in the world" (113). On the whole of Rosenzweig's relation to Gnosticism and his own conversion: B. Pollock, *Franz Rosenzweig's Conversions – World Denial and World Redemption*, Bloomington 2014.

stand still in front of his glance. The same is true for the 'spiritual' God, in whom everybody so easily and voluntarily believes, and at the same time is afraid, to believe in the One, who has created the world in order to rule over it."[32]

But his main conclusion held that Old and New Testament were thus always already interrelated in a double participation, competition and mutual enmity towards eschatological truth.

"In front of God both, Jew and Christian, are engaged in the same work. Nobody can dispense with the other. Between the two God has set enmity and yet he has united them mutually and with each other in the most intimate way. To us he gave eternal life, by igniting in our hearts the fire of the star of his truth. These he sent on the eternal path, by letting them run after the rays of that star of truth until the eternal end. (...) The truth, the whole truth, belongs neither to them nor to us. Although we carry it within us, we nevertheless have to lower our glance into our own inwardness, if we want to see her, and there we see the star, but not the rays. It would belong to the full truth, that we could see not only the light, but also what is illuminated by it. And those (Christians) are meant for all time, to see what is illuminated, but not the light."[33]

Thus Baeck, Buber and Rosenzweig laid the foundations for a post-canonical structure of the relation between Judaism and Christianity beyond eschatological suspension, orthodox resistance and Gnostic detachment from a Jewish point of view which in fact reflected an alternative type of post-canonical modernity.

VIII

Reading the leading Catholic intellectuals of the moderate interpretation of Vatican II, namely, the theologians of the Communio circle, Hans Urs von Balthasar, Cardinal Josef Ratzinger and others, it becomes clear that the awareness of the three issues – political Messianism, Gnosticism and Judaism – especially after the Holocaust – became central for what one could call the creation of a "Catholic version of the modern ternary canon" that resists both eschatological suspension and Gnostic rejection.

"The shock of the Shoah," Ratzinger wrote, has radically changed the background of the canonical constitution of Christianity. "Can Christians, after all that has happened, still claim in good conscience to be the legitimate heirs of Israel's

32 F. Rosenzweig, *Der Stern der Erlösung*, 1930, Frankfurt/Main 1988, 461.
33 Ibid., 462.

Bible? Have they the right to propose a Christian interpretation of the Bible, or should they not instead respectfully and humbly renounce any claim that, in the light of what has happened, must look like usurpation?"[34]

From the perspective of this shock, Pope Benedict XVI managed to formulate an impressive outline for the implicit Catholic understanding not only of the Biblical canon but of the whole of the modern canon. Of special interest here are his reflections in the opening remarks to the document on the Holy Scriptures and the encyclical declaration "Spe Salvi," which was issued in 2007, three years after the debate with Habermas. In fact it seems that the declaration is an echo to this debate, as can be sensed in the following remarks on Kant's vision of the Kingdom of God and the dialectics of enlightenment.

Against Kant's Religion of reason, which was supposed to translate the Christian eschatological hope, belief and love into a rational project of historical action, the Pope quotes from a later essay of Kant, "On the end of all things," and turns it, with direct reference to Adorno, into a kind of confession of the inner dialectics of enlightenment. "If Christianity should one day cease to be worthy of love ...then the prevailing mode in human thought would be rejection and opposition to it, and the Antichrist (...) would begin his (...) albeit short regime." The Pope develops this line of critique against modern political theology in the case of Marx's project to take a definitive step towards salvation, "towards what Kant had described as the Kingdom of God," which, because it "forgot man's freedom (...) and man's freedom for evil," could lead only into a dictatorship.[35]

This Catholic critique of modern eschatological politics in the name of freedom and democracy is only the specific modern post-secular aspect of the same move, which turns against the classical eschatological attitude of Christianity versus Judaism and the radical Gnostic tendency of Protestant theology to detach the Old from the New Testament. The Pope in fact points to a strange affinity between Harnack's demand to detach the Old from the New Testament and the attitude, determined significantly by the "Shock of the Shoah," questioning the relation between the two Testaments.

In fact, Harnack's strategy of detachment turns against Judaism as well as it turns against Catholic theology which, against the Gnostic heresy in the second century, created the double canon of Old and New Testament; this suggests an unexpected alliance, which the Pope wants to rethink in light of his reflections

---

34 J. Ratzinger, Preface to *The Jewish People and their Sacred Scriptures in the Christian Bible*, Rome 2001.

35 Pope Benedict XVI, *Spe Salvi*, Paragraph 20 to 23. Compare J. Ratzinger, *Glaube, Wahrheit, Toleranz. Das Christentum und die Weltreligionen*, Freiburg 2003, 94.

on the "shock of the Shoah." He reminds the reader first of Harnack's radical conclusion at the end of his investigation in Marcion: "The rejection of the Old Testament in the second century (=Marcion) was an error which the Greek Church was right in resisting; holding on to it in the 16th century was a disaster from which the Reformation has not yet been able to extricate itself; but to maintain it since the 19th century in Protestantism (...) that is the result of religious and ecclesial paralysis."[36] In light of this threat and its political results, Ratzinger states categorically: "without the Old Testament the New Testament would be an unintelligible book, a plant derived of its roots and destined to dry up and wither," and he does so in order to propose an interesting double hermeneutics for the dual structure of the canonic texts.

"In light of what happened, what ought to emerge now, is a new respect for the Jewish interpretation of the Old Testament (...) The Jewish reading of the Bible is a possible one, in continuity with the Jewish scriptures of the Sacred Temple period, a reading analogous to the Christian reading, which developed in parallel fashion."[37] While Christians are supposed to learn from the Jewish reading and interpretation of the Bible, Ratzinger can only express his hope "that Jews could profit from Christian exegesis."

This post-canonical Hermeneutics of the Bible opens the dynamics of interpretation beyond the classical diachronic succession for a synchronicity in which all texts enter interaction without closure. It leaves open the possibility to read the Old Testament as an independent and meaningful path, which – although in Christian terms it leads to Christ – in Jewish terms can still be understood in its open view of the messianic issue.

So Ratzinger seems to offer a possibility to adopt a position towards Judaism which in many ways resembles the new Catholic position towards secular society, as developed in his debate with Habermas: modernity has developed out of Christian culture, but it does not coincide with its aims nor can it detach itself from Christianity! The diachronic succession has to be counterbalanced then by a synchronic perspective where the partners involved do not lose their own respective independent characters, while still depending on each other.

---

36 Josef Ratzinger, Preface to *The Jewish People and their Sacred Scriptures in the Christian Bible*, Rome 2001; P. Hofmann, *Benedikt XVI. Einführung in sein theologisches Denken*, Paderborn 2009. See the chapter on the relation between scripture and tradition, 85 ff.

37 Ibid.

IX

Habermas' own position seems to show affinities with Blumenberg's interest to define modern secular culture from within, namely, without any need for external legitimization. But Habermas, like Ratzinger, was always deeply concerned with the German past; indeed, his theory of communicative action and his ethics of memory were philosophical strategies created in light of the Shock of the Shoah. Habermas wanted the legitimacy of a solid secular enlightened political culture to be founded on the basis of constitution and public debate, as these presupposed an ethical practice of solidarity as the fundament for the present political culture as well as for its relation to the German past: "To the extent that collective frameworks of living afforded less partnership, the more they survived by virtue of conquest and destruction of the lives of others, the greater the onus of reconciliation, the burden of facing up to the situation and the burden of self-criticism placed on succeeding generations."[38]

If solidarity was the ethical fundament for political and legal interaction in the democratic society, it had to be expanded for the victims of the past, as it was the answer to all forms of political eschatology which intended to establish a totalitarian system. Habermas not only declared war on the nationalist right wing traditions of the past, but he was no less aware of the radical tendencies of the 1968 student movement. As a student of Adorno and Horckheimer and a critical member of the 1968 movement he sympathized with the idea of a more pluralistic and individualistic society; however, he strictly rejected all radical forms of a violent political messianism which turned against the democratic fabric of society. It was the same Kantian tradition of enlightenment which Habermas mobilized against these anti-democratic forms of political theology and which was supposed to define the framework of his response to the religious challenge, a framework which demanded a change of attitude towards religious communities. Still this change was built on the very Kantian idea of a possible rationalist translation of the true meaning of religion, the same translational process which allowed for an ethical adoption of the idea of the kingdom of God and hold the legalistic frame of Jewish belief for not "secularizable," thus already hinting at the possible ultimate differences between Habermas' and Ratzinger's respective understandings of the post-secular relation. "Secularized citizens, insofar as they act in their role as citizens of a state, may neither deny out of hand the potential for truth in religious conceptions of the world nor dispute the right of believing

38 J. Habermas, Eine Art Schadensabwicklung, Frankfurt am Main, Suhrkamp Publishing House, 1983, 93

fellow citizens to make contributions to public discussions that are phrased in a religious language. Liberal political culture may even expect its secularized citizens to participate in efforts to translate relevant contributions from a religious language into a publicly accessible one."[39]

But Habermas nevertheless offered a secular vision of communicative interaction between the partners of the modern canon based on freedom, solidarity and mutual critique. In this sense he initiated his own conception of an open modernity beyond the eschatological mechanism, orthodox rejection and Gnostic repudiation. The emerging differences would be only a challenge for the canonic partners involved in the "undistorted" communicative action he envisioned, an opportunity where the citizens would "take seriously each other's contributions to controversial themes in the public sphere."[40]

These three different positions or points of departure thus seem to reflect the crisis of modern political theology, the modern canon and the Gnostic threat. It is through the dialogical confrontation with the modern ternary canon that each of the involved canonical partners discovers its adequate identity beyond messianic suspension, Gnostic detachment, or orthodox resistance, but within the modern canonic framework. The idea of a post-secular relation between secular and religious society thereby demands a reconstruction of the modern canon in post-canonic terms which opens the diachronic succession for a synchronic dialogue between independent partners. But since the post-secular relation defines first the interrelation between religion and modernity, it seems that the interreligious dimension of this relation, between Christianity and Judaism, presupposes the clarification of this first political relation. Therefore it seems that only a religion and a modernity which have come to terms with the conditions of the post-secular relation would be able to enter into dialogue with other religions without creating messianic superimpositions or orthodox resistances! Thus the post-canonic Canon is in no way exclusive. Against anti-Islamic constructions of the Judeo-Christian tradition it is certainly intended as an invitation to Islam to enter the canonic and dialogical partnership on the preposition of mutual recognition.

The post-secular relation, rather than describing a situation or offering a closed system of propositions, is meant then as a path, a method of dialogical cooperation and critique both of "pure secular reason" and of "pure dogmatic belief." It thus aims at a new balance between reason and belief, philosophy and theology "after post-modernity" which will enable coordination and integration of the simultaneous processes of modernization, in the different contexts

39 J. Habermas, "On the Relations between the Secular Liberal State and Religion," 260.
40 Ibid., 258.

of modernity with their accelerations and delays. The post-secular relation thus includes a dynamics of anticipation and memory of its theoretical and practical ideal – not forgetting its own failures and violent compensations. In its hope for a second global enlightenment, it reveals, at least partly, strong affinities to what the Jewish philosopher Leo Strauss called "the pre-modern enlightenment"[41] – namely, the medieval expression of this ideal of coordination and balance between philosophy and theology – which, after all, was initiated by the culture of Islam.

Bibliography

Asad, T. *Formations of the Secular: Christianity, Islam, Modernity*. Stanford: Stanford University Press, 2003.

Ascher, S. *Eisenmenger der Zweite. 4 Flugschriften*. Berlin: Aufbau Verlag, 1991.

Baeck, Leo. *Das Evangelium als Urkunde der jüdischen Glaubensgeschichte*. Berlin: Schocken, 1938.

Baur, F.C. *Das Christentum und die christliche Kirche der ersten drei Jahrhunderte*. Tübingen: Fues, 1853.

Bloch, E. *Das Prinzip Hoffnung*. Frankfurt/Main: Suhrkamp, 1954.

Blumenberg, H. *The Legitimacy of the Modern Age*. Massachusetts: MIT Press, 1985.

Blüher, Hans. *Secessio Judaica. Philosophische Grundlegung der deutschen Situation, des Judentums und der antisemitischen Bewegung*. Berlin: Der Weisse Ritter Verlag, 1921.

Blüher, Hans. *Die Erhebung Israels gegen die christlichen Güter*. Hamburg: Hanseatische Verlagsanstalt, 1931.

Boeckenfoerde, E. *Staat, Gesellschaft, Kirche*. Freiburg: Suhrkamp, 1982.

Brague, R. *La Loi de Dieu*. Paris: Folio, 2005.

Buber, M. "Zwei Glaubensweisen." *Schriften zur Philosophie*. Heidelberg: Buber, M: Zwei Glaunbensweisen, Lambert Schneider, 1965, 1962.

Casanova, J. *Rethinking Secularity. A Global Perspective*. http://www.iasc-culture.org.October 26th 2015

Feuerbach, L. *Gesammelte Werke. Vol. V: Das Wesen des Christentums*. Berlin: Akademie Verlag, 1979.

Grundmann, H. *Studien über Joachim von Floris*. Leipzig: Springer Verlag, 1927.

Habermas, Jürgen. *Glauben und Wissen, Dankesrede für den Friedenspreis des deutschen Buchhandels*, 2001. http://www.glasnost.de/docs01/011014habermas.html October 26th 2015.

Habermas, Jürgen. "On the Relations Between the Secular Liberal State and Religion. Pope Benedict XVI: Prepolitical Moral Foundations of a Free Republic." *Political Theologies*.

41 L. Strauss, *Philosophie und Gesetz*, Berlin 1935. R. Brague, *La Loi de Dieu*, Paris 2005 has formulated a similar idea of the Middle Ages, and, like Strauss, has elaborated on the secular process as a path of possible reductions denying the medieval openness.

Public Religions in a Post-Secular Word. Ed. H. de Vries and L. Sullivan. New York: Fordham University Press, 2006. 251–260.

Habermas, Jürgen. "Politics and Religion." *Politik und Religion – Zur Diagnose der Gegenwart*. Ed. F. W. Graf and H. Meier. München: C.H.Beck Verlag, 2013. 287–300.

Habermas, Jürgen. *Eine Art Schadensabwicklung*, Frankfurt am Main: Suhrkamp Publishing House, 1983.

Harnack, A. von. *Marcion. Das Evangelium vom fremden Gott. Eine Monographie zur Geschichte der Grundlegung der katholischen Kirche*. Leipzig: J.C.Hinrichs, 1921.

Hegel, G.F.W. "Vorlesungen über die Philosophie der Religion." *Werke in zwanzig Bänden, Band 17. III. Teil: Die absolute Religion*. Frankfurt/Main: Suhrkamp, pages 1975, 185 – 346

Hofmann, P. *Benedikt XVI. Einführung in sein theologisches Denken*. Paderborn: Ferdinand Schoeningh Verlag, 2009.

Kant, I. "Die Religion innerhalb der Grenzen der blossen Vernunft." *Werkausgabe VII*. Ed. W. Weischedel. Darmstadt: Wissenschaftliche Buchgessellschaft, 1968, 649–883.

Kasper, W. *Wahrheit und Freiheit. Die Erklärung der Religionsfreiheit des II. Vatikanischen Konzils*. Heidelberg: Winter, 1988.

Lessing, G.E. "Die Erziehung des Menschengeschlechts." *Lessings Werke VI*. Zurich: Stauffacher Publishers, 1965, 52–77.

Löwith, K. *Meaning in History*. Chicago: Chicago University Press, 1949.

Lubac, H. de. *Le Drame de l'humanisme athee*. Paris: cerf publishing house, 1945.

Marx, Karl. "Zur Judenfrage". *Werke, Vol. I*. Karl Marx and Friedrich Engels. Berlin: Dietz Verlag, 1976. 347–377.

Moeller Van den Bruck, Arthur. *Das dritte Reich*. Hamburg: J.C.C.Bruns Verlag, 1923.

Moltmann, J. "Theologie im Projekt der Moderne." *Gott im Projekt der modernen Welt. Beiträge zur öffentlichen Relevanz der Theologie*. Gütersloh: Kaiser Verlag, 1997.

Pollock, B. *Franz Rosenzweig's Conversions – World Denial and World Redemption*. Bloomington: Indiana University Press, 2014.

Pope Benedict XVI. *Spe Salvi*. Evangelical Letter w2vatican.va/.../benedict.../hf_ben-xvi_enc_2007 last Checked 27 october 2015.

Ratzinger, Josef. Preface to *The Jewish People and their Sacred Scriptures in the Christian Bible*. Rome: www.ccjl.us/.../documents...Statements/.../pope – benedict
Date October 26th 2015.

Ratzinger, Josef. *Glaube, Wahrheit, Toleranz. Das Christentum und die Weltreligionen*. Freiburg: Herder Verlag, 2003.

Rosenstock-Huessy, Eugen. *Judaism Despite Christianity. The 1916 Wartime Correspondence Between Eugen Rosenstock-Huessey and Franz Rosenzweig*. Chicago: Chicago University Press, 2011.

Rosenzweig, Franz. *Der Stern der Erlösung*. 2nd edition 1930. Frankfurt/Main: Suhrkamp, 1988.

Schleiermacher, F.D.E. Über die Religion – Reden an die Gebildeten unter ihren Verächtern. First published 1799. Hamburg: Tübingen Siebeck, 2004.

Slenczka, N. "Die Kirche und das Alte Testament." *Marburger Jahrbuch für Theologie* XXV (2013): 83 -119

Strauss, Leo. *Philosophie und Gesetz*. Berlin: Schocken Verlag, 1935.

Taubes, J. *Abendländische Eschatologie*. München: Koenigshausen Neumann Verlag 2001, 1991.

Taylor, C. *A Secular Age*. Harvard: Harvard University Press, 2007.

Voegelin, E. *The New Science of Politics. An Introduction*. Chicago: The University of Chicago Press, 1952.

Michael Fagenblat

10 "Fraternal Existence": On a Phenomenological Double-Crossing of Judaeo-Christianity

1 The Judaeo-Christian mood

In the notes Levinas penned as a French POW during his captivity between November 1940 and May 1945 we find two comments on Friedrich Sieburg's biography of Napolean in which the question of Judaeo-Christianity is raised. These comments are no more than sketches, and often ambiguous ones; given their context this is not surprising. It is clear, however, that Levinas engages with Sieburg's portrayal of Napolean in order to draw two contrasts. The first is between the categories of paganism and Judaeo-Christianty; the second, drawn on the basis of the first contrast, seeks to distinguish between the Judaic and the Christian alternative to paganism. In the spring or summer of 1942, from Fronstalag 133 (Rennes, in north-west France) or Frontstalag 142 (Vesoul, in north-east France), Levinas sketched these distinctions:

> Sieburg, in his considerations on Napolean. Categories: The heroic (an individual who has raised himself to the universal – who erupts and succumbs) and the harmonious individual, the man of measure realizing the universe in himself. Both categories are pagan. To this is opposed a Judeo-Christian category: the just who suffer – research this category through biblical figures – goodness and meekness (*douceur*), for example, not as psychological features but also as cosmic structures – their ontological significance. To research.
> A Judeao-Christian category? This is perhaps the point where one could separate them. The Christian ones are applied to pagans problems. The Greek world is included in Christianity; a Judaism for men with pagans problems.[1]

1 The final clause is in my view difficult to decipher without a slight adjustment to the printed edition. The full passage appears as follows:

> Sieburg dans ses considérations sur Napoléan, Categories: l'Héroïque (le particulier qui s'est haussé jusqu'à l'universel – qui éclate et succombe) et le particulier harmonieux, l'homme de la mesure réalisant l'univers en lui. L'un et l'autre sont des catégories païennes. À cela s'oppose une catégorie judéo-chrétienne : le juste qui souffre – à rechercher cette catégorie à travers les figures bibliques – la bonté et la douceur par exemple, non pas comme traits psychologiques, mais aussi comme structures cosmiques – leur signification ontologique. À rechercher.

Levinas sets himself a research project. What exactly is the categorical distinction between Greco-pagan accounts of the cosmos, with their anthropological implications, and Judaeo-Christian accounts? Already here, having digested Heidegger's radical notion of *Befindlichkeit*, according to which being itself is affectively disclosed by Dasein's attunements, Levinas contemplates the difference between the pagan and the Judaeo-Christian categories in terms of different affective moods disclosing different aspects of being. The affective distinction between paganism and Judaeo-Christianity is not merely an emotive or psychological difference; it has "ontological significance" bearing on being itself. Levinas's formidable research project involves developing this categorical contrast so as to understand how being discloses itself differently according to its respective ways of being-Greco-pagan or being-Judaeo-Christian. If the Greco-pagan cosmos discloses itself as heroism and harmony, Judaeo-Christianity discloses the world itself as just but suffering. But this distinction, which is itself ontologically significant, should not conceal the distinction within Judaeo-Christianity – "one could separate them," he suggests. For Christianity, the suffering of the just becomes a problem of heroism and harmony, as by a type of migration across the categories of being. On this basis one could speculate about the epochal, synthetic success of Christian science and art or, as Levinas will soon do, of Christian politics. For "the Greek world is included in Christianity" by its slow conversion throughout the course of European history of the tribulations of suffering into the adventures of heroism and harmony. Hence Christianity is a "Judaism for men with pagans problems."

This intriguing note from *Carnet* 5 condenses reflections that Levinas will unfold in the course of the ensuing decades. On the one hand, Judaeo-Christianity is a prized category that enables the distinction with Greco-paganism. On the other hand, it is a category that risks masking the essential difference between Judaism and Christianity. Another of Levinas's POW notes reveal him in the midst of this distinction: "ἐἰδωλον – the visible – this is the essential for idolatry. *Deus absconditus* – mystery – the only trait of Judaeo-Christianity which distinguishes it from all purely numerical monotheisms (Levinas 2009, 152)." Here too the Greco-pagan cosmos in which the real is measured by its visible forms – hence the role of the hero who actualizes the forms in virtuoso extreme, and the emphasis on harmony, in which forms are balanced – is contrasted with the Judaeo-Chris-

---

Catégorie judéo-chrétienne? C'est peut-être là le point où l'on puisse les séparer. Chrétiennes, elles s'appliquent aux problèmes païens. Le monde grec est inclus dans le christianisme. Judaïsme pour hommes aux problèmes païens.

tian world in which truth is invisible, concealed and often inverted with respect to the forms of beauty and truth. This note was penned in the midst of Levinas's reading of the ultra-Catholic writer Léon Bloy (d. 1917), whose account of the theological mystery of both suffering and femininity made a great impression on Levinas. Like Bloy, Levinas is interested in the difference between visible (Greco-pagan) and invisible (Judaeo-Christian) renderings of the real. As if adding to his nascent research program, he proposes that the "same work [as Bloy does for Catholicism is] to be undertaken for J[udaism]" (Levinas 2009, 151).

2 Begging to differ: "Judaeo-Christianity" or "major divergences"?

In modern times, with the help of course of the Greco-Roman tradition, Judaeo-Christianity sought answers to one its defining problem – that of the suffering of the just – in secular political institutions designed in part to protect those vulnerable to unjustified suffering. But as Levinas noted many years later, in a 1973 convention of Jewish educators, the political solution raises the very problem he confronted in the Frontstalag in a secular key. "Can the whole of Western humanism pass for a secularization of Judaeo-Christianity? Have the rights of man and of the citizen and the new spirit that conquered the eighteenth century not fulfilled in our minds the promises of the prophets?" The question afforded Levinas the opportunity to reflect once again on the Jewish remainder that no hyphenated Judaeo-Christian unity accommodates. If the ultimate justified purpose of secularizing 'Judaeo-Christianity' is liberal humanism, what does the particularism of being Jewish still have to contribute in an already secular, emancipated age?

What Levinas here called "the very crisis of Jewish education in emancipated Jewish society" consists of the trembling of this hyphen, whether registered or unfelt. As citizens of a secular state founded on 'Judaeo-Christian values,' emancipated Jews risk being political agents for the assimilation of Judaism to liberal values such as the equality of dignity and the rule of law. Sympathetic to the political benefits of secularization and the post-Vatican II ecumenical mood, Levinas was as much concerned with the problem these positive developments produce for Judaism, for under such conditions the enduring, distinct claim of Judaism on Jews becomes increasingly inaudible. The promises born by the hyphen of correcting a centuries old calumny also ring of a secular supercessionism in which the distinct conceptual contribution of Judaism is assimilated without remainder into the indistinct unity of an alleged 'Judaeo-Christian' humanism. "The notion of Judaeo-Christianity, which is on everyone's lips, certainly expresses an evolution and an ideal to be realized in a synthesis inspired by the ecumenical age," he concurred, before demurring: "but not every contradiction has yet been raised... Judaeo-Christian friendship: there is a phrase that employs an absolutely proper use of this synthetic adjective. But on the level of doctrine, as regards the very finality of the human, major divergences remain" (Levinas 1973, 278 f., trans. slightly modified).

A similar concern goes back to Levinas's first reflections after the War on the purpose, or lack thereof, of 'being-Jewish'. German Jewish thinkers from Mendelssohn to Cohen, like their twentieth century American successors, had identified the distinctive contribution of Judaism as consisting of liberal, humanist values. But Judaism itself, as a living spirit with an abiding contribution, was thereby reduced to a mere memory of "services rendered" to liberalism. "It justified its survival by the need to watch over the maturing of these sown seeds," but since these seeds have long flowered amid Christian and democratic peoples, Judaism would seem to have nothing left to offer an emancipated world. The contribution of Jewish monotheism, of the Decalogue and the great moral prophets, to liberalism would therefore appear to consign contemporary Judaism to "a colorless ancestor worship" (Levinas 1947, 206). Unless Judaism still bore "divergences" that are worth preserving. What might they be? Is there a Jewish remainder that cannot be assimilated to 'Judaeo-Christianity'?

A theistic answer affirming a Supreme Person governing the world was, and for many still is, no longer possible. "This was the century in which God died," Levinas insists, "- that is to say, in a very precise sense, in which a certain discourse on God became increasingly impossible... One still hears it in certain assemblies where one does not hesitate when faced with phrases such as 'God wished, God chose, God ordered'; we are told about God as we might be told about someone's doctor or mother-in-law (Levinas 1973, 280)."

Since traditional theism will not do, Levinas explores the possibility that the tremor of the hyphen consists of a secularism that Judaism alone makes audible. Judaism by itself would bear secular doctrines that are elided by the Judaeo-Christian liberal form of secularism that emphasizes individual rights. Attending to this tremor does not involve denying the validity of individual rights but invites us to consider that Christian humanism might fall short "of the very finality of the human" in so far as this finality or purpose exceeds the scope of individual rights. A division of labour between Judaism and Christianity is thereby implied. Christianity is credited with the secularization that yields liberal humanism and its political articulation in the form of individual rights, while Judaism is credited with the secularization of the relationality and implicatedness for which liberal individualism fails to account. Christianity is secularized as the ethics of liberal humanism, while Judaism is secularized as the ethics of anti-humanism. And since ours is an age in which humanism finds itself in crisis, it is also the time wherein the specific contribution of Judaism become manifest. "We therefore needed a crisis of humanism in our society," he told the Jewish educators, so that the "major divergences" of Judaism can become explicit. "That is a sad thing to say," he admitted, since the "crisis of humanism... began with the inhuman events of recent history" (Levinas 1973, 281).

Levinas's line of thinking, whose contours take form under very particular intellectual and political pressures, produces two conspicuous difficulties. The first, as he freely admits, is the risk that accompanies every critique of individual rights.[2] Levinas is cognizant of the risk, for it goes without saying that if the severance of Judaism from the hyphen of 'Judaeo-Christianity' enables the possibility of a secularism that goes beyond individual rights, this does not mean that Jewish antihumanism is in any way immune from *falling short* of liberal individualism, for example by "rejoining the forces of conservatism and the retrogressive morality of the family, work and the Fatherland, in which the name of freedom is not even pronounced (Levinas 1973, 287)." If such a risk was evident then, how much more so today.

The second risk Levinas faces in severing the hyphen and dividing the moral labor between Christian liberalism and Jewish antihumanism is that of an exclusive *geo-theo-political alliance* of two faiths which together would exhaust our ethical and political exigencies. No one could doubt that in the decades after the Holocaust it was, and in many respects remains, reasonable and desirable for Jews and Christians to seek to overcome the theological and political enmity of their shared history. Their shared biblical heritage and history was readily transformed from the zero-sum game of exegetical rivalry, conversion and persecution into "a new period in Jewish-Christian relations...a new peace" (Levinas 2001, 70–71; see also 137, 263). The problem of course is that this geo-theo-political alliance is grist to the mill of a so-called 'Clash of Civilizations' by which billions of non-Judaeo-Christians bear the brunt of an imaginary covenant resulting from internal developments, ironies and catastrophes of nineteenth and twentieth century European history. The imaginary flag of a "Judaeo-Christian" civilization risks legitimizing new forms of post-Holocaust and post-colonial Western imperialism. The "new peace" forged after Auschwitz thereby recalls the covenant of *pieces* given to Abram when he beheld a "smoking furnace" and then

2 Marx's critique of rights and Heidegger's critique of individualism are the most significant comparisons to Levinas's project, and of course he understood the risks of this enterprise as well as anyone. On Levinas and Marx see Gibbs 1992, ch. 10.

received the promise to occupy a conquered land (Gen. 15:17-18). I will return to this geo-theo-political objection in the final section.

For now, I want to suggest that the constraints within which Levinas explores the question of Judaeo-Christianity are also in large measure the parameters within which politically emancipated, liberal Jews continue to approach the Jewish remainder or remnant. On the one hand, the secularization of Judaeo-Christianity in the form of liberal humanism sells Judaism too cheaply, deflating the Jewish remainder by conflating emancipation and the ultimate purpose of Judaism with assimilation to a secularized Christian politics of individual rights. There are, Levinas insists, "major divergences" that require reckoning. On the other hand, traditional theism, with its resort to a God of providential design and efficacy, exacts too high an intellectual price to account for such divergences. Levinas's constraints are the parameters within which the Jewish divergence from Judaeo-Christianity remains to be sought. If neither theism nor secular liberal humanism affords an adequate way of breaking the hyphen, where might the divergences of Judaism lie?

3 Double-crossing Judaeo-Christianity: the Passion of Israel

The philosophical constraints on the question of what constitutes the Jewish remainder resulted in a double-crossing of Judaeo-Christianity: the Jewish divergence is depicted in terms that clearly allude to Christianity, that of "the Passion of Israel," thus crossing Judaism with a distinctly Christian trope, while the Christian trope of divine Passion is typologically appropriated, thus virtually – and in one case literally – crossed out. This peculiar strategy emerges from Levinas's Jewish experience of the Holocaust, in the biblical sense of a 'burnt offering,' penetrating the philosophical and Catholic contours of his intellectual horizon.

We first glimpse the elaborate gesture in published form in 1947 precisely while the inhuman events of recent history were still searing in his mind. "Being Jewish" is a programmatic essay that Levinas oddly never reissued in his several volumes of essays on Judaism, perhaps because the theme of 'ethics' is present only as a seed beneath the surface. Nevertheless, the essay illuminates his views on the relation between Judaism and Christianity with forthright clarity. Although closely related – "to a very large extent it [Christianity] is a Judaism" – there is a phenomenological difference that Levinas finds decisive. Christianity emphasizes the fulfillment of meaning in the present: the logos is made manifest in the incarnate Son who walks among people and, therefore, through whom "God is the Christian's brother, that is, his contemporary". This *presence* of the Father in the Son is the secret to Christianity's remarkable *political* flexibility. It can endure any number of hierarchical political arrangements as well as the separation of Church and State because in spirit Christianity renders people absolutely free of external domination and able to attain salvation by the renewal of their "wholly interior" life. The direct presence of the Son that is available for the Christian privileges the inner life of the individual as the locus of spirit, grace and salvation. By contrast, in Levinas's view of Judaism as it emerges in POW camps between 1940–45, being-Jewish yields a surplus of *passivity* that one can never get behind, establishing being-Jewish as a relation with a past that can never be brought entirely into presence, as with a Father who can never be adequately encountered in the Son, "this Father to which the Jew is attached as to a past" (Levinas 1947, 208). Being-Jewish, he says elsewhere, is a "category of being" that goes beyond Sartrean 'facticity' and Heideggerian 'thrownness,' and as such expresses a phenomenological reality, "a human situation, and in this the human soul is perhaps naturally Jewish (1947, 208)."[3] Being-Jewish is an excess of passivity in which human freedom, projection and authentic resolve are traumatically attached to the unappropriatable origins of one's being, an attachment that therefore has the structure of filiality and creatureliness.

There is, then, a division of phenomenological labour: Christian theology indicatively points toward the secular forms of liberalism, egalitarianism and humanism, while the theological passivity of being-Jewish indicatively points to the passion of an ethics that is antihumanist, or rather an ethics that is ante-humanist, ante-individualistic and ante-liberal. "Humanism has to be denounced only because it is not sufficiently human," he says in his major philosophical work, published at the same time as his address on "Antihumanism and Education" (Levinas 1974, 127–28). Naming this divergence of Judaism from Judaeo-Christianity as "the Passion of Israel" first occurs I believe, in 1957, in "A Religion for Adults," where it clearly alludes to the 1947 descriptions of "Being Jewish":

> I should like to remind you of what the years 1933 to 1945 were like for the Jews of Europe... They experienced a condition inferior to that of things, an experience of total passivity, an experience of Passion. Chapter 53 of Isaiah was drained of all meaning for them. Their suffering, common to them as to all the victims of the war, received its unique meaning from racial persecution which is absolute, since it paralyses, by virtue of its very intention, any flight, from the outset refuses any conversion, forbids any self-abandonment, any apostasy in the etymological sense of the term; and consequently touches the very innocence of the being recalled to its ultimate identity (Levinas 1957, 11–12; cf. Levinas 1947, 209).

3 On Judaism as a "category of being," see Levinas, 2009, 75; 1963, 181; 1965, 51.

Through to the late 1980's Levinas consistently returns to the idea of "the Passion of Israel" and indeed "the Passion of Israel at Auschwitz"; of "what one calls the *shoah*" as "the passion of Israel in the sense in which one speaks of the passion of Christ" (Levinas 2001, 92).[4] Here, then, is Levinas's double-crossing of Judaeo-Christianity, designating way of marking the Jewish remainder with a Christian trope (the very sign of the cross) while typologically appropriating Christianity (thus crossing it out). How did Levinas come to this view? And can it be justified?

4 The Eros of Election:"the flame of the divine kiss"

In the eulogy Jacques Derrida delivered for Emmanuel Levinas's in Pantin cemetery on December 27, 1995 he recalled "the day when, listening to a lecture by André Neher at a Congress of Jewish Intellectuals, Emmanuel Levinas turned to me and said, with the gentle irony so familiar to us: 'You see, he's the Jewish Protestant, and I'm the Catholic" – a quip that would call for long and serious reflection (Derrida 1995, 12)." The release of Levinas's wartime diaries affords a new and valuable perspective on such reflection. The diaries make it clear that Levinas began viewing *Jewish existence as a Passion* in late 1944. The thought can be traced to his reading of Léon Bloy while in captivity as a French POW in north-west Germany. Toward the end of 1944, Levinas read Bloy's *Letters to His Fiancée* (1889–1890) and was greatly impressed with how, for Bloy, "the whole of humanity is lodged in the categories of Catholicism" (Levinas 2009, 151). In Bloy, Levinas found contents and affects that he would later reproduce in a Jewish idiom, "absolute thoughts and absolute expressions borrowed from the Christian drama" through a curious theological language "cleared of all sleekness," a type of theological "slang as absolute language" (Levinas 2009, 160). In theological *argot*, Bloy denounces bourgeois decadence and, elsewhere, does so by recourse to the figure of the wandering Jew who, in his very pre-Vatican II view,

4 We find reference to the Holocaust as the Passion of Israel in confessional works that were mostly presented in a Jewish context, for example, in essays on Franz Rosenzweig, Moses Mendelssohn, and Vladimir Jankelevitch, in interviews with Myriam Anessovic, in his "Forward" to *Beyond the Verse*, in "Demanding Judaism," "Assimilation and New Culture," "Revelation in the Jewish Tradition," and "From Ethics to Exegesis" and in several Talmudic readings ("Who Plays Last?", "For a Place in the Bible," "The Translation of Scripture", "Beyond Memory").

enjoys a privileged intimacy with God precisely by virtue of his affliction (Calin and Chalier 2009, 23–25; Hand 2013). Caught up in an identity that cut through his integration into French culture, Levinas found refuge in Bloy's Catholic conviction that fundamental mystery can only be accessed by lifting the veil of bourgeois blindness that fails to see the signs of Christ manifest in affliction and abandonment. For Bloy, "the very abjectness of that Race [of Jews] is a divine Sign, the very manifest sign of the constant lingering of the Holy Spirit over these men so scorned (Bloy 1911, 305; cited by Moore 2013, 272)."[5] Amid his captivity and despair we read Levinas drawing inspiration from, and admiringly transcribing, Bloy's enraptured vision of "the immensity of the suffering of Christ, the grandiose, transcendent horror of the Passion" and the "unheard of dream of this love of God which demands a paradise of tortures" (Levinas 2009, 154, citing Bloy's Letter 21). As Levinas glosses it, Bloy's "dialectic through suffering" amounts to an "abandonment – but precisely there election" (2009, 159). Inspired by Bloy's sanctification of abjection, Levinas exalts the proximity to mystery afforded by the intoxicating pain of fire and blood and envisages a Judaism, grasped at the nadir of its persecution, making manifest this mystery (2009, 151 and *passim*). Otherwise than Being will render this inspiration in its most concretely expressive form (Brezis 2012). But the experience of war and Holocaust that gives rise to it.

A radio talk Levinas delivered on 25 September 1945, shortly after his release from captivity, shows how his identification as a Jew involved a phenomenological crossing of being-Jewish with the mystery of the Passion glimpsed in Bloy. Titled "The Jewish Experience of the Prisoner," Levinas describes the existence of the Jewish prisoner of war as having a distinctly religious quality even to a secular person like himself who, since his Bar Mitzvah, had renounced religious language and refused to understand his life in religious terms (2009, 210). Faced with no place to go and a menacing, unknown, inhuman future, the condition of this irreligious prisoner was one of "loneliness with God, even if through pride or prejudice one dared not speak his name" (2009, 211). Like Abraham, not like Isaac, the prisoner was not a martyr or sacrificial victim but one compelled to bear the weight of a lengthy, silent journey interrupted only by a traumatic question from the son, en enigmatic response from the father, and the silence of all that was left implied (*sous-entendus*). For the prisoner Levinas, this lengthy,

5 Drawing on Moyn (2009), Moore sensibly portrays Bloy's account of the Jews as a "philosemitism that relies upon antisemitic discourse and symbols in the putative service of Jews so as to dismiss, reject, or reverse the evaluation of stereotypes against them, 'flirting with the taboo' of anti-semitism in unstable ways (Moore, 273; citing Moyn 2009, 15)."

silent journey in captivity, where neither death nor hope provided release, gave rise to his philosophical account of being-Jewish by relating it positively to a dark theology of Judaism as a Passion. "Driven to their Judaism, they sought refuge in it. Jewish history, Hebrew, the Bible, all seemed worthy of interest and study; even religious worship became possible" (Levinas 2009, 211).[6]

Levinas then proceeds to recount how Judaism began once again to take on meaning for a prisoner driven into being-Jewish. With the allies at their nadir and the world divided into the triumphant Evil of pure force lording over the feeble powers of the Good, history seemed to revert to an unlikely story from the liturgy of old: impotent Jews praying for the mighty hand of the Lord to save them from the tyrant, Jonah crying out to God from the depths of the abyss, God's eternal love for Israel concealed and then revealed, and at the bottom of it all the conviction that amid the pain and doubt which these Jewish prisoners suffered was God's love. "In total passivity of abandonment, in the detachment from all ties – to feel oneself in the hands of the Lord, to feel his presence. In the burning of suffering to distinguish the flame of the divine kiss" (Levinas 2009, 213). The philosophical elaboration of this infinitely personal experience, verging on a mystical testimony, is inspired from its very depths with literal, even carnal sense of Jewish liturgy. As he put it in the rawness of September 1945, "To think that all these [liturgical] words must be taken as they are said, that they are true to their elementary truth...their popular truth, their vulgar truth... To read an archaic text and be able to take it literally without adapting it to an interpretation, without searching for a symbolic or metaphorical meaning for it!" (Levinas 2009, 214). The philosophical categories of passivity, creation, election, filiality, eros, paternity and much else were factically indicated to Levinas by the Jewish theological experience of history.

But of course passivity and persecution, filiality and election, and the abyssal depths wherein God's presence is touched, are equally constitutive of Christ's passion as they are of a Jewish theological experience of the war and the Holocaust. These early characterisations of "being-Jewish" and "Judaism" already anticipate Levinas's later use of the term Passion. Indeed in the transcript of the radio talk from which I have been quoting, the phrase "total passivity of abandonment" which I cited a moment ago was originally written as the "total passion

---

6 Note that Levinas does not yet include the Talmud among that which is worthy of study in the Jewish tradition. It was in 1947 that Levinas met Chouchani, with whom he studied Talmud in the years following. The *Carnets* help us understand Levinas's philosophical *motivations* for studying the Talmud, precisely as a way of exploring the divergence of Judaism from Judaeo-Christianity.

of abandonment," and the reference on the same page to Jonah referred at first to Jesus crying "from the depths of the abyss," before Levinas re-Judaized those formulations (2009, 213 notes a. and b.). It is therefore clear that, thrown into the historical specificity of being Jewish, Levinas evidently sensed that he had approached that which is specifically Christian, where one "discovers the mysterious returning of supreme suffering to happiness". But mindful of this indiscrete proximity between Jewish historical experience and the passion of Christ, Levinas resisted. "All of Christianity is already contained in this discovery that comes well before it," he says, before immediately reiterating: "In the final account then, what is Judaism – in what way does it differ from other religions that are also full of moral teachings and precepts of the good, they too acceding to the unity of the divine principle – what is Judaism if not the experience, since Isaiah, since Job, of this possible returning – *before hope, in the depths of despair* – of pain to happiness, the discovery in the very suffering of the signs of election" (2009, 213).

5 Covenant as Com-Passion

If the likeness of Jewish passivity to the Passion of Christ is initially characterized by an anxiety or a refusal of intimacy, Levinas soon develops a different, bolder approach that incorporates, rather than elides, the notion of Passion. This is carried out on the basis of an increasing awareness of the midrashic warrant for the idea, or something very close to it, within the Jewish tradition. In 1945 Levinas's understanding of Judaism consisted of familiarity, to what extent it is difficult to say, with the Hebrew Bible, Jewish liturgy, Maimonides' *Guide of the Perplexed*, modern Jewish philosophical works by Rosenzweig and Hermann Cohen, and no doubt other desultory sources, but he had not yet embarked upon his belated though earnest study of Talmudic Judaism. Many years later, for example in his 1979 essay "Demanding Judaism," he offers an interpretation of Isaiah 58 that places this Judaeo-Christian text squarely on the left side of the hyphen by contextualizing it within the liturgy of Yom Kippur. For the Jewish tradition:

> the feeling that its destiny, the Passion of Israel, from the bondage in Egypt to Auschwitz in Poland, its holy History, is not only that of a meeting between man and the Absolute, and of a faithfulness; but that, if one dare say so, it is constitutive of the very existence of God... Not that this destiny, Passion and History 'finally' provide the proof of God's existence which the philosophers lacked. Rather, they are the spreading out of this very existence, a concrete spreading out right into the Diaspora where, according to an enigmatic saying by the Talmudic scholars, God followed Israel (Levinas 1994a, 6–8)

The History of Israel is a Passion in which Godself is splayed from the Exodus to the diasporic existence of the Jewish people and the horrors of Auschwitz. To the carnal passivity with which Levinas identified Judaism in the mid-40's, which was already a relation of election, creation and filiation by God, the word Passion now adds the idea of God's abandonment to, or participation in, this very destiny. The History of Israel – which for Levinas is not exactly the same as the history of the Jews – like the Christ for Christians, is the very site and modality by which God's participation in the ordeals of human history is "manifest" and "concretized," as a phenomenologist might say, or "revealed" and "incarnated," as a theologian would put it. "The History of Israel in its daily patience, in its Passion and even in its despair and death in the concentration camps, is closely bound – bound by covenant – to the presence itself and the unfolding of the existence of the divine" (Levinas 1982a, 30; see also 29).

The Passion of Israel reveals and incarnates (in the language of religion), or manifests and concretizes (in the language of phenomenology), the com-passion that makes being first intelligible (as being-for-each-other, or "one-for-the-other", as Levinas puts it). Compassion is a word Levinas generally avoids, primarily because it suggests empathic identification with the other (e.g. Levinas 1961, 271; 1974, 117, 128, 146 and 166).[7] But I am using compassion in the sense that Jean-Luc Nancy employs it, as the "contagion, the contact of being with one another [*d'être les uns avec les autres*] in this turmoil. Compassion is not altruism, nor is it identification; it is the disturbance of violent relatedness [*l'ébranlement de la continguïté brutale*]" (Nancy 2000, xiii). It can be called coventantal com-passion, if one keeps in mind the violent choicelessness of the covenant, held like a mountain over our heads, that Levinas proposes we cannot but accept if we are to live human lives.

Levinas refers this covenantal compassion to an "enigmatic saying by the Talmudic scholars" that is first attested in the *Mekhilta de-Rabbi Ishmael* (*Bo'* 14): "wherever Israel went into exile, the *Shekhinah*, as it were, went into exile with them". If Levinas initially conceived being-Jewish as a Passion through his familiarity with Catholic writers, after the War he readily found this very idea in the heart of rabbinic Judaism. In the course of working on the research project he sketched in captivity he discovered that it was not only Jewish liturgy but also rabbinic mythology and exegesis that locate the presence of God amid Israel's

7 But see Levinas 1974, 195 n. 12 for a use of 'compassion' that is compatible with the sense I am giving it.

suffering, exile and persecution, a presence that confirms Israel's election as beloved child by virtue of the suffering undergone by Godself on their behalf.[8]

Moreover, Levinas's reading of Judaism adopts characteristic features of traditional Jewish readings of Isaiah 53 that go back to Rashi (1040–1105) who, responding to the First Crusade, regards the Jewish people as the servant of God whose suffering expiates the sins of humanity, a form of vicarious suffering for the sake of the welfare of *all* people.[9] The idea that the Suffering Servant was "pierced for our transgressions" and "the punishment of our peace/welfare (*shlomenu*) was upon him" (Isa. 53:5) was understood by Rashi as referring to the vicarious suffering that was brought upon the Jewish people "so that the whole world can have peace (*shalom*)" (ad. loc.). This exegetical tradition was adopted, and often adapted, by many subsequent Jewish readings of the Suffering Servant, through to the "mission theology" of Jewish *maskilim* (followers of the Enlightenment). The influential historian Heinrich Graetz, for example, advocated that the Suffering Servant was none other than the "Messiah-nation" of the Jewish people whose exilic history of affliction has the didactic purpose of showing how mercy and humility, morality and justice, ought to be borne. Hermann Cohen understood this concept of Israel's messianic vicarious suffering as a "lofty ideal" that "has the value almost of a new revelation". By being the representative or iconic vicar of suffering, the messiah-nation serves the whole of humanity by giving rise to an ethical concept of world history.[10] Levinas's wartime experience and his philosophical account of Judaism are based on just such a "new revelation". His whole work aims to elucidate the phenomenological, that is to say, the embodied and historically *revealed* sense by which the Passion of Israel manifests the vicarious suffering by which compassion lies the basis of cognition. In this way the

8 *Mekhilta de-Rabbi Ishmael*, 3 vols, edited and translated by J.Z. Lauterbach (Philadelphia, 1933), vol. 1, 113. In a related article (Fagenblat 2015) I bring some of the main rabbinic sources that describe Israel's covenant with God in terms of com-passion, of suffering with and for one-another and show how this rabbinic heritage is adopted not only by Levinas but also by Rabbi Kalonymus Kalman Shapira, the Rebbe of Piaseczno, in his extraordinary work *Holy Fire*, written in the Warsaw Ghetto during its liquidation.

9 The first part of this paragraph is indebted to Rembaum, though translations are my own. I am grateful to George Kohler for drawing this material to my attention. For a thorough discussion of nineteenth century Jewish "mission theologies" in which Israel is often depicted as the Messiah-nation who suffers vicariously for the sake of a world cause, see the texts and introduction in Kohler.

10 Cohen 1995, ch. XIII. The relation, both conceptual and historical, between Cohen's and Levinas's respective accounts of messianic history deserves more attention than I can give it here.

exegetical line drawn from Rashi to Hermann Cohen or from Isaiah to Auschwitz articulated by Levinas in phenomenological terms.

Viewing Levinas's recourse to the Passion of Israel within the factical life of the Jews – from the Hebrew Bible and Jewish liturgy through exilic midrashim, medieval exegeses, nineteenth century German-Jewish mission theologies, and the *Holy Fire* of the Warsaw Ghetto – suggests that at issue here is a typological expropriation of Christ's Passion. Moreover, I have tried to show, as others have done in more detail, that the notion of God's suffering *in*, *with* and *amid* the suffering of the Jews is an "authentic" Jewish motif, prevalent in rabbinic, Kabbalistic and Hasidic thinking. And of course Levinas is not alone in appropriating the Passion as an interpretative frame for understanding Jewish history.[11]

The "Passion of Israel" elaborates Levinas's account of being-Jewish according to which individualism is transcended from the very beginning, through creation and filiation, and through which the com-passion of being-together outstrips liberal values of respect, equality, and rights. This ante-humanism involves

---

11 Elie Wiesel invites a Christological readings of the Holocaust. In *Night* (72) the narrator imagines Rabbi Akiva Dumer confronting God "in this Calvary". Naomi Seidman suggests that Wiesel accommodated the French revision (which the English translates) of his Yiddish memoir to the sensibilities of the Catholic Nobel Laureate François Mauriac, who played a decisive role in its publication; see Seidman (1996) and also Idinopulos (2006). David Roskies (1984) suggested that with Mauriac, "possibly for the first time, the Holocaust survivor was compared to Christ" (Roskies 1984, 262), but as we have seen Levinas was engaging in this line of thinking earlier. Bloy plays an analogous role for Levinas to the one perhaps played by Mauriac for Wiesel. Roskies shows how other authors such as Uri Zvi Greenberg and artists such as Samuel Hirszenberg and Marc Chagall had already figured Judaism Christologically in the preceding decades in response to Eastern European pogroms. This research is extended further by Stahl (2012), though one should note how Levinas diverges from the various modern Jewish and Israeli self-representations for whom a liberal-Protestant Jesus is the exemplar of Jewish experience, as Leora Batnizky (2012) shows in her chapter in Stahl (2012).

Christian theologians likewise viewed the Holocaust as a Passion, sometimes by way of Elie Wiesel's account the boy on the gallows in Auschwitz as illustrating the "creative suffering" of God (Fiddes 1998, 3–4) or the "inner mystery of God himself in which God himself confronts us" (Moltmann 1974, 284). Such was the view of Pope John Paul II, whom Levinas met on several occasions, and who called Auschwitz the "Golgotha of the modern world" and who, when confronted with pictures of Jewish corpses bulldozed into mass graves, declared that "there is the body of Christ". Marcel Dubois, a Catholic priest who lived and taught in the state of Israel, also proposed that in the Shoah "Israel...announces and represents, even without knowing it, the mystery of the Passion of the Cross" (Dubois 1974). The problem of course is that such thoughts inscribe the decisive event of European Jewish modernity within a Christian narrative of salvation from which Jews *qua Jews* are excluded. Not only were the victims killed *because* they were Jews but their Christ-like Passion would thereby testify to the triumphant truth of Christianity over Judaism. Hence the novelty of Levinas's typological re-ex-propriation of the Passion.

a violence of the Good, a divine violence, but not an impersonal violation of each one's uniqueness. In Stalag XI-B in the shadows of Bergen-Belson, Levinas began to wonder if it might be possible think of Judaism as an alternative category of being to the *Geworfenheit* of Dasein, for the "mystery" of 'being-Jewish,' of election by the flame of a divine kiss, presented itself to him as significantly different to simply finding oneself thrown into a situation.[12] The facticity of being-Jewish demanded more than could be made phenomenologically visible, because it exposes one to intrasocial dimensions of subjectivity that can never be made manifest. For Levinas, this opening affords access to the human condition of election without salvation, of how one's own finitude, even unto suffering, is bound with the suffering of others, across the distance that separates individuals. Twenty year later, Levinas will call this "substitution," once again deploying a Judaeo-Christian term to formally indicate the sense of ethics. This, finally, is how we should understand the idea of a Passion of Israel at Auschwitz. It is not a theological concept and much less a dogma. It is a point of access through Judaism – non-liberal, liturgical, midrashic, mythic, factical, ante-individualistic and in these respects antihumanist Judaism – to the divine comedy of existing. It sees in Judaism ways of indicating implicit features of the human condition as such while suspending, for these philosophical purposes, the particular, determined "Jewish identity" to which they are commonly attributed. Thus if the Passion of Israel at Auschwitz typologically appropriates a central Christian concept within a phenomenology of Judaism, it does so while neutralizing the identitarian significance of being-Jewish. It confirms neither Jews nor Christians as historically elected but describes the covenantal com-passion of human existence. Perhaps here is the final figure, without identity yet without abstraction, of the true Israel.

6 Substituting Judaeo-Christianity: for our Muslim brothers and sisters

Levinas's account of being-Jewish as a Passion was generated through exposure to ultra-Catholic writers. Léon Bloy was perhaps the first, and Paul Claudel, who

12 See the opening remarks of *Time and the Other,* lectures Levinas delivered in 1946/47, which makes it clear that Levinas is trying to indicate a different starting point for understanding the intrasociality of the self than *Geworfenheit* provides. Toward the end of these lectures, Levinas sketches a problematic notion of 'the feminine' which he credits to Bloy.

deliberately figured (or disfigured) the Jews in similar terms, would impress him even more:

> Claudel knew that, under Hitler, the Jews endured an ordeal that is without name, and cannot be placed within any sociological category. ...The Jewish people lay at the very bottom of the abyss into which humanity was thrown between 1939 and 1945...But Claudel cannot look away from a suffering that is experienced as the abandonment of everything and everyone, a suffering at the limit of all suffering, a suffering that suffers all sufferings. That is no doubt what he is referring to when, without being flippant or guilty of trotting out a tired cliché, he uses the term 'holocaust'. From that point on, Claudel makes possible an attitude that is adopted by a Christian for the first time: he *sees* that the Jew as Jew is fully his contemporary (Levinas 1969, 129–130).

Again we see how Levinas understands Judaism as an election akin to a Passion which becomes, in philosophical terms, a com-passion; election involves a *substitution* whereby one's own soul is bound with that of the suffering of the other. Substitution extends while further complicating the relation between Judaism and Christianity in Levinas's thought. To a conference of Catholic intellectuals in April 1968 Levinas explicitly linked the Christian notion of kenosis with the idea of God's substitution of himself for us in a radical com-passion – "a self-inflicted humiliation on the part of a Supreme Being..."becomes a "passivity pushed to its ultimate degree in the Passion, the idea of expiation for others, that is, of a substitution. The identical par excellence, the noninterchangeable, the unique par excellence, would be substitution itself (1968, 54–54). Although "at first blush theological," Levinas assured his Catholic audience that philosophical, secular sense could be made out of their faith; far less reassuringly, perhaps their faith could *only* have a secular meaning: today, "the only possible modality of transcendence," he proposed, "manifest[s] itself as humble, as allied with the vanquished, the poor, the persecuted (1968, 55)." Levinas's central later notion of substitution – of one's ownmost or utmost self, one's proper uniqueness, as "one-for-the-other" – clearly develops his account of the filial and creaturely relations which Passion, as com-passion, also secularize.

The notion of substitution is, however, by no means only or entirely Christian.[13] The rabbinic notion of *arevut* has a similar connotation. A famous adage, which Levinas would undoubtedly have known, has it has "every one of Israel substitutes for every other," *kol yisrael arevim zeh la-zeh*. Following the blessings

13 For a comparison between Levinas's notion of substitution and the Catholic existentialism of Gabriel Marcel, whom Levinas admired and with whom he associated, see Gibbs 1992, ch. 9, who notes, however, that Marcel rarely uses this term (Gibbs 1992, 197).

for proscribing idolatry and keeping the Sabbath in Leviticus 26, blessings that include God's "walking among you" (26: 12), Leviticus 26:37 intones a series of curses, and among them the curse that "each one shall stumble over another." A rabbinic midrash interprets: "This does not merely mean that each one shall stumble over another but that each one shall stumble over the sins of the other – which teaches that each Israelite substitutes for the other."[14] Levinas's account of substitution as an expiatory com-passion is rooted in Rabbinic as well as Catholic theology. "The Judaism with a historic reality – Judaism, neither more nor less – is rabbinic. The paths that lead to God in this Judaism do not cross the same landscapes as the Christian paths" (Levinas 1957, 13). Once again, however, in his search for the "major divergences" of Judaism, Levinas double-crosses Judaeo-Christianity by typologically crossing out the Catholic concept of God's kenotic substitution of his suffering for human sin.

But this is not to say that for Levinas adopts a theo-geo-political alliance between Judaism and Christianity, as some seem to think. There is no covenant of pieces between Judaism and Christianity forged on the altar of the Holocaust. Rather, Levinas understands the division of labour between Christianity and Judaism in the context of a post-European and post-Christian age:

> On to the world stage come peoples and civilizations who no longer refer to our Sacred History, for whom Abraham, Isaac and Jacob no longer mean anything. As at the beginning of Exodus, a new king arises who does not know Joseph.
> I do not in any way want to qualify this rise in materialism because we hear in it the cry of a frustrated humanity, and while one certainly has the right to denounce one's own hunger as materialist, one never has the right to denounce the hunger of others. But under the avid eyes of this countless multitude who wish to hope and live, we, the Jews and Christians are pushed to the margins of history, and soon no one will bother any more to differentiate between a Catholic and a Protestant or a Jew and a Christian, sects that devour one another because they cannot agree on the interpretation of a few obscure books. They are a religious collectivity that has lost all political cohesion in a universe that is henceforth built around different structures (Levinas 1961b, 165).

There can be no political alliance between Judaism and Christianity because both Jewish and Christian theology have entered a secular, post-Christian age. The English translation of this passage renders "les yeux avides de ces foules innombrables" as "the greedy eyes of the countless hordes". But this construes the tone as frightened and pitiless, when in truth, in this text called "Jewish Thought Today," published in the same year as *Totality and Infinity*, Levinas is expressing compassion for the innumerable people on this planet from developing countries

14 *Sifra Behukotai* 2:7; BT Sanhedrin 27a.

who go hungry on a daily basis. Of the age-old theological double-crossing of Judaeo-Christianity, what is left today is not a geo-political alliance but a covenantal com-passion borne of the decentering of the Judaeo-Christian historical axis for the sake of contemporary humanitarian exigencies.

> Perhaps, in this enormous world now rising up before us, Marxism still unites us in an immediate and unique way, as a doctrine in which we can glimpse its Judaeo-Christian legacy. But surely these Marxist infiltrations will themselves be lost in the vastness of these foreign civilizations and impenetrable pasts. Is it not the case that evolving beneath such a gaze helps Jews and Christians to rediscover a forgotten kinship? It is not a kinship that leads to some syncretism or other, or a few common abstractions. Instead, a new feeling of fraternity is born in our childhood return from the depth of ages. And the current concerns of Christian ecumenism will surely go further than wherever their first steps take them? The dialogue this time will go beyond the level of the Graeco-Roman ideas common to Jews and Christians in the nations where until now they have lived on (Levinas 1961b, 165).

If a residual alliance between Judaism and Christianity extends into the post-Holocaust world, Levinas thinks of it in Marxist and post-colonial terms, as a shared emancipatory vision that opens a dialogue with equal partners from beyond the horizon of Eurocentric ecumenicism. The shared Judaeo-Christian attunement to the suffering of the innocent affords only a strategic alliance for the sake of emancipatory com-passion, based on their *fraternity*, issuing from the same Father, to whom Judaism is attached on its own terms and in its own way, as are all His children.

Thus despite his reiterated double-crossing of Judaeo-Christianity, Levinas does *not* reiterate Rosenzweig's view that Judaism and Christianity jointly articulate the sacred sociality of being. As Levinas characterized it, for Rosenzweig "Truth, in itself, would entail a double manifestation in the world" and "is consequently experienced in a dialogue between Jew and Christian" (Levinas 1990, 163).[15] But for Levinas, *monotheism is a philosophical truth*, not one that Judaism and Christianity divide between themselves. Philosophical monotheism

15 Note that for Rosenzweig the Jewish people attest to God's coming into *the present* and Christianity to redemption's *future*, whereas for Levinas it is Christianity that reflects the possibility of God *in the present* while for Judaism God, as Father, is essentially *past*. Moreover, for Rosenzweig, the liturgical rhythms of Judaism and Christianity complement each other in order to actualize the Absolute or "the All" in the world, a view that some exponents of "the New Paul" see as compatible with the *Sonderweg* or bi-covenantal approach to the mystery of election. This is not the case for Levinas, who is both *more Catholic* in his Judaism and *more Jewish* in his philosophical divergence from Judaeo-Christianity than I had previously appreciated (in Fagenblat 2010); and see Aronowicz (2011).

is *revealed to reason*, when reason is understood in its proper phenomenological modality (as one-for-the-other). There is no privileged alliance between Judaism and Christianity but only a common patrimony that makes manifest their shared fraternity with all human beings:

> Israel is not defined by opposition to Christianity, any more than it is defined as anti-Buddhism, anti-Islam or anti-Brahminism. Instead, it consists in promoting understanding between all men who are tied to morality. It seeks their understanding, in the first instance, with Christians and Muslims, who are its neighbours or companions in civilization. But *the base of this civilization is the Reason that the Greek philosophers revealed to the world.* ... Our feeling for Christianity is wholehearted, but it remains one of friendship and fraternity. It cannot become paternal. We cannot recognize a child that is not ours. We protest against its claim on the inheritance and its impatience to take over, since we are still alive and kicking (Levinas 1955–56, 109).

Levinas's account of Judaeo-Christianity is thus complex and nuanced. On the one hand, the Judaeo-Christian tradition makes phenomenologically manifest a realm of invisible significations that the Greco-pagan view fails to notice. These significations concern the phenomenological grounding of cognition in compassion, thus establishing the coventantal and created character of the intelligible world. Double-crossing this tradition "formally indicates" to the phenomenologist both the liberal/humanist (Christian) and ante-liberal/anti-humanist (Jewish) aspects of the world. On the other hand, this phenomenological access does not reinforce a privileged geo-theo-political alliance but on the contrary reveals the notion of a fraternal existence in which human beings substitute for one another. "The possibility of a fraternal existence – that is to say, one that is precisely synchronic, without any 'underdeveloped' or 'primitive' peoples – is perhaps the decisive test of the spirituality of the spiritual (Levinas 1969, 130)." *Fraternal existence*, siblings standing in mutual separation in relation to a common Father, is how Levinas thinks of the relation between Judaism and Christianity.[16] This

16 The notion of fraternal existence is also crucial to the argument of *Totality and Infinity*, where it appears as the relation that separates form the commonality of concepts and genus through unique relation to the father. "the human community instituted by language, where the interlocutors remain absolutely separated, does not constitute the unity of genus. It is stated as a kinship of men. That all men are brothers is not explained by their resemblance, nor by a common cause of which they would be the effect, like medals which refer to the same die that struck them. Paternity is not reducible to causality... Fraternity is radically opposed to the conception of a humanity united by resemblance... Human fraternity involves the commonness of a father, as though the commonness of race would not bring together enough. ...Monotheism signifies this human kinship (Levinas 1961a, 214). This passage clearly echoes Mishnah Sanhedrin 4:5 (cf. Q'uran Surah 5:32), on which see Fagenblat 2010, 29–32.

fraternal existence is attested by all monotheistic religions, with Islam no less than Christianity:

> Islam is above all one of the principal factors involved in this constitution of humanity. ... It united innumerable peoples and races. It understood better than anyone that a universal truth is worth more than local particularisms. It is not by chance that a talmudic apologue cites Ishmael, the symbol of Islam, among the rare sons of Sacred History, whose name was formulated and announced before their birth. It is as if their task in the world had for all eternity already been foreseen in the economy of Creation (Levinas 1959, 179).

Indeed the first public mention of Judaism as a Passion, to a forum of Catholics in an Abbey in Morocco in 1957, marks this fraternal monotheistic existence of separate siblings related through a common Father who creates them independently of each other:

> Like Jews, Christians and Muslims know that if the beings of this world are the results of something, man ceases to be just a result and receives 'a dignity of cause', to use Thomas Aquinas's phrase, to the extent that he endures the actions of the cause, which is external par excellence, divine action. We all in fact maintain that human autonomy rests on a supreme heteronomy and that the force which produces such marvellous effects, the force which institutes force, the civilizing force, is called God... Catholics, whether secular, priests or monks, saved Jewish children and adults both in France and outside France, and on this very soil Jews menaced by racial laws heard the voice of a Muslim prince place them under his royal sovereignty (Levinas 1957, 11–12).

In the end, both Judaism and Christianity, like Islam, like other religions too, of which Levinas almost never spoke, are justified by virtue of reason, understood in phenomenological terms as illustrating the covenantal com-passion of existing fraternally, as one-for-the other. Indeed the very notion of substitution, of this affective attunement of one-for-the-other in which one's own suffering *incorporates* the suffering of the other, is not only a philosophical interpretation of the Jewish notion of arevut or the Christian concept of kenotic solidarity but refers, perhaps above all, to the notion of *Badaliya*, which Louis Massignon, whom Levinas knew, found in Islam. It refers to a substitutory com-passion which Derrida first noted but, as far as I know, has not been noticed since.

> This discourse of substitution is to be read from out of the depths of an abyssal history. We spoke just a moment ago, citing Levinas, of a "Judeo-Christian spirituality." It will one day be necessary, so as to recall and understand Islam, to question patiently many of the affinities, analogies, synonymies and homonymies, be they the result of a crossing of paths, sometimes unbeknownst to the authors, or of necessities that are more profound, though often perplexing and oblique. The most pressing (and no doubt least noticed) example in France is to be found in another thought of substitution, one that, under this very name,

> traverses the entire oeuvre and adventure of Louis Massignon. Inherited from Huysmans–whom Levinas in fact evokes early on in *From Existence to Existents*, "between 1940 and 1945"–and at work throughout the tradition of a certain Christian mysticism (Bloy, Foucauld, Claudel, the author of The Hostage, etc.) to which Massignon remains faithful, the word-concept "substitution" inspires in Massignon a whole thought of "sacred hospitality," a foundational reference to the hospitality of Abraham, or Ibrahim, and the institution, in 1934, of Badaliya–a word that belongs to the Arab vocabulary of "substitution": "these souls for which we wish to substitute ourselves '*fil badaliya*,' by paying a ransom for them at our expense, is a replacement," say the Statues of the *Badaliya*, here the word "hostages" is written in bold letters: "we offer and we commit our lives, beginning now, as hostages" (Louis Massignon, *L'hospitalite sacree* [Paris: Nouvelle Cite, 1987], 373–74...(Derrida 1997, 145–146, n. 71; cf. Derrida 2002)

As pertinent as the Islamic notion of *Badaliya* was in France in 1997, it is even more pressing today, and of course not only in France but throughout Europe and the Middle East, including Israel. The double-crossing of Judaeo-Christianity that enables a philosophical articulation of the covenantal com-passion of fraternal existence must be crossed again, with Islam, among others, till it becomes a knot that unbinds, so that theological alliances undo geo-political alliances. To research.

Bibliography

Aronowicz, Annette (2011). "On Michael Fagenblat's *A Covenant of Creatures*." *AJS Review* 35.1: 105–114.

Batnizky, Leora (2012). "Jesus in Modern Jewish Thought." In Stahl, Neta. *Jesus among the Jews: Representation and Thought.* London and New York: Routledge.

Bloy, Léon. *Le vieux de la montagne* (1911). Rpt. in *Le Vieux de La Montagne; Pour Faire Suite Au Mendiant Ingrat, a Mon Journal, a Quatre ans de Captivite a Cochons-Sur-Marne Et A L'Invendable; 1907–19.* Nabu Press, Paris, 2011.

Brezis, David (2012). *Levinas et le tournant sacrificiel.* Paris: Hermann.

Calin, Rodolphe and Catherine Chalier (2009). "Préface au present volume." In Levinas, *Carnets de captivité et autres inédits.* Ed. Rodolphe Calin and Catherine Chalier. Paris: Bernard Grasset/IMEC, 2009, 13–41.

Cohen, Hermann (1995). *Religion of Reason: Out of the Sources of Judaism.* Oxford. Oxford University Press.

Derrida, Jacques (1995). "Adieu." Eulogy for Emmanuel Levinas, Dec. 27 1995. *Adieu to Emmanuel Levinas.* Trans. Pascale-Anne Brault and Michael Naas. Stanford: Stanford University Press.

Derrida, Jacques (1997). "A Word of Welcome." *Adieu to Emmanuel Levinas.* Trans. Pascale-Anne Brault and Michael Naas. Stanford: Stanford University Press, 1999.

Derrida, Jacques (1999). *Adieu to Emmanuel Levinas.* Trans. Pascale-Anne Brault and Michael Naas. Stanford: Stanford University Press.

Derrida, Jacques (2002). "Hostipitality." *Acts of Religion*. Ed. Gil Anidjar. New York: Routledge, 356–420.
Dubois, Marcel (1974). "Christian Reflections on the Holocaust." *SIDIC Periodical* VII.2 (1974): 4–15.
Fagenblat, Michael (2010). *A Covenant of Creatures: Levinas's Philosophy of Judaism*. Stanford: Stanford University Press.
Fagenblat, Michael (2015). "'The Passion of Israel': the True Israel according to Levinas, or Judaism 'as a Category of Being'." *Sophia: International Journal of Philosophy and Traditions*, 54:3, 297–320.
Fiddes, Paul (1998). *The Creative Suffering of God*. Oxford: Clarendon Press.
Gibbs, Robert (1992). *Correlations in Rosenzweig and Levinas*. Princeton: Princeton University Press.
Hand, Seán (2013). "Salvation through Literature: Levinas's *Carnet de captivité*." *Levinas Studies* 8: 45–66.
Idinopulos, Thomas A (2006). "Jesus' Cross in Elie Wiesel's *Night*". *Literature and Belief* 26: 1 (2007): 43–52.
Kohler, George, Y. *Der jüdische Messianismus im Zeitalter der Emanzipation: Reinterpretationen zwischen davidischem Königtum und endzeitlichem Sozialismus*. Berlin: De Gruyter, 2013.
Levinas, Emmanuel (1947). "Being Jewish." Trans. Mary Beth Mader. *Continental Philosophy Review* 40 (2006): 205–210.
Levinas, Emmanuel (1955–56), "The Spinoza Case." In *Difficult Freedom: Essays on Judaism*. Trans. Seán Hand. Baltimore: The Johns Hopkins Press, 1990, 106–110.
Levinas, Emmanuel (1957), "A Religion for Adults." In *Difficult Freedom: Essays on Judaism*. Trans. Seán Hand. Baltimore: The Johns Hopkins Press, 1990, 11–23.
Levinas, Emmanuel (1959), "Monotheism and Language." In *Difficult Freedom: Essays on Judaism*. Trans. Seán Hand. Baltimore: The Johns Hopkins Press, 1990, 178–180.
Levinas, Emmanuel (1961a). *Totalité et infini: essai sur l'exteriorité*. The Hague: Martinus Nijhoff. Trans. Alphonso Lingis as *Totality and Infinity: An Essay on Exteriority*. Pittsburgh: Duquesne University Press, 1969.
Levinas, Emmanuel (1961b). "Jewish Thought Today." In *Difficult Freedom: Essays on Judaism*. Trans. Seán Hand. Baltimore: The Johns Hopkins Press, 1990, 159–166.
Levinas, Emmanuel (1963). "Between Two Worlds" (The Life of Franz Rosenzweig). In *Difficult Freedom: Essays on Judaism*. Trans. Seán Hand. Baltimore: The Johns Hopkins Press, 1990, 181–201.
Levinas, Emmanuel (1965). "Franz Rosenzweig: A Modern Jewish Thinker". In *Outside the Subject*. Trans. Michael B. Smith. Stanford: Stanford University Press, 1994, 49–66.
Levinas, Emmanuel (1968). "A Man-God?" In *Entre Nous: on thinking-of-the-other*. Trans. Michael B. Smith and Barbara Harshav. New York: Columbia University Press, 53–60.
Levinas, Emmanuel (1969), "Poetry and the Impossible." In *Difficult Freedom: Essays on Judaism*. Trans. Seán Hand. Baltimore: The Johns Hopkins Press, 1990, 127–132.
Levinas, Emmanuel (1973), "Antihumanism and Education." In *Difficult Freedom: Essays on Judaism*. Trans. Seán Hand. Baltimore: The Johns Hopkins Press, 1990.
Levinas, Emmanuel (1974). *Otherwise than Being or Beyond Essence*. Translated Alphonso Lingis. The Hague: Martinus Nijhoff, 1981.
Levinas, Emmanuel (1982a) "For a Place in the Bible". *In the Time of the Nations*. Trans. Michael B. Smith. London: Continuum, 1994, 11–32.

Levinas, Emmanuel (1990a). *Difficult Freedom: Essays on Judaism*. Trans. Seán Hand. Baltimore: The Johns Hopkins Press, 1990.
Levinas, Emmanuel (1990b). *Time and the Other*. Trans. Richard A. Cohen. Pittsburgh: Duquesne University Press, 1990.
Levinas, Emmanuel (1994a). *Beyond the Verse: Talmudic Readings and Lectures*. Trans. Gary D. Mole. London: Continuum, 1994.
Levinas, Emmanuel (1994b). *In the Time of the Nations*. Trans. Michael B. Smith. London: Continuum, 1994.
Levinas, Emmanuel (1998). *Entre Nous: on thinking-of-the-other*. Trans. Michael B. Smith and Barbara Harshav. New York: Columbia University Press.
Levinas, Emmanuel (2001). *Is it Righteous to be? Interviews with Emmanuel Levinas*. Ed. Jill Robbins. Stanford: Stanford University Press, 2001.
Levinas, Emmanuel (2009). *Carnets de captivité et autres inédits*. Ed. Rodolphe Calin and Catherine Chalier. Paris: Bernard Grasset/IMEC, 2009.
Midrash Psalms [*Midrash Tehilim Shoḥer Tov*]. Ed. Solomon Buber. Vilna: Romm, 1891.
Moltmann, Jürgen. *The Crucified God: The Cross of Christ as the Foundation and Criticism of Christian Theology*. London: SCM Press, 1974.
Moore, Brenna (2013). "Philosemitism Under a Darkening Sky: Judaism in the French Catholic Revival (1900–1945)." *The Catholic Historical Review* 99.2: 262–297.
Moyn, Samuel (2009). "Antisemitism, Philosemitism, and the Rise of Holocaust Memory." *Patterns of Prejudice* 43.1 (2009): 1–16.
Nancy, Jean-Luc (2000). *Being Singular Plural*. Trans. Robert D. Richardson and Anne E. O'Byrne. Stanford: Stanford University Press.
Rembaum, Joel E (1982). "The Development of a Jewish Exegetical Tradition Regarding Isaiah 53." *Harvard Theological Review* 75.3 (1982): 289–311.
Roskies, David G. (1984). *Against the Apocalypse: Responses to Catastrophe in Modern Jewish Culture*. Cambridge M.A., Harvard University Press.
Seidman, Naomi (1996). "Elie Wiesel and the Scandal of Jewish Rage." *Jewish Social Studies* 3.1: 1–19.
Shapira, Kalonymus Kalman (1960). *Holy Fire*. Jerusalem: The Piaseczno Council, 1960 [Hebrew].
Stahl, Neta (2012). *Jesus among the Jews: Representation and Thought*. London and New York: Routledge, 2012.
Wiesel, Elie (1982). *Night*. New York: Bantam Books, 1982.

Part 3: **Political**

Warren Zev Harvey

11 The Judeo-Christian Tradition's Five Others

Ever since the term "Judeo-Christian tradition" became popular in the USA in the 1940s,[1] it has been used in opposition to five different Others: (1) the Christian tradition; (2) Greco-Roman culture; (3) modern secularism or atheism; (4) other religious traditions, e.g., Hindu, Zoroastrian, Shinto, Confucian, Buddhist, Taoist, African, Islamic, Sikh, or Native American; and (5) the Judeo-Christo-Islamic tradition, i.e., the Abrahamic or monotheistic tradition. In my following remarks, I should like to say some words about these five different usages of the term "Judeo-Christian tradition," which correspond to its five significant Others.

I wish to emphasize at the outset that the distinction between these five different usages is no trivial matter. It is not academic nitpicking. It is very important to be able to distinguish between these five usages. When one hears someone affirm or deny the existence of the "Judeo-Christian tradition," one must determine which of the five usages of the term is intended before one can decide if the user is a liberal or a conservative, a progressive or a reactionary, a tolerant person or an intolerant one, a philo-Semite or an anti-Semite, a do-gooder or an Islamophobe.

1 The Judeo-Christian Tradition vs. the Christian Tradition

I begin with the first significant Other of the term "Judeo-Christian tradition," namely, the Christian tradition.

1 See Mark Silk, "Notes on the Judeo-Christian Tradition in America," *American Quarterly* 36 (1984), 65–85: in the 19th century, the term "Judeo-Christian" "served only to designate connections between Judaism and Christianity in antiquity," but in the 1930s it began to be used "to refer to values or beliefs shared by Jews and Christians, to a common western religious outlook" (65–66); and in the 1940s the use of the term "Judeo-Christian tradition" in this sense became common. Cf. his *Spiritual Politics: Religion in America since World War II*, New York: Touchstone, 1988. See also Deborah Dash Moore, "Jewish GIs and the Creation of the Judeo-Christian Tradition," *Religion and American Culture* 8 (1998), 31–53: "During World War II, a new understanding of American Jewish identity crystallized... At its core lay a powerful concept...the Judeo-Christian tradition" (47).

In the 1940s and 50s, the term "Judeo-Christian tradition" was used by Jews and liberal Christians in America in order to counter Christian exclusivism. A Christian might in the past have said, "The Christian tradition teaches love of neighbor." This statement, innocent in itself, was often understood to mean that the Jewish tradition does *not* teach it. Jews responded that Judaism too teaches love of neighbor, as it is written in Leviticus 19:18: "Thou shalt love thy neighbor as thyself." Thus, one should *not* say, "the *Christian* tradition teaches love of neighbor," but "the *Judeo-Christian* tradition teaches love of neighbor." This ecumenical use of the term was intended to combat anti-Semitism, and to give Judaism a more accepted status among American religions.

Those who used the term "Judeo-Christian tradition" in this sense were not satisfied to interpret a verse here or a verse there. Their goals were much more ambitious. They argued that American values were not based on the *Christian* tradition, but on the *Judeo-Christian* tradition. The implicit premise of this argument was that Judaism and Christianity were somehow equals in American religious life. This sense of equality was perhaps most clearly expressed in the title of Will Herberg's best-selling sociological book about religion in America: *Protestant-Catholic-Jew* (1955). Herberg considered this equality of "the three great religions" (viz., Protestantism, Catholicism, and Judaism) to be something distinctively American, and entirely incomprehensible to Europeans.[2] Herberg wrote of the "Americanization" of Protestantism, Catholicism, and Judaism. He argued that in America, as opposed to Europe, the pluralism of religions was a basic value, and all religions were considered equal: "In America religious pluralism is...not merely a historical and political fact" but "an essential aspect of the American way of life."[3] The robust American use of the term "Judeo-Christian tradition" eventually had an influence on European intellectuals and ecumenicists, but the influence was limited and conflicted.[4]

---

2 Will Herberg, *Protestant-Catholic-Jew: An Essay in American Religious Sociology*, Garden City, NY: Doubleday, 1955; Chicago: University of Chicago Press, 1983, 82–90, 94–98. There were, however, exceptional Europeans, like the French Catholic philosopher Jacque Maritain, who did use the term "Judeo-Christian tradition" in roughly the American sense. See Silk (cited above, n. 1), 66, 77.

3 Herberg, 85; cf. 96, n. 44.

4 It is amazing that in the profound 1993 book by the French Jean-François Lyotard and the German Eberhard Gruber on the meaning of the adjective "Judeo-Christian," the phrase "Judeo-Christian tradition" does not appear even once, as if its very utterance were *outré*. See Lyotard and Gruber, *The Hyphen: Between Judaism and* Christianity, trans. P.A. Brault and M. Naas, New York: Humanity, 1999. French original: *Un trait d'union*, Sainte-Foy: Le Griffon d'Argile, 1993.

Historians are confidently able to identify the precise day, nay, the precise *hour*, the term "Judeo-Christian tradition" achieved its vaunted victory over the term, "Christian tradition." It was December 22, 1952, around noontime. On that hour of that day, then President-elect Dwight David Eisenhower made the following remark in the course of a speech: "[O]ur Government has no sense unless it is founded in a deeply-felt religious faith, and I don't care what it is. With us, of course, it is the Judeo-Christian concept, but it must be a religion that [teaches] all men are created equal."[5] On the eve of his first inauguration, Eisenhower thus stated clearly: *our* religion, *our* deeply-felt religious faith is "the Judeo-Christian concept." In other words, according to Eisenhower, when the Declaration of Independence of the United States proclaimed "that all men are created equal" and "endowed by their Creator with certain unalienable Rights," it did not allude to the Christian tradition, but to the *Judeo-Christian* tradition.

Earlier in 1952, the distinguished liberal Protestant theologian Paul Tillich published a very influential essay, "Is There a Judeo-Christian Tradition?" This essay was *so* influential that it determined the title of a conference in far-away Belgium 62 long years later. It may also have influenced Eisenhower's comment. Tillich answered that there definitely *is* a Judeo-Christian tradition. Judaism and Christianity, he explained, are inextricably connected in history. However, he continued, this does not mean that they are identical or even compatible. Indeed, he observed, from the point of view of Christianity Judaism is a "Christian heresy" (the Jews rejected the Messiah) and from the point of view of Judaism Christianity is a "Jewish heresy" (the Christians rejected the Law). As a Christian theologian, Tillich insisted that Christianity must not try to deny its Jewish roots. Indeed, he intimated, a Christian who denies the "Judeo-Christian tradition" is guilty of the heresy of Marcion, who tried "to cut out of the [Christian Bible] not only the Old Testament but also everything in the New Testament reminding him of the Old."[6]

The idea that historically-speaking Christianity cannot be severed from Judaism had been affirmed three centuries earlier by Baruch Spinoza, who held that one cannot understand the Greek of the New Testament if one does not know Hebrew, for although the external language of the New Testament is Greek, its underlying language is Hebrew.[7] Spinoza held that Christianity cannot be under-

---

5 Patrick Henry, "And I Don't Care What It Is: The Tradition-History of a Civil Religion Proof-Text," *Journal of the American Academy of Religion* 49 (1981), 35–49. Cf. Herberg, *loc. cit.*

6 Paul Tillich, "Is There a Judeo-Christian Tradition?" *Judaism* 1 (1952), 106–109. Cf. Bernard Heller's response, "About the Judeo-Christian Tradition," ibid., 257–261.

7 Spinoza, *Theologico-Political Treatise*, ch. 7, *Opera*, ed. C. Gebhardt, Heidelberg: Carl Winter, 1925, vol. iii, 100: "*nam quamvis aliis linguis vulgati fuerint, hebraizant tamen.*" See also ibid., ch.

stood apart from the Hebrew or Jewish tradition. It cannot be separated from the language, beliefs, and customs of the Jews. Had he known the term, he might have said that the New Testament is part of the Judeo-Christian tradition. Whatever heresies the Jew of Amsterdam was guilty of, he was not guilty of Marcionism.

In 1966, the prominent historian Jack H. Hexter published his erudite book, *The Judaeo-Christian Tradition*, which in effect gave the term "Judeo-Christian tradition" an academic respectability among historians. According to Hexter's historical analysis, Christianity, in its initial stages, was simply Judaism without the Law: "Christianity shared with Judaism...a profound vision of God, a rigorous standard for the conduct of life, a highly organized community life in synagogue or church, and the requirement of conversion." Hexter explained that Christianity was more "successful" than Judaism in converting gentiles because it rejected "the minute and exacting requirements" of the Law, including circumcision, thus offering the potential convert "those aspects of Judaism that the gentiles found most attractive," while removing "the obstacles."[8]

The liberal ecumenical campaign on behalf of the term "Judeo-Christian tradition" was successful in the United States beyond all expectations. Indeed, for many Jews, it was *too* successful. Far too successful! The differences between Judaism and Christianity were being forgotten.[9] Judaism was beginning to be seen as a Christian sect that had one or two idiosyncrasies – like preferring the *menorah* to the Christmas tree, or the *matzah* to the Easter egg. Jews now feared that this blurring of distinctions between Judaism and Christianity could lead to assimilation and intermarriage. The same well-meaning progressives who had energetically campaigned *for* the slogan "Judeo-Christian tradition" now energetically campaigned *against* it. The term "Judeo-Christian tradition" had become a sort of Frankenstein or Golem, audaciously turning against its creators and arousing fear in them. The term that had once represented the hope of civil equality had now suddenly come to represent the threat of religious assimilation.

10, 150, where it is said that the New Testament was originally written in Hebrew. Cf. Epistle 75 (to Oldenburg), *Opera*, vol. iv, 315, on the Hebrew nature of the Gospel of John.

8 See Jack H. Hexter, *The Judaeo-Christian Tradition*, New York: Harper & Row, 1966, 93–94; 2nd edition, New Haven: Yale University Press, 1995, 94–95. The 2nd edition adds a section (45–47) on the significance in Jewish history of "the Diaspora," when "a religion of animal sacrifice became a religion of teaching" (46).

9 Cf. Alan Brill, *Judaism and World Religions*, New York: Palgrave Macmillan, 2012, 86, 103, who speaks of "the Judeo-Christian optimism of the 1950s," and adds: "[b]y 1960, this ecumenism had progressed beyond mutual tolerance into a liberal campaign for the blurring of divisions between churches and creeds."

In an essay published in 1964, Rabbi Joseph B. Soloveitchik, the eminent Talmudist and philosopher, argued that the term "Judeo-Christian tradition" was justified *culturally*, but not *religiously*: "[I]t is quite legitimate to speak of a cultural Judeo-Christian tradition... However, when we shift the focus from the dimension of culture to that of faith...the whole idea of a tradition of faiths... which are by their very nature incommensurate...is utterly absurd, unless one is ready to acquiesce in the Christian theological claim that Christianity has superseded Judaism."[10]

The pros and cons of the term "Judeo-Christian tradition" were presented thoughtfully in a 1965 lecture by Robert Gordis, a well-known rabbi and prolific scholar. His lecture was entitled, "The Judeo-Christian Tradition – Illusion or Reality." He explained that the concept "came to flower" sometime during "the first half of the twentieth century" in response to "practical needs," encountered little opposition "in its heyday," but recently had come under attack. Some Jewish theologians, he continued, "dismiss[ed] it as an imaginary notion concocted to serve apologetic ends or political purposes." In the end, he concluded, the concept has difficulties since there are basic differences between Judaism and Christianity, but it is not an "illusion" or a "myth," since Judaism and Christianity do have partially common Scriptures and a partially common history.[11]

Emblematic of the negative reaction to the big success of the "Judeo-Christian tradition" slogan was the Jewish theologian Arthur Cohen's 1969 essay, "The Myth of the Judeo-Christian Tradition." Gordis, three years earlier, had marshalled much damning evidence against the concept of a "Judeo-Christian tradition," but ultimately affirmed it and denied it was a "myth." Cohen rehashed much of the same evidence but concluded that the concept is indeed a "myth." The "Judeo-Christian tradition" was thus not real, not historical – but a fiction, a *myth*. How, asked Cohen, could one speak of a "Judeo-Christian tradition" when one religion says the messiah has *not* come and the other says he *has* come?[12] Cohen ignored the fact that only people who belonged to the same Scriptural tradition could fervently debate whether cryptic proof-texts from Isaiah or Daniel referred or did not refer to a certain Jew named Jesus of Nazareth.

---

10 Joseph B. Soloveitchik, "Confrontation," *Tradition* 6.2 (1964), 22–23.

11 Robert Gordis, *Judaism in a Christian World*, New York: McGraw-Hill, 1966, 154–156, 177–180. Cf. Silk, "Notes on the Judeo-Christian Tradition in America" (cited above, n. 1), 79: "by the mid-sixties a certain Hegelian twilight was beginning to settle over the Judeo-Christian tradition: writers pro and con became conscious of it as a historically conditioned concept."

12 Arthur A. Cohen, "The Myth of the Judeo-Christian Tradition," *Commentary* 48 (November, 1969), 73–77. Cohen's essay was reprinted in his popular book, *The Myth of the Judeo-Christian Tradition*, New York: Schocken Books, 1971, ix-xxi, 85–94.

Many Jews tended to agree with Cohen that the "Judeo-Christian tradition" was a "myth," but they argued against him that it was a useful myth, or what Plato would have called "a noble lie." The poet Edward Kaplan responded pensively: "even the myth, so-called, of the Judeo-Christian tradition is...a powerful and expedient religious posture, valid for most people here and now, and bearing witness to a...relationship with very real meaningfulnesses."[13] The response of Rabbi Jacob Chinitz was more pragmatic: "But what lies in store for...the Zionist venture?... The State of Israel makes sense to a world brought up on the Bible, but not to a secular, humanist world... There is, therefore, a political stake, to put it bluntly, in the retention of the concept of the Judeo-Christian tradition, even though, admittedly, it does not stand theological analysis."[14] In effect Chinitz was saying: As a rabbi I reject the notion of a "Judeo-Christian tradition," but as a Zionist I affirm it. As a Jewish theologian, Chinitz had no use for the notion of a "Judeo-Christian tradition," since it obscured the distinctiveness of the Jewish religion. However, as a supporter of Israel, he recognized its "political" usefulness: the reestablishment of Jewish independence in the Land of Israel was, in a real sense, a return to the Bible – and this return could be best appreciated by those who know the Bible and believe in it. Christians who perceive the modern State of Israel as part of their own biblical tradition could be expected to have sympathy for the Zionist cause.[15]

The counter-campaign to denigrate the term "Judeo-Christian tradition" was itself very successful. For example, the celebrated Christian philosopher, Alasdair MacIntyre, wrote in 1989 that Christians "need badly to listen to Jews," but "not speak in their name"; for "the attempt [of Christians] to speak for [Jews], even on behalf of that unfortunate fiction, the so-called Judeo-Christian tradition, is always deplorable." According to MacIntyre, the "so-called Judeo-Christian tradition" is an "unfortunate fiction," and it is "deplorable" when a Christian speaks

---

13 *Commentary* 49 (January 1970), 6.

14 Ibid., 4, 6.

15 While the notion of a "Judeo-Christian tradition" is wholly alien to internal Israeli discourse, representatives of Israel, when addressing Christians, regularly appeal to the common religious tradition of Jews and Christians. Cf., e.g., David Ben-Gurion's letter to President Charles de Gaulle of France (6 December 1967), who was a devout Catholic: "[T]he entire...Christian world considered Palestine...to be a single country, which the Jewish people had hoped would someday belong to it again, as was promised by the Bible and the Prophets... [F]or thousands of years we believed in the vision of our prophets... When a British royal commission [= the Peel Commission] came to Jerusalem at the end of 1936 to weigh the future of the Mandate, I said to it, '*Our Mandate is the Bible.*'"

on its behalf.[16] MacIntyre, I would bet, had previously been criticized by Jewish colleagues for using the term "Judeo-Christian tradition," and accepted the criticism uncritically. I do not know how MacIntyre would defend himself against the charge of Marcionism.

In 1987, there was an important scholarly conference on the "Judeo-Christian Tradition and the U.S. Constitution," held at the prestigious Annenberg Research Institute in Philadelphia (now the Herbert D. Katz Center for Advanced Judaic Studies of the University of Pennsylvania), just a few blocks away from Independence Hall. It was reported there that many Americans, Jews and Christians alike, now considered the term "Judeo-Christian tradition" to be "apologetic, euphemistic, hypocritical" and "no[t] authentic."[17]

Writing in 1986, the noted American Lutheran historian, Martin E. Marty, keenly distinguished between the early use of the term "Judeo-Christian tradition" in the 1940s and 1950s and the "new" use that became common in the 1970s. Agreeing with Cohen that the term was "essentially an invention of American politics," he exclaimed: "Three cheers for that earlier political use, for it grew out of an effort to promote interfaith concord and to put an end to ageless prejudices." However, he complained, the term had now been appropriated by "conservative intellectuals, politicians, and populists," and was obscuring the important historical and theological differences between Judaism and Christianity, while at the same time excluding Muslims, Buddhists, secular humanists, and many others.[18]

In short, the first of the five abovementioned usages of the term "Judeo-Christian tradition" is in contradistinction to the "Christian tradition." It was a liberal and ecumenical usage. This is the usage that made the term voguish in the United States, but its popularity caused a violent backlash against it.

---

16 Alasdair MacIntyre, *Whose Justice? Which Rationality?*, Notre Dame: University of Notre Dame Press, 1989, 10–11. I wonder what MacIntyre considers "deplorable." There are many non-Jewish scholars who are capable of presenting Jewish teachings just as competently as any Jew, and similarly there are many Jewish scholars who are experts in the teachings of other religions. Moreover, how can MacIntyre interpret Aristotelian ethics, if he's not a Greek?

17 Louis Henkin, "The Constitution and Other Holy Writ," in David M. Goldenberg, ed., *The Judeo-Christian Tradition and the U.S. Constitution*, A *Jewish Quarterly Review* Supplement, Philadelphia: Annenberg Research Institute, 1989, 58.

18 Martin E. Marty, "A Judeo-Christian Looks at the Judeo-Christian Tradition," *The Christian Century* 103 (5 October 1986), 858–860. Cf. Marty's introduction to the 1983 edition of Herberg's *Protestant-Catholic-Jew* (cited above, n. 2); and his *Modern American Religion*, vol. iii, "Under God, Indivisible: 1941–1960," Chicago: University of Chicago Press, 1996.

2 The Judeo-Christian Tradition vs. Greco-Roman Culture

The second major Other of the "Judeo-Christian tradition" is Greco-Roman culture. Here the term "Judeo-Christian tradition" is used in the sense of "*Hebraism* vs. Hellenism" or "*Jerusalem* vs. Athens." A good example of this usage is found already in 1941 in a lecture by James Luther Adams, the renowned Unitarian Universalist theologian. Replying to Nietzsche's *The Birth of Tragedy* (1872), Adams presented "the Judeo-Christian tradition" as a worthy alternative to Apollonian intellectualism and Dionysian voluntarism. "According to the Judeo-Christian view," he said, "God is a righteous will fulfilling his purpose in history."[19] Adams argued that while the ancient Greek view of life was melancholic, the Judeo-Christian view is moral, purposeful, and optimistic.

In the widely-used 917-page college sourcebook, *The Traditions of the Western World*, edited by Jack Hexter, together with J.W. Snyder, P. Riesenberg, F.L. Ford, and K. Epstein, it was affirmed: "The principal sources of the traditions of the Western world are two – Judeo-Christian and Greco-Roman"; and these two traditions are sometimes complementary and sometimes in "confrontation."[20] A fundamental task of students of Western civilization is thus to try to distinguish between its "Judeo-Christian" and "Greco-Roman" elements. For example, philosophy and democracy are Greco-Roman elements, while love of God and love of neighbor are Judeo-Christian elements.

This usage of the term "Judeo-Christian tradition" is often best replaced by the term "biblical tradition."

3 The Judeo-Christian Tradition vs. Modern Secularism or Atheism

The third rival of the "Judeo-Christian tradition" is modern secularism or atheism. Here the term is used in the loose sense of *religion* vs. irreligion. An instructive example is found in a 1955 essay by the historian Irving G. Williams, who stated

19 James Luther Adams, "The Changing Reputation of Human Nature" (Berry Street lecture), *Journal of Liberal Religion* 4 (1942), 1–48. See Gary J. Dorrien, *The Making of American Liberal Theology*, Louisville: Westminster John Knox Press 2006, 133–143.

20 Jack H. Hexter, ed., *The Traditions of the Western World*, Chicago: Rand McNally, 1967, 17, 137–160.

that the "cold war" is the "definitive struggle" between "Western Judeo-Christian civilization with its concepts of freedom" and "atheistic nihilistic Communism."[21] In response, the philosopher Mordecai Roshwald wrote: the author forgets that atheists like "John Stuart Mill and Bertrand Russell have a share in Western Civilization and its tradition of freedom" and "Communism is a Western product [which] may to some extent be traced back to Judeo-Christian tradition (e.g., the eschatological element in Marxism)."[22]

This usage of the term "Judeo-Christian tradition" as a synonym of "religion" is problematic for two reasons: first, it ignores the fact that there are religions other than Judaism and Christianity; second, many versions of modern secularism and atheism, including (but not exclusively) Marxism, exhibit distinct Judeo-Christian elements.

4 The Judeo-Christian Tradition vs. Other Religions

The fourth opponent of the "Judeo-Christian tradition" is any of the other religions, e.g., Hindu, Zoroastrian, Shinto, Confucian, Buddhist, Taoist, African, Islamic, Sikh, or Native American. Thus, for example, in a discussion of Japanese Bible translations, one might say: "There are some terms in the Judeo-Christian tradition that are difficult to translate into Japanese." Tillich concluded his article on the Judeo-Christian tradition as follows. If someone raised on Hinduism, Buddhism, Confucianism, or Greek religion, were to be told about Judaism and Christianity, with all their disputes and conflicts, he would be "astonished at the identity of structure at all points, and at the identity of content in most," and would affirm unhesitatingly that there is a Judeo-Christian tradition.[23]

It may be noted that the use of the term "Judeo-Christian tradition" in this sense is relevant even with regard to the third Abrahamic religion, Islam. Thus, one might contrast the portrayal of biblical characters, like Abraham, Joseph, Miriam, or Ezra, in the "Judeo-Christian tradition" with their portrayal in Islam. This does not, of course, mean that Judaism is always closer to Christianity than to Islam. There is also a "Judeo-Islamic tradition," which may be contrasted with

---

21 Williams, "Freedom and Government," in Carl W. Grindel, ed., *Concept of Freedom*, Chicago: Henry Regnery, 1955, 149.

22 Mordecai Roshwald, Review, *Philosophy and Phenomenological Research* 18 (1957), 279.

23 Tillich, "Is There a Judeo-Christian Tradition?" (cited above, n. 6), 109.

Christianity. Islam was formatively influenced by Jews and Judaism, and Jews living in Islamic lands were profoundly influenced by Islam and Arabic.[24] In many – possibly most – areas, Judaism is closer to Islam than to Christianity. One might say, for example, "The place of law in the Judeo-Islamic tradition is more central than it is Christianity," or "Theologians in the Judeo-Islamic tradition developed theories of strict monotheism, while Christian theologians were committed to the Trinity."[25] In sum, the use of the term "Judeo-Christian tradition" should not be taken to mean that Judaism is necessarily closer to Christianity than to other religions, just as the use of the term "Judeo-Islamic tradition" should not be taken to mean that Judaism is necessarily closer to Islam than to other religions. Is Judaism closer to Christianity or to Islam? Compelling arguments may be advanced for both opinions, and each historian or theologian is welcome to espouse his or her preferred narrative.[26]

---

24 See, e.g., Abraham S. Halkin, "The Judeo-Islamic Age," in Leo W. Schwartz, ed., *Great Ages and Ideas of the Jewish People*, New York: Modern Library, 1956, 213–263; and Bernard Lewis, "The Judaeo-Islamic Tradition," in his *The Jews of Islam*, Princeton: Princeton University Press, 1984, 67–106. The term "Judeo-Islamic tradition" has in the past been used mostly by Jews and rarely by Muslims, but this is changing; see, e.g., the recent writings of Muhammad Al-Hussaini, Karim Chaibi, Adnan A. Husein, Atif Khalil, and Razib Khan.

25 In the judgment of historian Norman A. Stillman, the idea of a "Judeo-Islamic tradition" is "far more real historically" than that of a "Judeo-Christian tradition" (Interview with Professor Norman Stillman, Woolf Institute Interviews, Cambridge University, 29.7.2013, https://vimeo.com/38611320). See his *Jews of Arab Lands*, Philadelphia: Jewish Publication Society, 1979. Cf. S.D. Goitein, *Jews and Arabs*, New York: Schocken Books, 1955; 3rd ed. 1974, 130: "Never has Judaism encountered such a close fructuous symbiosis as that with the medieval civilization of Arab Islam."

26 Needless to say, most Europeans presume that the "Judeo-Christian" connection is more important than the "Judeo-Islamic" one. Cf., e.g., Lyotard's remark: "The hyphen...in the expression 'Judeo-Christian'...is distinct from the other hyphens that associate or dissociate the name of the Jew from those of other nations where Jews are dispersed or exiled: Judeo-Arab, Judeo-Spanish, Judeo-Roman. For it is not at all the result of the diaspora or the *galuth*" (Lyotard and Gruber [cited above, n. 4], 15; French, 26). Cf. Gil Anidjar's introduction to Jacques Derrida, *Acts of Religion*, ed. Anidjar, New York: Routledge, 2002, 10, n. 32: "Lyotard seems not to consider how the term *Arab Jew* could singularly disrupt the hyphen of *Judeo-Christian*." Lyotard's point regarding the Land of Israel vs. the Exile has its merits. However, one would not want to argue that the Jerusalem Talmud is culturally more significant than the Babylonian Talmud since the former was composed in the Land of Israel and the latter in the Diaspora.

5 The Judeo-Christian Tradition vs. the Judeo-Christo-Islamic Tradition, i.e., the Abrahamic or Monotheistic Tradition

Let us now turn finally to the fifth and most recent competitor of the "Judeo-Christian tradition." Today, with the increase in the Muslim population in Europe and America, there has emerged a new polemical use of the term "Judeo-Christian tradition." The term is now used by conservatives – and sometimes by Islamophobes – in opposition to what may be called the Judeo-Christo-Islamic tradition, which is also known as the Abrahamic tradition, the monotheistic tradition, or, in the phrase of Harry Austryn Wolfson, the tradition of "the three religions with cognate Scriptures."[27] According to this fifth usage, someone might say, "Religion in the European Union today is mostly part of the Judeo-Christian tradition." However, since there are currently about 15 million Muslims in the European Union and only about 1 million Jews, it would be more accurate to say, "Religion in the European Union today is mostly part of the Judeo-Christo-Islamic tradition." Thus, the term "Judeo-Christian tradition," which was originally used to *include* Jews is now used to *exclude* Muslims.[28]

To say that the term "Judeo-Christo-Islamic tradition" should sometimes be used in place of the term "Judeo-Christian tradition" is obviously not to say that it should *always* be used in place of it. Thus, an author discussing concepts of love might reasonably write: "In the Judeo-Christian tradition theories of love are often based on the Song of Songs, while in the Islamic tradition they are often based on Qurānic verses." Again, a social historian might reasonably write: "The Judeo-Christian tradition underwent a process of secularization in the 19th century to a greater extent than did the Islamic tradition." Such statements may sometimes be debatable, but are not anti-Islamic. However, our author discussing concepts of love should not write: "The great religious love poems written in medieval Spain belong to the Judeo-Christian tradition"; for they belong to the Judeo-Christo-Islamic tradition. Again, our social historian should not write: "The Judeo-Christian tradition is amenable to secularization because it is a monotheistic tradition"; for it is the Judeo-Christo-Islamic tradition that is monotheistic and therefore amenable to secularization. In these latter cases, the term

---

27 Wolfson, *Religious Philosophy*, Cambridge, MA: Harvard University Press, 1961, p. v.

28 Cf. Jehan Sadat, *My Hope for Peace*, New York: Simon & Schuster, 2009, 30: "In Europe and America, people talk about the Judeo-Christian tradition, yet Islam is also part of this tradition and indeed shares many of the fundamental tenets set down in the Torah and the Gospels."

"Judeo-Christian tradition" is used to exclude Islam. The exclusion is unreasonable and reflects a bias against Islam. In such cases, the term "Judeo-Christo-Islamic tradition" is appropriate.

The best example of the Judeo-Christo-Islamic tradition is the Medieval period in the history of Western philosophy. Medieval Philosophy was common to philosophers of all three Abrahamic religions. It sought to interpret the Greek philosophical tradition in accordance with the values and visions of the three cognate Scriptures. With regard to their philosophic positions, Medieval philosophers were *not* divided along confessional lines. For example, an Aristotelian such as the Christian Thomas Aquinas was much closer in his philosophical position to the Muslim Averroes or the Jew Maimonides than he was to the Christians Augustine, Anselm, or Bonaventure.

An explicit use of the term "Judeo-Christian tradition" (or "Judeo-Christian inspiration") in this fifth sense is found in the controversial book by the French medievalist Sylvain Gouguenheim, *Aristote au Mont Saint-Michel* (2008): "Fundamentally, European civilization remained of Greco-Roman and Judeo-Christian inspiration... Islam was, since the redaction of the Qurān, the bearer of a different comprehensive system."[29] Gouguenheim argues that one can explain the renaissance of science in 13th- century Christian Europe without having recourse to the influence of the Islamic world. That great scientific renaissance was, according to him, inspired by the Judeo-Christian tradition, not by the Judeo-Christo-Islamic tradition. If one evaluates Gouguenheim's thesis from the point of view of the history of philosophy, one concludes that he is right regarding Bonaventure but wrong regarding Aquinas. You could have Bonaventure without Alfarabi, Avicenna and Averroes, but you could not have Aquinas without them – yet it was Aquinas, not Bonaventure, who was the great revolutionary of 13th-century philosophy, who changed the direction of all future Western philosophy. Medieval philosophy was a "Judeo-Christo-Islamic tradition."

Thus, for the sake of accuracy and ecumenism, one should in certain contexts substitute the term "Judeo-Christo-Islamic tradition" for the term "Judeo-Christian tradition." To be sure, the term "Judeo-Christo-Islamic tradition" may itself sometimes be exclusivist, e.g., when it is used polemically with the intent to depreciate non-Abrahamic religions.

---

29 Sylvain Gouguenheim, *Aristote au Mont Saint-Michel: Les racines grecques de l'Europe chrétienne*, Paris: Seuil, 2008, 201: «Fondamentalement, la civilisation européenne est restée d'inspiration gréco-romaine et judéo-chrétienne... L'islam était, dès la rédaction du Coran, porteur d'un autre système global.»

Conclusion

To conclude, the term "Judeo-Christian tradition" has been used in five different senses since it became popular in the United States in the 1940s. Some of its uses have been praiseworthy, some blameworthy, and others indifferent. If you hear someone use the term, please, please, be sure to clarify its context before you assign praise or blame.

Bibliography

Adams, James Luther. "The Changing Reputation of Human Nature" (Berry Street lecture). *Journal of Liberal Religion* 4 (1942): 1–48.

Anidjar, Gil. "Introduction" to Jacques Derrida, *Acts of Religion*. Ed. Gil Anidjar. New York: Routledge, 2002. 1–39.

Brill, Alan. *Judaism and World Religions*. New York: Palgrave Macmillan, 2012.

Cohen, Arthur A. "The Myth of the Judeo-Christian Tradition." *Commentary* 48 (November, 1969): 73–77. (Reprinted in id., *The Myth of the Judeo-Christian Tradition*. New York: Schocken Books, 1971).

Dorrien, Gary J. *The Making of American Liberal Theology*. Louisville: Westminster John Knox Press, 2006.

Goitein, S.D. *Jews and Arabs*. New York: Schocken Books, 1955. (3rd edition, 1974).

Gordis, Robert. *Judaism in a Christian World*. New York: McGraw-Hill, 1966.

Gouguenheim, Sylvain. *Aristote au Mont Saint-Michel: Les racines grecques de l'Europe chrétienne*. Paris: Seuil, 2008.

Halkin, Abraham S. "The Judeo-Islamic Age." *Great Ages and Ideas of the Jewish People*. Ed. Leo W. Schwartz. New York: Modern Library, 1956. 213–263.

Heller, Bernard. "About the Judeo-Christian Tradition." *Judaism* 1 (1952): 257–261.

Henkin, Louis. "The Constitution and Other Holy Writ." *The Judeo-Christian Tradition and the U.S. Constitution*. A *Jewish Quarterly Review* Supplement. Ed. David M. Goldenberg. Philadelphia: Annenberg Research Institute, 1989. 57–70.

Henry, Patrick. "And I Don't Care What It Is: The Tradition-History of a Civil Religion Proof-Text." *Journal of the American Academy of Religion* 49 (1981): 35–49.

Herberg, Will. *Protestant-Catholic-Jew: An Essay in American Religious Sociology*. Chicago: University of Chicago Press, 1983. (1st edition, Garden City, NY: Doubleday, 1955).

Hexter, Jack H. *The Judaeo-Christian Tradition*. New York: Harper & Row, 1966. (2nd edition, New Haven: Yale University Press, 1995).

Hexter, Jack H. ed. *The Traditions of the Western World*. Chicago: Rand McNally, 1967.

Kaplan, Edward. "Letter to the Editor." *Commentary* 49 (January 1970): 6.

Lewis, Bernard. "The Judaeo-Islamic Tradition." *The Jews of Islam*. Princeton: Princeton University Press, 1984. 67–106.

Lyotard, Jean-François and Eberhard Gruber. *The Hyphen: Between Judaism and Christianity*. Trans. P.A. Brault and M. Naas. New York: Humanity, 1999. (French original: *Un trait d'union*. Sainte-Foy: Le Griffon d'Argile, 1993).

MacIntyre, Alasdair. *Whose Justice? Which Rationality?* Notre Dame: University of Notre Dame Press, 1989.
Marty, Martin E. "A Judeo-Christian Looks at the Judeo-Christian Tradition." *The Christian Century* 103 (October 1986): 858–860.
Marty, Martin E. *Modern American Religion*. Vol. III: *Under God, Indivisible: 1941–1960*. Chicago: University of Chicago Press, 1996.
Moore, Deborah Dash. "Jewish GIs and the Creation of the Judeo-Christian Tradition." *Religion and American Culture* 8 (1998): 31–53.
Roshwald, Mordecai. Review of C.W. Grindel, *Concept of Freedom*. *Philosophy and Phenomenological Research* 18 (1957): 278–279.
Sadat, Jehan. *My Hope for Peace*. New York: Simon & Schuster, 2009.
Silk, Mark. "Notes on the Judeo-Christian Tradition in America." *American Quarterly* 36 (1984): 65–85.
Silk, Mark. *Spiritual Politics: Religion in America since World War II*. New York: Touchstone, 1988.
Soloveitchik, Joseph B. "Confrontation." *Tradition* 6.2 (1964): 5–29.
Spinoza, Baruch. *Theologico-Political Treatise*. In Spinoza, *Opera*. Ed. C. Gebhardt. Heidelberg: Carl Winter, 1925, vol. iii.
Stillman, Norman A. *Jews of Arab Lands*. Philadelphia: Jewish Publication Society, 1979.
Stillman, Norman A. *Interview with Professor Norman Stillman*, Woolf Institute Interviews. Cambridge University, 29.7.2013. https://vimeo.com/38611320.
Tillich, Paul. "Is There a Judeo-Christian Tradition?" *Judaism* 1 (1952): 106–109.
Williams, Irving G. "Freedom and Government." *Concept of Freedom*. Ed. Carl W. Grindel. Chicago: Henry Regnery, 1955. 149.
Wolfson, Harry Austryn. *Religious Philosophy*. Cambridge, MA: Harvard University Press, 1961.

Itzhak Benyamini

12 The Hyphenated Jew: Within and Beyond the "Judeo-Christian"

The train of progress, that terribly over-worn image of the historical principle of World Spirit, a train carried not by the horses of some Über-Napoleon but by its own self-inertia; this train, though but a vulgar metaphor, hurtles towards the unending terminus of Universal Salvation – that teleological termination of the meta-narrative of progress that also seduces other nations, non-Western and non-Christian alike. This train will be asked to halt its self-spurring, to press Pause on history's film projector, to retrospectively freeze its own image, so as to inform us of its very movement, and to reveal the sub-theological element that perpetuates its consumption: that which we shall call the *Jew-Object*. The power and truth of this metaphor, vulgar as it may be, seems to lie more at the level of its image than at its actual meaning – despite the metaphor being an allegedly superficial guise for masking reality. For what is the historical reality manifest in our daily lives if not the superficial banalization of our Sisyphean attempt to explain our most fragile and intimate experiences? Is it not the vulgarization of our deepest and most complex principles, which are themselves indirect response to that same vulgarization? The question of the relation between Western discourse and the status of the Jew as its product must, in this sense, include discussion of the (Christian) theology of victimhood, which, as will be argued here, is itself a radicalization of a specific Jewish theme. The bleeding Passion of Christ will thus be shown to be an acute actualization of a certain core within Judaism: namely, the submissive surrender before the Other, God.

This essay will discuss the concept of "the Jews" and the status of the compounding hyphen in the term "Judeo-Christian," using the later works of Jean-François Lyotard (1990, 1999) as a convenient starting point. Lyotard made a highly important albeit, as I argue, hardly unproblematic attempt both to come to terms with this hyphenated structure and to think beyond it.[1] Against the

1 Lyotard's concept-in-quotation-marks, "the Jews," inspired no small amount of criticism. Boyarin seems like the cutting-edge of contemporary Jewish thought in this context, especially in energetically promoting the positive reinvigoration of the debate surrounding the Judeo-Christian hyphenated concept, following his previous work on St. Paul (Boyarin 1997, 220–222; Boyarin 2006). An earlier representative of modern Jewish thought who attempted to theoretically promote the Judeo-Christian concept is, of course, Franz Rosenzweig, whose *Star of Redemption* (Rosenzweig 2005) presents the religion of the Father and that of the Son as complementary, all

background of his project of punctuating the flow of philosophical discourse by using such terms as *différend*, *post-modernism* and *meta-narrative*, Lyotard examines what philosophers have so pretentiously dared to conceive as the engine or perhaps fuel that propels the *train of progress*, that urges it forward so faithfully and efficiently, even if less so in our current age, as this train confronts the post-modern shift that supposedly halts its progression.

This essay, in seeking to question the actual wonderment that forms the basic axis of Lyotard's discussion, inquires into the specific placement of the hyphen connecting the concept of the "Judeo" with that of the "Christian" and examines the possibility of *dis*connecting the two. I shall argue that in light of the theological and historical "stickiness" between these two religious traditions, we are encouraged to think about the relations between them in a manner more complex than that which is connected or disconnected through a hyphen; to consider other relationships not bound to the graphics of a connecting line or to its negation through spacing; to allow meandering shades and lines of repression, breaking above, under, and alongside the two, yet realizing that even such alternative graphics do not offer any simple release from the truly embroiled intertwining of these legacies. In other words, we will have to ask ourselves whether the concept "The Jews" – which, as Lyotard rightly argues, contains and thereby also constitutes Jewish existence, and which might be understood through the metaphor of a receptacle, a *vase*, into which Jewish existence is implanted and cultivated – has perhaps managed to grow independent of its original bounds. This constructing-constraining form of the concept concerns the role of the Jew as the Object of Western culture, as the definite article of "*the* Object," as something constituted by Western discourse yet also simultaneously constituting that discourse itself for itself. In other words, a reciprocally echoing construction that is entirely initiated by Western discourse, which forces itself upon the Jew by constituting the latter as its other. At the same time, however, I shall ask whether it is also possible to regard this concept as an animating factor that exists in its own right, and is not merely an object of consumption for the Western-discursive engine that uses it

---

the while disposing this romantic coupling of the "third" religion, Islam. This anti-Muslim sentiment is prevalent in current political, or rather theo-political, discourse, especially in the wake of 9/11. Ordinary politicians, especially from the US and Israel, speak of the Judeo-Christian tradition and its liberal and humanistic values as allegedly antithetic to those of Islam. It is obvious that such a position is misleading at best, seeing as Islam is undoubtedly part of the Abrahamic tradition, and since neither one of the other two nor their devotees are quite so morally virtuous, as history has so painfully reminded us, especially in regards to the alleged morality of the Religion of Love. See also the compilation of Rosenzweig's comments followed by an accentuated critical discussion in Gesine and Schwartz (2003).

as fuel. Finally, I shall argue for a different kind of alternative to this graphics, one dissimilar to Lyotard's Levinasian "rescue" of a certain form of Judaism: the alternative figure of the traditionalist or "everyday Jew."

***

The lesson revealed by the European historical adventure is that the Jew-Object underwent a thorough process of objectification, being always-already an object in the eyes of the alleged native Westerner, who supposedly has been well-situated within the European *Heimat* since time immemorial. In other words, it is an objectification of an object already-known-via-concept rather than an objectification of a living subject. Likewise, it is an objectification that seeks to swallow and internalize its object along with its innermost kernel as imagined by its objectifier.

To this lesson we might add that we are today uncomfortably situated within a post-critical discourse – one that disallows even the simplest distinctions or separations between paragraphs and sentences, between identities, between the respective essences of Christianity and Judaism, indeed between any element and its alleged contradictory one. In light of this we might argue, vis-à-vis Lyotard, that the fuel consumed by the progress-train, the *consumerdered*, as I suggest referring to it, which screams its own soon-to-be-retrospective murder, is not only the Jew-as-body, as raw material in the most real, non-metaphorical sense, but also the *concept* of "the Jew." It is a singular concept subsumed within a plural one, and is thereby twice contained: first as an individual-concept, and second within the collective-concept of "The Jews." As such, this concept is but a purified projection serving the intra-Christian debate regarding *its own* essence, that is, the essence of Christianity, with its ambitions, destiny, and fate, which is also the fate of Europe.

The position developed here is inspired by, among others, Jean-Paul Sartre's central observation in his 1944 text on antisemitism (Sartre 2002, 292–341). For Sartre, the Jew's most internal essence is intricately connected to its socio-historic condition as it emerged in Europe, including the fundamentally antagonistic relation towards him, and the channeling of this relation into certain questionable roles.[2] It is thus antisemitism that makes the Jew. Sartre's position is related to his existential doctrine of the subject, developed in *Being and Nothingness*, as that which is constantly under the constitutive Gaze of the Other. The ideas developed here are in dialogue with that same philosophical substrata, which

---

2 This should be compared with the position of historian Israel Yuval (2006) regarding how the Jewish essence was formulated as a consequence of its positioning in an alien environment, specifically that of Middle Ages Christianity.

had been further mediated by the psychoanalytic position, manifest in Jacques Lacan's Seminar XI (Lacan 1994), in which he discusses the Other's Gaze and how the subject is constituted in relation to it.[3]

Yet this argument becomes entangled in an almost unbearable manner in light of a further thesis, namely, that Judaism – if indeed it can be understood as a trans-historical essence with a persisting core – is, in its most crude and fundamental biblical sense, a lacuna that both contains and represses within itself a "Christian complex": a complex seemingly rooted in an era "prior" to the foundation of the Religion of Love in all its glory. Crucial here is Freud's text *Moses and Monotheism*, which paved the way for investigating this primary repression within the monotheistic field (Freud 1939). The quotation marks around the word "prior" are meant to suggest that this contained repression seems to have always dwelt there, awaiting deep within the Jewish position, with its constant temptation for the status of victimhood and for appeasing the wrath of God-the-Father.

***

In the face of Christianity's messianic victimhood – rolling along the wheels of History, peacefully living under the moralistic cover of Compassion and Love – there stands the Jew. On one hand, he is regarded as a believer who is no stranger to the sphere of Law yet who simultaneously evades the Law's authority. He is not enslaved to it, or at least not enslaved *enough*. He is represented as hypocritical, scheming, and hence as unwilling to participate in the festival of altruism and the orgy of brotherly love. On the other hand, by the same token, namely, by not being ready to serve the role of the self-sacrificed in its Christian sense, the Jew "achieves" the tragic status of being victimized, of the Object of Christianity as told by history: the partner that has become a reluctant part, that is, a crucial component in the messianic plan, yet one that is simultaneously both this plan's *abjected* object and the fuel for its progress machine. But moreover and ironically, he who as such becomes the object of his own Christian core of self-sacrifice.[4]

I wish to pinpoint both this lacuna as an empty place of seductive phantasmatic content, and the role of the Jew-Object functioning as the nucleus around which this messianic content orbits. This raises the further question of how the

3 In the 1930s both Sartre and Lacan participated in the famous seminar conducted by Alexandre Kojève on Hegel's master-slave dialectic, later incorporating this theoretical enquiry into their own respective thoughts.

4 It is perhaps in the same sub-theological sense that the philosophy of the early Hegel saw release from the Jewish spirit as the first condition, as well as the first means, for the actualization of Western Christian progress (Hegel 1975). See also Cohen (2005).

concept of "The Jew" refers to real bodies as opposed to beings-towards-being-murdered, namely, to the real, everyday, physical lives of men, women, and children, free of such conceptual quotations. How does this concept, understood here as a reductionist invention serving the program of messianic victimhood, contain, like a receptacle or vase, a community indifferent to the alleged external gaze, despite the very internalized other that is repressed within it, despite this other of victimhood, despite Isaac, who hides behind the antagonist laugher Abraham?

At the same time we might wonder whether there is not a paradigmatic difference between these two religions with regards to their self-sacrificing axis. In this context it is important to reiterate that we are always contending with self-sacrifice, be it the arch-Father sacrificing his son, Jesus, or Isaac being victimized by his arch-Father, Abraham (himself an agent of the arch-arch-Father). Both arch-Fathers sacrifice their arch-beloved-sons, the objects of our identification – we, readers, believers, who are everyday sons. We who are called to fulfill our own self-sacrifice to the arch-Other, simultaneously a Father sacrificing and a Son sacrificed, with the Father being not an external force but rather a Subject whose moral and spiritual demands are constituted by us. We are called upon to transfer the Son within us, to sacrifice our empty core while filling it with the presence of faith.

***

In light of this, perhaps the correct strategy is not to attend directly to Lyotard's compounding hyphen, either siding with or against its dis/connecting quality, but rather to offer a two-dimensional, critical engagement with it. The first dimension, stemming from the psychoanalytic orientation, attempts to trace a different tension between Judaism and Christianity, and points to a logic of repression being the constitutive element in the theological relation between the two. This tension of repression can take us only so far, however, teaching us that, at the *discursive* level, the Jew and the Christian are in fact one and the same subject, the difference between them being confined to shifting levels of repression and degrees of consciousness. The second dimension involves not discursive difference but rather how discourse is expressed; this dimension concerns the *tone*s of the discourse of Law and the *manner* in which subjectivity exists within it.

Lyotard suggests an observation regarding the respective manners in which Jews and Christians regard the Voice of God, and how this is translated into the context of human understanding. Whereas Christianity speaks of the Incarnation as a mysterious act in which the Voice is translated into the sanctified flesh, as an act in which signifier is directly aligned with signified, for Judaism the Voice remains enigmatic and as such does not lend itself to a single, definitive interpretation. The Voice remains ever capricious – a term Lyotard does not invoke but rather hints at, and one that appears to be related to the monotheistic God already in St. Paul – thereby leaving unclear in which direction He is leaning towards. Thus, the word of the Voice must be re-read and re-interpreted time and again, absent any ability to reach a definitive answer regarding God's desire. This is God as the absolute Other and Stranger. Along the same lines, the Jewish subject is one who intensely and obsessively grapples with this enigma of the Voice and of Godly desire via his interpellation by it. In this respect, the law of Jewish *Halacha* gives form to the enigma of the Voice of the Law, providing it comprehensible symbolic value, offering a compulsive type of relief. The Christian, however, does not require the mediating law, since he has Love in his heart, in the form of a tautological principle, one which, as Lyotard stresses, operates under the logic of "Love because there is Love": God loves me because he loves me, and I believe because I believe. This is a tautology grasping onto the mysterious entanglement in which signifier and signified are tightly and intimately connected (Lyotard 1999, 20, 24).

Lyotard's picture of the "Jew" thus cannot but serve the stereotypical image of the Jew as he who is truly liberated, in the postmodern sense, from the dogmatic position by adopting a position of endless interpretation. We shall wonder whether this image is perhaps not somewhat romantic, even if philosemitic, subscribing to an agenda of a postmodern meta-narrative as a hyper-liberating discourse within which various sub-narratives can be liberated as well.[5] Lyotard is certainly conscious of this trap, explicitly referring to how the Pauline discourse understands Jews. Yet with this comment he then plunges into the Pauline paradigm he himself subverts, precisely because he wishes to describe what the Jews *really* are or are *really* supposed to be, over and above Paul. A Pauline catch, then. Lyotard's contemporary Jacques Lacan, like other non-Jewish French thinkers, was inclined to retain an idealistic outlook toward the *Talmudic* Jew, while striving to reveal the *real* Jew as the epitome of an ethical understanding of Judaism, namely, an image of a subject stooped over the *Gemara*, ever studying (Lacan 2001, 428–429). Although adequate discussion of Levinas's thought on this matter is beyond the scope of this essay, we should ask whether his opinion is not far from that of his Parisian colleagues, despite it being more complex – even taking into account his concept of the Absolute Other, and the premise that at the basis

---

5 Lyotard treats this postmodern position of supposedly infinite liberated *othernesses* in an ironic manner. In this regard, see his story "Merry in Japan", opening his collection of postmodern legends (Lyotard 2003).

of *Chazalic* Jewish hermeneutics one can locate an almost infinite possibility of reading the Bible and extracting the Ethical from it (Levinas 1968, 1977, 1996).

***

At this stage of the discussion we must face a fundamental question: Is there such a thing as the Judeo-Christian Tradition? Whether it is addressed to our professional understanding of history or to our worldly experience of the present, this is a question pertaining to a concept born from a specific historical junction in modern time, yet it is a question that appears to have been present since the dawn of Christianity. Our contemporary understanding of the birth of this concept maintains complex relations with the concept itself, in a sort of circus of Freudian *overdetermination*. If this is indeed the case, then what is the supplement in this question that makes it unique?[6] How does this specific question present itself as bearing the question of the *contemporary* subject? Indeed, we might say that this question is *the* question of our times, or at least that it is at the heart of many of the questions that drive contemporary conflicts.

For what is common to present-day believers? What connects them beyond their being defined as "religious" (itself already a Western-Christian determination)? What links them in a manner that is always increasing at the expense of that which separates them? To be clear, underlying this view is the premise that different spiritual positions – whether their objects of worship are transcendent or immanent Beings, or constituted according to a maternal or paternal model – serve as the mental infrastructure for most types of identification, including religious, national, socio-political, and perhaps even gender; such identifications include today's allegedly atheistic society (so that the problem of identifying and differentiating religions or forms of faith can be extrapolated to the question of the difference between cultural identities). At stake is thus a *subject-question* so urgent that it supplants other questions, presenting them as merely secondary. It seems that Jews, Muslims, and other religious identities are trapped in an attempt to contend with – mostly against their will – the question of interfacing with the Christian element in World Spirit. This subject-question can also be regarded as the question concerning the status of *Sonhood*, which demands that the subject worship another subject that is close to – although not quite similar to – its being, and which like him is also a son. In fact, the same applies for Christians from different churches, especially in Western societies, the only difference being that, for them, their identity as sons challenges them in the most direct sense (Benyamini 2012).

6 Zagury-Orly (2011) serves as my point of departure regarding *the question of the question*.

The question that is posed to (and imposed on) the subject – a question which penetrates to the core of the subject's being in such a manner that even the question's tense existence becomes a precondition for the very essence of his subjectivity – is the question of the relation between the Christian motif and the other motifs which comprise our world symphony. Sometimes it seems that the Christian motif has become less prominent than it was in the past; other times it seems more dominant and controlling than ever. Yet it is always a *hyphenating* motif, in the sense that it always poses itself as being opposed to, complementary to, or equal to one or more additional motifs or elements, be they Jewish, Muslim, or pagan. The same starkly Christian motif is latently manifest even in its secularized version, when the Western world posits its democratic-liberal values as the basic, albeit not exclusive, platform for interpellation of the other. However, to address this hyphenation effectively, one should prioritize its paradigmatic case, namely, that of *Judeo-Christian*. For this latter hyphenation commences the Christian self-formation via its opposition, which launches a continuous dialectics with the framework of the identical-other (the "old Jew") (Lyotard 1999, 13–27; Nancy 2007). For this new and challenging field of thought, this project which seeks to renew our understanding of this hyphenation, I would like to suggest the term *Critical Theology* (Benyamini and Hotam 2015).

***

The Christian orientation sees in both Judaism and Christianity a single continuous Messianic framework, one historically linked under a tautological narrative that terminates in the Son's embrace. It is well-known that this Christian position stems from an ambivalent sympathy to Judaism and to Jews, one that relies on either a tolerant or intolerant patience of awaiting either the Jews' mass conversion or their partial acceptance of the Christian message. This is a continuation of Paul's conception in Romans 11 of the *patient waiting* on behalf of the believers in the Messiah for the moment the "old" Israelites will achieve their faith. The term "Judeo-Christian" announces that Judaism is historically and developmentally prior to Christianity, hence also teleologically prior: *Judeo* and then *Christian*, not vice versa. The adjective "Judeo-Christian," when attached to such nouns as "tradition," "culture," and "religion," couples two concepts, each pertaining to a different religion; the hyphen emphasizes a singular and unitary trend: a combination of two forces into a single orientation, which, at the same time, *is Christianity itself.*

In short, it is mostly one side of this relation that is a full partner in the joint venture. The phrase "Judeo-Christian tradition," for example, stems primarily from *Christian* self-understanding and serves as its self-definition, so much so that the phrase is nearly interchangeable with and equal to the term "Christianity." The graphic sign of the compounding hyphen is thus a manifestation, incarnated into the signifier's flesh, of Christian Being in all its glory. This small line coupling Christianity and Judaism *is* Christianity itself; the hyphen is the Christian message, and it captures precisely the message's position with respect to Judaism. To generalize this possibly strange-sounding point, we can say that here we have a set that contains an element which is identical with the set. Thus the unique mathematical essence of this set is that it simultaneously contains both the element that is most different from it and the set itself, while also defining itself as the continuation of that different element.

This does not imply that in European history there were no apostate Christian trends that sought to delete this hyphen and to either deepen or eliminate their connection with Judaism, as if (hyphenated) Christianity was born *ex nihilo*. Indeed, certain Gnostic groups ostentatiously held onto a radical antisemitic message, as in the work of the second-century Gnostic Marcion of Sinope, who rejected early Christianity's Jewish roots, and the incarnation of this view in the works of the Lutheran theologian Adolf Von Harnack. Lyotard, however, attempts to imagine a different possibility of separation, despite the strong attachment between the two and despite the presence of the Christian voice at every turn. In doing so he is identifying with the Jewish position, for what is the root of such possible separation if not Judaism's reluctance to accept Christianity, as well as any other religious position, as a continuation of itself, as a replacement that renders Judaism obsolete? It is in this manner that certain orthodox and other more suspicious varieties of Judaism attempted to remain indifferent to Christianity, as if Christianity had never been born, and so with it other "ailments," ancient as well as modern.

***

The modern ideology of progress stands upon the shoulders of the Pauline "upgrade" to the authority of the Law, as it applies to the Jew-as-subject and to the subject-as-Jew. The latter, in turn, was based on how contemporary Second Temple Judaism, then nearing its demise, was regarded, at least by Paul and other Hellenistic Jews, as a religion of Divine Law (Benyamini 2012). All this is true regardless of whether there were any Jews who actually fit this Hellenistic definition. In fact, it seems that at that period there were no longer any such *Maccabee*-type Jews (the anti-Hellenizing fraction who had rebelled against the Seleucid empire's rule of Judea) acting as if completely immune from the influence of Greco-Roman universalism. However, there were certain old-fashioned Jewish zealots of Jehovah and his Temple who imagined themselves as these former *Maccabees*, even behaving as if completely estranged from Hellenism. This fundamentalist Judaism was based on the same logic of otherness: an identity entirely constructed as opposition to a rival object. As such, this fundamentalist Jew is already-an-other alienated even from itself, trying, in a tragicomic manner, to escape his ambiguous shell, to evade the unbearable yet terribly present spirit of the age.

Moreover, Hellenism, with its self-esteem as a Constitution-based international Nation and a form of Universalism, manifested itself in the eyes of its contemporary slaves as a new kind of Babylonian Imperialism. As such, it tainted early devout Christian desire (with what may well be another example of Jewish fundamentalism), a desire to escape the Judaism of the Law. This alternative sought to adopt an apologetic position in relation to the Hellenic world – as with Philo of Alexandria – by presenting itself as also based on a Constitution, albeit one grounded not just politically but also divinely. This is the politico-theological basis of the Christian revolt against every Law whatsoever, including its Hellenic-Roman version, a revolt that becomes further subjugation to the Law, in an even more internal sense, under the logic of an internal subjugation that in turn unleashes a lighter form of subjugation.

Thus, Christianity too, which some regard as a Hellenistic deviation of Second Temple Judaism, was actively rebelling against the constitutional ethos of the Greek polis, drawing its passionate mentality from Eastern Mysticism; it was merging itself with the repressed nucleus of Judaism, the nucleus containing the desire for self-sacrifice, its very imagined core, yet never neglecting the universalist trend of Hellenism. For the Christian, this masochist core of self-sacrifice has become Universal Truth through the determined and fated concept of Love. From here it is but a short way towards submission to the ethos of secular emancipation, this active messianic-masochism being only a step prior to a *narcissist universalism*, in which the ego is but focused on its own wounded being. In other words, there is room to suspect that this masochistic, sacrificial orientation is motivated from the start by the very proto-secular desire for self-constitution, in which the *subject* is released from the burden of the Father through complete *subjection* to Him.

Thus we would not be entirely wrong to ironically title Second Temple Judaism, prior to the birth of Christianity, as Judeo-Christian. If the enveloping shell and its core content were indeed fused, then at a particular historical moment the proto-Judeo-Christian legacy split, in the wake of the destruction of Temple, into two major branches. The first branch was the *Chazalich* version of Judaism, which, disgusted by the zealous religiosity of the self-sacrificial ethos, attempted to restrain it by formulating the discourse of *Halacha* in its stead, as a regulative authority that operates as Divine Law. The former temptation of the victim's mentality was now integrated into the everyday human context as a regulator of life. Once this Judaism faced diaspora homelessness, however, it adopted the Letter in place of this lost Home as the source of religious joy. The second branch was the newly born Christian religion of faith, sublating the internalized Law, regressing directly to the core of victimhood found in Biblical Judaism, thereby forming the substratum required for the Morality of Love. Perhaps this principle of love was nothing but an ideological cover for the principle of victimhood that was, and still is, the core of Christian subjective Truth, that is, relating the love of one's neighbor to love of the fundamental Other, Jesus. In this regard, the bleeding passion of Christ is an iconic actualization of a certain hard core found within Judaism: the core of submissive surrender before the Other-God

As concerns the Jesus-Object, there is no denying that there was indeed an *incarnation*, and that it can be accepted regardless of faith and belief. And here is the proof. The submissiveness of the Jewish subject before the law – a law which he formulated for himself as its beneficiary – allowed him the status of being crushed not only under the Torah's Law but also, and especially, under the occupation of foreign empires. This is beautifully expressed in the famous pre-Jesus myth of the Slave of God (*eved Yehova*) found in the book of Isaiah (52:13–53:7). The figure of Jesus retroactively colors the myth's movement as its own – similarly to how Borges argues that Kafka's writing retroactively colors certain pre-Kafka literary works as Kafkaesque. In Isaiah the figure of the faithful slave of God, which some claim is a portrayal of the figure of the soon-to-arrive Messiah and others claim is a manifestation of the actual suffering of the Jewish people, is incarnated in Jesus, who, as those verses put it, is humiliated by the will of God.[7]

This mythical incarnation of the spirit-in-the-flesh of the slave-Jesus, who believes in his fate on the Cross, expresses the seminal pivot against the homely-Jewish evasion of the Law and of absolute obedience to it. Here is thus the unconscious Christian desire: to completely subject the subject under the status of a loyal lover/slave. Hence the dialectical relation of the Christian to the Jew: an admiration and idealization of the figure of the Jew as it fulfills the potential enslavement to the Godly Law, in the sense that the Law places Love at its core, while being constantly suspicious that the Jew is playing an elusive game with the Law as much as with the Love of the Law.

Paul then steps forward to forge a new Law, one upgraded by love, in light of which Abraham is presented as the admirable character who manifests complete self-negation in the face of God's demand. And what does Jesus of the Gospels come to challenge if not Jewish hypocrisy with respect to the Law and its spiritual depth? The verbal actualization of the Letter of the Law is contrasted to the actu-

7 Compare "slave morality" to Nietzsche's (1990) doctrine of that motive in Judaism and Christianity, as well as his use of the term "Judeo-Christian."

alization of the depth of spirituality manifest in the Law. Hence for the Christian there will always remain a suspicious core that something in Abraham is not entirely devoted to God: something about him remains independent, loyal to himself, to his home and family.

Thus, throughout the history of European Jewry, the antisemitic claim, was, on one hand, that the Jew is not truly idealistic, that he is hypocritical, morally evasive, and unprincipled – a position evident even to the end of all possible ends of the relation between the two, even in its secular manifestation, in Hitler's complaint in *Mein Kampf* that the problem with Jews is first and foremost that they are not idealistic. On the other hand was the ever-present suspicion of certain European thinkers (including the secular, post-Jewish Karl Marx of "On the Jewish Question"[8]) that Jews cannot ever really participate in the Christian European project of salvation and liberation, even if they devoutly and demonstrably take part in all its required manifestation.

In light of these points we can clarify the question. What is the Jew if not the one who manifests the universal aspect, even if in a radical manner, of the internal tension within the soul between the needy self-confining Law and the constant desire to evade it – especially when facing a Law the subject formerly put before himself as a locked gate, as if it were independent of his control, when what is in fact first locked is none other than subjectivity itself in the face of the agent of that Law, which cannot stand the recurring evasion tactics in relation to it. We have thereby come full circle to the closed cycle in which "the Jew," in light of the recognition of his experience, becomes a universal concept. This circular quality is the disintegration of Judeo-Christianity, bound together by the compounding hyphen, which stitches together the dialectical circuit in such a faithful and snug manner.

***

But a further question then arises. Namely, whether the figure of the Jew as the Sisyphean Talmudic interpreter of the voice of the Absolute Other can be projected onto all other Jewish figures, including those of non-European diasporas. What about the *Mizrachi* Jew of the Middle East or North African diaspora, whose

8 See Marx's defense of the Jews' entitlement to receive full political rights in his famous early text "On the Jewish Question" (Marx 1992). However, this defense is undertaken from a position which does not believe in the Jews' willingness to release themselves from the "God of *Mammon*." Of course, Marx, in light of the prevalent antisemitic mood of the times, connected the Jews' constant and intimate dealing with their own worldly material condition to the their political condition, which designates them to engage only in commerce and finance, and as such described them as "non-idealistic" and "non-spiritual."

identity was not shaped through exposure to Christianity (but rather, if anything, to Islam)? What about the so-called traditionalist (*Mesorati*) Jew? How to characterize his more "relaxed" relation to the Law and the Voice of God? Is the latter truly, for him, an ambiguous Absolute Other? To address these questions, we must turn to a different level of analysis regarding the relation between Christianity and Judaism: one that involves not a repressed relation to a Christian hard core of enslaved submission before God, but a *soft core* of daily faith. As I argue elsewhere, these two cores or attitudes can already be found struggling with one another in the arena of Abraham's soul, which serves as a common *theological stage* prior to the split between the two legacies (Benyamini 2011). I would like to suggest that, ultimately, it seems that what motivates the Jew (and perhaps also the Christian) in his daily life is this second, soft core, which offers a release from this self-inflicted, sanctimonious, sacrificial enslavement. It is an attitude that forms an additional route of *side-stepping or negotiating* the Judeo-Christian array, albeit not by way of completely evading or escaping the compounding hyphen – which would be truly impossible – but through the discovery of a different Jewish manner of dealing with the repressed-Christian.

Take, for example, the "other Abraham" positioned alongside a number of additional, other Abrahams envisioned by Kafka (1977) in a letter to a friend; other Abrahams unlike the Kierkegaardian one of the equation between Christianity and the Binding of Isaac; an Abraham who returns to his human core in its most intimate, daily, and simple sense, that of *familyhood*. The same Intimate whose door is locked before the Voice of the Law, so that the Law's representative must toil against the subject's enigmatic desires, a subject who is constantly maneuvering in an attempt to construct and sustain this sphere of homeliness and familyhood in relation to lofty principles emanating from that Voice. All this is in contrast, as an upside-down mirror, to the image of the Law as that is barred for the subject – that other image of Law found in Kafka's works, and the Christian way of presenting divine Jewish Law as seemingly inaccessible to the miserable subject. The "other Jew" or "other Abraham," on the other hand, manages to slip away, evading the desire of the Other/Law through winding roads that remain attentive to intimate, homely needs, day-to-day needs which the Other cannot comprehend without shedding His Absoluteness. And even then, He would be forced to labor even harder in order to enforce His desire in face of the rolling laughter of that other (different) Jew: a laughter like that of Abraham and Sarah; perhaps also like the one Freud (1991) spoke of when writing about the democratic nature of Jewish Joke, where even God is subject to the self-irony of the miserable Jew.

This emphatic description presents a different kind of Jewish figure, one whose focus is day-to-day life, and for whom religion is subjugated to daily needs, mediating Absolute principles through traditionalist practices. At this point, however, the Western Judeo-Christian concern seems to re-surface, once again raising the suspicion that this figure is precisely the stereotypical Christian figure of the Jew as hypocritical and spiritually untrue. Once again, we find ourselves entangled in the Christian-Pauline paradigm of Judaism, thus raising the question of whether it might indeed be impossible to evade this paradigm and its concept of the Jew.

This investigation has focused on the tension between the "The Jew" as a concept and the Jewish subject as a real worldly existence, a subject which far exceeds the confines of its concept and evades its definition. At stake is how the subject – Jewish or Christian – relates to the Law. The Christian – in the predominant Pauline sense – builds his life around complete subjection to the Law in its most masochistic sense, while supposedly evading this Law through love; thus, in the end, he is even more enslaved to it as a singular absolute principle, namely, the principle of the Law-of-Love. The Jew, however – or at the very least, the other kind of "daily" Jew described here as an alternative that evades, even if it does not completely negate, the Judeo-Christian complex – does not abandon the Law in its entirety; rather it acts within the dimension of the Law, albeit in a manner that is sensitive to and aware of both the Law and the subject's *discursive* being, in a manner that allows for the existence of an intimate sphere independent of the Gaze of the Other/God. It is a surplus of enjoyment (*jouissance*) to which Jewish existence flees when forced to face the concept of "The Jew." And it is this dimension that must be added to Lyotard's and other such conceptualizations of Judaism: recognizing the existence of an additional sphere or figure of being that exceeds the status of being an Object-for-God or an Object-for-Western-Progress. A being beyond being *consumurdered*.

Bibliography

Benyamini, Itzhak. *Abraham's Laughter: Interpretation of Genesis as Critical Theology*. Tel Aviv: Resling, 2011 [Hebrew].

Benyamini, Itzhak. *Narcissist Universalism: A Psychoanalytic Reading of Paul's Epistles*. New York: Continuum, 2012.

Benyamini, Itzhak and Yotam Hotam. "An Outline for Critical Theology: An Israeli/Jewish Perspective." *Journal of Modern Jewish Studies* 14.2 (2015): 333–339.

Boyarin, Daniel. *A Radical Jew: Paul and the Politics of Identity*. Berkeley: University of California Press, 1997.

Boyarin, Daniel. *Border Lines: The Partition of Judaeo-Christianity*. Philadelphia: University of Pennsylvania Press, 2006.

Cohen, Joseph. *Le Spectre juif de Hegel*. Paris: Galilée, 2005.

Freud, Sigmund. *Moses and Monotheism*. London: Hogarth Press, 1939.
Freud, Sigmund. *Jokes and their Relation to the Unconscious (The Penguin Freud Library, vol. 6)*. Trans. James Strachey. London: Penguin Book, 1991.
Hegel, G.W.F. "The Spirit of Christianity and its Fate." *Early Theological Writings*. Trans. R. Kroner and T.M. Knox. Philadelphia: University of Pennsylvania Press, 1975. 182–301.
Kafka, Franz. "Letter to Robert Klopstock, Matliary, June 1921." *Franz Kafka: Letters to Friends, Family and Editors*. Trans. Richard and Clara Winston. New York: Schocken Books, 1977. 284–286.
Lacan, Jacques. "Of the Gaze as Objet petit a." *The Seminar of Jacques Lacan, Book XI: The Four Fundamental Concepts of Psychoanalysis*. Trans. Alan Sheridan. London: Penguin Books, 1994. 67–122.
Lacan, Jacques. "Radiophonie." *Autre écrits*. Paris: Seuil, 2001. 403–448.
Levinas, Emmanuel. *Quatre lectures talmudiques*. Paris: Minuit, 1968.
Levinas, Emmanuel. *Du sacré au saint: cinq nouvelles lectures talmudiques*. Paris: Minuit, 1977.
Levinas, Emmanuel. *Nouvelles lectures talmudiques*. Paris: Minuit, 1996.
Lyotard, Jean-François. *Heidegger and "the Jews."* Trans. Andreas Michael and Mark S. Roberts. Minneapolis: University of Minnesota Press, 1990.
Lyotard, Jean-François. *Moralités postmodernes*. Paris: Galilée, 2003.
Lyotard, Jean-François and Eberhard Gruber. *The Hyphen: Between Judaism and Christianity*. Trans. Pascale-Anne Brault and Michael Naas. New York: Humanity Books, 1999.
Marx, Karl. "On the Jewish Question." *Karl Marx: Early Writing*. Trans. Rodney Livingstone and Gregor Benton. London: Penguin, 1992. 211–241.
Nancy, Jean-Luc. "The Judeo-Christian." *Judeities: Questions for Jacques Derrida*. Ed. Bettina Bergo, Joseph Cohen, and Raphael Zagury-Orly. New York: Fordham University Press, 2007. 214–233.
Nietzsche, Friedrich. "The Antichrist." *Twilight of the Idols and The Antichrist*. London: Penguin Books, 1990. 123–199.
Palmer, Gesine and Yossef Schwartz, eds. *'Innerlich bleibt die Welt eine': Ausgewählte Texte von Franz Rosenzweig über den Islam*. Berlin: Philo, 2003.
Rosenzweig, Franz. *The Star of Redemption*. Trans. Barbara Galli. London: University of Wisconsin Press, 2005.
Sartre, Jean-Paul. "Le regard." *L'être et le néant*. Paris : Gallimard, 2002. 292–341.
Yuval, Israel Jacob. *Two Nations in Your Womb: Perceptions of Jews and Christians in Late Antiquity and the Middle Ages*. Trans. Barbara Harshav and Jonathan Chipman. Berkeley: University of California Press, 2006.
Zagury-Orly, Raphael. *Questionner encore*. Paris: Éditions Galilée, 2011.

Amanda Kluveld

13 Secular, Superior and, Desperately Searching for Its Soul: The Confusing Political-Cultural References to a Judeo-Christian Europe in the Twenty-First Century

The phrase 'Judeo-Christian' became an important factor in the American political landscape in the twentieth century, even if the term itself is heavily contested for obscuring the bloody history of persecution of the Jews by Christians and the deep religious differences between the two traditions. The term has steadily increased in popularity in Western Europe as well and is now used in political discussions on both sides of the Atlantic. There are however important local differences in the use of the term. In twenty-first century Europe 'Judeo-Christian' is predominantly used in discussions on Europe's identity and the perceived threat of Islam. The term 'Judeo-Christian' is also popular with liberal, Christian-Democratic and populist politicians who are keen to present Judeo-Christian and humanist or Enlightenment values as one package, even if this is historically debatable. The term 'Judeo-Christian' has turned into a synonym for tolerance and human rights and is at the same time used to signify both a culture contrasting Islam and as something that needs protection from Islam. Judeo-Christian does not signify any religious affinity. Jewish religious customs such as the wearing of the kippah or religious slaughter are dismissed in favour of secular values such as the neutrality of the state. The same goes for Christian values and the teachings and sayings of Jesus Christ. Most politicians who stress the importance of Judeo-Christian culture, at the same time dismiss important elements of Judaism and Christianity. Few politicians see the actual renewing of the Jewish or Christian faith as an answer to the threat of Islam; instead they portray the Judeo-Christian tradition as essentially secular. This is very different from the United States where the idea of a Judeo-Christian tradition is part of a civil religion. In Europe, however, the term is not connected to either the Christian or the Jewish tradition. It is an instrument in a toolbox of political rhetoric that appeals to a secular search for an identity or even Europe's soul.

1.1 The term 'Judeo-Christian' in the United States

In 2011 Shalom Goldman, Duke Professor of Religion, discovered that there is an online Judeo-Christian Voter Guide for the USA.[1] Intrigued by this phenomenon and "as one who identifies with the 'Judeo' part of Judeo-Christian"[2], genuinely interested in the advice on whom to vote for, he clicked on the icon for his State. Goldman ended up with information about the Christian-right American Family Association.[3] Whereas once these kinds of organisations would describe their values as 'Christian', they now choose to use the seemingly more inclusive 'Judeo-Christian', Goldman explains. Of course, it is, in fact, the opposite of inclusive. In recent decades, conservative Christians have "successfully projected thick, sectarian meaning onto the purportedly inclusive symbols and observances of Judeo-Christianity".[4] According to Goldman 'Judeo-Christian', is nowadays a "quintessentially American term" with "considerable political value if not intellectual or spiritual weight".[5] Influenced by *The Myth of the Judeo-Christian Tradition* (1969) by theologian Arthur A. Cohen, this initially surprised Goldman. In his essay Cohen clarifies that there is an essential theological and unbridgeable difference between Judaism and Christianity namely, as paraphrased by Goldman: "The Jews expected a redeemer to come out of Zion; Christianity affirmed that a Redeemer had come out of Zion, but that he had come for all mankind. Judaism denied that claim".[6] A crystal-clear summary of the Israeli Orthodox Jewish theologian Eliezer Berkovits goes as follows: "Judaism is Judaism because it rejects Christianity and Christianity is Christianity because it rejects Judaism".[7] Without context, this last remark is problematic because it seems to imply that it is only possible to define Judaism from the existence of Christianity onwards, which is evidently not the case. Before Christianity, there was Judaism, and it did not come into existence because of Christianity. Of course, it was not Berkovits' intention to proclaim the opposite. He wanted to stress that Christianity is morally bankrupt and that the Holocaust had showed this. He thought it best if Judaism had nothing to do with Christianity and was against interfaith dialogue and joint humanitar-

---

1 Shalom Goldman, "What Do We Mean By 'Judeo-Christian'?," *Religion Dispatches*, January 15, 2011, http://religiondispatches.org/what-do-we-mean-by-judeo-christian/.

2 Ibid.

3 http://www.judeo-christianvoterguide.com/.

4 Frederick Mark Gedicks and Roger Hendrix, "Uncivil Religion: Judeo-Christianity and the Ten Commandments," *West Virginia Law Review* 110 (2007): 276.

5 Goldman, "What Do We Mean By 'Judeo-Christian'?."

6 Ibid.

7 As cited by Ibid.

ian or social activities.[8] "We have to go our own way", he stated.[9] Consequently, his perspective rejects a hyphen to serve as a bridge between Judaism and Christianity. Those who want to build a case for the contrary would be wise not to base it on the long history of the relationship between Christians and Jews.[10] They will find this is a past of relentless and bloody persecution of Jews by Christians.

Goldman explains that, despite all this evidence, the term Judeo-Christian did not fall out of use in the United States although, within today's political rhetoric it has a different meaning than at the beginning of the nineteenth century in Europe. Then Protestant missionaries in England used it to indicate baptised Jews. In the same period, German Protestant theologian Ferdinand Christian Baur specified with Judeo-Christian a historical phase during which Christianity was born in the "narrow and cramping" environment of Judaism and struggled to break free in order to reach its full potential.[11] A century later, Americans who opposed fascism and anti-Semitism, stressed that Western culture was not exclusively Christian and reintroduced the term Judeo-Christian to fight the exclusion of Jews.

1.2 The use of the term Judeo-Christian in contemporary Europe

In post-war twentieth century Europe, references to a Judeo-Christian tradition were different. In *The Myth of the Judeo-Christian Tradition* Cohen remarks: "The concept of the Judeo-Christian tradition has particular currency and significance in the United States. It is not a commonplace in Europe as it is here; rather, Europeans since the war have become habituated to speak of Jewish-Christian amity, to define the foundations and frontiers of community, to describe and, in describing, to put to rest, historic canards and libels."[12] In post-war West Germany this

8 Allan Brill, *Judaism and World Religions: Encountering Christianity, Islam, and Eastern Traditions* (London: Palgrave Macmillan, 2012), 71.
9 As cited by Ibid.
10 Marshall Grossman, "The Violence of the Hyphen in Judeo-Christian," *Social Text* 22 (Spring 1989): 115–122.
11 Lee Irons, "The Use of 'Hellenistic Judaism' in Pauline Studies", *The Upper Register*, January 18, 2006, http://www.upper-register.com/papers/hellenistic_judaism.pdf.
12 Arthur Allen Cohen, David Stern, and Paul R. Mendes-Flohr, *An Arthur A. Cohen Reader: Selected Fiction and Writings on Judaism, Theology, Literature, and Culture* (Detroit: Wayne State University Press, 1998), 211.

was certainly the case. In the West German Parliament 'Judeo-Christian' was mentioned for the first time in 1953 and has since been used some dozens of occasions, mostly to refer to cooperation and dialogue between Jews and Christians. From the 1980s onwards, with a seemingly growing confidence in West Germany's say in such matters, the term has increasingly been used to refer to an overall worldview that is considered to be a foundation for universal human rights and shared values amongst people. In 1990, several months before the German reunification, Chancellor Helmut Kohl spoke of the common Judeo-Christian tradition of Europe.[13] He considered the Jewish artist Marc Chagall to be the embodiment of this culture. With his art, for example, the church windows in Metz and Mainz, Chagall built bridges between the European peoples. Kohl used the term 'Judeo-Christian' to indicate universal values. In that respect, Kohl's mention of Chagall serves its purpose because Chagall tried to challenge "the notion of antithetical traditions" in his artistic work, for instance by stressing the universality of suffering.[14] Kohl was not the only one who was intrigued by this particular quality of Chagall. Raïssa Maritain considered him to "bridge the Old and New Testaments".[15]

Although Kohl presented a Roman-Catholic perspective on liberal democracy, he never distinguished between Roman Catholicism and Protestantism or, for that matter, between Christianity and Judaism, when he referred to a Judeo-Christian tradition. He never gave a precise definition of the term Judeo-Christian. Instead, he provided a colourful, visible and, aesthetic illustration of the tradition he believed to exist. Like Jacques Maritain he thought the Judeo-Christian tradition was "a source of the West's enduring values".[16] Kohl even presented an example of a person who embodied all of what the Chancellor considered to be significant to this tradition that was first and for all European. Through the embodiment by Chagall, it is European in a broad sense: the Russian empire where Chagall was born, France where he lived, and Germany, where he made the glowing blue stained glass windows for the relatively simple Gothic Saint Stephen's church in Mainz. Saint's Stephen's church was touched by history. It was severely damaged, first in the nineteenth century, then again during the Second World War. Mon-

---

13 "Deutscher Bundestag Stenographischer Bericht. 217. Sitzung, Bonn, Donnerstag den 21. Juni 1990", *Deutscher Bundestag*, http://dipbt.bundestag.de/doc/btp/11/11217.pdf.

14 David Fraser Jenkins, *John Piper: The Forties* (London: Philip Wilson Publishers, 2001), 26.

15 Judith D. Suther, "Images of Indestructible Israel: Raïssa Maritain on Marc Chagall," in *Jacques Maritain and the Jews*, ed. Robert Royal (Mishawaka: University of Notre Dame Press, 1994), 157.

16 Mark Silk, "Notes on the Judeo-Christian Tradition in America," *American Quarterly* 36.1 (Spring 1984): 66.

seigneur Klaus Mayer contacted Chagall in 1973 with the request to set a sign for Jewish-Christian attachment and international understanding.

Following Ernest E. Griffith, whose interest centred on cultural attitudes and mores that will sustain democracy, Kohl believed that the Judeo-Christian religions served as the best foundation to "maintain democratic institutions".[17] By stressing that very few people embody the Judeo-Christian tradition and by choosing an artist and not a politician or an intellectual as the only example he mentions, Kohl presented the Judeo-Christian tradition as something that is as strong as it is fragile and as associative as it is clear. Kohl seems to say that it is easier to find the Judeo-Christian tradition in the arts, where it can exist in all its delicacy, than in politics, let alone policies. Following Kohl, one does not automatically become an agent of this tradition in one day or by being born in Europe.

In Europe, Cohen states, "they are not addicted as we are here to proclaiming a tradition in which distinctions are fudged, diversities reconciled, differences overwhelmed by sloppy and sentimental approaches to falling in love after centuries of misunderstanding and estrangement."[18] Cohen is right in that sense that in Europe there is no Judeo-Christian Voter Guide, and it is unlikely this will ever be the case. A reference to the Judeo-Christian roots of Europe never materialised in the EU Constitution, and Europe is not thought to have one uniform civil religion that is considered to be Judeo-Christian as it is in the United States. However, since the beginning of the Millennium Judeo-Christian has become a term that is increasingly used in sweeping statements about national and international current affairs, not only by populist politicians but also political leaders who are generally accepted as respectable and mainstream. Various politicians of twenty-first century Europe, for example in The Netherlands, in The United Kingdom and, in Germany, refer to the 'Judeo-Christian' tradition of their respective countries, usually without describing what they actually mean by Judeo-Christian culture, tradition or, heritage. This chapter explores these references and aims to clarify why they are brought forward and what they signify. The central point of this analysis is that in contemporary political and public debate in Europe "Judeo-Christian" is predominantly used in a secular sense, rather than in a theological or a religious one. In regard to the secular cultural identity of Europeans, José Casanova's definition seems to have the best fit.[19] He states that on the

17 Christian Wicke, *Helmut Kohl's Quest for Normality: His Representation of the German Nation and Himself*, (New York/London: Berghahn Books, 2015), 81.

18 Cohen, Stern, and Mendes-Flohr, *An Arthur A. Cohen Reader*, 211.

19 José Casanova, "Religion, European secular identities, and European integration," *Eurozine*, July 29 2004, http://www.eurozine.com/articles/2004-07-29-casanova-en.html.

one hand, more and more Europeans do not participate in "traditional religious practices" but on the other hand they maintain individual religious beliefs.[20] It concerns a process of religious individualization and 'unchurching' rather than secularization, meaning that Europeans consider themselves to have some Christian cultural identity that is "implicit, diffused, and submerged".[21] According to Casanova, this results in secular and Christian identities that "are intertwined in complex and rarely verbalized modes among most Europeans". In this particular situation of intertwined identities, it is very hard, also for European politicians, to define what a Christian identity of Europe is, let alone a Judeo-Christian identity.

Although in today's European politics the signifier Judeo-Christian is indeed used to define the foundations and frontiers of community it would be intriguing to know if Cohen would still consider that twenty-first century Europe stands out positively compared to the United States when it comes to references to the Judeo-Christian tradition by its politicians. If Cohen were alive today (he died in 1985), he would undoubtedly notice that there is a difference between Kohl in 1990 and German Chancellor Angela Merkel some twenty years later. Addressing a congress of her Christian Democratic Party (German: *Christlich Demokratische Union Deutschlands*, CDU) in 2010, Merkel stated rather bluntly that multicultural society had failed utterly. Merkel explained that this was not so much due to the growing existence of Islam in Germany. The problem was, according to the Chancellor, that German society had "too little Christianity".[22] "We have too few discussions about the Christian view of mankind."[23] Merkel stated that Germany was in need of more public discussion of its guiding values, of its Judeo-Christian tradition. "We have to stress this again with confidence, and then we will also be able to bring about cohesion in our society."[24] Merkel explained that the Judeo-Christian tradition always had, and in the present still has, a defining power. Also in 2010, Merkel's fellow party member and Minister of State Maria Böhmer stated in parliament that the Judeo-Christian tradition was, and would remain, the foundation of the German system of values and Germany's Constitution.[25] Merkel seems to have a different and perhaps less sophisticated approach

---

20 Ibid.

21 Ibid.

22 Tom Heneghan, "Merkel: Germany Doesn't Have 'too Much Islam' but 'too Little Christianity'," *Blogs.reuters.com/faithworld*, November 15, 2010, http://blogs.reuters.com/faithworld/2010/11/15/merkel-germany-doesnt-have-too-much-islam-but-too-little-christianity/.

23 Ibid.

24 Ibid.

25 "Deutscher Bundestag Stenografischer Bericht. 65. Sitzung Berlin, Donnerstag den 7. Oktober 2010", *Deutscher Bundestag*, http://dipbt.bundestag.de/doc/btp/17/17065.pdf.

to the matter at hand than Kohl. In Merkel's view, most Germans are agents of their Judeo-Christian tradition, but they are sleeping and lack confidence. They should be woken up or empowered by a public debate. In Merkel's narrative the Judeo-Christian tradition is more domestic than in Kohl's in that sense, that it is meant to serve as a solution to a problem that Merkel explicitly links to German society, namely a scarcity of Christianity intertwined with a lack of social cohesion and a complex debate about the place of Islam. The reasoning of Merkel goes as follows: when social cohesion is weak, this leads to discomfort about immigration, the State address this problem by facilitating public debate about Christian values and Judeo-Christian tradition. Through this intervention, Germans will integrate the values and tradition, which will strengthen societies' cultural identity and with that, its cohesion.

1.3 "Our culture!"

As pointed out above, both Merkel and Böhmer are not alone in making indiscriminating statements on the importance of the Judeo-Christian tradition. Evidently, this is not the first analysis that touches upon the signifier Judeo-Christian and how it is part of the discourse of twenty-first century European politicians. In a chapter called 'Europe and its others', in his book *Art Power*, Boris Groys points out that nowadays European politicians repeatedly like to stress that Europe is something more than a "community of economically defined interests".[26] Europe is also a "community of shared cultural values and these should be asserted and defended".[27] According to Groys, remarks about shared values should be understood as follows: "Europa cannot and should not expand unlimitedly, but should end where it's cultural values end".[28] Groys explains that these kinds of remarks usually imply that who comes to Europe should conform to an internally homogenous community with a distinct cultural identity. He states that the European politicians usually define these values "as humanistic values that have their origin in the Judeo-Christian legacy and in the tradition of the European Enlightenment".[29]

26 B. Groys, *Art Power* (Cambridge MA: MIT Press, 2008), 172.
27 Ibid.
28 Ibid.
29 Ibid.; See also: Peter Gay, *The Party of Humanity: Essays in the French Enlightenment* (New York: Knopf, 1964).

This combination of Judeo-Christian and the Enlightenment is in a way ironic because, if we were to follow Cohen in his analysis in *The Myth of the Judeo-Christian Tradition*, the Enlightenment undertook a critique of political repression and social discord. It considered Christianity one of the main causes of this societal situation. Christianity, therefore, had to lose its authority, and one of the ways to accomplish this was by studying its beliefs and history. Because of this, Cohen states: "It could not be helped that in the attack on Christianity Judaism should suffer for Christianity depended upon Judaism for the internal logic of its history".[30] Cohen explains that the *philosophes* confronted Christianity with its dependence on the Hebrew Bible and while doing so defined a 'Christo-Jewish tradition' that was considered to be irrational and fanatic. In Cohen's opinion, this Enlightenment construct was not a myth. "The Christian religion depended for its essential theological groundwork upon the religious vision of the Jews and, for that reason, the Christo-Jewish legacy was both affirmed and opposed."[31]

The Enlightenment linked Judaism and Christianity because they supposedly shared a common untruth.[32] Mark Silk pointed out that that Cohen later explained that he had Voltaire, Diderot, and D'Alembert in mind. Silk claims that Cohen "might with greater plausibility have sought Enlightenment roots in the thought of Lessing and Mendelssohn, which, while likewise critical of revelation, portrayed Judaism and Christianity as positive religions partaking equally of the same truth".[33] The Enlightenment thinkers were not all primarily focused on targeting Christianity or for that matter explicitly and intentionally out to destroy religion as such. Still, European politicians, who define Judeo-Christian tradition by connecting it with Enlightenment values, realise that some explanation is required. One has to take only one look at the debates amongst historians about the question if Voltaire was simply anti-Biblical or anti-Semitic, to understand that every eclectic reference to the Enlightenment can cause problems.[34]

Some twenty-first century European politicians solve the seemingly problematic combination of Christianity and Enlightenment by presenting Judeo-Christian and Enlightenment ideals as one package. They do so by pointing out the crucial importance of Christianity in the development of science and the spread of knowledge. Others see an important role for Jewish thinkers like Spinoza in

30 Cohen, Stern, and Mendes-Flohr, *An Arthur A. Cohen Reader*, 209.

31 Ibid., 209.

32 Silk, "Notes on the Judeo-Christian Tradition in America," 80.

33 See footnote 42 in: Ibid.

34 Gay, *The Party of Humanity: Essays in the French Enlightenment.*; Bertram Eugene Schwarzbach, "Voltaire et les Juifs: Bilan et Plaidoyer," *SVEC* 358 (1997): 27–91.

the process of Europe's culture developing itself through history as the breeding ground for freedom of expression, rationality and, the principle of the separation of church and state. There are also politicians who combine elements of this line of reasoning by presenting the Enlightenment as a necessary filter that made Christianity 'Enlightened'. An example is former Dutch Member of Parliament for the liberal People's Party for Freedom and Democracy[35] and critic of Islam, Ayaan Hirsi Ali, who now lives and works in the United States.[36] Hirsi Ali claims: "Christianity went through that process of reformation and enlightenment and came to a place where the mass of Christians, at least in the Western world, have accepted tolerance and the secular state, the separation of Church and State, respect for women, respect for gays."[37]

Whatever line of reasoning is followed, European politicians who use the combination of Judeo-Christian and humanist, use humanist as a synonym for enlightened principles and indeed, as is suggested by Groys, for universal values. This is especially true in the Dutch political debate that started at the beginning of the Millennium with the rise of a new populist political party that was led by Pim Fortuyn. His views on, what he considered to be a Judeo-Christian humanist culture, are still of influence on other politicians in The Netherlands, both populist and Christian Democratic. Initially a communist, Fortuyn became a member of the Dutch Labour Party[38], which he left in 1989 for the People's Party for Freedom and Democracy. In 2001 he took on the leadership of the newly founded populist political party Liveable Netherlands[39] but he was forced to step down several months before the national elections in 2002, because of controversial statements about immigration and Islam in a national newspaper. Fortuyn founded a new party, List Pim Fortuyn[40] and was expected to do very well in the national elections of 2002. He was in favour of a restrictive immigration policy yet he also aimed to grant citizenship to a large group of illegal immigrants. Nine

---

35 Dutch: *Volkspartij voor Vrijheid en Democratie* (VVD).

36 Born in Mogadishu, Somalia in 1969, Ayaan Hirsi Ali grew up in Saudi Arabia, Egypt and Kenya before fleeing to The Netherlands where she gained political asylum. She became one of the most prolific critics of Islam. She became a Dutch MP for the People's party for Freedom and Democracy in 2002 but in 2006 came under public scrutiny when questions were raised about her asylum procedure. Ayaan Hirsi Ali acquired US citizenship in 2007.

37 Peter Malcolm, "Hirsi Ali Confronts Jon Stewart About Islam," *Truthrevolt*, March 24, 2015, http://www.truthrevolt.org/news/hirsi-ali-confronts-jon-stewart-about-islam.

38 Dutch: *Partij van de Arbeid* (PvdA).

39 Dutch: *Leefbaar Nederland.*

40 Dutch: *Lijst Pim Fortuyn* (LPF).

days before the elections he was shot and killed by a left-wing political activist who was afraid that Fortuyn would persecute Muslims and immigrants.

The interview that led to his dismissal as leader of Leefbaar Nederland included the remark that the he did not hate Islam, but that he considered it a 'backwards culture'. Although Fortuyn used the Dutch word '*achterlijk*' in the sense of backwards, it was a problematic choice of words because '*achterlijk*' is used in The Netherlands as a synonym for 'retarded'. Although this choice of words may have surprised his fellow party members, his views on immigration, Islam and culture were already known. In 1990, Fortuyn had written a book against the Islamisation of 'our culture' and he also had written a book on what he thought this culture entailed.[41] According to Fortuyn, modernity is based on Christian, Jewish and humanist cultural traditions. Although he hardly explains the adding of 'humanism', he thus places himself unconsciously in a longer tradition of thinkers about Europe, such as Edgar Morin who presented travelling humanists like Erasmus as "the carriers of Judeo-Christian culture in a worldly (rather merely Christian) context", thus shaping a European civilization of science, freedom and humanism and rationality.[42] Through this process, a different variety of Judeo-Christian European culture came into being.

In his book 'The orphaned society'[43] first published in 1995 and in an updated edition in 2002, Pim Fortuyn entitled one of the chapters 'The Judeo-Christian humanist culture: our culture!'.[44] In this chapter he states that historically, Christianity follows directly from Judaism while humanism is a product of Christian Renaissance. Fortuyn goes on to describe the essential character of the three traditions. The Jewish tradition is the eldest and is characterized by the idea of Law. Although the Law is important in the Christian tradition as well, he contends that Christianity is defined by a sense of community. The Roman-Catholic Church has a unique place in the development of Western culture because it brings a common language, it contributes to a culture of knowledge, and it provides a model for developing states. Finally, the humanist tradition is defined by the birth of the individual. Fortuyn meant by humanist tradition, the values and principles of the Enlightenment and this fits in Groys' description of the used definition of

41 Pim Fortuyn and Abdullah R. F. Haselhoef, *De Islamisering van Onze Cultuur: Nederlandse Identiteit als Fundament*, Geheel geactualiseerde en herz. ed., 5. (Uithoorn: Karakter: Speakers Academy, 2002).

42 Cited in G. Verstraete, *Tracking Europe: Mobility, Diaspora, and the Politics of Location* (Durham NC: Duke University Press, 2010), 28.

43 Dutch: *De verweesde samenleving.*

44 Dutch: *De Joods-Christelijk humanistische cultuur: onze cultuur!* Pim Fortuyn, *De Verweesde Samenleving*, (Rotterdam: Karakter Uitgevers, 2002), 44–54.

Judeo-Christian. Judaism, Christianity and humanism are according to Fortuyn the three primary cultural sources that produced the culture of Western modernity that is far superior to any other culture because it provides a political, cultural, social and, military system that is the best setting for economic progress, an even distribution of wealth, the emancipation of women, children, and (sexual) minorities, development of the rule of law firmly rooted in parliamentary democracy and the best opportunities for personal development connected to individual responsibility. Fortuyn explained the nine principles of modernity in his 1998 book '50 years Israel: how long will it last: Against tolerating fundamentalism' (Dutch*: 50 jaar Israël: hoe lang nog? Tegen het tolereren van fundamentalisme*): the separation of church and state, freedom of speech, market economy based on private initiative and free enterprise, parliamentary democracy, the principle of the separation of powers, equality of man and woman, individual responsibility, a collective system of shared core standards and values, respect for universal human rights and international treaties.[45] Fortuyn wanted a second Cold War, this time not against communism but Islam. However, he stated that he did not want discriminatory laws against Muslims.

Fortuyn's view on Judeo-Christian humanist culture and values is exemplary for the use of the phrase Judeo-Christian culture in the current Dutch political debate. According to Ernst van den Hemel, who discussed this particular topic in a chapter of the book *Transformations of Religion and the Public Sphere: Postsecular Publics* (2014) the Dutch political use of Judeo-Christian can be characterised by the fact that 'classical Dutch values' such as "tolerance, secularism, gay rights and feminism" have been "reframed as secular, yet Judeo-Christian accomplishments".[46] Generally speaking, politicians who refer to Judeo-Christian do not dive deeply in the process of gathering historical data to find evidence for their claim. References to a theological unity or a confessional identity are rare, and mentions of personal faith or religious experiences are absent. Van den Hemel explains that in any case almost all descriptions of or references to Judeo-Chris-

45 Pim Fortuyn, *50 Jaar Israël, Hoe Lang Nog?: Tegen het Tolereren van Fundamentalisme* (Utrecht: Bruna, 1998); Johan ten Hove, "Fortuyn zet zijn kruistocht tegen het fundamentalisme voort," *Trouw*, June 5, 1998, http://www.trouw.nl/tr/nl/4512/Cultuur/article/detail/2742572/1998/06/05/Fortuyn-zet-zijn-kruistocht-tegen-het-fundamentalisme-voort.dhtml.

46 Ernst van den Hemel, "(Pro)claiming Tradition: The 'Judeo-Christian' Roots of Dutch Society and the Rise of Conservative Nationalism," in *Transformations of Religion and the Public Sphere: Postsecular Publics*, ed. Rosi Braidotti, Palgrave Politics of Identity and Citizenship Series (Basingstoke: Palgrave Macmillan, 2014), 53–76.

tian culture entail that these "are perceived as in need of protection from threats, most notably of Islam".[47]

1.4 Protecting Judeo-Christian Europe

The notion that Europe's Judeo-Christian culture has to be protected is not typical of the Dutch political debate. The question is of course of what or from whom is it to be protected or even defended since it is certainly not the case that only Islam is considered to be a threat. In the United Kingdom Rabbi Lord Jonathan Sacks, Member of the House of Lords seems to be more concerned with secularising forces in today's Europe, which ridicule and challenge the faith of both Jews and Christians. According to Sacks Britain now pays the price for the radical moral and cultural revolution of the 1960's that entailed the abandonment of "its entire traditional ethic of self-restraint", giving way to the process of secularisation.[48] All you need, sang the Beatles, is love. The Judeo-Christian moral code was jettisoned. In its place came: whatever works for you. The Ten Commandments were rewritten as the Ten Creative Suggestions. Or as Allan Bloom put it in The Closing of the American Mind: "I am the Lord Your God: Relax!"[49]

Without faith, Sacks explains, there is no future for civilisation. "If Europe loses the Judeo-Christian heritage that gave it its historic identity and its greatest achievements in literature, art, music, education, politics, and economics, it will lose its identity and its greatness."[50] Jews and Christian should, therefore, "stand side-by-side in order to renew our faith and its prophetic voice", thus saving the soul of Europe "for the sake of our Children".[51] The financial crisis and the riots in London were for Sacks reasons to again point out the importance of faith. He explained that the birth of modern economy is inseparable from its Judeo-Christian roots and that the market economy emerged in a Europe "saturated with

47 Ibid., 54.

48 Jonathan Sacks, "Reversing the Moral Decay Behind the London Riots ", *The Wall Street Journal*, August 20, 2011, http://www.wsj.com/articles/SB10001424053111903639404576516252066723110.

49 Ibid.

50 Marcus Dysch, "Chief Rabbi and Pope Discuss Fears for Europe", *The Jewish Chronicle Online*, December 13, 2011, http://www.thejc.com/news/uk-news/60227/chief-rabbi-and-pope-discuss-fears-europe.

51 Rabbi Jonathan Sacks, "Has Europe Lost Its Soul? Address given at the Pontifical Gregorian University (December 12, 2012)", *Catholic Education Resource Center*, http://www.catholiceducation.org/en/religion-and-philosophy/social-justice/has-europe-lost-its-soul.html.

Judeo-Christian values".[52] Now, that same market undermines these values. This is why Sacks sees an important role for both Jews and Christians and he refers to them as 'us': "The time has come for us to recover the Judeo-Christian ethic of human dignity in the image of God. Humanity was not created to serve markets. Markets were created to serve humankind".[53] In other words, civilisation came into existence because of faith and consequently has to be saved by faith. For politicians who are not religious leaders, the narrative is slightly different although we have seen that Merkel wanted to turn the tide by adding more Christianity to society, something Sacks would approve of.

Sacks' references to Judeo-Christian culture are not the same as those of for example Fortuyn. Whereas Sack explicitly connects Judeo-Christian civilisation to the faith of Jews and Christians, Fortuyn was happy with the alleged outcome of modernity namely, a secularised and therefore neutralised Christianity. He felt threatened, particular by Islam because this religion had not gone through the filter of Reformation and Enlightenment that Fortuyn and Hirsi Ali seemingly considered to be a historical reality. Although Fortuyn's and Hirsi Ali's views differ from Sacks' idea about the importance of faith, they all agree that religious fundamentalism is a threat to Western freedom and Judeo-Christian civilisation. Sacks stated that it is impossible to defend a civilisation against religious fundamentalism with only secular individualism and relativism. A century after a civilisation loses its soul it will lose its freedom, Sacks prophesied. "The precursors of today's scientific atheists were Epicurus in third-century BCE Greece and Lucretius in first-century Rome. These were two great civilisations on the brink of decline. Having lost their faith, they were no match for what Bertrand Russell calls 'nations less civilised than themselves but not so destitute of social cohesion'. The barbarians win. They always do."[54]

What is the strategy of defence of the Europe's political advocates of the Judeo-Christian tradition who do not think the solution lies in increasing faith? Most populist politicians are of the opinion that there should not be tolerance towards intolerance. Fortuyn already brought this up in the subtitle of his book about the 50th anniversary of the state Israel.[55] But how does one act against intol-

52 Jonathan Sacks, "Finance and the Golden Calf," *The Jerusalem Post*, December 15, 2011, http://www.jpost.com/Opinion/Op-Ed-Contributors/Finance-and-the-golden-calf.
53 Ibid.
54 Jonathan Sacks, "Chief Rabbi: Atheism Has Failed. Only Religion Can Defeat the New Barbarians The West Is Suffering for Its Loss of Faith. Unless We Rediscover Religion, Our Civilisation Is in Peril," *The Spectator*, June 15, 2013, http://www.spectator.co.uk/features/8932301/atheism-has-failed-only-religion-can-fight-the-barbarians/.
55 Fortuyn, *50 Jaar Israël, Hoe Lang Nog?*.

erance. Reducing freedom is problematic because of the humanist or Enlightenment values that are part of the Judeo-Christian imaginary. Groys points out that the paradox of the appeal to the Judeo-Christian values is that they are on the one hand too general and universal to differentiate from other cultures and on the other hand not sufficient "to do justice to the immense wealth of the European cultural tradition".[56] Groys explains that this leads to the following problem: if European cultural values are humanistic and universal and this is what the European cultural identity consists of, it can only mean that other cultures are antidemocratic, inhuman and intolerant.[57] However, to describe other cultures as inhuman is not considered to be compatible with a humanistic approach that considers cultures as of equal value although they are different.

It happens nevertheless, explains Elizabeth Shakman Hurd. Indeed, Judeo-Christian seems to serve mainly to "define what one is *not*, over against other groups".[58] Where Groys uses the notion cultural identity Shakman Hurd cites Charles Taylor's description of a social imaginary: "the ways in which people imagine their social existence, how they fit together with others, how things go on between them and their fellows, the expectations that are normally met, and the deeper normative notions and images that underlie these expectations."[59] She argues that 'Judeo-Christian secularism' is part of the European social imaginary and by 'Judeo-Christian secularism' she means "a political project in which what are represented as Christian, or sometimes Judeo-Christian, religious values and modern secular politics are understood to commingle in a particular way, each strengthening the other".[60] Fortuyn describes this process. He pointed out that Judaism and Christianity were thankfully almost completely secularised, and secular fundamentalism such as communism and socialism were effectively beaten.[61] Modernity had prevailed and it had to be protected against fundamentalist tendencies of Islam.

Because Western religious traditions are understood as the foundation of secular democracy, the European-Style secularisation may be tied to a particu-

---

56 Groys, *Art Power*,173.
57 Ibid., 173.
58 Brian M. Britt, "Secularism and the Question of Judeo-Christian," *Relegere: Studies in Religion and Reception* 2.2 (2012): 343.
59 Elizabeth Shakman Hurd, "What Is Driving the European Debate about Turkey?", *Insight Turkey* 12, no. 1 (2010): 185–203. http://www.academia.edu/898024/_What_is_driving_the_European_debate_about_Turkey_. For the original citation see Charles Taylor, "Modern Social Imaginaries," *Public Culture* 14.1 (2002): 106.
60 Elizabeth Shakman Hurd, "What Is Driving the European Debate about Turkey?", 191
61 Ten Hove, "Fortuyn zet zijn kruistocht tegen het fundamentalisme voort."

lar cultural identity, Shakman Hurd explains. Judeo-Christian secularism promotes this exclusivist approach to the cultural boundaries of democracy: "This religio-secular formula for "Europe" rests upon the assumption that full secular democracy can only be fully realized in societies possessing this particular religious heritage. In this view, the Christian or Judeo-Christian foundation of European secularism and democracy, and of Europe itself, is the only foundation possible."[62] Because of all this, the accession of Turkey to the EU will always be problematic because Turkey can never be a secular democracy based on a shared Judeo-Christian tradition. Shakman Hurd is probably right because most defenders of Judeo-Christian Europe even find it problematic to accept certain values, expressions and beliefs that are part of Judaism and Christianity, let alone of Islam. In Hirsi Ali's remark about Christianity, we can find only a certain amount of trust in Christianity of the West. Christianity in other parts of the world apparently has not had the benefit of being toughed by a particular European history of the Reformation, Enlightenment and, Secularism that eventually has led Christians to accept tolerance.

Some politicians find it necessary to, for defensive purposes, promote a legal ban on both Islamic and Jewish religious slaughter, or even like populist politician Geert Wilders of the Dutch Party for Freedom[63] on possession and distribution of the Koran. In 2014 Oliver Roy stated with regards to these developments: "In France Marine Le Pen of the National Front has called for banning both the hijab and the *kippah* (but not the priest's cassock) in public places.[64] In this respect, the defence of Europe's Christian identity is taking on an especially ugly quality: It echoes the anti-Semitic regulations of Nazi Germany and other European countries in the 1930s. So much for the Judeo-Christian roots of European culture; once again, the Jews of Europe are made to feel like foreigners."[65]

At the same time most European politicians who refer to the Judeo-Christian tradition and indicate that they want to defend it, point out the importance of Israel. Their reasoning is that having a Judeo-Christian heritage means that one is democratic and free and, therefore, different from the Muslim world. However, Christopher L. Schilling points out that Israel being "Jewish" means "being a state in contrast to the Western states of secular character." Customs, national holidays, education and civil law are to some extent guided by Jewish religious

62 Elizabeth Shakman Hurd, "What Is Driving the European Debate about Turkey?", 192.

63 Dutch: *Partij voor de Vrijheid* (PVV).

64 Oliver Roy, "The Closing of the Right's Mind", *The New York Times*, June 4, 2014, http://www.nytimes.com/2014/06/05/opinion/the-closing-of-the-rights-mind.html?_r=0 .

65 Ibid.4,27s

law, Schilling explains.[66] This goes far beyond what Europeans are used to. At the time Schilling wrote his book, pigs were not allowed in Israel (although this is now under debate), and there was only a partial recognition of civil marriage. For secular Europeans these regulations would be incompatible with both a secular and enlightened self-proclaimed cultural identity. This means that an appeal to this shared heritage could not only lead to the conclusion that Europe differs from the Islamic world but also that it is different from Israel in a way that will not be accepted by a pure secular idea of a state and for that matter of "the West".[67] Schilling points out that Michael Barnett already explained that Israel has an ambivalent relation to "the West".[68] Such consideration is no part of the reflections of the defenders of Judeo-Christian Europe when they proclaim their love, admiration and, solidarity with Israel. During a visit to Israel in 2010 Italian Prime Minister Silvio Berlusconi, who was an inspiring example for the Dutch Pim Fortuyn, indicated that someday he hoped to see Israel as a member of the EU. He understood, he said that the terrible past of the Jews was always paramount in Israel's considerations. With this visit, Berlusconi explained, the Italian cabinet wanted to demonstrate: "our love, our closeness, our desire to collaborate, to show our recognition of the fact that our two countries and our two peoples share a close bond. We are here to show our recognition and our pride in the fact that we are part of a Judeo-Christian culture that is the basis for European culture".[69] Prime Minister Benjamin Netanyahu recognised the cultural links between Israel and Italy. "One hundred years ago, when the state visionary, Theodore Herzl...was asked about the prospects for a future Jewish state in such a dangerous region, he said that the fate of the Jewish state would ultimately be linked to the fate of the West".[70]

Wilders visited Israel many times and considers Israel the state that fights for 'us' against the Jihad. In his view the fight against Israel is the fight against 'us' because if Jerusalem falls, Rome and Athens will fall, he warns. Therefore Israel is, according to Wilders the central front in the defence of the West and this is summarised by him in the motto "We are Israel". In his speech in Australia in 2013 Wilders stated: "Indeed, the only place in the Middle East where Christians are safe to be Christians is Israel. Israel is also the only democracy

66 Christopher L. Schilling, *Emotional State Theory: Friendship and Fear* (Lanham: Lexington Books, 2014), 65.

67 Ibid.

68 Ibid.

69 Herb Keinon, "Berlusconi 'Dreams of Israel Joining EU,'" *The Jerusalem Post*, February 2, 2010, http://www.jpost.com/Israel/Berlusconi-dreams-of-Israel-joining-EU.

70 Ibid.

in the Middle East, a beacon of light in an area of total darkness. We should all support Israel."[71] During a speech in Los Angeles before the American Freedom Alliance, Wilders said he would like to see the relocation of embassies in Israel from Tel Aviv to Jerusalem. In Los Angeles he told his audience of the American Freedom Alliance: "Let us fly the flags of all the free and proud nations of the world over embassies in Jerusalem, the only true capital of Israel and the cradle of our Judeo-Christian civilization."[72]

In Israel there are mixed feelings about such declarations of admiration. Complex motives lie behind the pro-Israel politics of Eurosceptic parties such as Vlaams Belang (Belgium) and the Sweden Democrats, an op-ed in *The Jerusalem Post* declared. "In ideological terms, their nativist ideology allows them to link Israel's security challenges to what they perceive as one of Europe's challenges – Islam. However, supporting Israel (and the Jews) also has a functional role: it allows these parties, especially the ones with a questionable past, to present a "cleaner" image. This is to some extent a "shield" that protects them from being accused of anti-Semitism. Austria, for example is the home of the FPÖ. The current leader of the party, Heinz-Christian Strache, visited Israel in 2010 and expressed his support. Two years afterwards, the party's true face was exposed once again. In 2012 the FPÖ organized an annual Waltz dinner which took place on the Holocaust Memorial Day, and in the same year Strache published an anti-Semitic cartoon on his Facebook page (with an EU banker featuring a hooked nose and Star of David cufflinks)."

One thing is clear. However Israel might be admired, Europe's Judeo-Christian culture or tradition apparently does not include acts or expressions of faith that are part of Judaism. It is also not appreciative of essential elements of Christian faith including teachings and sayings of Jesus. Frits Bolkestein, who was European Commissioner for Internal Market and Services until 2004 and one the political tutors of Geert Wilders, stated for example in 2010 that Western civilisation is based on the Judeo-Christian and humanist culture.[73] Just like Fortuyn he proclaims Western civilisation to be superior to Islamic civilisation. However, he also states that the pervading influence of Christianity on Western culture had its downside. According to him Protestantism had created an 'away-with-us culture'.

---

71 Geert Wilders, "Speech Geert Wilders, Melbourne, Australia February 19, 2013,", *Geert Wilders Weblog*, http://www.geertwilders.nl/index.php/in-english-mainmenu-98/in-the-press-mainmenu-101/77-in-the-press/in-the-press/1822-speech-geert-wilders-melbourne-australia-tuesday-february-19-2013.

72 Ibid.

73 "Frits Bolkestein over Het 'Christelijk Schuldgevoel' van Het Westen," *Moraalridders*, February 2, 2010, https://www.youtube.com/watch?v=Pf4pB_3Vyzg (14 April 2015).

The Sermon on the Mount has soaked European culture with concepts such as 'to turn the other cheek'. Such Christian notions have decreased the self-esteem and confidence of Christianity in general and of Europe in particular. Bolkestein refers to the philosopher Nietzsche and his concept of slave morality in Christianity of which the democratic movement obsessed with equality and freedom is its heir.[74] Apart from the fact that Bolkestein seems to be rather selective in how he picks his 'facts' from the Bible, Western philosophy and for that matter history, he is obviously not prepared to include the whole package when he places a hyphen between Judeo and Christian. No politician is. Bolkestein wants Judeo-Christian civilisation to be more confident in defending itself but at the same time he wants to get rid of some essential elements of Christian faith. Perhaps the conclusion is justified that Bolkestein and other advocates of the superiority of Judeo-Christian civilisation are not so sure if this civilisation actually has what it takes to defend itself or whether it is worthy of trust in its foundations. This leads to a very selective and even abbreviated form of Christianity that is acceptable to these 'cultural Christians', but has very little to do with a living faith of Jewish and Christian believers.[75] Whereas Sacks sees serious flaws in contemporary culture due to the lack of faith, most politicians see a serious flaw in the Judeo-Christian tradition because notwithstanding the triumph of modernity, faith and accompanying religious practices still exist. Sacks finds the solution for this flaw within the Judaic part of the Judeo-Christian tradition itself. Faith provides the solution and therefore both Jewish and Christian faith has to be restored. Other politicians also see serious flaws in Judeo-Christian culture but do not attempt to explain them by referring to questions of faith or theology. They choose a more populist approach that consists of attacking the political elite. During a debate in the European Parliament about the terror attacks in Paris in January 2015 the British politician and leader of the UK Independence Party (UKIP) Nigel Farage, called for the defence of Judeo-Christian culture in response to Islamist terrorism.[76] Farage stated that the fifth column utterly opposed to our values lived within our countries. "We're going to have to be a lot braver and a lot more courageous in standing up for our Judeo-Christian culture".[77] Tim Farron, spokesman for foreign affairs for the

74 Friedrich Nietzsche, *Zur Genealogie der Moral. Eine Streitschrift* (Hamburg: tredition, 2011).

75 Bart Wallet, "Zin en Onzin van de Joods-Christelijke Traditie," *Christen Democratische Verkenningen*, (2012): 100–108.

76 "UKIP's Nigel Farage Urges 'Judeo-Christian' Defence after Paris Attacks," *BBC News*, January 12, 2015, http://www.bbc.com/news/world-europe-30776186.

77 Carey Lodge, "Is Britain Still Christian? Should We Even Care?," *Christian Today*, January 15, 2015, http://www.christiantoday.com/article/what.is.judeo.christian.culture.and.should.we.be.defending.it/45980.htm.

British Liberal Democrat party reacted to the fifth column statement by framing Farage's politics as a 'politics of blame' "that has no place in modern, diverse and tolerant Britain".[78] Indeed, Farage's rhetoric's can be defined as politics of blame but the question remains: who exactly is blamed? By criticising the fifth column remark and pointing out that Britain is diverse and tolerant, Farron suggests that Farage's politics of blame is about blaming Islam or blaming Muslims. However, Farage logically cannot blame Muslims or Islam. If Muslims and Islam are the opposite of the Judeo-Christian culture, as Groys explained is automatically the case in this discourse of Judeo-Christian humanist values, they cannot be blamed for being different and thus dangerous for the culture that has to be defended. Farage blames first and for all the British Government and the EU for not defending the Judeo-Christian culture and for failing to acknowledge that it should be defended. In 2014 while discussing the problem of home grown Islamic militants, Farage blamed 'us' and not 'them': "A lot of this is our own fault," he said. "We have been too weak. My country is a Judeo-Christian country. So we've got to actually start standing up for our values."[79]

At first sight this seems to be a tautological analysis: populist criticise the political elite, which is why they are populists. However, it is still important to see whom exactly they are blaming. They do not blame Muslims, who radicalise and travel to Syria to fight on the side of IS, they blame the Government for allowing them to come back. The anti-terror proposals of David Cameron are acceptable to Farage so he points out that Cameron would have trouble implementing his new proposals because of the European Convention on Human Rights. Farage, in other words, manages to find an even higher elite to blame. Farage is not alone in blaming the political elite. In April 2015 Geert Wilders, a member of the Dutch Parliament for the populist anti-Islam party PVV (Party for Freedom) held a speech in Dresden for PEGIDA (Patriotic Europeans Against the Islamisation of the West).[80] Wilders applauded his audience for being proud patriots. He knew,

---

78 Hether Saul, "Nigel Farage Urges the West to Admit Some 'Culpability' in the Charlie Hebdo Attacks," *The Independent*, January 13, 2015, http://www.independent.co.uk/news/uk/politics/nigel-farage-urges-the-west-to-admit-some-culpability-in-the-charlie-hebdo-attacks-9974176.html.

79 Ibid.

80 "Wilders noemt Pegida-aanhang moedige patriotten," *NOS*, April 13, 2015, http://nos.nl/artikel/2030056-wilders-noemt-pegida-aanhang-moedige-patriotten.html. The PEGIDA movement originated in Dresden in 2014 and wanted to protest against 'the islamization' of Germany and to call for stricter immigration laws. After staging a series of very successful mass protests that attracted many thousands of protesters, the movement now seems to be in decline.

he said, how difficult it is, especially in Germany, to be proud patriots because there is a lot of resistance against such sentiments.[81]

> In my eyes, you are all heroes. And I applaud you. Because there is nothing wrong with being proud German patriots. There is nothing wrong with wanting Germany to remain free and democratic. There is nothing wrong with preserving our own Judeo-Christian civilisation. That is our duty. Our own culture is the best culture there is. Immigrants should adopt our values and not the other way round. Our freedom and democracy must be defended. It is our duty to defend it. That is why we are here tonight. In the tradition of Kant, Schiller, and Stauffenberg. In the tradition of freedom of speech, in the tradition of speaking the truth and acting accordingly.[82]

Wilders rhetorically asked his audience if he should take Chancellor Merkel home with him to The Netherlands. Merkel had said that Islam was also part of Germany and Wilders stated that the majority of the German people thought this was not the case. We do not want a Monokultur (monoculture), explained the Wilders, "but we want our own Judeo-Christian culture to remain the Leitkultur (leading culture, core culture) in our country."[83] Again, Wilders doesn't blame Islam or Muslims, but the Chancellor who does not acknowledge the duty to defend Germany, a defence that Wilders frames in the tradition of Enlightenment, high culture and resistance against Nazism.

Both the populists and the Christian Democrats refer to a Judeo-Christian tradition or culture. Although none of the politicians provides a definition of the Judeo-Christian tradition of Europe or the West (both seem to be interchangeable) they seem to agree on what it entails. They also agree on the premise that this culture or tradition is under threat. However, they differ on how one should defend or protect the Judeo-Christian tradition. Representative of Dutch Christian Democratic Party[84] Sybrand van Haersma Buma reacted to the 2015 terrorist attacks in Paris in Dutch Parliament by stating that ruthless Muslim radicals had shaken the very foundations of Western society with their attacks on Charlie Hebdo and a Jewish supermarket in Paris. He considered the terror of radical Islam the greatest threat to our security. Apparently anticipating the reaction of the Party for Freedom he indicated that 'we' stand together for a free society and democracy but that politicians should ask themselves what they do to support these words. "We have a lot to defend", the leader of the Christian Democrats said in Parliament. "Our continent is formed by an ancient Judeo-Christian and

81 Ibid.
82 Ibid.
83 Ibid.
84 Dutch: *Christen-Democratisch Appèl* (CDA).

humanist tradition. Freedom entails that you see to your neighbour, that you respect each other and that you take responsibility for your actions. It is all right to fight these terrorists because in this part of the world you can believe what you want, but the values that arise from our Judeo-Christian tradition, are non-negotiable. You must not misuse the freedom to undermine the rights of others. The recent terror is an attack on the democratic rule of law and our way of living."

The Christian Democrat also looks to the Dutch Muslim community to take its responsibility to fight Muslim radicalism by contributing to a peaceful, democracy and freedom oriented Islam. According to Van Haersma Buma "this happened in Germany and France and should also happen in The Netherlands." In other words Muslims in Germany and France are better Muslims than the Dutch Muslims because they participate in national events where victims of Islamic terrorism are mourned, outrage about the attacks is expressed and the non-negotiable values of the Judeo-Christian and Humanist society are collectively embraced. In other words, perhaps faith is required to solve the problems that taunt Judeo-Christian Europe. However it is not religious faith, but a secular faith or to be more precise, a civil religion that comprises symbols and rituals that signify shared values. Muslim, Jews and Christians are supposed to join in on the celebration of this civil religion but are not provided instructions. They simply have to accept that the Judeo-Christian tradition is a secular one, a construct, as Cohen called it, which does not actually recognise the religious dimension of that tradition.

This notion brings us back to the United States, where the civil religion is considered to be Judeo-Christian because references to a Judeo-Christian foundation are part of the imaginary of the nation's foundation. An example of this Judeo-Christian imaginary is the design of the Great Seal of the United State proposed by Benjamin Franklin: "Pharaoh sitting in an open chariot, a crown on his head and a sword in his hand passing thro' the divided waters of the Red sea [sic] in pursuit of the Israelites: rays from a pillar of fire in the cloud, expressive of the divine presence, ... and command, reaching to Moses who stands on the shore and, extending his hand over the sea, causes it to over whelm Pharoah [sic]".[85] Early Americans considered their flight from Europe as a new exodus and America as the new Promised Land, separated, according to Jefferson from the tyrannies and corruptions of the continent they left. Judeo-Christian values dis-

85 Rafael Alberto Madan, "The Sign and the Seal of Justice," *Ave Maria Law Review* 7.1 (Fall 2008): 123.

tinguish America from all other countries, Dennis Prager states.[86] The Christians who founded America considered themselves heirs to the Hebrew Bible as much as to the New Testament. Americans identify with the Jews' chosenness. "It is a belief that America must answer morally to this God, not to the mortal, usually venal, governments of the world."[87] If one day America will not be Judeo-Christian anymore, it will become secular and amoral like Europe, Prager warns.[88]

The imaginaries Prager mentions are not part of a shared idea about the foundation of Europe and in European politics 'Judeo-Christian' does not refer to religious notions of being a chosen people, nation or, geographically speaking, continent. Prager is correct when he sees a difference concerning the secular dimension of Europe and because for him the signifier Judeo-Christian has a religious and theological meaning, he does not even consider that European politicians would identify with Judeo-Christian values. From his perspective on Judeo-Christian, they indeed do not. Europe does not have a Judeo-Christian tradition and whether it has a civil religion is debatable. On a national level there certainly are aspects of a civil religion but Europe itself, or in a smaller setting the EU, has no such thing, although Marko Ventura has built an argument for the idea that Europe's civil religion consists of an alliance between religious freedom and socio-economic freedom.[89] Such a civil religion is interchangeable and does not have a soul for there is nothing to believe. If Cohen were alive today he might see that in Europe the phrase Judeo-Christian is just a small element from a toolbox filled with political rhetoric that is easily replaceable and comfortably vague and not in any way connected to either Judaism or Christianity or faith for that matter. There is no Judeo-Christian Europe. Europe does not even have a powerful myth that says there is.

Bibliography

Brill, Allan. *Judaism and World Religions: Encountering Christianity, Islam, and Eastern Traditions*. London: Palgrave Macmillan, 2012.

Britt, Brian M. "Secularism and the Question of Judeo-Christian." *Relegere: Studies in Religion and Reception* 2.2 (2012): 343–352.

86 Dennis Prager, "What Does 'Judeo-Christian' Mean?," *The Dennis Prager Show*, March 30, 2004, http://www.dennisprager.com/what-does-judeo-christian-mean/.

87 Ibid.

88 Ibid.

89 Marco Ventura, "The Changing Civil Religion of Secular Europe," *The George Washington International Law Review* 4 (2010): 947–961.

Casanova, José. "Religion, European secular identities, and European integration." *Eurozine*. July 29, 2004. http://www.eurozine.com/articles/2004-07-29-casanova-en.html (20 April 2015).
Cohen, Arthur Allen, David Stern, and Paul R. Mendes-Flohr. *An Arthur A. Cohen Reader: Selected Fiction and Writings on Judaism, Theology, Literature, and Culture*. Detroit: Wayne State University Press, 1998.
"Deutscher Bundestag. Stenographischer Bericht. 217. Sitzung, Bonn, Donnerstag den 21. Juni 1990." *Deutscher Bundestag*. http://dipbt.bundestag.de/doc/btp/11/11217.pdf (21 April 2015).
"Deutscher Bundestag. Stenografischer Bericht. 65. Sitzung Berlin, Donnerstag den 7. Oktober 2010." *Deutscher Bundestag*. http://dipbt.bundestag.de/doc/btp/17/17065.pdf (20 April 2015).
Dysch, Marcus. "Chief Rabbi and Pope Discuss Fears for Europe." *The Jewish Chronicle Online*. December 13, 2011. http://www.thejc.com/news/uk-news/60227/chief-rabbi-and-pope-discuss-fears-europe (21 April 2015).
Fortuyn, Pim. *50 Jaar Israël, Hoe Lang Nog?: Tegen het Tolereren van Fundamentalisme*. Utrecht: Bruna, 1998.
Fortuyn, Pim. *De Verweesde Samenleving*. Rotterdam: Karakter Uitgevers, 2002.
Fortuyn, Pim and Abdullah R. F. Haselhoef. *De Islamisering van Onze Cultuur: Nederlandse Identiteit als Fundament*. Geheel geactualiseerde en herz. ed., 5. Uithoorn: Karakter: Speakers Academy, 2002.
"Frits Bolkestein over Het 'Christelijk Schuldgevoel' van Het Westen." *Moraalridders*. February 2, 2010. https://www.youtube.com/watch?v=Pf4pB_3Vyzg (14 April 2015).
Gay, Peter. *The Party of Humanity: Essays in the French Enlightenment*. New York: Knopf, 1964.
Gedicks, Frederick Mark and Roger Hendrix. "Uncivil Religion: Judeo-Christianity and the Ten Commandments." *West Virginia Law Review* 110 (2007): 273–304.
Goldman, Shalom. "What Do We Mean By 'Judeo-Christian'?" *Religion Dispatches*. January 15, 2011. http://religiondispatches.org/what-do-we-mean-by-judeo-christian/(25 April 2015).
Grossman, Marshall. "The Violence of the Hyphen in Judeo-Christian." *Social Text* 22 (Spring 1989): 115–122.
Groys, B. *Art Power*. Cambridge MA: MIT Press, 2008.
Hemel, Ernst van den. "(Pro)claiming Tradition: The 'Judeo-Christian' Roots of Dutch Society and the Rise of Conservative Nationalism." *Transformations of Religion and the Public Sphere: Postsecular Publics*. Ed. Rosi Braidotti. Palgrave Politics of Identity and Citizenship Series. Basingstoke: Palgrave Macmillan, 2014. 53–76.
Heneghan, Tom. "Merkel: Germany Doesn't Have 'too Much Islam' but 'too Little Christianity'." *Blogs.reuters.com/faithworld*. November 15, 2010. http://blogs.reuters.com/faithworld/2010/11/15/merkel-germany-doesnt-have-too-much-islam-but-too-little-christianity/(27 April 2015).
Hove, Johan ten. "Fortuyn zet zijn kruistocht tegen het fundamentalisme voort." *Trouw*. June 5, 1998, http://www.trouw.nl/tr/nl/4512/Cultuur/article/detail/2742572/1998/06/05/Fortuyn-zet-zijn-kruistocht-tegen-het-fundamentalisme-voort.dhtml (28 April 2015).
Irons, Lee. "The Use of 'Hellenistic Judaism' in Pauline Studies." *The Upper Register*. January 18, 2006.
http://www.upper-register.com/papers/hellenistic_judaism.pdf (28 April 2015).
Jenkins, David Fraser. *John Piper: The Forties*. London: Philip Wilson Publishers, 2001.

Keinon, Herb. "Berlusconi 'Dreams of Israel Joining EU'." *The Jerusalem Post*. February 2, 2010. http://www.jpost.com/Israel/Berlusconi-dreams-of-Israel-joining-EU (5 May 2015).
Lodge, Carey. "Is Britain Still Christian? Should We Even Care?" *Christian Today*. January 15, 2015. http://www.christiantoday.com/article/what.is.judeo.christian.culture.and.should.we.be.defending.it/45980.htm (7 May 2015).
Madan, Rafael Alberto. "The Sign and the Seal of Justice." *Ave Maria Law Review* 7.1 (Fall 2008): 123–203.
Malcolm, Peter. "Hirsi Ali Confronts Jon Stewart About Islam." *Truthrevolt*. March 24, 2015. http://www.truthrevolt.org/news/hirsi-ali-confronts-jon-stewart-about-islam (4 May 2015).
Nietzsche, Friedrich. *Zur Genealogie der Moral. Eine Streitschrift*. Hamburg: tredition, 2011.
Prager, Dennis. "What Does 'Judeo-Christian' Mean?" *The Dennis Prager Show*. March 30, 2004. http://www.dennisprager.com/what-does-judeo-christian-mean/(17 April 2015).
Roy, Oliver. "The Closing of the Right's Mind." *The New York Times*. June 4, 2014. http://www.nytimes.com/2014/06/05/opinion/the-closing-of-the-rights-mind.html?_r=0 (23 April 2015).
Sacks, Jonathan. "Finance and the Golden Calf." *The Jerusalem Post*. December 15, 2011. http://www.jpost.com/Opinion/Op-Ed-Contributors/Finance-and-the-golden-calf (7 June 2015).
Sacks, Jonathan. "Reversing the Moral Decay Behind the London Riots ", *The Wall Street Journal*, August 20, 2011, http://www.wsj.com/articles/SB10001424053111903639404576516252066723110 (20 April 2015).
Sacks, Jonathan. "Has Europe Lost Its Soul? Address given at the Pontifical Gregorian University." *Catholic Education Resource Center*. December 12, 2012. http://www.catholiceducation.org/en/religion-and-philosophy/social-justice/has-europe-lost-its-soul.html (7 June 2015).
Sacks, Jonathan. "Chief Rabbi: Atheism Has Failed. Only Religion Can Defeat the New Barbarians The West Is Suffering for Its Loss of Faith. Unless We Rediscover Religion, Our Civilisation Is in Peril." *The Spectator*. June 15, 2013. http://www.spectator.co.uk/features/8932301/atheism-has-failed-only-religion-can-fight-the-barbarians/(7 June 2015).
Saul, Hether. "Nigel Farage Urges the West to Admit Some 'Culpability' in the Charlie Hebdo Attacks."
The Independent. January 13, 2015. http://www.independent.co.uk/news/uk/politics/nigel-farage-urges-the-west-to-admit-some-culpability-in-the-charlie-hebdo-attacks-9974176.html (14 April 2015).
Schilling, Christopher L. *Emotional State Theory: Friendship and Fear*. Lanham: Lexington Books, 2014.
Schwarzbach, Bertram Eugene. "Voltaire et les Juifs: Bilan et Plaidoyer." *SVEC* 358 (1997): 27–91.
Hurd, Elizabeth Shakman. "What Is Driving the European Debate about Turkey?" *Insight Turkey* 12.1 (2010): 185–203. http://www.academia.edu/898024/_What_is_driving_the_European_debate_about_Turkey_ (14 April 2015).
Silk, Mark. "Notes on the Judeo-Christian Tradition in America." *American Quarterly* 36.1 (Spring 1984): 65–85.
Suther, Judith D. "Images of Indestructible Israel: Raïssa Maritain on Marc Chagall." *Jacques Maritain and the Jews*. Ed. Robert Royal. Mishawaka: University of Notre Dame Press, 1994. 157–167.
Taylor, Charles. "Modern Social Imaginaries." *Public Culture* 14.1 (2002): 91–124.

"UKIP's Nigel Farage Urges 'Judeo-Christian' Defence after Paris Attacks." *BBC News*. January 12, 2015. http://www.bbc.com/news/world-europe-30776186 (20 April 2015).
Ventura, Marco. "The Changing Civil Religion of Secular Europe." *The George Washington International Law Review* 4 (2010): 947–961.
Verstraete, G. *Tracking Europe: Mobility, Diaspora, and the Politics of Location*. Durham NC: Duke University Press, 2010.
Wallet, Bart. "Zin en Onzin van de Joods-Christelijke Traditie." *Chisten Democratische Verkenningen*, (2012): 100–108.
Wicke, Christian. *Helmut Kohl's Quest for Normality: His Representation of the German Nation and Himself*. New York/London: Berghahn Books, 2015.
Wilders, Geert. "Speech Geert Wilders, Melbourne, Australia February 19, 2013." *Geert Wilders Weblog*. http://www.geertwilders.nl/index.php/in-english-mainmenu-98/in-the-press-mainmenu-101/77-in-the-press/in-the-press/1822-speech-geert-wilders-melbourne-australia-tuesday-february-19-2013 (12 April 2015).
"Wilders noemt Pegida-aanhang moedige patriotten." *NOS*. April 13, 2015. http://nos.nl/artikel/2030056-wilders-noemt-pegida-aanhang-moedige-patriotten.html (23 April 2015).

Anya Topolski

14 A Genealogy of the 'Judeo-Christian' Signifier: A Tale of Europe's Identity Crisis

Even though the European Union Parliament did not endorse the reference to Europe's 'Judeo-Christian' roots in its constitution, the question nonetheless provoked an on-going debate on Europe's symbolic foundation and its future identity. On the one side of the debate are those who cite the 'Judeo-Christian' commandment to care for the stranger as central to European civilization, while on the other side are those who argue for the exclusion of Islam from Europe in the name of the 'Judeo-Christian' tradition. There has been extensive discussions of the theological meaning of the term 'Judeo-Christianity' (Levinas 1977; Lyotard 1999) (Cohen 1971, Silk 1984, and Gruber 1999; a political debate on its meaning in America after the Shoah); a dialogue on its exclusionary potential (Anidjar 2003; Anidjar 2007; Anidjar 2014; Bunzl 2007); yet there is a lack of analysis of the discursive relationship between Europe's transnational identity construction, symbolically rooted in the 'Judeo-Christian' tradition, and its controversial relationship to Islamophobia in Europe.

While there are certainly many differences between anti-Semitism and Islamophobia, in terms of social and economic factors, my claim is that there is an important parallel in terms of mechanisms of exclusion visible in the rhetoric used to symbolize inclusion.[1] To explore this, it is necessary to comprehend the process of identity formation in relation to the construction of enemies. A critical discursive analysis of the symbolic representation of European identity as 'Judeo-Christian' makes tangible how society constructs its outsiders and allows us to consider how such exclusions can be avoided. It is in the aim of averting violence that Europe needs a notion of community not defined by exclusion. If Europe seeks to embrace an identity of diversity and tolerance, it must repudi-

1 I think it is worth emphasising that a comparison between anti-Semitism in the 20th century, and specifically the Shoah, and Islamophobia today is problematic. The implicit parallel I am making is a comparison, but to compare is not to equate. The historical context is different and this must not be overlooked. To ignore this is problematic as it permits the entire history of anti-Semitism, and its precursor in theological anti-Judaism, to be reduced to the Shoah. This allows anti-Semitism to be reduced to its biological manifestation and dismisses all other manifestations of racism that are non-biological. To be explicit the parallel I am implicitly drawing is between anti-Semitism in the 1870s-1920 to Islamophobia in the 1970s-2015.

ate divisive binary identities that are all too often the product of fear rather than hope.

In this chapter, I develop this claim by tracing the story of the signifier Judeo-Christianity to demonstrate how it, both in the 19th century and today, was used to create an illusory unity by way of an exclusionary identity construction. I consider two very different tales of the signifier Judeo-Christianity. Over the span of two centuries and two continents, the signifier has been almost entirely emptied of its signification, what remains is its function in terms of an exclusionary identity-construction. Both its European apparitions[2], the first in the 1830s and the second after the Shoah when the first steps were being taken towards unifying Europe, serve to create unity by constructing an exclusionary identity-formation. Let us not forget that "until just after World War II, European Jews were marginal too, but since that break the emerging discourse of a 'Judeo-Christian tradition' has signalled a new integration of their status in Europe" (Asad 2003, 168). This discourse – with its diverse meanings and uses, previously excluded Jews; it now excludes Muslims, another of Europe's historical others. The fact that this signifier remains exclusionary even when its signification has been totally emptied is 'enlightening'. Given that the term 'Judeo-Christian' has several different and often opposing meanings (concepts)[3], the continued use of this one signifier is perplexing. By way of this genealogy of the signifier Judeo-Christianity, I expose the problematic political stakes of European identity constructions.

My hope is that if Europe is to be a community that is not constituted on violence and exclusion, we must begin by seeking alternatives to such exclusionary identity-formations. The first step in creating such a community is in rejecting the need for a unifying or shared identity. Such a possibility exists in taking the link between identity and exclusion seriously. By taking responsibility for the exclusionary violence which has its origins in endeavours to define Europe's identity, there may be hope to create an inclusive community, a Europe 'to come', that is free from the spectre of identity currently haunting Europe. By way of conclusion I briefly consider an alternative to a union based on identity. I turn to the political notion of *communitas*, as developed by Roberto Esposito, in which there is no

---

2 The American story differs significantly, see introduction to this volume.

3 To my count there are at least 7 different ways in which the term 'Judeo-Christian' is being used in European discourse today: 1) as a synonym for secularism, 2) as exclusionary of Islam, 3) as a form of Christian supersessionism (often in relation to Pauline theology), 4) by Jews as a contemporary form of Jewish *stadlanut*, 5) in terms of shared morals either positive or negative (e.g. Nietzschean meaning), 6) as a post-Shoah apology rooted in guilt and, 7) as a synonym for faith. While there is no space to develop each of these, several of these meanings are present in this paper.

common identity but rather a shared responsibility that binds different people and peoples together.

The Origins of Europe's Judeo-Christian Identity Formations

Let us begin with the first appearance of the signifier Judeo-Christianity[4], which can be dated to an 1831 publication by Ferdinand Christian Baur, the founder of the German Protestant Tübingen School. Tübingen, where Hegel, Schelling (who were roommates) and Hölderlin all studied philosophy and theology (in the 1790s), was an important player in terms of German idealism. Baur, who saw his theological contribution as an essential supplement to German idealism, coined the term Judeo-Christianity as part of a crude Hegelian dialectic. The thesis was a combination of Judaism and paganism, its antithesis Judeo-Christianity – by which he specifically meant Catholicism that was still tainted by Judaism, and its synthesis was Pauline or Gentile Christianity – akin to the Protestant theology espoused by scholars of the Tübingen school. The latter was a Christianity purified of all traces of Judaism, paganism and orientalism. In this vein, Baur declares that "the relation of [Pauline] Christianity to heathenism and Judaism is defined as that between the absolute religion and the preparatory and subordinate forms of religion. We have here the progress from servitude to freedom ... from the flesh to the spirit" (as quoted in Lincicum, 2012, 148).

In essence, Baur – like Hegel – had a strongly supersessionist view of the relationship between Judaism, Catholicism, Islam (which was then known as Mohammedanism) and Protestantism.[5] Supersessionism, also known as fulfilment theol-

4 See introduction to this volume for an explanation of why this term is said to have been coined by Baur in 1831.

5 A few citations from Hegel with regard to Jews and Orientals: 1) From Hegel's Philosophy of Mind: "Of the oriental, especially the Mohammedan, modes of envisaging God, we may rather say that they represent the Absolute as the utterly universal genus which dwells in the species or existences, but dwells so potently that these existences have no actual reality. The fault of all these modes of thought and systems is that they stop short of defining substance as subject and as mind" (Hegel 2015, 257); 2) From Hegel's Logic: "It is true that God is necessity, or, as we may also put it, that he is the absolute Thing: he is however no less the absolute Person. That he is the absolute Person however is a point which the philosophy of Spinoza never reached: and on that side it falls short of the true notion of God which forms the content of religious consciousness in Christianity. Spinoza was by descent a Jew; and it is upon the whole the Oriental way of seeing

ogy or replacement theology, defends the position that the new covenant replaces the old. Christianity, according to this theological stance, reforms and replaces Judaism, which is defected. Supersessionism can be defined as follows:

> The concept of a Judeo-Christian tradition comfortably suggests that Judaism progresses into Christianity – that Judaism is somehow completed in Christianity. The concept of a Judeo-Christian tradition flows from the Christian theology of supersession, whereby the Christian covenant (or Testament) with God supersedes the Jewish one. Christianity, according to this myth, reforms and replaces Judaism. The myth therefore implies, first, that Judaism needs reformation and replacement, and second, that modern Judaism remains merely as a 'relic'. (Feldman 1998, 18)

Supersessionism is by no means new to Christianity which has defended this position since its institution in the 4th century. What was new was Baur's *secondary* supersession – that of Protestantism, or Pauline Christianity, over Judeo-Christianity. This secondary supersessionism is clearly influenced by Hegel's 1831 *Lectures on the Philosophy of Religion.*

> To look at God in this light, as the Lord, and the Lord alone, is especially characteristic of Judaism and also of Mohammedanism. The defect of these religions lies in their scant recognition of the finite, which, be it as natural things or as finite phases of mind, it is characteristic of the heathen and (as they also for that reason are) polytheistic religions to maintain intact. (Hegel et al. 1991, para. 112)

This secondary supersessionism is necessary according to Baur as Catholicism has become contaminated by its interactions with paganism, Judaism and Islam. Again, this idea can be found in Hegel's work (among other German Idealists):

> In the Protestant conscience the principles of the religious and of the ethical conscience come to be one and the same: the free spirit learning to see itself in its reasonableness and truth. In the Protestant state, the constitution and the code, as well as their several applications, embody the principle and the development of the moral life, which proceeds and can only proceed from the truth of religion, when reinstated in its original principle and in that way as such first become actual. (Hegel 2015, 242)

Baur turns to Paul's letters for textual evidence and by means of the 'scientific' method of higher biblical criticism finds support for this supersessionism.

---

things, according to which the nature of the finite world seems frail and transient, that has found its intellectual expression in his system. This Oriental view of the unity of substance certainly gives the basis for all real further development. Still it is not the final idea" (Hegel et al. 1991, 226) Hegel's racism is further explored in (Bernasconi and Cook 2003; Outlaw 1996; Taylor 2013).

According to Baur, Paul's importance lies in his ability to have brought about a victory between two warring factions (or parties) in the early church (between the 2nd – 4th century CE). Paul thereby ensures that Pauline Christianity would eventually, guided by the spirit, supersede Judeo-Christianity. Baur claims that in the 19th century the spirit of Judeo-Christianity is dominant and thus seeks to correct this historical error by making clear that Pauline Christianity is superior to the Judeo-Christian factions (espoused by James, Peter and the Ebionites, etc). Baur sees the latter opposing parties as hindering progress,[6] with Judeo-Christianity standing in the way of the spirit. His conclusion was that in order for Pauline Christianity to guide history, it must be freed from all traces of Judeo-Christianity.

Baur's importance cannot be relegated to the realm of academic theology. His conclusions are critical to European politics because nineteenth-century historical thought, "was not a mere academic and intellectual pursuit but underwrote, in various ways, many of the major social and political movements of that period" (Zachhuber 2014, 3). In this vein, Baur's work, and those of his many students at the Tübingen school, was immensely influential in the long 19th century (from the 1789 French Revolution to 1914 WWI). Much like today, questions of religion were central to politics and questions of identity in most European nation states. From at least the 17th century, religious categories served to categorise and organise the world (Topolski, 2014).[7] Until the French revolution, Europe was an *explicitly* Christian continent, and Europeans organised the world in terms of four nations (groups, peoples, tribes or races): Christianity, Judaism, Mohammedans, and the rest (heretics, pagans, heathens, idolaters, polytheists). It was only during the 19th century that these categories came under scrutiny and theology was forced to compete with other 'sciences' for the 'privilege' to 'organise' or 'categorise' humanity. Baur's contribution was an attempt to return theology – specifically Protestant biblical criticism – to its rightful position as the queen of the sciences. Theology's greatest competitor, as is clear from Nietzsche's work written in the same period, was philology.

> What went on in the course of reshuffling the old categories – seemingly a purely conceptual exercise – was in fact part of a much broader, fundamental transformation of European identity ... undoubtedly reflecting a sea change in the European relationship to the rest of the world ... but most immediately it was facilitated by an influential new science of

6 Ernst Käsemann, a 20th century member of the Tubingen school, more polemically, perceived Judeo-Christianity to be impeding divine history.

7 Historians such as R. I. Moore argue that this was the case from at least the 13th century (see Moore 2007).

> comparative philology ... This strong drive to hellenize and aryanize Christianity paralleled another tendency that originated around this time: to semitize Islam. (Masuzawa 2005, xii)

In the 19th century, theology and philology both sought to play a critical role in terms of the idea of Europe. While Christendom had always been the unspoken identity of Europe (Delanty 1995; Delanty and Rumford 2005; Hay 1966; Pocock 1994; Pagden 2002), this now came to be challenged with the rise of atheism and its appeal to the sciences. Philologists did not, however, begin with a *tabula rosa* – they in fact borrowed the categories created by 19th century theologians such as Baur. The most compelling example is that of Ernest Renan. Renan, who was trained as theologian before becoming a philologist and diplomat, was a young scholar in the 1840s and believed that philology was the queen of the sciences. Nonetheless he, in his early years as a student of theology, had been convinced of Baur's claims. Thus, by separating Pauline Christianity from Judeo-Christianity, Baur enabled theologically inclined linguists – such as Ernest Renan – to associate Pauline Christianity with the Indo-European or Aryan languages which was proven to be superior to the Semitic languages. In this vein, Baur's secondary supersessionism of Judeo-Christianity was translated by scientists into linguistic *cum* identity markers for particular groups of people. According to Renan, only philology could provide solid evidence for such supersessionism. Thus, in his highly successful 1847 *General History of Semitic Languages*, he proved the linguistic superiority of Indo-European or Aryan languages over that of Semitic languages.

> Although initially a term referring to a certain cluster of languages, 'Aryan' increasingly was taken to mean an ethnic or, purportedly, racial grouping of peoples ... It is singularly ironic that by the time the name 'Aryan' had taken on the virulently racist connotation familiar to us today, the noble Persians and Indians of yore were all but expunged from its meaning, as the term came to signify a certain idea of European identity, that is, the 'whiteness' that excluded, above all, the Jews, who in turn were deemed – though not for the first time-'oriental'. (Masuzawa 2005, 152)[8]

In this manner Baur's Judeo-Christian vs. Pauline Christianity dichotomy was translated into an Orient-Occident division. While Baur never made such claims,

8 "In due course, it became customary among Europeans, in speaking of "the Aryans" to set aside the Persians and the Indians altogether, and to use the term to refer to and distinguish themselves from "the Semites" – above all, from the Arabs (now equated with Muslims) and the Jews" (Masuzawa 2005, 171). Worth noting, the term Arab was popularised in the 19th century as a racialised form of Mohamedanism or Turkish.

it was believed that "the Orient to Baur represents closed, nationalistic systems, whereas the Occident, Europe, especially Greece, is the origin of freedom" (Gerdmar 2009, 113). This misreading of Baur was especially problematic as these political theological struggles occurred while colonialism and antisemitism were on the rise at the end of the 19th century. What was taken from Baur was his highly influential teleological Protestant history of ideas, a strong notion of progress and of history being 'hindered' by Judaic, Oriental and pagan influences. In a nutshell, Baur's views, and those of his followers, were used to prove that once the purified idea of Europe to be found in Pauline Christianity was free of the chains of Judeo-Christianity, Europe would return to its rightful place in the civilised world. While Baur believed that higher biblical criticism could bring about this transformation, others were not so patient and believed the spirit needed to be supported by means of the sword. While the biological connotations of the Aryan supremacy of Semitism did not come to dominate until the very end of the 19th century, the roots are clearly to be found in this theological distinction.[9] Baur clearly never intended nor could have envisioned the 20th century genocide justified in terms of biological Aryan superiority, nonetheless his thought is by no means free of such traces:

> Paul places Judaism and Christianity together under the light of a great religio-historical contemplation, and of a view of the course of the world before the universal idea of which the particularism of Judaism must disappear as qtd. in. (Lincicum 2012, 153) [10]

In the end, it is clear that Baur's theological distinction between higher Pauline-Christianity and lower Judeo-Christianity, served philologists and politicians

---

9 "Scientifically based distinctions first grounded race separation before being biological justified ... Science categorized Jews and Arabs as being 'of the same stock', conjointly epitomized the character of the Semitic race ... The 'scientific' guise in which a man of great learning could dress-up the philological distinction between Semites and Indo-Europeans gave support and strength, among wide intellectual circles, to the popular biological distinction between Semites and Aryans that was increasingly widespread at this time" (Sand and Renan 2010, 10).

10 "Despite these weaknesses, Baur's greatness cannot be denied. The discipline of New Testament studies owes him more than any of those who came before him. On the wall in Käsemann's living room study hangs a copy of the University of Tübingen's portrait of Baur, a gift to the New Testament scholar upon his retirement. Once outside Baur's direct influence, the one-time pupil of Bultmann finally came to write of Baur as the true 'progenitor' of a criticism at the root, a criticism conceived not merely as scientific method but as a presupposition for the life of the spirit. One summer day he pointed to that portrait on his study wall and said, 'greater even than Bultmann'" (Harrisville and Sundberg 1995, 130).

to create exclusionary identity-formations that justified antisemitism and the exclusion of Jews from the European public sphere.

Europe's Judeo-Christian Identity Formations Today

After a prolonged and controversial debate, the EU Parliament voted not to include a reference to Europe's 'Judeo-Christian' heritage in the 'EU Constitution.'[11] This is not surprising since "the question of religion in the constitution has been described by some as 'the most emotive' issue its drafters have had to negotiate" (Heyward 2005, n. 3). The question of religion emerged in discussions about the constitution's preamble that sets out to define the 'shared values' of the Union. Again this is not surprising as religion organised public life in Europe until the end of the long 19th century.[12] Christendom was for much of Europe's history a synonym for the 'idea of Europe'; as such, the question of religion is indispensable for any consideration of Europe's history, identity, and values. While today many Europeans consider themselves secular, it is quite clear to all those who are non-Christians, that secularism is a post-Christian project and that European societies are still very much organised according to a Christian logic (Asad 1993; Asad 2003). This connection between religion and identity was palpable in the national media headlines in Europe from 2003 to 2005 related to the intense parliamentary debates and public discourse on the draft constitution, which tied the question of religion directly to that of European identity.

In the end, the drafters of the European constitution compromised by defining Europe's values as a 'cultural, religious and humanist inheritance'. This compromise flouted the heated political discussions which had stirred so many European citizens; it refused to engage the question of the relationship between the past 'idea of Europe' and Europe 'to come' – the project now clearly tied the European Union. While Europe is divided between those that support the European

11 Draft Treaty Establishing a Constitution for Europe (Secretariat of the EC, 18 July 2003) CONV 850/03 was adopted by consensus by the EC on 13 June and 10 July 2003, and submitted to the President of the European Council in Rome on 18 July 2003.

12 "Changes began in the seventeenth century, but came to a head at the end of the eighteenth with a number of transformations that can summarily be described as the historicization of European intellectual life ... All areas of public discourse, and rational enquiry were increasingly inscribed in, and reconstructed as, historical development or evolution. It was a paradigm shift in European thought if ever there was any." (Zachhuber 2013, 4).

project and those that see it as a failure, neither camp has been able to answer the 'million Euro' question: what is Europe? The question of Europe's identity – and specifically the future identity of Europe – is a political question of the greatest importance if there is to be a Europe 'to come'. Paradoxically, ideologically opposed political parties agreed that a European identity is lacking and without it there can be no Europe. Those critical of the EU claim there is no European identity and thus there can be no European Union. Those in favour of the EU believe there is a European identity but are often mired in discussions about what this identity is. Neither camp has considered whether *an identity is necessary for unity*. Is identity the best means to unify a potential political community or does identity presuppose exclusion and thereby create division? It is my contention that if Europe 'to come' seeks to be a community it cannot be based on an exclusionary identity-construction such as was attempted by means of the signifier Judeo-Christianity.[13]

Today, almost two centuries later, the signifier Judeo-Christianity is once again being used to create an exclusionary European identity. Paradoxically the term "Judeo-Christianity" now includes Jews but excludes another 'Semitic people' – Muslims. While the actual signifier is contingent, its reappearance with a completely new signification is not. The current usage of the term "Judeo-Christianity" illustrates the intertwined political and theological stakes still at play in the idea of Europe. The recent rise (2004–2014) in references to Europe's "Judeo-Christian" heritage, traditions, faiths, identity etc., especially those by populist right-wing parties (whose substantial victory on May 25th, 2015 can no longer be ignored), is another attempt to construct an exclusionary identity-formation. To demonstrate this, I now consider the debate on the draft constitution for Europe that took place in 2003–4 as well as several representative quotes from political and theological leaders in Europe. These reveal the different ways in which the signifier Judeo-Christianity is being used today in reference to the construction of an exclusionary European identity.

Unlike most EU parliamentary debates, the one about the preamble to the draft constitution was full of politics, a rare case for Europe which is more often than not policy without politics.[14] First, the nature of the reference to Judeo-Chris-

---

13 I am neither saying identities do not exist nor that we must totally rid ourselves of the notion of identity. This question is beyond the scope of this article. My critique is of the abuse of identity as a political instrument for exclusion.

14 Contrary to traditional EU debates which according to Vivian Schmidt are usually 'policy without politics' in contrast to national level polities which are 'politics without policy' ('Interview of Vivien A. Schmidt, Professor at Boston University, to the' 2014).

tianity was discussed: was Judeo-Christianity to be understood historically or symbolically? The historical approach was strongly rejected after the 6th amendment (from France) defined Europe's history as 'a river of blood'.[15] The proposed amendment stated we "believe that the peoples of Europe, while remaining proud of their identity and their national history, are determined to transcend their ancient divisions"[16] and included the following explanatory note:

> The argument to condense the history of the currents of thought that crossed Europe and contributed to civilization in a short list of two paragraphs of the preamble is absurd. The history of Europe is also a river of blood, as the construction of the Union succeeded in slowing down: let history without historians manipulate for political purposes.[17]

The initial response to the symbolic use of Judeo-Christianity came in the 2nd amendment (from Spain) that wanted to recognise that Europe was "marked by the spiritual impulse of Christianity that has been encouraging and is still present in its heritage"[18] and Ignace Berten added that the term Judeo-Christianity is "unacceptable and outrageous, it is a true historical forgery, it is the expression of a deliberate attempt to eliminate Christianity in European memory. If you explicitly acknowledge our debt to the Greek and Roman civilizations and the culture of the Enlightenment, it is deeply dishonest not to recognize at the same time our debt to Christianity, Christianity having been the crucible and the unifying form of European culture, in most part of the continent, largely for over a thousand years. [Citing Roberto Formigoni, President of Lombardy, he states:] A pathetic attempt to ignore the Christian roots of the European Union"[19]. This view was quickly reinterpreted by those who argued for the inclusion of the reference to Judeo-Christianity as a symbolic means to correct the exclusive reference to Europe's Christian religious heritage. Other supporters of the reference to Judeo-Christianity saw this as complementary to references to Europe's enlightenment, secular and humanist traditions (Amen. 7), and wanted to change the preamble to state that Judeo-Christianity was a notable spiritual impulse, a change that would allow for a more faithful reflection of history. Only after several days of debate was it explicitly stated that this signifier was similarly exclusive but of Islam (in Amen.15).

---

15 All citations are from the proposed amendments to the text of the articles of the treaty establishing a constitution for Europe can be found at: http://european-convention.europa.eu/EN/amendments/amendments519b.html?content=1000&lang=EN. All translations are my own.
16 Ibid.
17 Ibid.
18 Ibid.
19 Ibid.

This itself is incredibly problematic and exemplifies at minimum the implicit bias against Muslims in the EU and at most its structural or explicit Islamophobia. Furthermore, the reply to this claim confirms what Arthur Cohen claimed in the 1960s with regard to the antisemitism implicit in the term Judeo-Christian (Cohen 1971). The reply to the suggestion of Islamophobia stated that those who used the term "Judeo-Christianity" actually meant it as synonymous with Christianity, without considering that this was a form of anti-Semitism.

Since these debates in 2003–4, similar positions about European history and identity continue to be expressed by some of the most important political and religious leaders. While Romano Prodi, then president of the EU (2007) and a member of the EPP party (as is Angela Merkel), wanted the specifically Catholic roots of Europe to be noted, a direct provocation and exclusion of Protestants, the statement he supported and declared was more inclusive:

> Europe's Judeo-Christian roots and common cultural heritage, as well as the classic and humanist history of Europe and the achievements of the period of enlightenment, are the foundation of our political family.[20]

While seemingly benign, Prodi was criticisng the draft constitution, which failed to explicitly make reference to either Judaism or Christianity. His choice to use the signifier Judeo-Christianity rather than simply Christianity is also one that can be understood as a recognition of the role Jews played in European history, an implicit apology for the Shoah, or a form of supersessionism in which the signifier Judeo-Christianity actually means Christianity. Secondly, Prodi's comments were interpreted as exclusionary of Islam, which according to his position is not part of Europe's *political family* – which of course begs the question – who decides who is part of Europe's 'Christian' family?

While Prodi's comments are intentionally diplomatic, those by Geert Wilders in 2008, here being cited as an example of how this signifier has become popularized by right-wing populists, are explicitly exclusionary.

> Leftists, liberals and Christian-Democrats are now all in bed with Islam. This is the most painful thing to see: the betrayal by our elites. At this moment in Europe's history, our elites are supposed to lead us. To stand up for centuries of civilization. To defend our heritage. To honour our eternal Judeo-Christian values that made Europe what it is today.[21]

---

20 European People's Party (EPP) 50th anniversary declaration/press release published: March 27th 2007. See: http://www.kas.de/upload/ACDP/CDU/Programme_Europaparlament/EPP_Long_Manifesto2009.pdf.

21 Greet Wilders Speech to the Hudson Institute: Neocon Express September 25, 2008.

The reference to 'being in bed' is not accidental. The trope of orientalism as a highly sexualized danger is central to politics from the 1880s onwards (Said 1979). The us-them rhetoric is also hammered in with the repeated use of the terms 'our' and 'us' and the war metaphors of defence, leadership and standing up. Judeo-Christian heritage and values are here explicitly opposed to, and threatened by, Islam, which has seduced the ruling political parties. While Wilder's explicitly Islamophobic comments were shocking in 2008 and were often dismissed as right-wing ranting, the sad reality is that other more centrist parties have begun to use this discourse today and groups such as Pegida are increasing in membership.

While no one is surprised to hear such exclusionary and violent claims by leaders such as Wilders or Le Pen, the fact that other religious leaders use this same signifier without qualification is alarming. In December of 2011, Rabbi Jonathan Sacks, then chief rabbi of orthodox Jews in the British commonwealth, said:

> If Europe loses the Judaeo-Christian heritage that gave it its historic identity and its greatest achievements in literature, art, music, education, politics, and as we will see, economics, it will lose its identity and its greatness, not immediately, but before this century reaches its end.[22]

Given that Sacks knows about the rise of the right in Europe today and understands the dangers of such populism in times of crisis, how can he make such a comment? What is Judeo-Christian for Sacks? It strikes me as a contemporary form of *shtadlanut* (intercession or lobbying practice), a communitarian self-protection mechanism (Guesnet 2005; Guesnet 2007).[23] Given what happened to the Jews on the continent (clearly different than the story of Jews in England during WWII), how can Sacks see this past European identity as great? Is Sacks possibly trying to exclude Islam as a means to support Israel? Sacks' historical dishonesty is disturbing all the more so when affirmed by the then Pope Benedict. In 2012, the pope warned American bishops of "powerful new cultural currents' which are not only directly opposed to core moral teachings of the Judeo-Christian tradition, but increasingly hostile to Christianity as such."[24] Apparently Judaism, now superseded and statistically insignificant, is not hostile (or at least not a threat) to

---

22 Speech on the question of 'Has Europe Lost its Soul?' given by Chief Rabbi Lord Sacks at The Pontifical Gregorian University.

23 See also my work on this topic at: https://kuleuven.academia.edu/AnyaTopolski.

24 Address of Pope to the Bishops of the USA on their 'Ad Limina' visit at Consistory Hall on Thursday, 19 January 2012. See: http://w2.vatican.va/content/benedict-xvi/en/speeches/2012/january/documents/hf_ben-xvi_spe_20120119_bishops-usa.html.

Christianity but clearly the new secular currents are. Given that the Pope seems to view the rise of secularism and atheism as a real threat, one would suppose that Islam would be an ally. Sadly, it is clear from the Pope's 2006 Regensburg speech that this is not the case.[25] Sadly it seems that the 'us' is Christianity strengthened by a hyphenated (castrated) 'Judaism' and opposed to on the one hand, secularism and on the other hand, supposedly unenlightened religions such as Islam.

What this genealogy of the signifier Judeo-Christianity brings to light is how functional it has been in creating exclusionary identity formations in Europe. Its meaning has shifted from originally excluding Jews and Catholics to now including them in order to fortify its exclusion of Muslims. Much like capitalism, or its present neo-liberal manifestation, this signifier has an ability to capitalise on oppositions by incorporating it. Nonetheless, the appeal to Judeo-Christianity as an inclusive signifier masks its persistent exclusionary identarian logic. Much like in the 1830s, the signifier Judeo-Christianity tells the story of a unity driven identity construction that necessitates exclusion. Given how present the media is in today's public sphere, it is irresponsible to deny that this type of us-them discourse has resurfaced in Europe. The signifier Judeo-Christian is one among many political discourses today that serves as a façade for a unity or identity driven by exclusion which at present singles out Muslims as well as other groups such as immigrants, refugees, sans-papiers, and Romas.

From A European Union to a European *Communitas*

This genealogy raises two fundamental philosophical questions. Firstly, is identity construction in a space determined by power relations possible without exclusion? Or in other words: is it possible to have a non-exclusionary political identity construction? According to Talal Asad:

> The general preoccupation in the social sciences with the idea of *identity* dates from after the Second World War. It marks a new sense of the word, highlighting the individuals' social location and psychological crises in an increasingly uncertain world ... The discourse of *identity* indicates not the rediscovery of ethnic loyalties so much as the undermining of old certainties. The site of the discourse is suppressed fear. The idea of a European identity ... concerns *exclusions* and the desire that those excluded recognise what is included in the

25 "Faith, Reason and the University: Memories and Reflections" University of Regensburg. 12 September 2006. See: http://w2.vatican.va/content/benedict-xvi/en/speeches/2006/september/documents/hf_ben-xvi_spe_20060912_university-regensburg.html.

> name one has chosen for oneself. The discourse of European identity is a symptom of anxieties about non-Europeans. (Asad 2003, 161)

Thus, if as Klaus Eder claims, "in a broader historical perspective, the EU can be seen either as a case of an emerging new type of collective identity-building or as a latecomer in the process of national identity building" (Lucarelli, Cerutti, and Schmidt 2012, 38), the current discourse on European identity cannot be inclusive. This leads to a second philosophical question: are identity constructions as politically necessary as assumed? Given that Europe, and specifically the EU, is a project that was stirred by the horrors of the Shoah, neither of Klaus's proposals offers an appealing path to be pursued. Perhaps it is time to consider an alternative, one that is often overlooked by political scientists who assume that "a collective political identity constitutes a political community" (Scheuer and Schmitt 2009, 551), an assumption that is also present in the writings of many political philosophers – especially those whose roots can be traced back to Hobbes or contract theories of community in which vertical immunity (*immunitas*), the protection and negation of life, is substituted for horizontal community (*communitas).*

By way of conclusion, I would like to propose an understanding of community, inspired by the writings of Roberto Esposito, that is fundamentally opposed to any notion of a collective identity. Esposito begins his analysis of the notion of *communitas* by trying to distinguish it from common political misunderstandings about community (Esposito 2009). He returns to the roots of the Latin term *communitas* to recover its original meaning which "is the totality of persons united not by a 'property' but precisely by an obligation or a debt" (Esposito 2009, 6). "The common is not characterized by what is proper [property] but by what is improper [what is not yet completed, the obligation]" (Esposito 2009, 7). To be part of *communitas* meant to participate in fulfilling a shared obligation, in which all have a role. Emmanuel Levinas, writing after the Shoah, also expresses such an idea:

> Echo of the permanent *saying* of the Bible: the condition – or incondition – of strangers and slaves in the land of Egypt brings man closer to his fellow man. Men seek one another in their incondition of strangers. No one is at home. The memory of that servitude assembles humanity. (Levinas 1977, 66).

While, according to Esposito, the Christian fusion of the theological term *koinonia* with that of *communitas* (in the 12th century) partially masks this meaning, the fundamental responsibility for the loss of the term *communitas* lies with Hobbes. Hobbes (intentionally or not) incorporates the theological story of Cain and Abel into his foundational myth and in so doing fuses the concepts of *communitas* and *immunitas*, which were previously opposed to each other. "This [Cain's crime] is what Hobbes sees in the dark depths of the community; this is how he interprets community's indecipherable law: the *communitas* carries within it a gift of death [as such] ... nothing else remains for us except to 'immunize us' beforehand and, in so doing, to negate the very same foundations of community" (Esposito 2009, 6). For Hobbes the danger of *communitas* requires us to immunize ourselves from this threat of death. Hobbes thereby founds modern political philosophy by destroying the bond or shared responsibility that previously defined community and replacing it with the vertical contract that is the template for most modern liberal nation-states.

Clearly, as the persistence of exclusionary identity constructions prove – whether those provided by nationalism, racism, sexism etc., – the contract proposed by Hobbes does not create a community.[26] It might create a nation, a race etc. but these are by definition exclusionary identities. In order to rescue the original and broad meaning of community as 'in common' (Esposito 2009, 15), we must reject its reduction to '*a* common subject' (whether in terms of people, territory, essence, etc.) in which "the community is walled in within itself and thus separated from the outside" (Esposito 2009, 16). It is in this sense that Esposito's notion of *communitas* avoids the exclusionary dangers of identity constructions that litter Europe's history. The question is: could Europe form such a *communitas?* Could the Europe 'to come' become a community of responsibility, bound together by the dominance, arrogance, and privilege that Europe has had over others across the globe, rather than a union based on an exclusionary identity-construction? As powerfully argued by Tony Judt "the idea of Europe stands as a convenient suppressor of collective memories of the widespread collaboration with Nazis crimes in East and West alike, as well as of mass brutalities and civil cruelties for which all states were directly or indirectly responsible" (as quoted in Asad 2003, 162). If, as Esposito argues, a debt can be the foundation for an inclusive community, why cannot the debt Europe has to all those it has excluded, be the cornerstone for the Europe to come?

Bibliography

Anidjar, Gil. *The Jew, the Arab: A History of the Enemy*. 1st ed. Stanford, CA: Stanford University Press, 2003.

Anidjar, Gil. *Semites: Race, Religion, Literature*. Stanford, CA: Stanford University Press, 2007.

26 Alex Tsipiras speech during EU campaign – searching for an inclusive form of community.

Anidjar, Gil. *Blood: A Critique of Christianity*. NewYork: Columbia University Press, 2014.
Asad, Talal. *Genealogies of Religion: Discipline and Reasons of Power in Christianity and Islam*. Baltimore, MD: The Johns Hopkins University Press, 1993.
Asad, Talal. *Formations of the Secular: Christianity, Islam, Modernity*. 1st ed. Stanford, CA: Stanford University Press, 2003.
Bernasconi, Robert and Sybol Cook. *Race and Racism in Continental Philosophy*. Bloomington: Indiana University Press, 2003.
Bunzl, Matti. *Anti-Semitism and Islamophobia: Hatreds Old and New in Europe*. Chicago: Prickly Paradigm Press, 2007.
Cohen, Arthur Allen. *The Myth of the Judeo-Christian Tradition, and Other Dissenting Essays*. New York: Schocken Books, 1971.
Delanty, Gerard. *Inventing Europe*. London: Palgrave Macmillan, 1995.
Delanty, Gerard and Chris Rumford. *Rethinking Europe: Social Theory and the Implications of Europeanization*. London: Routledge, 2005.
Esposito, Roberto. *Communitas: The Origin and Destiny of Community*. Trans. Timothy Campbell. Stanford, CA: Stanford University Press, 2009.
Feldman, Stephen Michael. *Please Don't Wish Me a Merry Christmas: A Critical History of the Separation of Church and State*. New York [etc.]: New York University Press, 1997.
Gerdmar, Anders. *Roots of Theological Anti-Semitism: German Biblical Interpretation and the Jews, from Herder and Semler to Kittel and Bultmann*. Leiden: BRILL, 2009.
Guesnet, François. "Textures of Intercession – Rescue Efforts for the Jews of Prague, 1744/48." *Simon Dubnow Institute Yearbook* 4 (2005): 354–375.
Guesnet, François. "The Turkish Cavalry in Swarzedz, or: Jewish Political Culture at the Borderlines of Modern History." *Imon-Dubnow-Institute Yearbook* 6 (2007): 227–248.
Harrisville, Roy A. and Walter Sundberg. *The Bible in Modern Culture: Theology and Historical-Critical Method from Spinoza to Kasemann*. Grand Rapids, MI: Wm. B. Eerdmans Publishing Company, 1995.
Hay, Denys. *Europe: The Emergence of an Idea*. New York: Harper Torchbooks, 1966.
Hegel, Georg Wilhelm Friedrich. *Hegel's Philosophy of Mind*. Trans. William Wallace. 1st ed. CreateSpace Independent Publishing Platform, 2015.
Hegel, Georg Wilhelm Friedrich. *The Encyclopaedia Logic: Part I of the Encyclopaedia of Philosophical Sciences with the Zusätze*. Indianapolis: Hackett Publishing, 1991.
Heyward, Madeleine. "What Constitutes Europe?: Religion, Law and Identity in the Draft Constitution for the European Union." *Hanse Law Review, The E-Journal on European, International and Comparative Law* 1.2 (2005). http://www.hanselawreview.org/pdf2/Vol1No2Art8.pdf October 20th 2015
"Interview of Vivien A. Schmidt, Professor at Boston University, to the *Crisis Observatory*". 6 May 2014. http://crisisobs.gr/en/2013/09/sinentefxi-tis-vivien-a-schmidt-kathigitrias-sto-panepistimio-tis-vostonis-sto-paratiritirio-gia-tin-krisi/October 20th 2015
Levinas, FIST NAME. *Du sacré au saint, cinq nouvelles lectures talmudiques*. Paris: Editions de Minuit, 1977.
Lincicum, David. "F. C. Baur's Place in the Study of Jewish Christianity." *The Rediscovery of Jewish Christianity from Toland to Baur*. Atlanta: Society of Biblical Literature, 2012. 137–66. *Open WorldCat*. Web. 12 Nov. 2013. LAST ACCESS http://www.sbl-site.org/assets/pdfs/pubs/063705P.front.pdf
Lucarelli, Sonia, Furio Cerutti and Vivien A. Schmidt. *Debating Political Identity and Legitimacy in the European Union*. 1st ed. London: Routledge, 2012.

Lyotard, Jean-Francois and Eberhard Gruber. *The Hyphen: Between Judaism and Christianity*. Trans. Pascale-Anne Brault and Michael Naas. New York: Humanity Books, 1999.

Masuzawa, Tomoko. *The Invention of World Religions: Or, How European Universalism Was Preserved in the Language of Pluralism*. Chicago: University of Chicago Press, 2005.

Moore, R. I. *The Formation of a Persecuting Society: Authority and Deviance in Western Europe 950–1250*. 2nd ed. Hoboken: Wiley-Blackwell, 2007.

Outlaw, Lucius T. *On Race and Philosophy*. New York: Psychology Press, 1996.

Pagden, Anthony, ed. *The Idea of Europe: From Antiquity to the European Union*. Cambridge: Cambridge University Press, 2002.

Pocock, J. G. A. "Deconstructing Europe." *History of European Ideas* 18.3 (1994): 329–345.

Said, Edward W. *Orientalism*. 1st Vintage Books ed. New York: Vintage, 1979.

Sand, Shlomo and Ernest Renan. *On the Nation and the Jewish People*. Original. London: Verso, 2010.

Scheuer, Angelika and Hermann Schmitt. "Dynamics in European Political Identity." *Journal of European Integration* 31.5 (2009): 551–568. *Taylor and Francis+NEJM*. Web. 22 Apr. 2014. http://www.tandfonline.com/doi/abs/10.1080/07036330903145856#.ViYmGdYri-I

Silk, Mark. 'Notes on the Judeo-Christian Tradition in America.' *American Quarterly* 36, no. 1 (1 April 1984): 65–85.

Taylor, Paul C. *Race: A Philosophical Introduction*. 1st ed. Cambridge, UK; Malden, MA: Polity, 2013.

Topolski, Anya. "Spinoza's True Religion: The Modern Origins of a Contemporary Floating Signifier." *Society and Politics* 8.1: 41–59. 2014

Zachhuber, Johannes. *Theology as Science in Nineteenth-Century Germany: From F.C. Baur to Ernst Troeltsch*. Oxford: Oxford University Press, 2013.

Zachhuber, Johannes. "The Absoluteness of Christianity and the Relativity of All History. Two Strand in F.Chr. Baur's Thought." *Ferdinand Christian Baur Und Die Geschichte Des Urchristentums, Tübingen*. Ed. C. Landmesser, M. Bauspieß and D. Lincicum. Mohr Siebeck, 2014.

Notes on Contributors

Itzhak Benyamini is a Lecturer at the University of Haifa and Bezalel, Jerusalem. His research interests are: Critical theology, Psychoanalytic theory, and Biblical studies. His most recent publications include: *Lacan's Discourse – The Revision of Psychoanalysis and Judeo-Christian Ethics* (in Hebrew, Tel Aviv: Resling, 2009), *Narcissist Universalism: A Psychoanalytic Reading of Paul's Epistles* (London: The Library of New Testament Studies, T&T Clark, 2012; in German: Berlin: Merve Verlag, 2013), and *A Critical Theology of Genesis: The Non-Absolute God (New York: Palgrave Macmillan, forthcoming in 2016).*

Michael Fagenblat is a Senior Lecturer at the Open University of Israel and Adjunct Senior Lecturer at Monash University, Australia. His research concentrates on phenomenology, philosophy of religion and Jewish thought. He is the author of *A Covenant of Creatures: Levinas's Philosophy of Judaism* (Stanford University Press, 2010) and "The Concept of Neighbor in Jewish and Christian Ethics," in *The Jewish Annotated New Testament*, edited by Amy-Jill Levine and Marc Brettler (Oxford University Press, 2011).

Warren Zev Harvey is a Professor Emeritus in the Department of Jewish Thought at the Hebrew University of Jerusalem. His research focuses on Jewish philosophy, e.g., Maimonides, Crescas, Spinoza. Among his publications are "Maimonides and Aquinas on Interpretation of the Bible," *Proceedings of the American Academy for Jewish Research* 55 (1988), pp. 59–77; and *Physics and Metaphysics in Hasdai Crescas* (Amsterdam: Gieben, 1998).

Peter C. Hodgson is a Charles G. Finney Professor of Theology, Emeritus, Divinity School, Vanderbilt University. His research interests include topics in systematic theology and several figures in nineteenth century studies: Hegel, Baur, Strauss, George Eliot. His most recent publications include edited translations of Ferdinand Christian Baur, History of Christian Dogma (Oxford: Oxford University Press, 2014), and (forthcoming) Lectures on New Testament Theology (OUP, 2016); and Georg Wilhelm Friedrich Hegel, Lectures on the Philosophy of World History (OUP, 2011), on which he wrote a monograph, Shapes of Freedom: Hegel's Philosophy of World History in Theological Perspective (OUP, 2012). Among his earlier books, he published Winds of the Spirit: A Constructive Christian Theology (Louisville: Westminster John Knox Press, 1994).

F. Stanley Jones is a Professor of Religious Studies and Director of the Institute for the Study of Judaeo-Christian Origins at California State University, Long Beach. His research interests are the New Testament and ancient Christianity, especially ancient Jewish Christianity. His recent publications include: *The Syriac "Pseudo-Clementines": An Early Version of the First Christian Novel,* Apocryphes 14 (Turnhout: Brepols, 2014), *Pseudoclementina Elchasaiticaque inter Judaeochristiana: Collected Studies*, Orientalia Lovaniensia Analecta 203 (Leuven: Peeters, 2012), and, as editor and contributor, *The Rediscovery of Jewish Christianity: From Toland to Baur,* History of Biblical Studies 5 (Atlanta, GA: The Society of Biblical Literature, 2012).

Ivan Kalmar is a Professor of Anthropology and Hon. Newton W. Rowell Professor at Victoria College, at the University of Toronto. His work investigates the relationship between western Christian representations of Muslims and Jews, as well as the Jewish response to these. In particular Kalmar has been interested in the role the trope of the "Jew" plays in the history of orientalism. He has published numerous articles on the subject, and co-edited with Derek Penslar *Orientalism and the Jews* (2005). More recently he authored *Early Orientalism: Imagined Islam and the Notion of Sublime Power* (2013, 2014).

Amanda Kluveld is an Associate Professor at the Faculty of Arts and Social Sciences, Maastricht University, The Netherlands. Her research interests include the cultural history of religion, depillarization and secularization in The Netherlands. Her publications include: *Pijn. De terugkeer naar het paradijs en de wens er weer uit te ontsnappen* (Amsterdam: De Arbeiderspers, 2007), *Mens en Dier. Verbonden sinds de zesde dag. Een cultuurgeschiedenis* (Amsterdam: De Arbeiderspers, 2009). She is working on a volume on the relation between freedom of conscience and freedom of religion to be published in 2016.

Marianne Moyaert is a Professor at Vrije Universiteit Amsterdam, The Netherlands, where she holds the Fenna Diemer Lindeboom Chair in Comparative Theology and Hermeneutics of Interreligious Dialogue. She has recently authored *In Response to the Religious Other: Ricoeur and the Fragility of Interreligious Encounters* (2014) and edited (with Joris Geldhof) *Interreligious Dialogue and Ritual Participation: Boundaries, Transgressions and Innovations* (2015). Her research focuses on the hermeneutical, ethical, and theological presuppositions of interreligious dialogue. She holds a research grant from The Netherlands Organisation for Scientific Research (NWO). The title of her project is *Crossing Borders: Interreligious Ritual Sharing as a Challenge to the Theology of Interreligious Dialogue.*

Emmanuel Nathan is a Lecturer in Biblical Studies and the Head of the School of Theology at the Australian Catholic University in Sydney. His research interests are in early Jewish and Christian origins, biblical hermeneutics, and interreligious dialogue. His most recent publications include: *2 Corinthians in the Perspective of Late Second Temple Judaism*, CRINT 14 (Leiden: Brill, 2014) [with R. Bieringer, D. Pollefeyt and P. Tomson], *Provoked to Speech: Biblical Hermeneutics as Conversation* (Leuven: Peeters, 2014) [with R. Bieringer, R. Burggraeve and M. Steegen] and, shortly, *Re-membering the New Covenant: New Perspectives on 2 Cor 3*, WUNT (Tübingen: Mohr Siebeck, 2016).

Gesine Palmer is a freelance author and public lecturer, running the Büro für besondere Texte in Berlin. Palmer holds a PhD in Religious Studies and is an expert in Jewish Thought of the 20th Century. Her most recent publications include Konversionen und andere Gesinnungsstörungen. Zur bleibenden Relevanz des Jüdischen Denkens nach Hermann Cohen und Franz Rosenzweig" (an edition in six small volumes, of which the first three are already available); "'In 100 Jahren hat die Welt wieder eine Form und wir wieder ein Gesetz.' Rosenzweig's Polemics on Law and Love", Rosenzweig Yearbook 8/9, Love, Law, Life (Freiburg/München: Alber 2014); a contributor to the cultural periodical, Ästhetik & Kommunikation (co-editor of the volume "Graue Literatur", Berlin, June 2015); "The Strange Heritage of Sin", in APuZ, 52/2014; and author of the literary work, Achilles. A Novel on Heroism and Insanity (Münster 2013).

Christoph Schmidt is an Associate Professor at the Department for Philosophy and Religion at the Hebrew University in Jerusalem. He works in the fields of political theology and phenomenology of religion, and has published numerous books and essays on these topics, such as "Theopolitical Hour – 12 Perspectives on the Eschatological Problem of Modernity"

(2009) and "Israel of the Spirits – The Philosophy of the '68 Students' Movement in Germany and Its Aftermath" (2015).

Noah B. Strote is an Assistant Professor of Twentieth-Century European History at North Carolina State University. His research interests are in German intellectual and political history, religion, and political economy. His first book, *Nation Builders: An Intellectual History of Germany's Collapse and Reconstruction, 1924–1964* is forthcoming with Yale University Press.

Anya Topolski is an Assistant Professor in Political Theory at the Radboud University of Nijmegen in the Netherlands. The work for this volume was completed as part of her research grant from the Research Foundation of Flanders (FWO). The title of her project is *European Identity and Exclusion: The Discursive Construction of the 'Judeo-Christian' Tradition.* Her research interests are in European identity politics, anti-semitism, islamophobia, racism, gender, Jewish thought, and radical political theory. Her most recent publications includes the monograph *Arendt, Levinas, and a Politics of Relationality* (Rowman & Littlefield, 2015) and the article *Tzedakah: The True Religion of Spinoza's Tractatus* (History of Political Thought, 2016).

CPSIA information can be obtained
at www.ICGtesting.com
Printed in the USA
LVHW081651150922
728431LV00009BA/145

9 783110 578706